Robert L. Dorman

Revolt

of the Provinces

The Regionalist Movement

in America, 1920–1945

The University

of North

Carolina Press

Chapel Hill

and London

Manufactured in the United States of America

Library of Congress Cataloging-in-Publication Data
Dorman, Robert L.
  Revolt of the provinces : the Regionalist Movement in
America, 1920–1945 / by Robert L. Dorman.
    p. cm.
  Includes bibliographical references and index.
  ISBN 0-8078-2101-2 (cloth: alk. paper)
  1. United States—Intellectual life—20th century.
2. Regionalism—United States—History—20th century.
I. Title.
  E169.1.D687 1993
973.91—dc20   92-31234
                                                        CIP

This book was published with the assistance of the H. Eugene
and Lillian Youngs Lehman Fund of the University of North
Carolina Press.

The paper in this book meets the guidelines for permanence
and durability of the Committee on Production Guidelines for
Book Longevity of the Council on Library Resources.

97 96 95 94 93   5 4 3 2 1

To my parents,
Jack and Sybil Dorman,
and to my grandmother,
Alta Dorman

Contents

Illustrations

A section of photographs of many of the regionalists appears on the following pages:

Preface

Presently we saw a curious thing. . . . On some upland
farm, a plough had been left standing in the field. The
sun was sinking just behind it. Magnified across the
distance by the horizontal light, it stood out against
the sun, was exactly contained within the circle of the
disc; the handles, the tongue, the share—black against
the molten red. There it was, heroic in size, a picture
writing on the sun.

Even while we whispered about it, our vision
disappeared; the ball dropped until the red tip went
beneath the earth. The fields below us were dark, the
sky was growing pale, and that forgotten plough had
shrunk back to its own littleness somewhere on the
prairie.
—Willa Cather, *My Ántonia*

During the two decades between the world wars, artists
and intellectuals across the United States awakened to
cultural and political possibilities that they believed to be
inherent in the regional diversity of America. This book is
an attempt to understand their motivations and expectations, and to trace the fortunes of the movement that they
launched for the utopian reconstruction of modern civilization. It is thus necessarily a case study in the experience of early twentieth-century American artists and intellectuals, seen performing their self-defined and socially
consigned roles. More broadly, however, this book is also
intended to be a chapter from a much vaster story, a
chapter that regionalists were both authors of and characters within: their movement as the signal of a critical
juncture in the centuries-long transformation of this country from a rural, frontier, decentralized, producerist,
farm and village society—the older America—into the

modern commercialized, consumerist, and mechanized mass society of the metropolis.

For the most part, the brief regionalist chapter in this vast story took place, literally and appropriately, not in the great capitals of art and culture, but rather in obscurer settings, small provincial cities, college towns, artist colonies, and still remoter locations where regionalists uncovered what they perceived to be the last remnants of the older America in their modern world. This book will therefore little concern itself with what was happening within most of the famous *cosmopolitan* artistic and intellectual circles of New York, Chicago, or Boston during this era, even though the various regionalist circles shared with them a number of basic modernist assumptions. Nor will this book examine—except as an erosive modernizing force—what has come to be known as *popular* culture, the (less flatteringly labeled) *mass* culture manufactured and promoted by Madison Avenue and Hollywood, as distinguished, by regionalists themselves, from the *folk* culture that was produced and preserved by unrefined groups and individuals in the hinterland, and that provided the raw materials for regionalism. In short, this book will not focus on urban America in the interwar years except as it represented (to regionalists) the congested, proletarianized, centralized, and standardized future toward which the country seemed irreversibly to be declining.

Instead, this work will recount how the *region* was posed against all of these modern tendencies as the means toward a richer, freer, and more humane way of life. As both a cultural and a political concept the region was introduced into the long-running debate over the nature of American nationalism and, in parallel, the problems and promise of cultural pluralism. Most immediately in the pre–World War I period, that debate had been given new turns by intellectuals and reformers such as Randolph Bourne and Jane Addams, who, confronted by millions of recent European immigrants in the cities, proposed more tolerant and multiverse alternatives to acculturative assimilation. So too were regionalists in the interwar years to develop their own ethic of pluralism, a pluralism on behalf of the survivals of older-stock and indigenous folk-rural cultures. To the extent that these cultures could be identified not merely as "American" but only in their association with particular geographic and historical regions of the country, the regionalist ethic of pluralism became more directly an ideological construct, commenting on the distribution of power among and within the various sections of the nation, and upholding heterogeneity over homogeneity. And to this end, the *region* was more concretely, indeed, programmatically envisioned to be the utopian means for reconstructing the nationalizing, homogenizing urban-industrial complex, redirecting it toward an accommodation with local folkways and local environments. The region, it was hoped, would provide the physical framework for the creation of new kinds of cities, small-scale, planned, delimited, and existing in balance with wilderness and a restored and rejuvenated rural economy. In all of these applications, then, regionalism must be considered not only as a critique of modernization, and not only as a noteworthy contribution to the historic dialogue over pluralism, but also as marking a significant stage in the still-unfolding history of conservationism, preservationism, urban planning, and environmentalism.

The regionalists of the interwar years were not the first to awaken to the possibilities of a regionally differentiated nation. Recognition of and identification with the diverse landscapes of North America are as old as European settlement on this continent, and the Native American saga of human adaptation to those environments is far older still. But it was under the pressures of modernization and industrialization, especially in the nineteenth and twentieth centuries, that the personal landscape of the region began to assume for a long line of artists and intellectuals a certain utility as a device for art, social commentary, and political expression. Some artists, in fact, some of the greatest—Nathaniel Hawthorne, for example—used the provincial and familiar as raw materials which they shaped according to presumably "universal" philosophical, psychological, and moral themes. Such was the case with a number of the most prominent regional artists of the 1920s and 1930s—William Faulkner, Robert Frost, Thomas Wolfe, and Georgia O'Keeffe—names that continue to live as definitive of modern American art and literature. This study, however, will focus primarily on individuals who strove to move beyond this style of personal confrontation with local culture, tradition, or landscape, and who wished instead to fashion regionalism into a democratic civic religion, a utopian ideology, and a radical politics. It was these individuals—Lewis Mumford, B. A. Botkin, Howard Odum, Mary Austin, Donald Davidson, and others—who sought not just to render aesthetically the unraveling of traditions, the dissolution of the familial and communal, and other bleak symptoms of modernity, but who proposed to reverse those processes, to ameliorate and heal them ideologically.

Yet it must be noted that the regionalist chapter in the vast story of the modernization of America was not limited to the anxieties and aspirations of these few visionary artists and intellectuals. For, of course, they were also observers and participants within larger regional and national cultures, and in their works they took up some of the most basic and most broadly held of regional-national myths: the myth of mobility, the myth of white supremacy, the myth of the frontier. A study like this one of their confrontation with myths thus obtains some vantage on the broader culture of interwar America; it becomes, implicitly, a further case study in the function of myth in society. As regionalists compared the values and assumptions of America's myths with the realities of past and contemporary history, they discovered and were obliged to report the critical degree to which some very fundamental preconceptions of the American public had fragmented and grown obsolete. The extent to which the public heeded such reports from the provinces was to be an object lesson for regionalists in the nature and persistence of myth, a lesson on which the fortunes of their movement would hinge in the end. Ultimately, regionalism was itself revealed to be a symptom of the passing of the older America, which, after this brief renaissance, "shrunk back to its own littleness" in the modern world.

I wish to express my gratitude to all of the archivists and librarians who offered me their kind assistance during thousands of miles of travel and research across regional America—at the following institutions: Brown University, Harvard University, the Museum of New Mexico, the Nebraska State Historical Society, Oklahoma State University, Southern Methodist University, the Texas State Archives, the University of Arkansas–Fayetteville, the University of Missouri–Columbia, the University of Montana, the University of Nebraska at Lincoln, the University of New Mexico, the University of North Carolina at Chapel Hill, the University of Oklahoma, the University of Texas at Austin, the University of Virginia, Vanderbilt University, and Yale University. The Graduate School and the Department of History at Brown University provided funding to help make this travel and research possible, for which I also express my appreciation.

In addition, I must acknowledge those individuals who contributed to this book through their advice and criticisms. Donald Fleming of Harvard University and Daniel Joseph Singal of Hobart and William Smith Colleges pointed out a number of needed improvements in earlier versions. I also extend my deepest thanks to Mary Gluck, James T. Patterson, and John L. Thomas, all of Brown University, who guided the work from the beginning. On not a few occasions, even their smallest comments led to significant stylistic improvements and interpretive breakthroughs. Jack Thomas, particularly, must be singled out. He gave what were several years ago my vague and general interests a focus and a name: regionalism. And at every point since that time he has shaped and inspired my understanding of it, to this result.

Revolt of the Provinces

Introduction

No Limits and No Oneness: Regionalism and the Regionalist Tradition in American History

It is nothing less than the effort to conceive a new world.

—Lewis Mumford, *The Golden Day*

To begin the task of defining the concept of regionalism, one might imagine a transhistorical discourse between two men of New York—J. Hector St. John de Crèvecoeur, eighteenth-century farmer, surveyor, and philosophe; and Lewis Mumford, twentieth-century cultural critic, regionalist, and urban planner. The setting is crucial to the conceit: first we see Crèvecoeur, composing his *Letters from an American Farmer* (1782) at Pine Hill, the substantial two-story house built around 1770 on a low rise in the midst of 250 acres near Goshen, a small, well-settled community in the southern part of the colony, not far situated from the frontier. Then the scene shifts—across a century and a half, moving southeastward over the vast megalopolitan expanse of New York City—to Mumford, writing *The Golden Day* (1926) in a cooperative apartment at Sunnyside Gardens, a planned housing development circa 1924, located next to the railroad tracks of industrial Long Island City, inexpensive, with small backyard plots and young trees along the sidewalks, twenty minutes by subway from Manhattan. Both philosophe and critic concern themselves with large issues, the largest, in fact. But one might begin by contemplating a simple observation or two. Crèvecoeur, while answering the famous question of Letter III—"What, then, is the American, this new man?"—describes a "great metamorphosis," expressed geographically:

Europeans . . . become, in the course of a few generations, not only
Americans in general, but either Pennsylvanians, Virginians, or provincials under some other name. Whoever traverses the continent must
easily observe those strong differences, which will grow more evident in
time. The inhabitants of Canada, Massachusetts, the middle provinces,
the southern ones, will be as different as their climates.

Mumford, who is also examining the transformation by which "Europeans
become Americans," characterizes the process as the "dispersion of Europe"
in the New World. As a starting point for understanding regional culture and
regionalism, what Crèvecoeur's word map and Mumford's catchphrase suggest together is the interrelationship of a regionally differentiated America
and, as Mumford elaborates, "the disintegration of European culture," more
particularly, "the breakdown of the medieval synthesis."[1]

The *Letters*, written from the vantage of Pine Hill, where "everything is
modern, peaceful, and benign," are a glad obituary for this passing order: "we
are strangers to those feudal institutions which have enslaved so many." Not
coincidentally, Crèvecoeur's is also an early vision, a "great and variegated
picture," of American pluralism, celebrating the cultural, economic, and political consequences of the myth that "there is room for everybody in America."
Part travelogue, part exceptionalist fable, the work as a whole provides an extended commentary for his word map of regional diversification and European
transmutation, beginning necessarily with the first-generation immigrant pioneers. "The variety of our soils, situations, climates, governments, and produce," Crèvecoeur declares, "hath something which must please everybody":

> No sooner does an European arrive, no matter of what condition, than his
> eyes are opened upon the fair prospect: he hears his language spoke; he
> retraces many of his own country manners; he perpetually hears the
> names of families and towns with which he is acquainted; he sees happi-
> ness and prosperity in all places disseminated.

Over time, social interaction and intermarriage conflate these immigrant
cultures, and "individuals of all races are melted into a new race of men," the
American. A more profound process of assimilation is also involved, a sort of
Rousseauean conversion. The European, according to Crèvecoeur, "leaving
behind him all his ancient prejudices and manners, receives new ones from the
new mode of life he has embraced, the new government he obeys, and the new
rank he holds." Indeed, the liberation from nationality and tradition is absolute: "He is neither an European nor the descendent of an European." And
thus, the rejoicing conclusion: "The American is a new man, who acts upon
new principles."[2]

As Crèvecoeur's word map indicates, this broader process of Americanization is closely bound up with the emergence of distinct regional cultures, with the transformation of the immigrant into the indigenous. To Crèvecoeur's Enlightenment sensibility, steeped in Linnaean taxonomies, "men are like plants; the goodness and flavour of the fruit proceeds from the peculiar soil and exposition in which they grow." More explicitly, his provincials are Lockean sensationalist agglomerations of their natural and cultural surroundings: "We are nothing but what we derive from the air we breathe, the climate we inhabit, the government we obey, the system of religion we profess, and the nature of our employment." For evidence, Crèvecoeur looks to the social context "as it appears in the middle provinces"—the tolerant, bountiful rural environs of Pine Hill and, more generally, that special landscape of the Enlightenment mind, Pennsylvania. Differentiating it from the whalers and "Presbyterians" of rocky Massachusetts as well as the slaves and planters of tropical South Carolina, he depicts a set of regional traits that *must* cause European culture to disintegrate: "Industry, good living, selfishness, litigiousness, country politics, the pride of freemen, religious indifference." The immigrant enters a land without "a despotic prince, a rich abbot, or a mighty lord," where Montesquieu's small-scale agrarian society seems to flourish and Rousseau's Golden Age of independence and equality appears actualized. In due course, like the archetypal Andrew the Hebridean, he is "soon enlightened and introduced into those mysteries with which we native Americans are but too well acquainted," such as the responsibilities of landowning, the agricultural techniques necessary for new soils and crops, and the requirements of Anglo-colonial political life. The immigrant's aspirations inexorably mean "the breakdown of the medieval synthesis": to "become a freeholder, possessed of a vote, of a place of residence, a citizen of the province of Pennsylvania."[3]

Yet of course, in the 1770s, the political culture of British America was itself dispersing out across the "great and variegated picture" of the colonies, fractured by the convergence of an emerging republican ideology (as modified from English, classical, and Continental sources by increasingly sophisticated and self-confident "native American" political theorists) with the vista of unlimited land and opportunity. Crèvecoeur clearly shares in the republican worldview. His early letters, written in the years just prior to the War for Independence, envision the disintegrated ancien régime giving birth to a new kind of community, constructed on the "natural" basis of self-interest and tied together consensually by practices of mutuality, justice, and benevolence. But the Anglophilic philosophe also asserts that the foundation for this new society must be built on "the laws, the indulgent laws" of the loosely governed colonial system, laws which are "derived from the original genius and strong desire of the people ratified and confirmed by the crown" and which facilitate the all-important individual acquisition of land.[4] Unfortunately, it was precisely the attempt of the British government to make the empire more efficient and less decentralized that persuaded American patriots, who dwelt not in imperial outposts but, like Crèvecoeur, in their own virtuous landscapes (the "City upon a Hill," the "state of Virginia"), that a sinister plot against their republican liberties was being laid in the corrupt capital of the Atlantic world.

Consequently, the Revolution unfolds as a shattering, tragically ironic event for Crèvecoeur, caught suddenly with his untenable neutrality in an America accelerating toward principles newer than his own, an America where suddenly "everything is strangely perverted." If in his early *Letters* such indigenous "middle settlements" as Goshen and Chester in the neighborhood of Pine Hill had served him as models of beneficent community life (inspiring, for example, the cooperative house-raising episode in the parable of Andrew), they become in the later "Distresses of a Frontier Man" and the appropriately fragmentary *Sketches of Eighteenth-Century America* the backdrop for real and fictive "scenes of low absurdity and tyranny" within a revolutionized countryside. There "Ecclestone," Crèvecoeur's stand-in and mouthpiece in the short morality play called "Landscapes," is beset by the Whig "committee rule" of "low, illiterate, little tyrants." And sometime after 1778, when the Tory-leaning Crèvecoeur must finally flee from his patriotic neighbors ("If I attach myself to the mother country, which is 3,000 miles from me, I become what is called an enemy to my own region"), Pine Hill is burned to the ground by Indian mercenaries working for the invading British army. Crèvecoeur in this manner comes to know despair of a peculiarly *modern* variety, not unlike that of his contemporary, the conservative Edmund Burke— the firsthand experience of cultural dissolution, of "the dearest bonds of society torn asunder": imperial incursions violating the sanctified regional settings of his provincial republics, destroying the diffuse configuration of power necessary for their existence; plebeian revolutionaries moving beyond mere republicanism toward the unsettling possibilities of democracy, confiscating land in the name of justice yet committing thereby the ultimate republican crime. The philosophe escapes from this disintegrating world to the deceptive stability of France, but finds imaginative sanctuary in what will become a favorite refuge for those seeking to repair the American cultural order—a friendly tribe of Indians. He writes: "There must be in their social bond something singularly captivating and far superior to anything to be boasted of among us . . . something more congenial to our native dispositions than the fictitious society in which we live . . . something very indelible and marked by the very hands of nature." He ends the *Letters* with a prayer:

Restore peace and concord to our poor afflicted country; assuage the fierce storm which has so long ravaged it. Permit, I beseech thee, O Father of nature, that our ancient virtues and our industry may not be totally lost and that as a reward for the great toils we have made on this new land, we may be restored to our ancient tranquillity and enabled to fill it with successive generations that will constantly thank thee for the ample subsistence thou hast given them.[5]

Crèvecoeur's conceptualization of regional culture is deeply rooted in eighteenth-century physiocratic assumptions, which view culture and nature as both external to and constitutive of the individual. His regional cultures, which are *new* cultures, emerge from the complex intermingling of diverse ethnic pioneer strains and, particularly, from the economic dimension of environmental adaptation. Yet certainly the provinces of America have a greater significance for him. Writing during the 1770s floodtide of the Enlightenment, he constructs them on the bedrock of universal Nature, endowing them with all the utopian implications of republican communitarianism, drawing the appropriate exceptionalistic conclusions. But ultimately, as Crèvecoeur learns to his sadness during the preview provided by the Revolution, these regional cultures would prove, over the course of subsequent history, to be fragile and unstable as repositories of values; the "dispersion" of culture would continue. With its Harringtonian emphasis on landed property, republicanism was by definition oriented toward personal acquisitiveness; and given the vast and vastly tempting context of the American continent, it served as well as a powerful goad for individual mobility and national expansionism. If these sheering forces were not enough for any communitarian ethos to try to contain, the gradual nineteenth-century infusion of market and capitalist mores, sanctioned by a classical liberalism that dispensed with prerogatives of social unity and responsibility, relegated cooperative values to the margins of American culture—where even as early as the 1770s Crèvecoeur must look for them, with his fictional flight to the Indians. Crèvecoeur's vision of the liberated "new man" transformed by the virtues of an "ample subsistence" so dimmed over the ensuing decades that, from Mumford's vantage point, the chief and very damaging cultural legacy of the pioneer is perceived to be "the burden of a vacant life," of "senseless external activity" for a fast buck: "On one side, the bucolic innocence of the Eighteenth Century, its belief in a fresh start, and its attempt to achieve a new culture. And over against it, the epic march of the covered wagon, leaving behind it deserted villages, bleak cities, depleted soils, and the sick and exhausted souls that engraved their epitaphs in Mr. Masters' Spoon River Anthology."[6]

The scene shifts now from New York the plenteous British colony to New York the Spenglerian world city, where Mumford is confined at Sunnyside Gardens as at an "enclave in the midst of an industrial desert." The crisis of culture the surcease of which Crèvecoeur so fervently prays for is in hindsight recognized by Mumford to be the permanent crisis of modernity, ever more "abstract and fragmentary," leaving Americans of the 1920s with only "a blankness, a sterility, a boredom, a despair." With Long Island City's "air-polluting factory district" and its "chaos of railroad yards" outside his apartment window, Mumford confronts the problems of urban-industrial existence within the larger context of a tired liberal order undermined by three decades of modernist attacks and still disoriented after the cataclysm of World War I. The view from Sunnyside is of a disintegrative "process of abstraction"— Protestantism, republicanism, science, capitalism, liberalism, utilitarianism, industrialism, pragmatism—playing out recklessly across three centuries of American history and, like the "meaningless" labors of the pioneer, failing "either to absorb an old culture or create a new one." As a consequence, Mumford's work *The Golden Day* is in one sense a longing eulogy for those very "feudal institutions" whose demise is celebrated by Crèvecoeur. "Something of value disappeared with the colonization of America," Mumford declares. "Why did it disappear?" In providing an explanation for this central question, *The Golden Day* unfolds as an exercise in *catastrophist* history, a chronicle of the decay and destruction of values and traditions. Yet Mumford is no apologist for guilds or state churches. If Crèvecoeur's work is fundamentally the story of utopian promise dying in cultural dissolution, Mumford's is an account of cultural dissolution giving birth to utopian promise—"something of value was created" as well out of the "dispersion of Europe" in America. The "medieval synthesis" represents to him "the notion of a complete society, carrying on a complete and symmetrical life," an organicist ideal that lies at the heart of the definition of regionalism put forward in *The Golden Day*, Mumford's solution to the perennial crisis of American culture.[7] Thus does his lamentation become a manifesto.

Mumford's belief, contrary to Crèvecoeur's, that "pioneer experience did not produce a rounded pioneer culture" stems directly from his conception of regionalism, in fact, from his understanding of the nature of culture itself. He implicitly rejects Crèvecoeur's physiocratic-republican assumptions regarding the cultural consequences of freehold property. The pioneer, according to Mumford, "lived only in extraneous necessities; and he vanished with their satisfaction: filling all the conditions of his environment, he never fulfilled himself." The historical ramifications of this utterly rootless and exploitative pioneer mentality, he argues, can be seen in a modern way of life "entirely absorbed in instrumental activities," purposeless and disconnected within an "abstract framework of ideas" that serve "in lieu of a full culture." As a basis for his regionalist counterdoctrine to this world of "nomadry, expansion, and standardization," Mumford contends therefore that "man is not merely a poor creature, wryly adjusting himself to external circumstances: he is also a creator, an artist, making circumstances conform to the aims and necessities he himself freely imposes." Mumford elaborates this conviction not in abstract theoretical terms but, aptly enough, through a series of historicist lessons, a survey of American cultural history that leads him to one unique time and place, the period 1830–60, when "the old culture of the seaboard settlement had its Golden Day of the mind," of "disintegration and fulfillment" as a "thriving regional culture": "The attempt to prefigure in the imagination a culture which should grow out of and refine the experiences the transplanted European encountered on the new soil, mingling the social heritage of the past with the experience of the present, was the great activity of the Golden Day."[8]

From this "great activity" of the antebellum New England renaissance, Mumford distills regionalism—the intellectual doctrine, the cultural movement—as essentially an aesthetic concept, integrally conservative in orientation. Although he draws on a very modern definition of culture, "prefigured in the imagination" by "a creator, an artist," Mumford steers clear of the radical philosophical consequences of the aesthetic approach to reality explored by Friedrich Nietzsche and others, with its endpoint in anarchic self-culture. If regionalism is an "art," and art is the attempt to unite "imaginative desire . . . with actuality," then regionalism, he qualifies carefully, is an art grounded in "desire sublimated and socialized." It is "socialized" because it is embedded in a common "social heritage," the "essential likeness which is a necessary basis for intimate communication": a set of values and traditions, ultimately European in origin, shared by a homogeneous, local, and humanly scaled community. Regionalism as a cultural movement arises, according to Mumford, when the modernizing "process of abstraction" threatens to "disperse" this social heritage, for "it is at the hour when the old ways are breaking up that men step outside them sufficiently to feel their beauty and significance." Most crucially, this regionalist self-consciousness manifests itself as a conservative "organic break" with the past, a response quite at odds with Crèvecoeur's disavowal of "ancient prejudices and manners" and equally distinct from the mere perpetuation of received traditions. As Mumford explains in the course of his concrete historicist illustration, socioeconomic change had by the antebellum period hollowed the remnants of New England Puritanism into "a shell." But instead of collapsing into anomie, this disintegrating Puritanism "begot" the transcendentalism of the Golden Day, a movement of regional self-cultivation, selecting, adapting, and transfiguring the remnants of its cultural inheritance to suit the needs of a secular and industrial age. This inheritance embodied for Emerson, Thoreau, Whitman, and others the ideal of an "integrated culture," of "what it means to live a whole human life," inspiring their creation of "new institutions, a new art, a new philosophy"—new and *indigenous*. The close-knit towns of New England, the "well-balanced adjustment of farm and factory," the "lecture-lyceum and the provincial college"—these also were the fruit, in Mumford's view, of a "thriving regional culture," an all-too-brief equilibrium between the medieval and the modern, a product of the regionalist "organic break."[9]

"That world was the climax of American experience," Mumford proclaims, holding to his catastrophist scheme and, more indirectly, to the purposes of his manifesto: "What preceded led up to it; what followed, dwindled away from it." Just as the "fine, fertile, well-regulated district" of Crèvecoeur's middle-provincial Pine Hill was "torn asunder" by despotic power, rampant individualism, and corrosive venality, so too does Mumford depict the achievements of New England's Golden Day as "for all practical purposes demolished" by the "inevitable dictatorship" of the Civil War and the "unchecked, unmodified" industrialism that "controlled the mind as well as the material apparatus of the country" during the subsequent Gilded Age. In the end, just as a regional culture emergent from the plantlike workaday coalescence of values and environment in Crèvecoeur's formulation proves to be evanescent, so too does a regional culture self-consciously developed by an intellectual movement show itself to be equally ephemeral, vulnerable to the fragmenting forces of modernization. But if Mumford believes that "'the promise of regionalism' was exterminated for fully two generations" after 1860, it is an observation that he makes from the vantage of Sunnyside Gardens, the "tiny patch of urban order" designed by fellow members of the Regional Planning Association of America and built as a regionalist beachhead in the "wasteland" of metropolitan New York. Perhaps the chief historicist lesson which he apprehends from the "fine minds of the Golden Day" is, ironically, that they were unafraid "to welcome the new forces that were at large in the world." He calls on his contemporaries to continue the New Englanders' "first exploration," to launch a new regionalist cultural project "more imaginative than the dreams of the transcendentalist," aimed at "reformulating a more vital tissue of ideas and symbols" that would extend beyond the high cultural bounds of philosophy and criticism to transform those "instrumental activities" in which American life had become "entirely absorbed." The new regionalism that Mumford begins to define in *The Golden Day* is much more than a phenomenon of cultural geography, and more than a literary renaissance. The regionalism guiding his hoped-for "programs of regional development" is more even than a blueprint for social and economic reform. It anticipates a virtual "re-settlement" of America. "It is," Mumford writes, ending his book on an exhortative note, "nothing less than the effort to conceive a new world. Allons! the road is before us!"[10]

The rough preliminary sketch of regionalism provided by our transhistorical conceit is necessarily skewed by Mumford's rhetorical strategies, not to mention Crèvecoeur's. Yet their particular biases, agendas, tensions, and blind spots will serve nevertheless to elucidate certain broader elements of a more general definition of regionalism, elements that recur, moreover, in the regionalist tradition unfolding across the decades intervening between them. For even as the tradition itself waxed and waned or took its particular twists and turns in the works of American artists and intellectuals from the late 1700s to the mid-1900s, the concerns of that tradition remained constant: to create a cultural order appropriate to America, with its centrifugal diversity, its continental immensity, a culture to fill the void of wilderness and modernity together—a culture for a country, in the words of Nathaniel Hawthorne, with "no limits and no oneness."[11]

Crèvecoeur's depiction of middle-provincial freeholders and Indians and Mumford's of New England villagers indicate part of the regionalist solution to this most fundamental problem: a genuine American culture must be grounded on the concept of the *folk*. Texas folklorist J. Frank Dobie in 1924 defined the word this way: "any group of people not cosmopolitan who, independent of academic means, preserve a body of tradition peculiar to themselves." As Mumford recognized from his contemplation of the descendants of the Puritans, this "body of tradition" is the central element in regional culture, the foundation for "intimate communication" among members possessed of "that living sense of history which makes one accept the community's past, as one accepts the totality of one's own life." Folk traditions were thus seen by regionalists to be *organic*, but not merely in the sense that they enfold and help to constitute the personal identity of the individual. They are organic as well to a place, symbiotic and indigenous to a specific regional environment— "men are like plants," in Crèvecoeur's conceptualization. The folk are settled, stable, a veritable human "climax-community," to borrow a term from ecology. As another of Mumford's contemporaries, sociologist Howard Odum, summed up, "The folk-regional society is bottomed in the relative balance of man, nature, and culture."[12]

A not unintentional by-product of our transhistorical conceit is that the specific folk-regional societies referred to by Crèvecoeur and Mumford are representative of three distinct sources for folk values that have commonly been appropriated by participants in the regionalist tradition: pioneer agrarian-republican communities, Indian tribal cultures, and immigrant-borne folk life. Each of these sources was *imperiled* by the modernizing "process of abstraction" of Mumford's catastrophist scenario, but each lingered across the nineteenth century and into the twentieth in the problematic and attenuated form of an ever more marginalized and forgotten Mumfordian "shell." The agrarian-republican watchwords of cooperation and independence, invoked less and less frequently by spreading numbers of agribusinessmen and share-cropping landlords, reverberated nevertheless throughout agrarian political discourse from the rise of Jeffersonianism and Jacksonianism in the early 1800s to the turn-of-the-century era of Populism, rural socialism, and the neo-populism of the 1930s, as farmers made the often painful conversion from self-sufficiency and small-scale local production to incorporation within a world-wide cash-crop economy. American Indians also clung to the remnants of their civilization—witness the failed restorations of Tecumseh and the Prophet, or Wovoka and his Ghost Dance—even as their culture was being eroded over the decades by racism, Christianization, and wars of conquest; by the 1920s, there were still old-timers on the reservations who remembered former days, and remote desert places where a few tribes performed the remaining uncensored ceremonies. Similarly, the process of immigrant assimilation into the American melting pot could mean the loss of languages, family names, religious affiliations, or perhaps whole histories and genealogies—the "fresh start." But contrary to the exceptionalist assertions of both Crèvecoeur and Mumford that the American was a "stripped European . . . uninfluenced by peasant habits or the ideas of an old culture," some vestiges of the old country endured the "dispersion" in the form of folklore and ballads and folk dances, vernacular furniture and architecture, and the dialects and accents of regional speech—only the most visible residues of the multigenerational transmutation of immigrant cultures from Europe (and Africa, one might add) into the indigenously American.[13]

As Mumford's conservative definition of regionalism implies, the values of folk-regional societies, when "imperiled," stimulate self-consciousness of what had previously been habitual values and practices and thereafter require deliberate reflective acts of recovery to ensure their perpetuation. His concept of the "organic break" presupposes that artists and intellectuals nurtured within an imperiled regional cultural context not only supply their region with, as it were, a consciousness of itself, but also move beyond their fragmenting "social heritage" to explore its essence and invent new possibilities for it. Inevitably, when such regional cultures are recovered and "pre-figured in the imagination" of the regionalist, a necessary amount of reification becomes involved, a projection of values onto reality. In their personal search for meaning, regionalists tend to believe that their particular region embodies—or in the past, embodied—timeless political principles, universalistic philosophical truths, even irrational mystical beliefs. Emerson gave this regionalist style of thought poetic expression in "The American Scholar" (1837): "Man is surprised to find that things near are not less beautiful and wonderful than things remote. The near explains the far. The drop is a small ocean." Regionalist literary and other cultural productions are said to be "at once local and national," as folklorist Dobie phrased it, because regionalists (like Crèvecoeur) interlace their regional portraits with powerful American myths, myths of exceptionalism, of the frontier, of the special virtue of people living close to the land.[14] When this mythicizing regionalist mind then confronts an often morally ambiguous regional reality (such as the disappointed Crèvecoeur, faced with his grasping patriotic neighbors), a wide range of scholarly and artistic responses might result: from uncritical antiquarianism and romanticized escapist tales of local color, to histories of decline and nostalgic elegies for irretrievable pasts, to broadsides of social criticism and works of art ambivalent toward inherited traditions. In fact, the feelings of loss and urgency attendant with the regionalist act of recovery, the sense of vanishing and violated ideals, might ultimately fuel a desire for political action.

Mumford, to whom the antebellum New England renaissance was the "climax of American experience," perceived only a single historical manifestation of this regionalist style of thought. Yet "we don't hear a word of what was happening south of the Potomac and Ohio all that time," or so complained his contemporary, the Southern poet Allen Tate, after reading *The Golden Day* in 1927. Our own conceit involving Crèvecoeur, as well as the perspectives of many of Mumford's predecessors and contemporaries, do suggest a far more multiplex regionalist tradition, a regionalist impulse recurring throughout the 1800s and early 1900s and cropping up all across the American continent in diverse cultural-historical settings. William Dean Howells, writing in 1892, evokes the proper context: "Our very vastness forces us into provincialism of the narrowest kind." And historian Vernon L. Parrington develops this idea of irreducible cultural heterogeneity at length in his influential *Main Currents in American Thought* (1927), perceiving not only an antebellum "Mind of New England" but also a prewar "Mind of the South"—including Edgar Allan Poe, Sidney Lanier, and William Gilmore Simms—with its own "Virginia Renaissance" featuring Thomas Jefferson, John Taylor, and John Pendleton Kennedy; a "Mind of the Middle East" focused on New York and the mid-Atlantic states, which encompassed the works of Washington Irving and James Fenimore Cooper; a distinctive "agrarian West" captured in the philosophies of Jackson and Lincoln; and a rebellious postwar Middle Border region given expression by Howells, Edward Eggleston, and Hamlin Garland. Complicating further still Parrington's own map of American cultural history are the critical concepts put forward by interwar regionalists such as *Midland* editor John T. Frederick of Iowa, who saw his regionalist tradition less in terms of a national cultural patchwork than of an evolving tendency within an individual region—in the case of the Midwest, from the early frontier efforts of James Hall and Timothy Flint in the 1820s and 1830s, culminating in the Gilded Age novels of Mark Twain, to the second "wave" centered on the Chicago World's Fair of 1893, to the third and continuing stage beginning around 1910 and counting among its productions the works of Sinclair Lewis, Edgar Lee Masters, and Carl Sandburg. "The literary tendencies that emerge from this complex of regional aspirations, as they interweave and form general movements," summarized Southern poet Donald Davidson in 1938, "furnish us with the only kind of literary history that we can call national." Instead of an overarching " 'national glow of thought and feeling,' " he concluded, "we have had a series of glows, appearing now in New England alone, now in the Middle States, now in the South or West."[15]

Davidson's concept of a "series of glows" comprised part of a general theory of "organic sectionalism" which he formulated with only mixed success in *The Attack on Leviathan* (1938). He provides, nonetheless, an additional set of insights that may be expanded upon for our own theoretical portrait of regionalism, and that will help in the construction of a synoptic "regionalist history of America" as a preface to the examination of the movement of 1920–45. Agreeing with Crèvecoeur's early observation of the importance of diversified "climates" in the differentiation of America into regional cultures, Davidson based his reading of national cultural history on the "physiographic areas into which the country is spatially divided" that "have determined the economics and, to some extent, the culture of the political sections." Other factors are also essential in fixing the "character" of a section, according to Davidson: "the tendency of population stocks to concentrate within definite areas, and to foster within those areas the cultural preferences to which they are accustomed," as well as the "attitudes remaining from frontier experience," which endure as "a more or less permanent cultural deposit." Altogether, geography, ethnicity, and frontier life interweave to create distinctive "folkways" that are "imponderable and almost indeterminate" and "have to do with the way in which people live and feel and think." These indigenous folkways make up " 'the immediate, organic sense of life in which the fine artist works,' " Davidson argues, quoting Allen Tate with approval, and thus he proceeds to his conclusion: the diversity of regional folkways means that "regionalism is a name for a condition under which the national American literature exists as a

literature: that is, its constant tendency to decentralize rather than to central-
ize; or to correct over-centralization by conscious decentralization."[16]

In opposition to the line of analysis running from Mumford's *Golden Day*
through Van Wyck Brooks's *Flowering of New England* (1936) to F. O.
Mathiessen's proclamation of the *"American" Renaissance* (1941), Davidson
contends therefore that "we have no centre," no representative region or
"intellectual capital." No single region or city could be considered "quintessentially American," because American culture is quintessentially pluralistic.
He agreed with Mumford that "if we had remained a nation of the Atlantic
seaboard, without a westward expansion or a great access of immigration, we
might have recapitulated European conditions" and developed a more homogeneous and unified culture. However, the "false nationalism that the metro-
politans have been disseminating" stemmed, he believed, from their "wrong
application" of a European Herderian nationalist analogy to the whole of
America's cultural life. To be sure, regionalist contemporaries who claimed
inspiration from great *national* cultural awakenings abroad, nationalist movements that were to serve as examples of cultural development for the disparate component *regions* of America, lend Davidson's argument some measure
of support. In Allen Tate's view, as one example, the interwar Southern
"renascence" was analogous to the "outburst of poetic genius at the end of the
sixteenth century" in Elizabethan England. Nebraska novelist Willa Cather,
for her part, discovered a model in the works of the poet Virgil, who hoped to
be the first "to bring the Muse into my country." And two Southwesterners,
folklorist B. A. Botkin and editor Henry Nash Smith, felt a kinship to the
makers of the Irish Revival, whose chief "prophet" was W. B. Yeats. In short,
for these and other regionalists, past and contemporary, Frederick Jackson
Turner's depiction of the United States as "a union of potential nations" was,
in a cultural sense at least, no overstatement.[17]

The notion of potential nationhood is particularly apt for Davidson's conception of regionalism, for although he reiterates the ideal pluralist configuration—"at once local and national"—which William Gilmore Simms in 1842
called the "republic of letters," Davidson centers his version of American
cultural history, of American *political* history, on acts of "conscious decentralization." If the goal of regionalists was to ensure, as Hamlin Garland wrote in
Crumbling Idols (1894), that "never again can a city or a group of States
overshadow the whole of literary America," the constant reality confronted
over the length of the regionalist tradition was perceived to be quite the
opposite, a regional-cultural "colonial dependency" on one center or another,
or so Davidson suggests. It was a perception rooted in the exceptionalistic
assumptions given their classic expression in Crèvecoeur's *Letters*: America,

as the seat of newness, must have a new and literally unprecedented cultural order—an attitude that was both cause and symptom of the "dispersion of Europe." As poet John Blair Linn wrote in the heady post-Revolutionary period, "These regions were not formed, only to echo the voice of Europe; but from them will yet sound a lyre that shall be the admiration of the world." Yet when Noah Webster wrote in 1783 that "for America to adopt the present maxims of the old world would be to stamp the wrinkles of decrepit age upon the bloom of youth and to plant the seeds of decay in a vigourous constitution," he began a worried refrain that, during the next century and a half, was to frame American concerns over emerging dangers of feudal-style despotism, aristocratic decadence, class stratification, and moral relativism *at home* in terms of the necessity to liberate the national mind from the influences of European and, especially, British culture. These concerns may be seen as projections of collective fears of social fragmentation and the loss of exceptionalism into the realm of arts and letters—with the consequent and perennial call for a genuinely American language and literature to reflect and reassert common moral and political values. As one writer in 1846 observed of "American Nationality": "In the fusion of all its elements in a generous union under the influence of a noble National Literature lies the best (if not the *only*) hope of perpetuity for the American Confederacy"—"a new art and music," as Edgar Lee Masters ninety years later described this still-worthwhile Whitmanesque enterprise, "in which the people would be celebrated instead of kings; and the liberty of Jefferson should be sung until it permeated the entire popular heart."[18]

"Imported" culture thus threatened American ideals because it signified continued connection to and dependency on the corrupt Old World. But more fundamentally, it ignored native history, tradition, folkways, and environment, constituting another of the forces imperiling folk-regional values and interfering with the integrative function of an indigenous cultural utterance. If Americans remained satisfied with an "imported" culture, inappropriate to and obscuring their unique experiences, it was a sign that they were not enjoying the positive freedom—culture as a way of living, not a consumer good—which could only come from understanding the sublimity of "the common . . . the familiar, the low," as Emerson put it. That Emerson's own fellow antebellum New Englanders remained satisfied showed them to be "a people too busy to give to letters anymore," a people without true culture and the personal autonomy and identity it entailed; in Mumford's words, they were well on the way to becoming "entirely absorbed in instrumental activities." It was therefore no coincidence that in the opening paragraph of "The American Scholar," Emerson himself engaged in an act of "conscious decentralization"—"Our day of dependence, our long apprenticeship to the learning of other lands, draws to a close"—and at the same time exhorted his audience to "fill the postponed expectation of the world with something better than the exertions of mechanical skill."[19] This first decentralizing step was not a complete disavowal of European cultural influences or antecedents, it must be noted, but the overture to the "organic break" whereby the regionalist act of recovery (and, in more general terms, the creative process) might begin.

Yet as Mumford's catastrophist historical scheme shows, neither Emerson's transcendentalism, despite his hope to unite North and South within the organicist Divine Soul, nor any of the other cultural productions of the antebellum height of literary nationalism, were successful in holding the American nation together within a new and indigenous cultural order. Davidson's version of antebellum developments furnishes one explanation:

> Emerson had no better principle of union to offer than the Yankee transcendentalism which, even at that moment, in another aspect than the literary, was about to attack and all but destroy the very foundations of Southern culture. His voice was not the voice of America, but of New England, and his plan of salvation was to result not in peaceful unification but in bloody disunion.

In the final analysis, Davidson declared, regionalism as "conscious decentralization," the interpretive framework of his cultural history, "is really sectionalism under another name." All of the resentments of cultural domination, the concerns over lost exceptionalism, the fears of new tyrannies, the anxieties about social dissolution—all of these could undoubtedly be directed into visions of democratic pluralism within a greater national unity. But disparate regionalist impulses might also become embroiled in domestic debates that involved competing definitions of the course and nature of American society, constantly pulling against national unity and, on one occasion, rending it. "Inevitably," Davidson writes, "the artist is driven, or at least the critical student of art is driven, into social and economic questions," those essentially political considerations that determine the destiny of a folk-regional society and its imperiled values.[20] Such questions—to qualify Davidson's flat equation of sectionalism and regionalism and distinguish between them—such questions might be turned *inward* as part of a larger *regional* cultural self-critique, as was the case with the New England transcendentalists at Brook Farm. Or, granting his general point, those questions might be projected *outward* against other sections depicted as the embodiment of evil and corruption, with one's own locality cast in the role of victim or potential victim.

Thus, when Ohio anthologist W. T. Coggeshall in 1858 warned his readers against "servile dependence on the Atlantic States" in the field of literature, he was voicing as well the grievances of a debtor West, virtuously agrarian and victimized, the true America, against the self-interested politicos and money-changers of a creditor East. In a similar way, when the *Atlantic Monthly* began publication by proclaiming to be an "exponent of what its conductors believe to be the American idea" (the emerging Northern free soil–free labor ideology), it aggravated the other great antebellum sectional polarization by stating its purpose to become "the new literary and anti-slavery magazine," the Southern Slave Power being the very apotheosis of aristocratic Old World evil.[21] Certainly Davidson's own anti-Northern characterization of "The American Scholar," a century or more later, demonstrates how deeply rooted and rankling sectional passions could be: to him, transcendentalism was a cultural manifestation of the Yankee imperialism that, after a final apocalyptic battle with the Jeffersonian South, was to saddle the rest of the country in the decades after the war with an ever more centralized European-style national state and an ever more standardized industrial order: Leviathan.

Mumford's is an even bleaker depiction of the postwar rise of this "domestic imperialism": "What the office-holders in the central government called 'the menace of sectionalism,'" he writes, "and what we may call equally 'the promise of regionalism' was exterminated for fully two generations. Local life declined. The financial centers grew. . . . All the crude practices of British paleotechnic industry appeared on the new scene without relief or mitigation." Admittedly, if until the 1850s the United States may be said to have occupied a basically peripheral status with regard to Great Britain and the other more advanced nations of Western Europe (possessing a largely extractive economy, politically vulnerable to the richer, more populous, more commercially advanced European "core"), then the Southern and Western two-thirds of the nation may be seen (and were so perceived) to have played that same role during the decades between 1865 and 1920 for the emerging "core" of the Northeast. Looming most ominously in the eyes of Southerners and Westerners was the rapid growth of New York City to Spenglerian dimensions, "*a city, a point*, in which the whole life of broad regions is collecting while the rest dries up."[22] There were other apparitions suddenly abroad in the landscape as well, equally menacing, all wrought by the "crude practices" of industrialization: robber barons, monopolies, labor unions, anarchists, landlords, tenants, financiers.

Yet in contradistinction to Mumford's assertion of a dwindling and empty cultural aftermath following the 1850s Golden Day, Davidson locates another moment of "conscious decentralization" in the 1890s, when the "new Northwest" of the Mississippi Valley, with its capital in Chicago, arrived at "full consciousness of the fact that they, too, no less than the now discredited South, had become a section which must fight a sectional battle." But if the "dangers of centralization," as Hamlin Garland saw them at the time, were real enough, here may be observed most clearly a tendency among regionalists both before and after the 1890s to conceptualize drastic social change as *incursions from outside* their regions. Such a perspective might provide fodder for conspiracy theories, but, more importantly, it allowed the regionalist to define and reassert the values of the regional-sectional community in opposition to an "alien" presence—a rhetorically and politically useful variation on the old nationalist theme of "imported" culture. Thus, in 1894, Populist sympathizer and Single Taxer Garland outlined some of the "reasons for the revolt against the domination of the East over the whole nation": "We deny that the East is to be the exclusive home of the broadest culture . . . a section which is really nearer the Old World than the New"; his purpose was "not merely to combat literary centralization, but also to build up local centres," for it was his belief that "the literature which is already springing up in those great interior spaces of the South and West is to be a literature, not of books, but of life," drawing inspiration from "original contact with men and with nature. . . . It is to outrun the old-world limitations." Garland concluded: ". . . it is my sincere conviction, taking the largest view, that the interior is henceforth to be the real America. From these interior spaces of the South and West the most vivid and fearless and original utterance of the coming American democracy will come."[23]

That utterance, of course, was widely recognized to be Frederick Jackson Turner's 1893 essay on the significance of the frontier, which traced the roots of American democratic culture to the interactions of pioneers in an "area of free land" not unlike the environment of the Mississippi Valley. Even Davidson admitted that the Turner thesis was "a bit of sectional rationalization," yet it was also the most compelling synthetic vision of regional history and national myth ever written, as well as the most convincing case for American exceptionalism. Turner was engaging, however, in a self-conscious regionalist act of recovery—the essay's final portentous lines marked the closing of the frontier. By the 1890s and early 1900s, it was a very late year in the life of the American folk: the last few scraps of Indian land were taken, immigrants were flocking more and more to the great cities, and the republicanism of Jefferson was sounding distinctly old-fashioned to those reformers trying to "mitigate" the effects of explosive industrial growth. For inspiration, most often these Progressive Era reformers looked to the rationalism of science or the innate fairness of constitutional government, or they mustered up a liberalized and rather desiccated Christianity, largely ignoring the possibilities of irrational organicist folk communitarianism. But they were confronted with (to paraphrase Davidson) a nationalizing influence of a more sweeping and seemingly irresistible character than anything out of the eighteenth or nineteenth centuries. The corrosive "process of abstraction," dissolving whole cultures, had continued to march onward, into the postfrontier age—no area of America was now out of reach. Turner himself placed his faith in "those manifestations of economic and social separateness involved in the existence in a given region of a set of fundamental assumptions, a mental and emotional attitude which segregates the section from other sections or from the nation as a whole," which could conceivably become "potential bases for forcible resistance" within a larger federalist unity.[24] But as the frontier receded across the continent and into history, and as the regionalist recovery of values became less and less a "sociological" and more and more a purely historical project, it was not clear whether such regional "bases of resistance" could withstand the unprecedented onslaughts of centralization and standardization that the twentieth century had in store.

One result of Turner's deed of "conscious decentralization," along with the efforts of fellow participants in the Midwestern "renaissance," was to fulfill Garland's call for a culture of the American interior beyond his most hopeful expectations. By the 1920s, few American intellectuals could dispute Turner's contention that "the true point of view in the history of this nation is not the Atlantic Coast, it is the great West," or deny that "Middletown" (Muncie, Indiana) was the typical American city. The assay of Midwestern life made by the Lynds and others in the 1920s, however, caught only glimpses of folk values that were now so imperiled as to be, perhaps, irrecoverable. The darkness in their depictions of the Midwest was the rapidly gathering twilight of the older America. As Sherwood Anderson wrote in *Winesburg, Ohio* (1919): "Much of the old brutal ignorance that had in it also a kind of beautiful childlike innocence is gone forever. The farmer by the stove is brother to the men of the cities, and if you listen you will find him talking as glibly and as senselessly as the best city man of us all"—which Sinclair Lewis illustrated in this famous exchange between George Babbitt and his manly backwoods guide, Joe Paradise, during a nature outing:

> "Joe, what would you do if you had a lot of money? Would you stick to guiding, or would you take a claim 'way back in the woods and be independent of people?"
>
> For the first time Joe brightened. He chewed his cud a second, and bubbled, "I've often thought of that! If I had the money, I'd go down to Tinker's Falls and open a swell shoe store."

The cultural blossoming of the Midwest was born of its despair at the withering of the heroic Jeffersonian-Turnerian tradition in the new America of stiflingly conformist small towns and interchangeable metropolises. "If I didn't love Main Street would I write of it so hotly? could I write of it so ragingly?"

Thus Lewis confessed in 1920, and he persisted in the hope of a "way-out" through "the democracy of a trained, taut, eager Common People making themselves worthy to rule and build." But to find the "way-out" meant freeing the "Common People"—people like Joe, like the "farmer by the stove"—from one of the most remarkable and insidious inventions of the new urban-industrial America: mass culture.[25] Coupled with the post–World War I resurgence of nativist "100 percent Americanism" and the "Anglo-Saxonism" of Prohibition, both crude and hurtful attempts at unifying the sprawling national heterogeneity brought on by industrial disorder and several recent waves of immigration, the advent of mass culture set the context for the homogenized caricature of community life that artists and intellectuals like Lewis found so oppressive in the 1920s. By the 1930s, mass culture was to furnish for them one of the most visible emblems of the corporate domination of America. In fact, it proved to be one of the central evils and challenges confronted by the "new regionalism" of the interwar period: how to salvage and preserve the culture of the folk from this perhaps most imperiling of all the forces of modernization.

The vast expansion of mass culture after World War I was only one dimension of a broader crisis of culture that was widely perceived to be afflicting all of Western civilization during this period, and that constituted the immediate context and stimulus for the emergence of the regionalist movement. Just as rapid—and to Henry Adams's mind, *accelerating*—socioeconomic change had made it a late hour in the life of the folk, so too did the perception grow that Western culture in general was being left behind, as it were, by the abstract and fragmenting urban-industrial order that Mumford was to lament in *The Golden Day*. High culture and workaday values alike came to be seen as *survivals* (in the new anthropological parlance), obsolete concepts and beliefs from earlier, less complex places and periods that could no longer bring coherence to a world that had evolved far beyond them. This crisis, and the *modernist* sensibility that was born out of it, were first extensively reported in America during the prewar "cultural revolt" centered at Chicago and at Greenwich Village, a revolt predicated on the radical and liberating implications of the insights of the chief prophets and critics of modernity—Nietzsche, Freud, James, Dewey, Bergson, Joyce, Zola, Marx, Dostoevsky, Santayana, Bourne, and Veblen, among others. George Santayana's formulation of the "genteel tradition" and Van Wyck Brooks's "high brow/low brow" dichotomy became the definitive conceptualizations of the crisis for both prewar and postwar artists and intellectuals. "America is a young country with an old mentality . . . a survival of the beliefs and standards of the fathers," Santayana counseled in 1911. One part of the American mind, he wrote, "has floated gently in the backwater, while, alongside, in invention and industry and social organization the other half was leaping down a sort of Niagara Rapids. . . . The one is all aggressive enterprise; the other is all genteel tradition." This tradition, rejected by disdainful prewar bohemians of all stripes, manifested itself in many guises: as a dusty, largely Anglicized literary canon (antiquity and moral transparency defining the bibliography); as a myopic idealist philosophy (divorced from a utilitarian praxis); as a hypocritically proscribed and overly complacent moralism (separate rules for home and office, business and pleasure); and as an unlovely patriotism and naive faith in progress (denying ethnic segmentation and class polarization). For many intellectuals, regionalists included, the term *genteel* came simply to connote a culture that had "lost its basis in American life," a culture purely "academic," ethereal, irrelevant. In *America's Coming-of-Age* (1915), Brooks cast the resultant crisis in more concrete terms: "Between university ethics and business ethics, between American culture and American humor, between Good Government and Tammany, between academic pedantry and pavement slang, there is no community, no genial middle ground." Consequently, the United States was, in effect, cultureless. Brooks conjured another vivid catchphrase image: "America is like a vast Sargasso Sea—a prodigious welter of unconscious life, swept by ground-swells of half-conscious emotion . . . everywhere an unchecked, uncharted, unorganized vitality like that of the first chaos. It is a welter of life that has not been worked into an organism."[26]

The prognosis after World War I seemed hardly improved. If the creative momentum of the prewar cultural revolt was all too quickly absorbed and dissipated by the pressures of wartime and the ensuing post-Versailles disillusionment, the perceptions of cultural crisis, of a "polite and conventional American mind" utterly disengaged from the polyglot and disordered social scene it purported to interpret, survived and were intensified by the diversion of the war and its aftermath. The collaborative critical survey *Civilization in the United States*, published in 1922, sets the contemporary scene out of which the regionalist movement was to unfold: a scene of despair mingled with utopian aspirations of building a new culture, a culture appropriate to, and integrative of, the modern age. "We have no heritages or traditions to which to cling except those that have already withered in our hands and turned to dust," survey editor Harold Stearns wrote, summing up the general thrust of the volume. "The most moving and pathetic fact in the social life of America today is emotional and aesthetic starvation." And yet, Stearns and his contributors believed, such "culturelessness" could have its liberating compensations: "American civilization is still in the embryonic stage, with rich and with disastrous possibilities of growth." Significantly, while outlining those possibilities, Stearns resorted to rhetoric and remedies evocative of the still-extant cultural-nationalist tradition attacking "imported" culture. For to avoid "disaster" would necessitate continued assaults on mainstream cultural ramparts in the universities, the publishing industry, the media, and the public at large—all of which "imported" the genteel tradition into the present. Numerous new cultural organs had been established during the prewar revolt for this very purpose, new magazines like the *Seven Arts*, the *Little Review*, the *Smart Set*, the *Masses*, and the *New Republic*, and new publishers like Alfred Knopf and Boni & Liveright. "We shall never achieve any genuine nationalistic self-consciousness," Stearns wrote, "as long as we allow certain financial and social minorities to persuade us that we are still an English Colony." Because "thought is nourished by the soil it feeds on," cultural reconstruction must involve a reengagement with the indigenous, requiring that "we begin seriously to appraise and warmly to cherish the heterogeneous elements which make up our life, and to see the common element running through all of them." Until this project took place, Stearns cautioned, "we shall make not even a step towards real unity," toward a "common concept of the good life"—what Brooks in 1915 had called a new "social ideal."[27]

Brooks's own *Civilization* essay on the national "Literary Life," however, foresaw only dim and possibly abortive prospects for any such project which was not nourished by a strong indigenous cultural *movement*—again, like Stearns, articulating a sentiment that was to be widely shared among interwar regionalists (already, at his writing, arriving in the provinces, forming friendships, and beginning to coalesce into groups and circles). The sad fact, Brooks wrote, was that "for half a century the American writer as a type has gone down in defeat," unable to fulfill the promise of his or her talent within a blighted environment of "general colourlessness and insipidity," of "isolation, nervous strain, [and] excessive work" generated by the "harassed, inhibited mob of our fellow-countrymen." Compared with the vital accomplishments of Europeans like George Bernard Shaw, Thomas Hardy, and Anatole France, or with the "spiritual force" of Emerson, Thoreau, and Whitman, nurtured within a long-lost "pastoral America," the "creative will in this country," Brooks believed, "is a very weak and sickly plant." To sustain the few "weeds and wild flowers" of the current prewar-launched literary revival through careers of "continuous growth" would require all the elements of cultural infrastructure common to Europe but so long absent from, if ever present in, America, such as an "enlightened publishing system" and a "strong and self-respecting literary guild." Above all, American writers needed "the sense that one is *working in a great line*," the inspiration of masters, past and contemporary. Most pointedly, because the whole of the "American environment is answerable for the literature it has produced," because the stunting of American creativity was "a sign of some more general failure in our life," it was essential, Brooks concluded, for the "half-artists" of the United States to act collectively. Adventuresome editors, literary forums, and cultural histories were not enough. "'What we want,'" he quoted from an 1862 letter by Henry Adams, indicating a perennial and as yet unfilled prescription, "'is a school. We want a national set of young men like ourselves or better, to start new influences not only in politics, but in literature, in law, in society, and throughout the whole social organism of the country—a national school of our own generation.'" This, Brooks declared, "is the one thing necessary; the reforestation of our spiritual territory depends on it."[28]

If the clear-cutting of that territory, to elaborate Brooks's metaphor, was a consequence of exponential and chaotic processes of urban-industrial growth unleashed by the very war in which Adams had made his premature reconstructionist proposal—growth so rapid that it seemed to rarefy the cultural atmosphere, making of American culture an anthropological survival—it was also the result of a subtler defoliation by radical new artistic and philosophical agents obtaining wider and wider currency in the decade before the *Civilization* survey appeared. The prewar cultural revolt, perceiving and precipitating crisis, had broken open the boundaries of cultural possibility. Regionalism, in the interwar period, became one of a loosely defined range of modernist cultural movements that would attempt to carry out (as Santayana had admonished) "the reconstruction that alone can justify revolution." Together with several of those other movements—the makers of the Harlem Renaissance, the *Partisan Review* cosmopolitans, the *New Masses* communists— regionalists would share a common faith in cultural radicalism, the belief that artistic and intellectual production (especially social art) can in itself help to bring about dramatic social change. Relatedly, they would with these others be disdainful of mass culture and devoted to artistic innovation and experimentation, to ungenteel subject matter and alternative forms of expression (in fact, some regionalists, like Allen Tate, would contribute to the *Partisan Review*). More broadly, regionalists would promote, like those other movements, their own special doctrine of cultural pluralism. In particular, regionalist defenders of Native American tribes would conjoin with Randolph Bourne– inspired cosmopolitan intellectuals as critics of acculturative assimilation. Regionalists too would believe, with the adherents of the 1920s Harlem Renaissance, in the "universality" of the culture of the Negro and other lowly folk, in such a culture's "lack of the self-conscious element" and its "nearness to nature," as two writers defined the importance of black folklore in *The New Negro* (1925), using almost identical terms to those written by regionalists about their own folk groups. (Perhaps not coincidentally, the original Harlem Renaissance manifesto—which became *The New Negro* volume—appeared in the March 1925 issue of the *Survey Graphic*, only two months before that magazine published the manifesto of Mumford's Regional Planning Association of America.)[29] And as that manifesto among others of theirs showed, regionalists, like the communists, would have a revolution in mind for their country, envisioning a radical democratization of ownership and control, and a humanization of technology.

Regionalists would, in sum, join this interwar modernist generation in the search for a new *integrated* culture and society. But if they were to share many modernist goals and assumptions, they often did so ambivalently, on their own terms and according to their own distinctive cultural and political agendas. Most simply yet significantly, those other largely New York–centered movements, reflecting the recent immigrant background and city backdrop of most of their members, were to be very much urban-oriented (and -confined), concerning themselves with the promise and problems of factory workers, ethnic neighborhoods, immigrant religious groups, and the transplanted "city Negro." The mainly older-stock regionalists, on the other hand, would of course be preoccupied with rural America, its traditions, folk, farms, towns, and wildernesses; even the prominent urban-planning wing under Mumford was to take as a chief project the "ruralizing" of the metropolis.[30]

Closely associated with this preoccupation of the regionalist movement, and further distinguishing it from the others (who virtually ignored the subject), would be regionalism's central emphasis on *place*, on the lived environment as a unique historical, cultural, and physical entity, and as a key to a fully human life. Such an emphasis on place implied a "particularism" that the "internationalism" of the communists and the (Marxist-leaning) cosmopolitans were to find objectionable, if not "reactionary."[31] And it is true, to distinguish the regionalists further still, that on balance their movement must be characterized as "nationalistic" (as it was), in perhaps this more positive connotation of the word: they believed that the materials for cultural reconstruction must be found at home, where time and nature had taught an appropriate wisdom; and thus, for example, diverging from the Harlemites, they were to look to African American but not African folk life for inspiration. And, diverging from the Marxists and communists, regionalists were to look to "native American" ideologies—such as republicanism, populism, or liberalism—rather than various "imported" creeds, to find their values and agendas, because, to their minds, such alien internationalist and industrialist doctrines ignored the saving diversifying and decentralizing graces of place (a sentiment not without a "conservative" thread, to be sure). That regionalists would draw on American political traditions, with their inherent squeamishness about class, collectivism, and coercion, is not surprising, given what was to happen to various "international" ideologies in the 1930s, the era of Hitler and Stalin. And that this "nationalistic" tendency would reveal a larger conservatism of sorts is also not surprising, because of all the interwar movements manifesting modernism, regionalists were perhaps to be the most ambivalent and uneasy about its radicalisms, relativisms, and uncertainties.

In retrospect, many of the divergences of the regionalist movement from these other cultural movements of the period might be traced to their determination to find a home for the older America of the folk in the fragmenting world of the twentieth century, a home not merely metaphorically but literally and concretely. Working with what they perceived to be the bedrock of America, its civic traditions, its folk cultures, its very landscapes, regionalists must have felt impelled in this project and reassured in it. Yet the obstacles to their goal, to cultural "reforestation" in general—modernizing pressures of all varieties, failure of vision, mediocrity of talent, stultifying chauvinism, public indifference—the obstacles were many, and if they were not insurmountable, they were to be enough. Regionalism, in the end, was to be splayed and hobbled by the modernist dilemma that Walter Lippmann, sighing, characterized this way in 1930: "The acids of modernity are so powerful that they do not tolerate a crystallization of ideas which will serve as a new orthodoxy into which men can retreat. And so the modern world is haunted by a realization, which it becomes constantly less easy to ignore, that it is impossible to reconstruct an enduring orthodoxy, and impossible to live well without the satisfactions which an orthodoxy would provide."[32]

Holding to the latter impossibility as an article of faith, regionalists were slow to yield the former. It would take many of them almost two decades of effort before they yielded it. Picking up the threads of the regionalist tradition and the ever more tenuous connections to the older America maintained by such pre–World War I caretakers as the Midwestern renaissance, the Arts and Crafts movement, the early works of Willa Cather and Mary Austin, the garden city plans of Ebenezer Howard, the wilderness advocacy of John Muir, and the sheer distance and preserving isolation of the provinces themselves, regionalists during the 1920s and 1930s would attempt, in the course of staging a "regional renaissance" of unprecedented national scope, to turn that tradition to unprecedentedly radical and ambitious ends. The times demanded it. As "cultural radicals" they confronted not only the disintegrative crisis brought on by the "acids of modernity," but also—in ominous, overlapping succession—the further catastrophe of the Great Depression, imperiling even the workaday pseudoculture of ordinary Americans, and the rise of totalitarianism abroad, which seemed to threaten the dissolution of civilization itself. In response, regionalists were to press their creed beyond its historic role as artistic seedbed and adversary culture: fulfilling Adams's prescription, they would seek to "start new influences . . . throughout the whole social organism of the country"—to save that "organism" from the acids of modernity.[33] In short, they would attempt to formulate regionalism as a full-fledged national *ideology*, showing the one "way out" that America must follow if it were to preserve the exceptionalism that had been the persistent worry of the regionalist tradition since at least the time of Crèvecoeur.

In the interwar years such a "re-settlement" of America still seemed possible: to reclaim the myths and ideals that had been abandoned and "dispersed" during the centuries-long march of Americans across the continent and into modernity. The manifold crises of the period seemed to open the range of cultural and political possibility. Much about the national life that had gone unquestioned was now questioned, particularly the perennial absorption of Americans in the abstract and empty "instrumental activities" of the modern urban-industrial economy, even to the exclusion of culture itself. Seeking with their new ideology to reintegrate that economy with the folk-regional myths and ideals it had so deeply violated, regionalists were to plot an alternative route for modernization. Their "programs of regional development" would call not for a return to a threadbare, simpler time, but for "the continuous cultivation and development of all the resources of the earth and of man," as Lewis Mumford wrote. Rejecting the "mine and move" philosophy that had laid waste to America's landscape as well as its democracy, they would proselytize a new guiding maxim: "stay and cultivate." Conducted on an *aesthetic* rather than a utilitarian basis, regional "cultivation" could never be business as usual; in this new order, economic development would proceed as a work of the imagination, shaped by the dictates of local tradition and environment, by an organic sense of place. "A complete culture," Mumford wrote near the end of *The Golden Day*, "leads to the nurture of the good life; it permits the fullest use, or sublimation, of man's natural functions and activities." Ultimately, this was what the regionalist movement, seeking to neutralize the "acids of modernity," was briefly to grasp in the two decades of chaos between the world wars—Mumford's "new world": "the conception of a stable and settled and balanced and cultivated life."[34]

Part One

The Regional Renaissance

1 This Earth So Deeply Yours

A Biographical Exploration of the Regionalist Sensibility

The history of every country begins in the heart of a man or a woman. —Willa Cather, *O Pioneers!*

The life and works of Willa Cather, treated emblematically, provide some helpful guideposts into the regionalist sensibility that emerged among a generation of American artists and intellectuals during the 1920s and 1930s. Born in 1873 and raised within the "old and conservative society" of the "Valley of Virginia," where "life was ordered and settled," Cather at age nine moved with her parents to the "new country" of the Nebraska frontier near the town of Red Cloud, the "end of everything." There, on the prairie land of the Divide between the Little Blue and Republican rivers, she got "acquainted with the neighbors"—immigrant Swedes, Danes, French Canadians, Norwegians, Bohemians, Germans, and Russians— "whose foreign speech and customs," Cather later remembered, she "found intensely interesting." After graduation from the University of Nebraska, a short career as journalist and teacher in Pittsburgh, and an editorial position with *McClure's Magazine* in New York, Cather gradually came to feel the need for a new direction in her thirty-eight-year-old life. "Being bored eats the heart out of me," she wrote in a fictionalized version of her ordeal a few years afterward. And so, escaping from the urban routine under which she was "half-anaesthetized all the time," Cather in 1912 departed for the canyonlands of northern Arizona, hoping, as does her frazzled character Thea Kronborg in *The Song of the Lark* (1915), to "get some of my spring back."[1]

In fact, as most of her biographers have noted, the 1912 trip to the Southwest was a turning point in Cather's life. "Everything that had happened to her since she had been there," Cather wrote in the story of Thea's recuperative confrontation with Panther Cañon, was "more than had happened in all her life before." Thea spends several weeks living near an ancient Indian cliff dwelling, bathing frequently in the waters of a stream on the cañon's floor. "In the rapid, restless heart of it, flowing swifter than the rest, there was a continuity of life that reached back into the old time," Cather observed. "Thea's bath came to have a ceremonial gravity. The atmosphere of the cañon was ritualistic." The centuries-old relics strewn about the rooms of the empty cliff houses also possessed profound meaning for her: "These potsherds were like fetters that bound one to a long chain of human endeavor," wrote Cather; they made "the world seem older and richer." Consequently, Thea's encounter with the landscape and tradition of the cañon enables her to gather together her true identity and purpose: "The things that were really hers separated themselves from the rest. Her ideas were simplified, became sharper and clearer. She felt united and strong." As Cather discerned of both Thea's and her own experiences in the Southwest, "The Cliff-Dwellers had lengthened her past"; she now had "older and higher obligations."[2]

The discovery of the "things which seemed destined for her" in the vanished culture of the Ancient People eventually led Cather back to the "windy Nebraska tableland" of the Divide country as another source for her art. Her awakening to the emotive, aesthetic, and spiritual power of folkways intertwined with natural environment brought her to "a new consciousness of the country . . . almost a new relation to it," a realization of "how much the country meant to her." Or so she described the parallel epiphany of protagonist Alexandra Bergson in *O Pioneers!* (1913), a novel which had lain in fragments before Cather's Southwestern trip but which she thereafter expanded and transformed, inaugurating a decade and a half of great productivity and literary achievement. If, like the poet Virgil, Cather hoped to be "the first . . . to bring the muse into my country," she intended the word *country* in the same sense as the *patria* of Virgil's *Georgics*: "Not a nation or even a province," she explained in *My Ántonia* (1918), "but the little rural neighbourhood on the Mincio where the poet was born . . . his own little 'country,'" a place that one knows intimately, its boundaries defined not merely by geographic features but by memory and experience, friendship and kinship. As Jim Burden remarks near the end of the novel, "I found that I remembered the conformation of the land as one remembers the modelling of human faces." Yet Cather's belief that her folkish source material represented "immemorial human attitudes which we recognize by instinct as universal and true" allowed her regionalism to transcend mere autobiography or local color, unifying the disparate "countries" that she visited and revisited over the course of her career—the Nebraska prairie with its immigrant folk communities, the Southwestern plateauland with its cliff cities, priests, and pueblos.[3] For, like patria, "country" could encompass a larger cache of meanings: the setting of an enriching rural life-style, the provinces that exist outside a cosmopolitan court and capital, and the national state whose central myths are encapsulated in the "little neighbourhood" of the poet.

In *My Ántonia*, there is a famous moment when Jim Burden and his friends the immigrant "country girls," out picnicking, contemplate the legendary sixteenth-century visitation of the Spanish explorer Coronado to a featureless Nebraska landscape suddenly become magical. "Presently we saw a curious thing," Burden recalls:

> On some upland farm, a plough had been left standing in the field. The sun was sinking just behind it. Magnified across the distance by the horizontal light, it stood out against the sun, was exactly contained within the circle of the disc; the handles, the tongue, the share—black against the molten red. There it was, heroic in size, a picture writing on the sun.

> Even while we whispered about it, our vision disappeared; the ball dropped and dropped until the red tip went beneath the earth. The fields below us were dark, the sky was growing pale, and that forgotten plough had sunk back to its own littleness somewhere on the prairie.

Cather spent much of her career trying to hold onto "the precious, the incommunicable past," the passing folk and frontier life that her narratives captured glimpses of at full noontime and inevitable twilight. On her trips from New York to see relatives in Red Cloud, she witnessed what Jim Burden witnesses: "The old pasture land was now being broken up into wheatfields and cornfields, the red grass was disappearing, and the whole face of the country was changing." The original prairie endured only in tiny, fenced-off "unploughed patches" over the graves of pioneers like *My Ántonia's* Mr. Shimerda and "Neighbour Rosicky." One by one as they passed away, the elderly farmwives whom Cather had known since childhood were crossed from her Christmas list. As she wrote of Niel Herbert in *A Lost Lady* (1923), "He had seen the end of an era, the sunset of the pioneer. He had come upon it when already its glory was nearly spent." Cather's sense of loss, her sense that "the world broke in two in 1922 or thereabouts," relegating the prewar period "back into yesterday's seven thousand years," contributed to a mid-life crisis in the early 1920s, despite all her worldly success. Like Gregory St. Peter in *The Professor's House* (1925), she "did not regret [her] life," but she had become "indifferent to it."[4]

Once again, Cather sought a solution in art, and a rejuvenation of her art in the culture of the Southwest, traveling to Santa Fe and Taos, New Mexico, in 1924–26, pursuing "those long, rugged, untamed vistas dear to the American heart" prescribed for the depressed and suicidal Professor St. Peter—"dear to all hearts probably," Cather believed, "at least, calling to all." On this trip, however, she immersed herself in a tradition not of folk culture, but of folk acculturation. In the history of the desert diocese of the French missionary priests, kindred spirits displaying open-mindedness and cultivation, she discovered a tradition that tolerated and appreciated "the Indian's way to pass through a country without disturbing anything . . . to vanish into the landscape, not to stand out against it" . . . to become "the landscape made human." As Cather's Bishop marvels in *Death Comes for the Archbishop* (1927), the mesa dwellers, "who must share the universal human yearning for something permanent, enduring, without shadow of change,—they had their idea in substance." Significantly, at the close of the novel, Cather describes the expulsion of the Navajo from their beloved Canyon de Chelly by the U.S. government in the late nineteenth century. "Their country," a chief objects futilely, "was a part of their religion; the two were inseparable . . . it had nourished and protected them; it was their mother." As Cather herself observes, "Their gods were there, just as the Padre's God was in his church." Finally, after five years of wasting away on inhospitable new lands, the Navajo are allowed to return to their "sacred places": "once more crops were growing down at the bottom of the world between the towering sandstone walls; sheep were grazing under the magnificent cottonwoods and drinking at the streams of sweet water; it was like an Indian Garden of Eden." In his old age, the Bishop expresses Cather's own hopes for the modern fate of regional America: "I do not believe, as I once did, that the Indian will perish. I believe that God will preserve him."[5]

To Cather herself, "art and religion" were "the same thing, in the end, of course." Folk-regional values constituted the "eternal material of art," sieved from memory and history and the "teeming, gleaming stream of the present," out on the "bright edges of the world." In these "countries" that her art made peculiarly her own, the "great grass plains" and the "sage-brush desert," Cather found renewal, a sense of freedom and of possibility: "Something soft and wild and free, something that whispered to the ear on the pillow, lightened the heart, softly, softly picked the lock, slid the bolts, and released the spirit of man into the wind, into the blue and gold, into the morning, into the morning!"[6] This discovery of the region as a basis for wholesale personal and cultural rejuvenation was one that a number of American artists and intellectuals arrived at in the course of the 1920s. Cather's exposition of the regionalist sensibility in her life and works, interpreted loosely as an archetype, suggests a pattern of biographical preconditions shared among many of these individuals who converged during the decade to form the sprawling set of intellectual circles and friendships that comprised the larger movement.

The most critical of these "preconditions" was an upbringing within or at least some measure of exposure to a folk group or broadly defined *traditional* social order, such as a rural or village life-style, and the landscape of which it was a part. Given this exposure, Cather's real and fictive biography indicates several consequent avenues that might lead toward the emergence of a self-conscious regionalist mind-set, none necessarily exclusive of the rest (as Cather's own life demonstrates). One fairly common and crucial path was the painful personal experience of the erosion and transformation of such folk cultures by the forces of modernization. Another possible path was the mobile and ambitious native son's or daughter's fruitless search for meaning out in the wider urban-industrial world, or an ill-starred career within it, resulting finally in a homeward yearning for the region. Conversely, still another path lay in a revelatory outsider's discovery of the exotic provincial by the aimless modern city dweller.

These various more direct regionalist-formative experiences were intertwined with a broader precondition of the conventional (or one might more precisely say, *unconventional*) personal experience of modern artistic and intellectual training, education, and development. Virtually all regionalist men and women were first-generation academics, scholars, and artists, and most came from older-stock, white middle- or lower middle-class origins—the sons and daughters of farmers, ranchers, rural–small-town schoolteachers, ministers, or shopkeepers. A few arose from humbler beginnings; folksong collector John Lomax, for example, described his roots as "the upper crust of the 'po' white trash.'" At least two—namely, Native American authors D'Arcy McNickle and John Joseph Mathews—were born to mixed-racial families, and thus their life experiences diverged significantly, if not essentially, from those of white regionalists (both McNickle and Mathews attended the very Anglo-white Oxford University, for instance). In any case, most future regionalists had been schooled from birth in the pervasive verities of late nineteenth- and early twentieth-century bourgeois culture, and most departed on a "road not taken" out of this background, self-consciously rejecting many of its pieties and expectations (such as revealed, organized religion, faith in historical progress, and commercial, consumerist values) even as they necessarily continued to be influenced, subtly, by those same beliefs.[7]

If this alienated road not taken carried some American interwar intellectuals toward Marxism, and others to New Humanism, and still others to cosmopolitanism, it took regionalists, of course, to and through the *region*. Not only their formal education but also the culture and history of their regions provided alternative pieties that served both to overcome and exacerbate their ambivalence regarding modernity. The region supplied materials for the artistic and scholarly production important to an unconventional career, and values which formed a new basis for personal action and belief as well as a critical, distancing perspective on the contemporary cultural consensus. Cather's own case amply shows that as a consequence of the attainment of this regional consciousness, personal identity could and did become enmeshed with regional identity. In practical terms, the exploration, cultivation, and preservation of a regional culture became the vocation of the individual artist or intellectual. Region and regionalist rose from the unknown and into the known together. His or her career hinged upon making the local and obscure into the national, universal, and significant. For some artistic explorers of the region, like Cather herself (or William Faulkner or Thomas Wolfe), this transmutation was conducted with an emphasis on individual characterization, psychology, the drama itself. As Faulkner once said, "The sociological qualities are only . . . coincidental to the story—the story is still the story of the human being, the human heart struggling."[8] Avoiding the "sociological" for whatever aesthetic or philosophical reasons meant, however, that artists such as Cather or Faulkner also largely avoided the political dimension of the regional settings their art so evocatively depicted. In contrast, those artists and intellectuals who composed the core of the regionalist movement proper perceived the region not primarily as a locality of unique, irreducible individuals but as an environmental, economic, and political entity, and thus, above all, as a sociological and *ideological* construct. For these regionalists, a national or "universal" perspective and definition of the problems and injustices—as well as the virtues—of a region were often the starting point of social and cultural criticism and, possibly, of individual political consciousness.

Manifestly, despite her other helpful guideposts, Cather's more atypical apolitical career underscores the unsurprising fact that no one individual can "emblematically" represent all of the diversity of artistic and intellectual orientations that emerged in these years with regard to the region. Indeed, the depiction of the coalescence of the regionalist movement proper out of such a multiplex confluence of individual lives and aspirations faces some difficulties because of the very nature of regionalism. Aptly enough, with its credo of decentralization, the movement itself had no center, no directing or dominating group. It was a *movement* less from its formal or organizational cohesiveness than from its simultaneity across the country, a simultaneity that stemmed, it is true, from common generational experiences and backgrounds (farmboys turned academics, for example), but that issued most crucially from a confrontation with common cultural, intellectual, and political problems (the future of rural America, to name one). Local knots and circles began forming particularly in the mid- to late 1920s, often taking shape as select cores of articulately self-conscious regionalist theorists (many of the main subjects of this chapter) surrounded by penumbras of bit players (such as Lew Sarett, Vardis Fisher, and Haniel Long), distinguished fellow travelers (Waldo Frank, Vernon Parrington, and Van Wyck Brooks), and brilliant lone wolves (William Faulkner, Robert Frost, Georgia O'Keeffe, and Cather herself). Tracing the strands of all of these lives as they were woven into an intricate national cultural map becomes a matter of choosing among a number of people and places equally appropriate as starting points, of finding where in the vista to drop down and begin following faint lines backward toward antecedents and outward to other centers, along the strong ties of friendship and the looser bonds of mutual awareness and common interest that linked the movement together.

The Santa Fe and Taos art colonies of New Mexico, dear to Cather's heart, will serve as well as any place as a starting point. Certainly these colonies have as good a claim as any to the oxymoronic title of regionalist capital. During the 1920s and 1930s, the flourishing artistic scene there exerted a powerful shearing pull against the New York–Hollywood cultural axis. The stark beauty of the mesas and mountains and the mysterious primitivism of the Pueblo tribes attracted the likes of Aldous Huxley, D. H. Lawrence, and numerous other high-cultural luminaries. More importantly for the movement itself, with its rare intraregional meetings and conferences, Santa Fe and Taos were the closest thing to a "nexus" (or perhaps, "touchstone") which sprang up in the interwar years. At one time or another, regionalists from the South, the Southwest, the Midwest, and elsewhere felt the need for a short visit or a longer stay.

Yet besides their substantial salon life (courtesy of Mabel Dodge Luhan), the New Mexican colonies were special because of their presiding spirit, Mary Austin. Like Cather, Austin was of an older generation than many of those who became the leading lights of the interwar regionalist movement. Her books, dating back to *The Land of Little Rain* in 1903, as well as her tireless promotional efforts helped to kindle over the years a national interest in American Indian and folk culture. In 1919, reflecting on the recent works of Edgar Lee Masters and Carl Sandburg, Austin told *Poetry* editor Alice Corbin Henderson that at last "Americanism is beginning to make itself felt in its own medium":

When I think of how I have struggled during the past fifteen years to help bring this about, how many letters of commendation to editors publishers and others who gave this medium its opportunity, how many bitter fights with the same gentry on my own account, how many times I have done it

up in pink jewelers cotton for Women's Clubs, or ripped up in its interest
the modest complacency of University professors, I feel as a woman must
who sees her children grow up and beyond the need of her.

More directly, Austin in her final years influenced and encouraged a number of
young writers and editors who were then working to develop an indigenous
culture for the greater Southwest beyond New Mexico. Expressing gratitude
to the budding young radical Carey McWilliams (then making his brief intersection with the movement) for dedicating his short study *The New Regionalism* (1931) to her, Austin confessed with a considerable degree of truthfulness
her role as a pre–World War I "caretaker" of the regionalist tradition: "I have
have been all my life looking toward just such a development as you describe."[9]

Cather herself wrote the final chapters of *Death Comes for the Archbishop*
in Austin's Santa Fe home, Casa Querida. The house, built in 1924 of traditional adobe, decorated in Navajo, Hispanic, and Pueblo motifs, was an important way station on the spiritual and artistic journeys of both women. The
fifty-three-year-old Cather completed there the book that signified the summit of her career. During the remaining two decades of her life, her ever-
darkening vision found diminishing solace in the early traditionalist days of
such "countries" as the Rock of Quebec. In the antebellum Virginia setting of
Sapphira and the Slave Girl (1939), one of her few and lesser works of the
1930s, the idyllic was more and more overwhelmed by the evil and the tragic
(and again, as will be seen, this change in Cather archetypified tendencies in
the larger movement). For Austin, lately of the intellectual and artistic communities in New York and Carmel, Casa Querida announced her arrival at the
center of the awakening cultural scene in Santa Fe and Taos and the Southwest as a whole. "What I felt in New Mexico," Austin later reflected, "was the
possibility of the reinstatement of the hand-craft culture and of the folk
drama," her patronage of the former especially evident in Casa Querida.
Even more than for Cather, New Mexico became her literal "Land of Journey's Ending," the place where she spent the last ten years of her life. As she
explained in her autobiography *Earth Horizon* (1932), "I liked the feel of roots,
of ordered growth and progression, continuity, all of which I found in the
Southwest."[10]

Earth Horizon, in fact, with its portrait of a mind gripped more powerfully
even than Cather's by the totalistic self-enfolding mysticism and communitarianism of folk culture, furnishes a further set of insights into the regionalist
mind-set, as well as additional archetypal variations and confirmations of the
biographical sources of the regionalist orientation. As preparation for the
work that came to be called *The Land of Journey's Ending*, Austin in 1918

made "one prolonged survey" of "the country between the Colorado and the Rio Grande." The trip, she wrote, "gathered all the years of my life; all my experience; my intentions; it determined the years that were left." Her regionalist sensibility, like Cather's, had been nurtured within diverse landscapes encountered since her "Middlewestern" youth in Macoupin County, Illinois, during the 1870s and 1880s. The "country neighborhoods" near the "Methodist small town" of Carlinville were then still marked by lingering influences of "the pioneer period in the history of which she reveled." Folk songs and old hymns, the art of farmhouse cooking, a book entitled *Progress and Poverty* ("which was something like the Bible, only more important"), her whole rambling childhood in and around "the house on Plum Street with its adjacent woods and pastures"—all left their imprint on Austin, even as the town and its environs petrified into something staid and respectable, and "culture" came to mean Chautauqua and the genteel parlor clutter of "Whatnot." As Austin observed, it was a time "when the early American tradition of beauty and suitability in household furnishings and the appurtenences of cultivated living was ebbing fast, and no new aesthetic, native to the time and experience, [was] rising in its place." Life in the central Illinois of that period, she concluded, had reached "a dead level of fulfillment." Thus, soon after her graduation from teachers' college in 1888, she accompanied her mother to the San Joaquin Valley of California, where her older brother had preceded them, and "where there was still to be had Government land for the taking."[11]

The years of homesteading in California were the next significant phase in Austin's regionalist education. On their way to the Tejon district during the late summer of 1888, in the arroyos of the chaparral, she became aware of an "insistent experiential pang" for such "beauty-in-the-wild," beauty, she sensed, that was "yearning to be made human," a "lurking, evasive Something, wistful, cruel, ardent; something that rustled and ran . . . and when you turned from it, leaped suddenly and fastened on your vitals." In the coming months, as Austin wrote of herself, "she was out every day and sometimes all day on her horse . . . making contacts with sheepherders, Indians, and tall Spanish-speaking vaqueros," not to mention miners, ranchers, other homesteaders, and migrant workers. "She attended round-ups, brandings, shearings," Austin remembered. "She began to learn how Indians live off a land upon which more sophisticated races would starve, and how the land itself instructed them." Finally, on a dry April morning in 1889, walking through a sandy hollow where flowers bloomed around pools of runoff, she had one of the strongest of a lifelong series of mystical experiences, a feeling of the "warm pervasive sweetness of ultimate reality . . . never to go away again, never to be completely out of call"—"ultimate, immaterial reality . . . the only true and absolute."[12]

This incident, according to Austin, ended a "long spiritual drought" and, although she analogized that "only the Christian saints" had "made the right words" to describe what had happened to her, it broke her "commitment to organized religion" as well. This ascent into personalized mysticism was in fact merely her first departure from bourgeois expectations. By the latter 1890s, trapped in a dreary marriage and cut off from a mother who had always been cold toward her, Austin sought escape and solace in a "study of Indian verse, strange and meaningful; of Indian wisdom, Indian art," especially of the California Paiutes. In her description, "she consorted with them; she laid herself open to the influences of the wild . . . she entered into their lives, the life of the campody, the strange secret life of the tribe." Out of this whole web of confrontation with folk culture, Austin began to weave her own unique brand of mysticism, expressed through such concepts as the "Earth Horizon":

> In the Rain Song of the Sia, Earth Horizon is the incalculable blue ring of sky meeting earth, which is the source of experience. It is pictured as felt rays of earth energy running together from the horizon to the middle place where the heart of man, the recipient of experience, is established, and there treasured. . . . At the Middle Place, where all influences of the Earth Horizon come to equilibrium, experience explains itself, flowers and fruits in the holder.[13]

The more prosaic ramifications of these alternative pieties of regional culture through Austin's personal life indicate a larger biographical pattern encompassing women regionalists particularly, a pattern in which the regionalist divergence from middle-class conventions was perhaps most manifest. Armored by her new folk-regional faith, Austin broke free from her "total disappointment" of a marriage—never to remarry—and, somewhat later, she placed her only child, a mentally handicapped daughter, in an institution. She struck off for an independent literary career, making her living from the material she had gathered in the outback of California. In this rejection of the middle-class destinies of dutiful wife and mother or dependent spinsterhood, a rejection relatively unusual in its time, both Austin and Cather were joined by the younger generation of the other prominent women artists and intellectuals of the interwar movement. Constance Rourke, Mari Sandoz, Angie Debo—each either never married or was married young and briefly, then permanently divorced. Each of them, in turn, supported herself largely by freelancing, because there were few or no career prospects in male-ruled academia. (By contrast, virtually all of the male regionalists enjoyed a conventional married and family life, and most were academics, though, as will be seen, this life-road too involved for many a personal revolt of sorts.)[14]

In books such as her first, *The Land of Little Rain*, Austin attempted to verbalize her individual experience of integrated tribal life and symbiosis with nature, and over the years this work and others brought her growing fame as an author and entry into the fashionable literary circles of Carmel, London, and New York. Yet, like Cather, Austin came to feel disenchanted with the self-absorbed focus of the urban salon life and lecture circuit. "The thing I suffered from worst in New York was boredom," she later recalled. "The people I met were seldom interested in the things that interested me." New York "missed the open order of the country west of the Alleghenies. . . . It lacked freshness, air and light. More than anything else it lacked pattern," Austin declared, "and I had a pattern-hungry mind." California as well, she wrote, "had slipped away from me," in more ways than one. By the 1910s, "changes at Carmel had made of it a faded leaf, pressed for remembrance." As for her beloved Inyo country, setting for *The Land of Little Rain*, "on the life there, the unforgettable life," developers had laid "a greedy, vulgarizing hand." In comparison, Santa Fe, which she discovered on her 1918 expedition in northern New Mexico, seemed to provide "such an abundance of fresh, workable material" that she would be able to escape the "labored staleness which overtakes one in older localities." This withdrawal to and celebration of the provinces was, of course, the definitive life-event for all regionalists, but it should be noted that as a decision it was a congeries of personal as well as artistic-intellectual motives. For example, like so many others who settled and visited there, Austin found that Santa Fe was a place of "simple pleasures inexpensively attained, such as gardening, the collection of folk art, and easy hospitality." But at the same time, the awesome surrounding landscape and the exotic local Indian and Hispanic traditions seemed to her to hold "the key to an understanding of the whole pattern of civilized society."[15]

The ten years following the construction of Casa Querida coincided with the rise and high-water mark of regionalism as a national movement, and during that period Austin, although increasingly bothered by ill-health, made her presence felt through books, essays, and reviews, as well as her shared leadership with Luhan and Witter Bynner of the important New Mexico wing, stretching from Taos and Santa Fe to Albuquerque and Las Cruces. She filled her life with the cause of regional America, working on behalf of the local Indian Arts Fund and Spanish Colonial Arts Society and, more significantly for the movement outside New Mexico, acting as critic, confidant, and adviser to a number of prominent regionalists scattered across the awakening West. From her, we can thus begin to sketch one exemplifying web of the kind of influences and exchanges that bound regionalists into their widely dispersed "movement." As one example, a decade or so after Austin's death in 1934 (her ashes sealed within a crevice in the Sangre de Cristo Mountains), editor John H. McGinnis of the Dallas-based *Southwest Review* recalled that Austin was the first to convince him that regionalism "*could* be a philosophy"—"I learned from her in person."[16] McGinnis's coeditor at Southern Methodist University, Henry Nash Smith, was also strongly under her influence (writing a 1931 examination of "Mary Austin's Prophesy"), as was Carey McWilliams, beginning his career out in their mutually adopted country of California. Others, at a further distance, gave Austin's editorial and philosophical opinions considerable weight—B. A. Botkin, while launching the *Folk-Say* anthologies in Oklahoma, and H. G. Merriam, who welcomed Austin to a 1932 Missoula, Montana, regionalist conference, hoping to invigorate the movement in the Northwest.

Each of these individuals, moving for a time within Austin's orbit, had discovered regionalism via a different path, each of them creating still further variations on the basic patterns of antecedents suggested by Cather and Austin. To focus on one example, McWilliams, like Austin, and like an array of other regionalists (among them, Walter Prescott Webb, Angie Debo, Bernard DeVoto, J. Frank Dobie, Mari Sandoz, and John Lomax), spent a youth in impressionable contact with what they perceived to be the closing frontier. McWilliams himself was born in 1906 and grew up near Steamboat Springs in the Yampa River region of northwestern Colorado. It was a rugged alpine country of large ranching operations, one of which was owned by his father. Here McWilliams lived among horses and cowboys, with periodic stays in Denver. "Growing up in such an extravagantly beautiful, long-isolated, sparsely settled mountain paradise induced in me, as a youngster, a strange sense of timelessness," he reflected years later. "To me the settlements seemed as timeless, as resistant to change, as the landscape." But after the heady days of high cattle demand during World War I, "this very special pastoral 'world' of the open-range cattle industry suddenly and dramatically collapsed," and, as McWilliams remembered, "the shock was the greater for being wholly unanticipated." The experience, he wrote, "turned my life upside down. My father died, the family fortune vanished, and my mother and her two sons became migrants." By 1922 (the year, he noted, that F. Scott Fitzgerald said the "Jazz Age actually peaked"), McWilliams found himself "a nearly penniless 'expatriate' in Southern California, just as the fantastic boom of the 1920s was beginning to gather momentum." There, having been expelled from one closed frontier (already the ski resorts that were to make Steamboat the "St. Moritz of the West" were being constructed), he witnessed over the course of a decade "the whole saga of frontier growth and westward expansion, the storybook version of the American Dream" given "its penultimate staging in a semi-tropical setting at the western edge of the continent . . . , the reenactment accelerated at such a pace that it attracted worldwide interest and attention." As part of the burgeoning bohemian community of Los Angeles, he came under the influence of H. L. Mencken, who encouraged him, along with many others, to "concentrate on the American scene." Thus, during the late 1920s and early 1930s McWilliams became "intensely interested in regionalism and regional culture," developing "a lively interest in American folklore and Californiana," writing a biography of Ambrose Bierce, and starting "an extensive literary correspondence" with Austin and other Western authors. His advice to aspiring regional artists and intellectuals? "Young Man, Stay West."[17]

Many of them, however, did go east, to New York, New England, and across the Atlantic, before returning to the American provinces. Henry Smith's experiences are instructive. Born in the same year as McWilliams, he grew up amid the explosive urban growth that transformed Texas cities like his hometown Dallas from small commercial centers—walkable cities with middle-class neighborhoods and shops—into would-be metropolises whose expansion was fueled by giant oil strikes. He graduated at age eighteen from Southern Methodist, and he departed for Harvard in 1926 to complete his master's degree. Even years afterward, when back at Harvard to pursue his doctorate, an older and more mature Smith would describe his status there as "a sojourner": "Behold me an exile," he wrote home only half-jokingly. His regionalist education continued after his return to Dallas in 1927, when he assumed a position on the "super-graduate seminar" (as Smith himself called it) of McGinnis's *Southwest Review*, already well on its way to becoming the focus of a broader Texas regionalist network including critic Howard Mumford Jones, folklorist J. Frank Dobie, and artist Jerry Bywaters. Smith's tour of Europe in 1930, moreover, must also be counted part of his educative process. He summed up all of his confrontations with traditionalism, and his search for the proper setting of the artistic vocation, in letters to Mary Austin and in a 1930 *Review* article, "On Living in America." Writing from Munich, he depicted a society that had reached a kind of cultural saturation point, caught in stasis, a stagnant place in which "one has the feeling that all the possibilities of life have been thought out and put into literature or painting or sculpture, so that all that remains for the artist of the present is to search out super-refinements and yet more delicate nuances, at grave risk of losing himself in the backward recesses and on the edges of consciousness." Expatriation was therefore no real solution for the American seeking a nurturing environment. Yet neither did the East Coast cultural establishment have much to offer. The "traditions" that he was schooled in at Harvard were merely rote derivatives, "parasitic attachments," of European values and ideas: "New York has been engaging in this idolatry of Europe for a little while, Boston much longer; and the universities have never pretended to do anything else." But there were, Smith concluded, "American alternatives" to expatriation or "insufferable" residence in New York. "It is possible to learn to get along very well without

most of such metropolitan stimuli," he wrote. "These things have a surface
air. They were not necessary for a Kant at Konigsberg, a Goethe at Weimar, a
Wordsworth at Cumberland. . . . There is more repose where things are not so
noisy; the air is fresher where it has not been breathed before, even by a
genius."[18]

But Smith, like many regionalists, did not reject traditionalism outright. If
he largely agreed that "living in America, it is said, is inhabiting a void," he
nevertheless believed that one might choose to live in "the void" in order "to
build." In fact, Smith thought an indigenous traditionalism was exactly the
prescription needed to fill the American void: "There will be no American
civilization"—in the sense that Europeans were civilized—"until a whole is
realized—a whole which is the integration, not merely the aggregation, of all
the complex of physical environment and government and religion and art, a
whole which includes all these and is all these." To begin this realization,
Smith looked to his own Southwest to acquire what to his mind was the most
American of traditions: "There is still need for pioneering," he wrote, "though
the wildernesses to be conquered are not the same." The long task of "making
this continent habitable" had hitherto degenerated into an industrialized
routine; pioneering must consequently shift to the "spiritual" realm and "form
a new world" out of this chaos. The American artist must reclaim the "intuition of the pioneer" because, Smith asserted in almost Hegelian terms, "more
than any other man may the pioneer feel himself part of the realizing process
by which the being of the universe is maintained and ever brought nearer to
complete expression." In this way "the individual may integrate his personality and realize his potentialities," for in helping to build a genuine American
civilization he becomes nothing less than "intimately concerned in creative
processes analogous to the formation of the Christian Church or the feudal
system."[19]

This was what brought Smith and others who went abroad from their
regions back home, and into the regionalist movement—"the privilege of
helping to make a civilization," as Smith put it. This same two-sided sense of
cultural malaise and possibility, gleaned from refined yet stale "older localities" in America and Europe, may be seen even more clearly in the case of
the far-ranging H. G. Merriam, who settled in the mountain Northwest at
Missoula, a small college town tucked into the folds of the Continental Divide.
Born in 1883 at Westminster, Massachusetts, he attended high school in
Denver, Colorado, and graduated in 1905 with a B.A. from the University of
Wyoming, where he earned a slot among the first group of American Rhodes
scholars. Two Oxford degrees later, Merriam returned to the United States
and a decade-long series of teaching posts in Washington, Wisconsin, and
Oregon, punctuated by an Austin fellowship at Harvard in 1910. He spent

World War I in France working for the YMCA, and after the armistice lived in London a year. Finally, in 1919, Merriam accepted a job at the University of Montana, where he remained until his retirement in 1954. And what impressions had all his ramblings left him with? "The present Greenwich Village makes me sick," he told poet Lew Sarett in 1927; moreover, "I lived so long in Europe that nothing can shake my Americanism." Many years afterward, he traced the origins of *The Frontier*—the Missoula-based magazine which he edited for nearly two decades and which was the center of the Northwestern regionalist wing—"to a day when, as a student at Oxford University, I sat in on a lecture by Ernest De Selincourt on Shelley, Keats, and other poets in the spring of 1906":

> In that lecture he aroused both musing and annoyance, for he apologized for lecturing on poets as recent as these writers. He felt that their place in literature had not been established although nearly three-quarters of a century had passed since their death.
>
> Was the enjoyment of a writing as a profound piece of human experience skillfully expressed to be limited to writings at least a hundred years old? A spirit of rebellion came over me.

To Merriam, the definition of a classic was a work grounded not in antiquity, but "founded in the universals of mankind's thought and feeling." The "idea of regionalism," he argued, which swept aside the tired ethereal haute culture of literary allusion and books about books, engaging the artist and intellectual again in the fundamentals of existence, "tends to be a releasing factor, a step, at least, towards the so-called universal." Like Smith, though, Merriam acknowledged that his region's "present intellectual life is lagging," and it was his hope to re-create his personal experience of the richness of the older cultural capitals right at home in Montana. As he wrote to skeptical Idaho native Ezra Pound in Italy in 1931, "I am interested in maintaining American mental life at something comparable to the European level."[20]

B. A. Botkin's discovery of the possibilities of this provincial "void" came during a life journey that was the reverse of that made by regional "native sons" like Smith and Merriam, one that instead took him out of the metropolis and into the provinces. Born and raised in Boston, Massachusetts, as a member of a close-knit Jewish family and educated at Harvard (1920) and Columbia (1921), he seemed an unlikely regionalist. Many young Jewish intellectual contemporaries, with similar backgrounds, were to establish their reputations in the flowering New York City intellectual community of the 1930s. With hindsight, Botkin later contended that his participation in the regionalist movement stemmed in part from his roots in rich Jewish traditions and folkways: "My adaptability and my devotion to the 'cause' are part of my heritage." Yet he was living in New York (and later would be drawn back there) when he received a job offer to teach at the University of Oklahoma beginning in the fall of 1921. Mustering some enthusiasm, he remarked in a letter written before his departure that "I desire a place where, with an adequate income, I can enjoy leisure and peace for thought without going into a state of suspended animation." In any case, he added, "if Main Street, Norman, is dull, then Main Street, New York, is as many times duller as it is longer. And for me the first has the advantage of being quiet and affording a quick escape to the country."[21]

Initially, Botkin was rather ambivalent about his new home in the small university town and county seat: "Here all is flat monotony, save for the sunsets and the green winter wheat. . . . Culture in Norman is illusory. . . . I shall never regret my year here, but should regret another year here." As anticipated, there were some compensations for him, such as morning walks in the countryside. For it was during one of these strolls that he had what was perhaps a revelatory outsider's encounter with the "exotic provincial"—in this instance, a local tenant farm family traveling by wagon. These were Botkin's somewhat romanticized impressions at the time:

> Now the wagons approached, with plodding mules, a boy in overalls mounted on a mule by the side. Two or three men occupied the seat, and within I had a glimpse of women and children, bedding and household goods. I drew in a breath: this was a taste of pioneering. . . . More curious than gypsies they were. . . . Outlandish, poor, sombre, they were my first view of the rough, shifting life of the west.

And if into the spring semester of that first year he remained disappointed with the intellectual climate of Norman, Botkin was already germinating an unconscious predisposition toward folklore and the life of the folk—though still, at this point, perceiving them from the vantage of the refined Harvard snob:

> On Saturdays the greatest source of interest for me is the wagon-yards, where the farmers herd their vehicles and some of their wives, in ridiculous hats, perched up on the seat. . . . I happened by on my way to the University Library and rubbed shoulders with and was stepped upon and narrowly escaped being spat upon by the gaunt, leathery-faced, unshaven farmers who assisted at the spiritless bidding for a huge yellow motor truck. . . . I was surprised to find a grain of wit among these hairy rustics.[22]

Ultimately, Botkin took a two-year leave of absence in the East, including (as he reminisced to "fellow Harvard man" Henry Smith in 1929) "an unsuccessful wooing of New York." It was only on his return to Oklahoma in 1925, he wrote, that "I began to realize what Oklahoma meant to me. I had grown a half-inch or so taller when I first came out, and now I began to grow mentally and spiritually. . . . The East was complete without me; there were no worlds left to conquer—this side of the Mississippi. But *jenseits* everything was plastic to my touch. First there were my students to mold, and then some public opinion in the University and the state of my adoption." After several more years on this cultural frontier, Botkin was able to articulate to Mary Austin "what it is that holds us here in Norman in spite of the physical and spiritual flatness of the place":

> We agreed that it was the community of cultural interests that binds a few congenial spirits together in a town small enough to be free from the mercenary self-seeking that taints friendship in the cities and large enough to lose oneself in when one wants to be alone, free from the snooping, hampering conventions of the usual small town—this and the physical freedom of space (the open country at one's back door and the broad sweep of sky always overhead) that constitutes the lure. I see in it an equilibrium of man and nature, for nature triumphs over man's attempts to mechanize the life of the region with the ubiquitous standardization of automobile, radio, talkies, electrical conveniences, etc. . . . and the ugliness of his buildings. . . . This is where I have learned and am applying what I flatter myself with calling a regional philosophy; and I am not only attached to this place but grateful to it.[23]

Many such "communities of cultural interest," binding "a few congenial spirits together," began assembling themselves across America during the mid- and late 1920s, all of them engaged in "learning and applying a regional philosophy." To complete in summary fashion this sketch of the cultural-intellectual map of the regionalist movement in America, circa 1930, we should note that, comprising the Greater West region, in addition to the New Mexican colonies, Albuquerque (T. M. Pearce's emerging *New Mexico Quarterly* group), Missoula in the Northwest, and Norman and Dallas in the Southwest, there were Midwestern circles at Lincoln, Nebraska (L. C. Wimberly and the *Prairie Schooner*, novelist Mari Sandoz), and at Iowa City, Iowa (John T. Frederick's *Midland*, artist Grant Wood). The Southwestern network also incorporated Austin, Texas (focal point of the "Texas Triumverate"—J. Frank Dobie, historian Walter Prescott Webb, naturalist Roy Bedichek). Concurrently, to the east, there were the regionalist centers of the South: Nashville, Tennessee (home base of the Agrarians), Chapel Hill, North Carolina (Howard Odum and his regional planning group, W. T. Couch's University of North Carolina Press), Charlottesville, Virginia (Stringfellow Barr's already nationally prominent *Quarterly Review*), and, emerging somewhat later, the Baton Rouge circle (Robert Penn Warren and the *Southern Review* editors). And to the north, headquartered, as it were, in and around the camp of the enemy—New York City—there were the members of Lewis Mumford's circle, especially, the Regional Planning Association of America.

The "regional philosophy"—or more precisely, *philosophies*—toward which all of these points of cultural activity were converging was not merely a matter, as has been implied thus far, of diverging from bourgeois conventions, or breaking from a European culture gone to seed, or disdaining a parochial and narcissistic New York literati, or rejecting a hoary academic canon— however liberating such "roads not taken" might seem. As Cather's second self-rescue in the benign acculturative tradition of her Archbishop suggests, the rediscovery of American traditions necessitated acts of recovery, of salvaging and preserving folk-regional cultural complexes under modernizing pressures from all sides. Botkin's persistent ambivalence about his adopted "country" of Norman and the state of Oklahoma encased a core of fundamental devotion, a devotion that devolved from his perception in the small university city of an accommodating middle ground—a ground self-consciously cultivated, *created* by "a few congenial spirits"—between the traditional and the modern, the rural and the urban, the natural and the cultural. Yet this middle ground, the heart of the regionalist vision, was constantly slipping out from under him (hence his ambivalence), as it was for others who perceived it in their own regions, because it was obscured and threatened by cultural change both subtle and catastrophic. "The struggle to be oneself in an environment that isn't always positively encouraging," Donald Davidson wrote to fellow Southern poet John Gould Fletcher, "isn't as hopeless as at times it has seemed." Nevertheless, he added, "the problem of *being* grows enormously acute for us; we cannot endure many more *Waste Lands*." But one had to continue the struggle: "I believe we are all trying to formulate . . . some kind of *modus vivendi* for Southern Americans. . . . Myths must undergo reanimation, or we must have new ones."[24]

Although shared by most of the various circles, this aspect of the regionalist sensibility, the experience of cultural dispersion and dissolution—the perception of traditions under threat—was perhaps best elucidated by the Southern contingent, particularly the famous Nashville Agrarians of which Davidson and Fletcher were key members. If, in broadest terms, the predominant theme of the component regions of the Greater West emphasized the myth of the frontier, both as a tradition and an activist posture (the cultural frontier of the modern "void"), then the idea of traditionalism and of the South as the special repository of tradition in America can be seen as the major note and rallying cry sounded by Southern regionalists. Our conceit here is only temporary, a matter of emphasis, for clarity's sake, to elaborate another layer of the regionalist mind. It should be noted, by way of qualification, that the Westerners' rhetoric of a shift from the "physical" to the "spiritual" frontier, for example, was itself a symptom of cultural dispersion and of their recognition of a postfrontier world. At the same time, many Southern writers by the 1930s had become preoccupied with their own region's frontier vestiges and antecedents. But what set the Southerners apart (as inevitably, it seems, they must always be) was their conservative "tradition of traditionalism" (of kinship, religiosity, and aristocracy) as well as their long-standing, overt *sectionalism* (defined handily by the borders of a brief nationhood), both tendencies kindling their sense of traditionalism under siege by the invading forces of modernity.[25]

Raised within this context, certain of the Agrarians—namely, Fletcher, Davidson, Allen Tate, and John Crowe Ransom—were predisposed to experience modernization with peculiar, and articulate, acuteness. As a child, Allen Tate (born in 1899) was on occasion taken by his mother for a wistful visit to the ruins of her family's Pleasant Hill plantation big house in Virginia. Years later, Pleasant Hill (not long before being sacked and the house burned to the ground by Yankee invaders) was to make this impression on the first-person narrator in Tate's novel *The Fathers* (1938):

> It is an old country, I thought, as my toes sank into the rusty clay, powdered by the sun; an old country, and too many people have lived in it, and raised too much tobacco and corn, and too many men and women, young and old, have died in it, and taken with them into the rusty earth their gallantry or their melancholy, their pride or their simplicity . . . and too many people have loved the ground in which after a while they must all come to lie.

While for some Southern artists and intellectuals such a looming pile of past generations might be suffocating, for Tate and his fellow Agrarians the central dilemma posed by their own modernist self-consciousness, at least as they came to view the crisis by the late 1920s, was how to reestablish and maintain contact with an Old South that was fast receding, hustled aside by Progress. As Tate described it, the antebellum South was a "formal" society, seemingly "timeless," one in which "the individual quality of a man was bound up with his kin and the 'places' where they lived." In contrast, his own childhood and youth in Kentucky and surrounding states were made chaotic by the bad marriage and frequent separations of his parents, which led to an endless series of moves from town to town. As an undergraduate at Vanderbilt and a member of the pre-Agrarian Fugitives group, Tate came to know a measure of stability in his life; but there and later for two years in Greenwich Village he was thoroughly schooled in the quandaries of modern poetry. "I'm afraid Eliot is about right in saying there are no important themes for modern poets," he wrote Davidson in 1926. "Hence we all write lyrics; we must be subjective." Yet, he observed, "minds are less important for literature than cultures; our minds are as good as they ever were, but our culture is dissolving. . . . You can't escape it even in Tennessee!" Tate's famous elegy for a mind confronting this dissolution ("Ode To the Confederate Dead"), written that same year, captured the would-be traditionalist predicament very powerfully, without offering a resolution. It left his friend Davidson cold: "And where, O Allen Tate, are the dead? You have buried them completely out of sight—with them yourself and me. God help us, I must say. You keep on whittling your art to a finer point, but are you not also whittling yourself."[26] No one was more aware than Tate that while the ambiguity of life in Henry Smith's "void" might inspire high modernist art, it could also wreak havoc with personal identity and philosophical certainty. Thus his Guggenheim Fellowship abroad in 1928–29 found him drinking in European traditionalism, writing a biography of another tormented Southern soul, Jefferson Davis, and otherwise beginning the immersion in Southernism that would by 1930 see him restored to a plantation house in Clarksville, Tennessee, from which he was to preach the faith of Agrarianism, to himself and to America, over the next several years.

Indeed, as John Crowe Ransom reminded Tate in 1927, "poets . . . are not merely the expression, they are also the prophets and teachers of their compatriots." These were roles that Ransom, the self-described "son of a theologian, and the grandson of another one," seemed preordained to fill, yet, he observed sadly, "the gift did not come down to me." His loss of conventional religious belief was caused not only by the decline and displacement of the rural middle Tennessee Methodist culture into which he had been born in 1888, but also by his own exposure to classical and modern philosophy under a Rhodes Scholarship at Oxford. Gradually, the evangelical emotionalism and irrationalism which were the heart of his forefathers' creed were stripped away from him, leaving a hard core of "rationality and Noblesse Oblige," as Tate perceived it, and which Ransom was glad to have identified with the morality of the Old South. For, like Mary Austin and many other regionalists, the secularized Ransom retained a religious temperament and sought to make a religion of the region. A broadly defined "religion," he believed, "is the only effective defense against Progress." Ransom's Agrarian counterpart, John Gould Fletcher, elaborated a similar sentiment in a 1924 letter to Van Wyck Brooks, albeit on behalf of a creed closer to the mysticism of Austin and her Orientalist Santa Fe neighbor, Witter Bynner, than to the rational humanist code of Ransom. The modern crisis, he wrote, necessitates a new spiritual communism, in the Medieval plan, but on an altogether different scale, adapted to modern conditions. Where that new communism is coming from, I don't know. . . . Now everything is being done to hamper that development which is necessary. Everything. We have false science, aestheticism, ignorance, hypocrisy, smut, the vested interests of a million institutions to fight at every turn. And most of the people who understand at all what is coming, are uprooted from the soil (like myself) struggling to keep alive, fighting ill health and worry night and day. . . . But someday I know—whether anyone will ever listen to me or not—someday there must be a reconstruction of the religious impulse inherent in human life, or else there will be a disaster to which the last war will appear childsplay.

When Fletcher wrote these words he was already beginning his own process of self-conversion and reassimilation to the traditionalist Southern way of life, which he, like Tate, had known through immediate family history, but from which he had expatriated himself to Europe almost two decades earlier. His state of "uprootedness" began when, as a long-sheltered youth, he was sent away from his native Arkansas to some traumatic experiences at Harvard, which he left in 1907 after the death of his father, a wealthy cotton broker and Civil War hero. Following a summer stint on an archeological expedition in the desert Southwest, he departed for Europe and a poet's vocation. His periodi- cally innovative and somewhat distinguished career had largely reached a dead end by the 1920s, when he happened onto the Nashville Fugitives during a lecture tour. Through them, he came to see a path toward his "new spiritual communism" by the poetic rendition, as Davidson put it to him, of "the metaphysical in shining terms of the physical." Just as Ransom declared that the resistance against Progress was "one peculiarly for the Conservative South to lead," so too did Fletcher finally learn "where that new communism is coming from."[27]

Davidson told Fletcher in 1926 that "you must know the minds of Tate, Ransom, myself and maybe others are running in the same direction. We have maybe found a Cause of a sort; we may be able, as you say, to 'do something for the South.'" Although Davidson was to become the most strident proponent of this cause, his biography was perhaps the most mundane of the group. Born in 1893 at Campbellsville, Tennessee, the son of a schoolteacher, a graduate of Vanderbilt with the briefest taste of combat in World War I, he was plagued by a waffling personality and feelings of inferiority toward his more accomplished and talented fellows (already in 1920, he expressed these feelings: "Did I just fail to keep up with the pattern of your thinking, and, though once worthy,

thus become unworthy?"). Compelled by these feelings, and goaded as well by
the Scopes trial, Mencken's abusive Southern commentary, and the whole
tendency of New South booster rhetoric, Davidson attempted in his epic *The
Tall Men* (1927) to define himself in terms of heroic Scotch-Irish pioneer
ancestors and, in a larger sense, to stake out a regional literary position
somewhere between the "Slough of Sentimentality" (his words) and Tate's
modernist Abyss—thus joining a national pattern of regionalist revulsion
against modernist styles and, more importantly, its moral relativism. "I have
fully decided that my America is here or nowhere," he told Tate. "I have been
going through a spiritual 'Secession.'" Davidson analyzed the meaning of
"The Resurrection" and "Epilogue" sections of *The Tall Men* for another
correspondent. They were, he wrote,

> built around certain lines from the Anglo-Saxon "Finnsburg Fragment";
> the warriors of Hnaef, besieged in the mead-hall, held the door against
> great odds; in modern times the struggle is to retain spiritual values
> against the gnawing of industrialism. . . . The South, I believe, has
> arrived at a crisis. It has always possessed great individuality which
> under modern influences it runs great risk of losing. To retain its spiritual
> entity the South (as other sections, for that matter) must become con-
> scious of and not repudiate whatever is worth saving in its traditions.[28]

By the late 1920s and early 1930s, as the manifestos announcing the regionalist movement started to appear, the question of how these regional traditions might be saved began to be explored by regionalists not only in Nashville
but also around the country as a whole. Did the answer require the emerging
sectional chauvinism of the Agrarians, who were (in the estimation of Tate)
"trying to make a political creed do the work of religion" and restore a proudly
insular community of values? Or was regionalism more properly a purely
artistic project—as Austin, Smith, Merriam, and Botkin were coming to
define it—a movement to revivify a moribund national culture through a
conservative return (as Botkin was to conceive it) "to the lower level of the
folk, to the source of all art in the wonder and faith that are also the mother of
religion"? Or was there another, alternate solution to the crisis, another route
to the "accommodating middle ground" between the modern and the traditional? Poets, folklorists, editors, historians, painters, and novelists were
codiscoverers of the *region* with sociologists, conservationists, urban planners, and architects, who saw in the organicism embodied by the region—and
its ethical and aesthetic implications as well—a sophisticated new tool for
mitigating the effects of Progress. As North Carolina sociologist Howard
Odum reflected, "Any adequate picture of the South must combine the poetic
with the scientific. It is as if a new romantic realism were needed to portray

the old backgrounds and the new trends and processes." Addressing an essential balance between these oppositions would necessitate, Lewis Mumford concluded, "the conservation of human values" and the "reinvigoration and rehabilitation of whole regions." That balance, he believed, could only be accomplished through the "art" of regional planning.[29]

The origins of the planners' circles of the regionalist movement—which included such figures as Benton MacKaye, Rupert Vance, Paul Taylor, and Arthur Raper—are traceable in Odum's and Mumford's own regionalist educations, their discovery of the region as the centerpiece of the next and critical stage in social evolution. Odum's regionalism was rooted in what he perceived to be two universals, folk culture and science; their marriage constitutes much of the story of his early life and career. He was born (1884) in the small town of Bethlehem, Georgia, to a father who was the latest generation of a long line of Southern yeoman farmers, and to a mother who (like Tate's) was the disappointed but ambitious daughter of slaveholders displaced and devastated by the War Between the States. Two rather pessimistic and pathetic grandfathers, Confederate veterans both, imbued Odum not only with a sectional consciousness but also with a strong sense of the tragic, a sense reinforced, as his biographers have emphasized, by the premature or accidental deaths of three younger siblings. College and graduate school, however, brought Odum two important, saving revelations. The first, at the University of Mississippi, was an exposure to the zealous Progressive Era faith in the transfiguring promise of objective social science for human improvement. (At least two other prominent regionalists, John Collier and Constance Rourke, also arrived at regionalism via Progressive reform, the former out of community activism, the latter from educational theory.) Odum's second revelation stemmed from his study of Southern black folk culture for doctoral work at Clark University and Columbia from 1906 to 1910. The old spirituals and work songs particularly spoke to his personal experience of life's vicissitudes, expressing seemingly fundamental truths with "humor, pathos, and poignancy," as he later characterized them, and representing "a sort of timeless and spaceless folk urge."[30]

In 1920, when Odum received an appointment at the University of North Carolina to head the school of social work and the sociology department, he arrived with these component worldviews; in coming years, he would mold them into a vision of the "folk-regional society"—"the relative balance of man, nature, and culture," the "equilibrium" of "social forces" and "common traditions." Yet the only commonalities that the contemporary South shared at present, Odum was to find in the course of many investigations, were the "pathological conditions" revealed by his department's rapidly growing body of sociological surveys—the breakdown of community and local institutions,

the widespread misery, poverty, and despair attending the rampant and un-
even urbanization and industrialization of New South development. The "new
romantic realism" of regionalism, Odum believed, would deal expertly and
unflinchingly with this ongoing tragedy of waste and degradation, guided by
the region as a quantifiable social scientific category (a complex set of physical
and social interrelationships) and the region as a wellspring of values and
wisdom, especially the old yeoman "background" with its ideals of decentralization, cooperation, and self-sufficiency.[31]

Many regionalists, both inside and outside the planners' circles, came to
share in this hope that regionalism could provide a map not just for cultural
reconstruction but for social, economic, and political reform as well. This
"utopian" or "visionary" tendency of the regionalist sensibility was given its
clearest exemplification in the life and works of the foremost philosopher of the
movement, Lewis Mumford. Like Botkin, he was a self-described "child of the
city," born and raised and educated in and *by* New York—"New York with its
libraries, its museums, its parks, its nearby landscapes . . . not least its
multitudinous human richness." He also felt the "sharp imprint" of a "round
of rural activities" savored during childhood summers spent on a Vermont
farm with his mother. If Mumford thus grew to understand the importance of
both urban and rural experience for a truly cultivated life, it was a synthesis of
these two settings, discovered in fast-disappearing pockets still existent in, as
he later reminisced, the "city of my youth," that most profoundly affected his
intellectual development: "From Sixty-fifth Street up, Broadway was still full
of vacant lots, with visible chickens and market gardens, genuine beer gardens like Unter den Linden, and even more rural areas. Since for the first
quarter of a century of my life I lived between Central Park and Riverside
Drive, wide lawns and tree-lined promenades are inseparable in my mind from
the design of every great city." As a young man about to graduate from high
school, during one of his frequent explorations of metropolitan New York,
Mumford admired a vista from the Brooklyn Bridge that precipitated an
almost mystical "fleeting glimpse of the utmost possibilities life may hold for
man":

> Here was my city, immense, overpowering, flooded with energy and
> light. . . . And there was I, breasting the March wind, drinking in the city
> and the sky, both vast, yet both contained in me, transmitting through me
> the great mysterious will that had made them and the promise of the new
> day that was still to come.[32]

Mumford's intensive self-education and scatter-shot formal schooling at
City College and Columbia were crystallized by the holistic teachings of the
Scottish biologist, philosopher, and pioneer ecologist Patrick Geddes. From

his insights into the organic "interdependence of city and country," Mumford took the bearings which, by the early 1920s, were to set his own mind on a course toward the middle ground of "a new kind of human environment—the regional community." In the 1925 collection of essays published together by *Survey Graphic* as the manifesto of the members of the Regional Planning Association, he tried to capture his still-evolving vision of what regionalism might achieve. "Regional planning asks not how wide an area can be brought under the aegis of the metropolis," Mumford wrote, "but how the population and civic facilities can be distributed so as to promote and stimulate a vivid, creative life throughout a whole region"—a life that Mumford's regionalist counterparts, dispersed in their cultural outposts across the South and the West, were even at that moment beginning to build for themselves. The "civic objective" of regional planning, he went on to assert, "aims equally at ruraliz-ing the stony wastes of our cities," a goal "summed up with peculiar accuracy in the concept of the garden-city," and a task destined particularly for Mum-ford and his metropolitan-centered planners' group—for "the hope of the city lies outside itself." Which would it be?, he asked in conclusion: "Regionalism or super-congestion? Will man in America learn the art of mastering and ordering his environment, to promote his fuller purposes, or will he be mas-tered by his environment, and presently . . . find himself without any purposes other than those of the Machine?"[33]

Like many regionalists, Mumford had a brief taste of expatriation in Europe shortly after World War I but chose to return to America because of "earlier and deeper allegiances." What brought him back from his "dip into the intel-lectual life of London" and, ultimately, to residence in the planned community of Sunnyside Gardens? "I knew in my bones," Mumford recalled years later, "I could not fit into this society without forfeiting something I valued in my own American past." The United States, he declared, echoing Henry Nash Smith, "by its very polyglot disorder, still gave me the sense of its being ready, responsive, and in some degree malleable, more open to favorable human pressures and plans and self-transformations." More directly, "despite the disillusion that set in after the First World War, we believed that we might give a more humane shape to American culture before our molten desires had cooled." Here, perhaps, was the fundamental motivation underlying the for-mation of the regionalist movement: "My part of the younger generation was still hopefully confident of reclaiming 'Our America.'"[34]

2 The Power of Art

The American Indian, the Aesthetic Society, and the Regionalist Civic Religion

Let come who may with an estranging hand,
Let touch who will this earth so deeply yours,
None of it ever goes away from you.
Your gods are here, deeper than any spade.
—Witter Bynner, "Indian Earth" (1929)

From 1922 to 1932, the great stone edifice of the new Nebraska state capitol was slowly raised above the city of Lincoln and surrounding prairie. Designed by Gothicist architect Bertram Grosvenor Goodhue—best known for his cathedral projects—the structure was monumental in every sense of the word. Its 400-foot domed tower was centered on a multistory base 437 feet square, and its long facades were decorated with sculpture and inscriptions depicting "nothing less than the history and symbolism of political freedom," or so observed Goodhue's collaborator and "coauthor" of the ornamentation, University of Nebraska philosopher Hartley Burr Alexander. "The building, indeed, was to be like a book," he wrote in mid-construction, "logically arranged, with introduction, body, and conclusion, no chapter to be displaced without bringing disorder to the whole." The Gothic "monumental totality" of Alexander's text was integral as well with the symmetry, massiveness, and austerity of Goodhue's overall "sort of Classic" conception. Yet, Alexander declared, "the Nebraska Capitol is neither Gothic nor Classic; it is a new architectural style." One Lincoln commentator, marveling how the building "reaches upward into the heavens out of the level of common things," concluded: "It can be

Figure 2.1 The Nebraska State Capitol in 1934. (Courtesy of the McDonald Studio
Collection, Nebraska State Historical Society)

termed nothing but American art; in fact, some say it is distinctly Nebras-
kan."[1] (Figures 2.1 and 2.2.)

The "text of the meaning of the building" began on the heavy balustrades
framing the steps to the north-oriented main entrance—"the American idea,
on the Indian side," Alexander explained. To "make the image autochtho-
nous," carved panels of stylized bison and maize were overlaid with translated sayings from the rituals of Nebraska Plains tribes "to represent Indian
thought," especially, the Indian's "sense of the *sacra* of the soil." At the top of
the steps, over tall bronze doors, a larger panel portrayed yoked oxen, men
and women on foot, and a covered wagon. "In this is commemorated," Alexander wrote, "the event which, if the Capitol stand, as it should, for thrice
a thousand years, will still be the greatest event in the life of the Plains
country—the coming of the homesteaders who transformed the virgin prairies into cultivated fields" (Figure 2.3). Then, beginning at the northwestern
corner and parading along the western, southern, and eastern facades, there
was a further sequential series of smaller panels, more detailed than the first,
overlooked at the south portal by a group of sculpted pilasters. For the

Figure 2.2 East balustrade, Nebraska State Capitol. (Courtesy of the Nebraska State Historical Society)

pioneers, Alexander's narration continued, had "brought with them something more than their toils; they brought Anglo-Saxon institutions, and infused in these the whole tradition of the civilization of Europe as embodied in the Law." Its progress was chronicled in bas-relief on the sides of the great building, from "Moses Bringing the Law from Sinai" and "The Codification of Roman Law under Justinian" to "The Writing of the Constitution of the United States" and "Lincoln's Proclamation of the Emancipation of the Negroes," until, lastly, "The Admission of Nebraska as a State in the Union." The pilasters culminated in the likenesses of lawgivers, among them, Minos, Hammurabi, Solon, Solomon, Charlemagne, and Napoleon. Finally, wrapping around the entire block-square monument, underlining panels, pilasters, and inscriptions, grounding it all in the local, there was a decorative band, engraved with the names of every county in the state.[2]

The "prophetic conclusion" to the capitol was provided by the tower with its golden dome, soaring high above the base building. In form, it was a "sort of classical" as well as vernacular rendering of that most American of architectures, the skyscraper. The 70-foot octagonal dome foundation, rising from among four small octagonal turrets, sat on top of eight floors of offices, 329 feet

Figure 2.3 Bas-relief panel of the Pioneers, Nebraska State Capitol. (Photograph by the author)

in the air. One critic observed that if "the Base is thus a symbol of the material plane upon which man's activities are spread," its decoration "derived from concrete episodes in the slow development of social life," then the Tower encouraged man "to lift his thoughts from the material plane . . . to the spiritual limitless spaces of his ideals." Just under the dome-cap itself were eight multicolored tile faces, each depicting the mythical thunderbird of the Plains tribes, "chief power in the heavens," yet also, as the bringer of rainfall, "that single power beyond their control upon which they depended for their very sustenance of living" (as one contemporary interpretation had it). The thunderbird therefore suggested not the separation but the unity of the spiritual and the material, a central concept of Native American cosmologies and a theme then brought to a climax by the statue of "The Sower," which crowned the dome. This figure, Alexander wrote, was intended to be at once "prophetic and retrospective," looking backward to "the Indian who first brought maize into the land" and "the Pioneer who made of the prairies a domain of fields," but forward also from "that deeper sowing effected in history of which the harvest is the fulfilled commonwealth" and toward "that

Figure 2.4 Thunderbirds and the Sower, Nebraska State Capitol. (Photograph by the author)

life of the future for which Nebraska's present hour is but the planting-time" (Figure 2.4). Thus ended "the program bequeathed by the architect to the sculptor," and Alexander had no doubts about the achievement of their attempt at social art: "There are great churches in the world which show symbolism as perfect, but is there another house of state which can vie with this in moving eloquence?" The Sower and all of the symbolic sculpture of the new capitol, he believed, "should well assure that reverence for high traditions which it is the office of public monuments to inspire."[3]

In 1928, while praising another of Goodhue's commissions, the Los Angeles Public Library (a building which owed much to the precedent of the Nebraska capitol), Lewis Mumford commented: "We live in an age that has still to create or re-create its symbols." Such a re-creation was precisely the result sought by Goodhue, the cathedral builder. As Alexander remarked of this scion of two old and prominent New England families, his art revealed "never anything less than the utter expression of his faith in the genuineness of the values that underlie both our humane and our religious ideals." Certainly Goodhue's convictions were manifest in the capitol design. "The common heritage of our

Western civilization is, it seems to me, perfectly clear, and came to us through a direct line," he wrote to Alexander in 1922. Yet the capitol was less ecclesiastical than fortresslike in its aggressively hortatory assertiveness of communal ideals. Like many other American artists and intellectuals during the post–World War I years (not a few of whom might have labeled his work in Nebraska a memorial rather than a monument), Goodhue was himself stricken by a growing sense of cultural disintegration. "The mere fact that one states one's belief proves that such a belief is open to doubt," he admitted shortly before his premature death in 1924. And in the 1922 letter, he confessed: "Now everything is so changed that I like to hold tight to what I have in the way of heritage, and I believe that countries and races must do the same." His task as an architect of monuments had become less one of celebration than of *reclamation*, of re-animation, effected through the "organic break" with the past of Mumford's *Golden Day* formulation. The Goodhue firm's original proposal stated:

> It has seemed to the authors that the traditions of ancient Greece and Rome and of Eighteenth Century France are in no wise applicable in designing a building destined to be the seat of Government of a great western commonwealth: So, while the architectural style may, roughly, be called "Classic," it makes no pretense of belonging to any period of the past. Its authors have striven to present . . . a State Capitol of the Here and Now, and naught else.

A Native American saying on the balustrades set the proper tone: "Arise with the dawn," it read, "Bathe in the morning sun." The realization of the "Goodhue Dream of a great building indigenous to the soil of their State and indicative of the highest aspirations of that State," one of Goodhue's collaborators exclaimed, meant that "perfection has come to dwell in the midst of the Nebraska country as it came to dwell once-upon-a-time, briefly, on the Akropolis in Athens."[4] A renaissance seemed upon them.

Appropriately enough, therefore, the construction of the new Nebraska state capitol furnishes us with theme, plan, and periodization. For in the decade or so after the war and prior to the onset of depression-era politicization, the regionalist movement took shape and rose to the task of cultural rejuvenation, seeking inspiration from the fresh materials of indigenous America—specifically, from Native American tribal cultures and from the European and African "folk epic" in the New World. At places like Lincoln, Santa Fe, Norman, Dallas, Austin, Chapel Hill, Nashville, and Missoula, regionalists sought to reconnect with, reinterpret, redefine, and establish wholesale a body of traditions expressive of regional and national life together. This cultural project, predominantly of the South and West, was in rhetoric broadly democratic, pluralistic, producerist, and communitarian, and in its governing assumptions at once conservative and modernist. "We have within us the means of our salvation," Nebraska poet laureate John G. Neihardt wrote in his 1925 work *Poetic Values*. "Only by the systematic stimulation of the art consciousness in men and its application to the problems of society can we hope to be saved from ourselves." Such a unifying "art consciousness" required the "systematic stimulation" of a communal aesthetic: "Though the fundamental greatness of a poem is commensurate with the mood of the whole," asserted the writer of the epic *Cycle of the West*, "even as the fundamental greatness of Nebraska's new capitol is in the totality of the architectural dream, yet either, to be of value, must be shared."[5] From the early 1920s to the early 1930s, the search for this integrating aesthetic, an aesthetic to heal the breaches of modernity—the void between subjectivity and objectivity, between society and culture, between mechanical civilization and humane values, between oligarchic reality and democratic ideals—was carried forward in the cultural outposts of regional America.

For Neihardt, poetry was "merely a means to an end—the preservation of a great race-mood of courage that was developed west of the Missouri River in the 19th century." The *Cycle of the West* was his personal attempt at "systematic stimulation of the art consciousness" in Americans, a saga of mountain men, pioneers, and Indian wars, the last vestiges of which he had witnessed during a youth spent on the sod-house frontiers of Kansas and Nebraska during the 1880s and among the Omaha Indians during the early 1900s. The works that Neihardt produced in the course of his subsequent literary career were, in fact, indicative of the two larger tendencies of the regionalist cultural project, both enshrined in the sculpture of Goodhue's civic cathedral. The *Cycle* was part of the postfrontier resuscitation and celebration of pioneer myths and traditions, arising in spite of and in opposition to the dominant interwar intellectual prosecution of the frontiersman and his allegedly perverting effect on American society, an important theme within a larger regionalist debate over the existence and persistence of folkness among European Americans in general and "Anglo-Saxons" in particular (the subject of our next chapter). Neihardt's *Black Elk Speaks* (1932) exemplified, in turn, the far less problematic effort by members of the movement to appropriate Native American cultures for the purposes of cultural reconstruction. If there was some controversy over the survivability of folk traditions among European settlers and their descendants—the citizens and builders of an industrializing and secularizing nation-state of great social and geographic mobility—there was relatively little doubt among regionalists that American Indians, although seriously threatened by modernization, nevertheless represented "ancient social orders, organisms of communal life from thousands of years ago" still extant in the contemporary world. In this Native American version of the

Golden Age ("us two-leggeds sharing in it with the four-leggeds and wings of
the air and all green things," as Neihardt's Black Elk intones, "for these are
children of one mother and their father is one Spirit") were the materials not
only for new styles of art, regionalists believed, but also the cultural means to
transform modern society.[6] Through this confrontation with the civilization of
American Indians, the utopian intentions of the regionalist cultural project
can thus most clearly be seen.

The recourse to American Indian civilization was in itself a hallmark of the
severity of the interwar cultural crisis. Implicitly and explicitly, the Native
American literature, narrative histories, and anthropological studies produced during the 1920s and early 1930s reflected the tragedy of modernization, not its progress. In terms of the frontier myth, modernization had
heretofore always meant the triumph of a superior white civilization over
barbaric, paganistic redskins. In the hands of interwar regionalist writers and
artists, working out of the paradigm of cultural relativism provided by anthropological theorists, this worldview was largely subverted. On the walls and
tower of the Nebraska capitol, the monumental representations of both civilizations seemed to coexist without tension, without contradiction. Yet in actuality the inclusion of Indian elements was an elevation, a legitimation, of
Indian culture. If they occupied "lower" positions on the exterior of the
building in relation to the Anglo-Saxon pioneers or the Sower, their placement
signified not subordination but rootedness and naturalness: the "autochtho-
nous." Furthermore, at certain points within the interior—the intricately
worked tribal chiefs on the leather-covered doors of the senate chamber, for
example—Native American motifs dominated. They were certainly the most
essential elements for codesigner Alexander, who during construction also
compiled a translation of Plains Indian drama and ceremonials entitled *Manito
Masks* (1925), which he considered "an effort to find out some of the sources of
a national idealism in the arts, and so in life," some "form of idealization of the
soil, some light of native imagination striking to the roots of our growth"; the
same might be said of his design work on Goodhue's capitol. "The country
almost has seemed to *go Indian*," Mabel Dodge Luhan (who was then married
to a Pueblo tribesman) commented with perhaps a degree of wishful thinking
to Mary Austin after a public meeting on Indian policy convened at Taos in
1923. "We want *interest & appreciation* of the indian life and culture to become
a part of our *conscious* racial mind," Luhan asserted, projecting her own
desires. "We want *as a nation* to *value* the indian as we value ourselves. We
want to *consciously* love the wholeness & harmony of indian life, & to consciously protect it." That such interest, such a yearning "began in politics,"
she supposed, "does not prevent its being channeled into aesthetics."[7] Regionalists hoped that the reverse might also be true.

But what was it that Native American cultures had to teach white civilization? What solutions did they offer to the modern crisis? What were the
particulars of an Indian Golden Age, of an "idealization of the soil," of "going
Indian"? Santa Fe, with its circle of writers, artists, and distinguished visitors, was the center of the search for answers to these fundamental questions.
In this role, the community was, to Alexander, "ideally gifted for the inauguration of a new humanism," or so he told one of the foremost researchers
located there, archeologist Edgar L. Hewett. The small capital's "aboriginal
roots," Mary Austin remarked to Hewett in 1920, were essential as well to
"the independent art movement growing up outside Manhattan."[8] It was
Hewett and Austin who explored, at a general sociological and philosophical
level, the reconstructive promise embodied by Indian culture, primarily focusing on the local Pueblo tribes. In this task they were both continuing and
transcending earlier efforts of the 1910s and 1920s to analyze and comprehend
Native American civilization, including works by Alexander on myths and the
anthropological surveys of Clark Wissler, curator of the American Museum of
Natural History.

Hewett himself had been exploring the Indian ruins of the Southwest
since the 1890s, cofounding in subsequent years the School of American Research and the Museum of New Mexico, both headquartered in the restored
centuries-old Palace of the Governors in Santa Fe; he had also participated in
the restoration of the cliff houses at Mesa Verde (inspiration for Willa Cather)
as well as the initial excavation of the giant Pueblo Bonito dwelling at Chaco
Canyon. This lifetime immersion in Anasazi culture turned Hewett into a
proselytizer of a reanimated native traditionalism as the one hope for Western
society. For him, the subject matter of archeology burst beyond dry academic
boundaries to form a deep and rich pool of transcendental values. As if re-
sponding to fellow curator Wissler ("the sole objective of anthropology is to
discover the origin and conditions which have produced the Indian and his
culture"), Hewett wrote in his popular-level archeological survey, *Ancient
Life in the American Southwest* (1930):

> If archeology had only to do with the rescue of dead things and their
> exhibition in museum halls, I could take little interest in it. But it is the
> science of things that live; that through the ages do not grow old; of things
> that disasters cannot kill; works of the spirit that, buried for millennia,
> rise again to new life and potency; the science which demonstrates that in
> races that have survived from a far past, powers lie dormant which may
> be energized anew.

Hewett assumed, as did Luhan, Austin, John Collier, and many others in New
Mexico embroiled in Indian policy fights during the 1920s, that the present-

day Pueblo Indian was a survival, "a contemporary of the village Indians of
half a millennium ago," who "orders his life to this day on lines laid down" in
ages past. He saw his own part in those policy battles as an attempt to
preserve this native wisdom, to realize it in the modern era and apply it to
modern problems. "The races called by us inferior," he declared, "have qualities that are priceless to human society and . . . in the discovery, recognition,
and cultivation of the special abilities in the less powerful races lies our
soundest insurance against spiritual decline and extinction by way of our own
violence."[9]

These regenerative qualities and abilities were elaborated by Hewett in
Ancient Life and by Austin in her examination of Indian songs, *The American
Rhythm* (1913, 1923, 1930). The two works—one a study of the archeological
record, the other a literary analysis of present-day Native American poetry—
conjoin as samplings at opposite ends of a vibrant and continuous body of
tradition. Hewett put the matter succinctly: "The most extraordinary characteristic of Indian culture is to be seen in the unification of all its elements.
Religion, art, social structure, industries—all coalesce in daily life." This
"orderly, integrated racial life" was brought about by long evolution in isolation on the American continent, he argued, "the first and only process of
Americanization that has been carried to completion." Aboriginal Americans,
"from Alaska to Patagonia," were a race that "took its character from the
soil," developing "a racial spirit keenly alive to forces which meant so much in
the life of the people." The Native American, Hewett wrote, "viewed nature
as the great source of all existence, found in contemplating its orderly processes the principle for ordering his own life, sought in its mysterious forces
not something to be captured and made to serve him, but harmonies that he
might share to the profound satisfaction of his soul." Mary Austin saw in this
symbiosis a basis for a group perception of the "shared stream" of "rhythmic
stimuli arising spontaneously in the environment," forging a "common urge
toward communality." Social integration was sealed, she hypothesized, by
ceremonial songs and poetry appropriating these natural rhythms and bringing them into "communication" with a pantheistic "Allness." This sense of
veneration, Hewett added, was expressed as well "in the building and embel-
lishment of temples for celebration" and "in the adornment of the body and of
articles of domestic and religious service"—all constituting a way of life
"preeminently esthetic and religious."[10]

Certain social and political configurations devolved from this "completely
integrated culture" of the New World, configurations that Hewett and Austin
believed the "Europeans" now dwelling there would do well to learn from. "In
esthetic, ethical and social culture," Hewett claimed, "the Indians surpassed
their conquerors." In this assertion and others he and Austin joined Crève-

coeur and a long line of American intellectuals, past and contemporary, in using Indian culture as a projection screen for social criticism—a tendency always symptomatic of the perceived failure of mainstream social and political institutions. For the purposes of this book, the accuracy of the cultural traits assigned to Indians (some of them, but not all, rather dubious) is less important than the revelation of intellectual preoccupations, of the culturally regenerative myths Hewett, Austin, and others were *making*. Hewett especially conceived native culture as a cure for some peculiarly postwar concerns. Because on the American continent "there was magnificent space in which tribes might develop without acute conflict of interest," he wrote, "the process by which America was humanized" had created a civilization in which "ethnic unity was established and preserved," a civilization "without nationality," without the "everlasting strife for supremacy that constitutes the major part of Old-World history." The vast spaces of America also prevented the rise of Caesarism, Hewett posited, extending the mantle of Turnerian exceptionalism to aboriginals: "The sense of individual freedom was too great to permit of dynastic government," he wrote. "Chieftaincy arose without resulting in kingship or overlordship." In fact, "the typical government throughout the Americas was republican." Hewett further implied that native societies were largely classless. "There was little specialization," and, moreover, "no record was kept of the achievements of warriors, priests, architects or artists save in the evidences of a splendid culture." Yet Indian civilization departed crucially from this predominant stream of white American myths with one central feature, the one that most captured the interest of interwar intellectuals for the very reason that it promised to fill a crippling void in modern society: the "aboriginal American race," Hewett observed, was marked by an almost complete "absence of individualism"—"to the community all individual activities were subordinated."[11]

The coordination of rampant, anarchic, self-interested individualism into socially benevolent directions had been an obsession of social critics in Europe and the United States for decades; finding a political framework which could achieve the common good without crushing self-expression and individual volition remained the basic dilemma. In Hewett's and Austin's conceptualizations of Native American culture, this dilemma—how one might attain a "sense of individual freedom" within a community in which "all individual activities were subordinated"—seemed to be reconciled. The key lay in the fact that all elements of Indian life were "essentially esthetic." Europe was a civilization, Hewett explained, "founded on force, dedicated to supremacy of force," to "the state organized by force, maintained by force, depending upon force for its existence." But "the success of Democratic organization," Austin argued, "depends finally on the establishment among its members of a state of uncoerced obedience to its ideals," a state of "affective group-mindedness." To this end, Native American civilization was predicated on an entirely different basis than force—"the integration of utility and beauty and religious thought." In Indian societies, there was no distinctive "class of trained artists," Hewett emphasized, because "all were artists," artists for whom a daily task such as hunting was "ceremonially ordered" and planting a "ritualistic performance." On more formal occasions, Austin suggested, the "poetic orgy" of Amerindian "dance drama," with its combination of collective rhythmic speech and chore-ography, was employed as the most effective means of bringing about the "coalescence of individual minds," ultimately "raising the plane of group consciousness."[12]

With such conceptualizations, Hewett and Austin well represented the imaginative and theoretical groping taking place during the 1920s phase of the regionalist movement, when participants were seeking to define concretely what shape a transformative application of folk-Indian values might assume in modern American society, not only in its environmental, but in its social and political relationships. Regionalists came to perceive that the essential genius of Native American civilization lay in its realization that all such relationships were intertwined: the organic coherence and stability of Native American social life rested on its nonexploitative, intimate relationship to nature. In the emerging regionalist conceptualization, the nature that had nurtured the Indian's superior culture was not the object-victim of Victorian and latter-day industrial conquerors; rather, it was the nature that the Romantics had intu-ited, the nature that the Darwinians had theorized and the post-Darwinians had cast man from the center of, the nature that the infant science of ecology— the study of "the relationship of everything to everything else," the "science of communities"—was by the 1920s revealing in all its organically intercon-nected complexity. The rhetorical focus of regionalist admiration incorporated many of these "natures," depicting the Indian as the living expression of timeless, changeless natural law (Cather's "landscape made human"), as the acolyte of a pantheistic universe (practicing Austin's "rhythmic communica-tion" with the "Allness"), and as an exponent of the permanent wisdom of symbiotic membership in a natural community (the "orderly processes" of which were instrumental in "ordering his own life," as Hewett wrote).[13]

That such a symbiotic community was also an aesthetic society, Hewett, Austin, and other students of the Indian believed, was no accident. "The Red Man adds the dignity of myth and poetry and religious feeling to what is at bottom his recognition of physical sustenance," wrote Hartley Alexander, demonstrating that for all of its wishful mythicizing, the regionalists' concep-tion of Native American cultures had some grounding in anthropological findings.[14] The aesthetic sensibility encompassed a recognition, an appreciation, a *respect* for objects in themselves, their forms, patterns, and rhythms. Yet this sensibility was demanded by predominantly oral societies trying to survive in often-harsh environments. The most effective techniques of agriculture and craft making, painstakingly discovered and evolved, were more easily perpetuated in the form of myth-narratives, ceremonies, and ritualized behavior. Proper raw materials, the correct seasons, weather, and lunations under which to plant and hunt—these aspects of existence required an acute sensitivity to the natural environment together with a readily accessed body of lore. Thus, in a village or tribe, "all were artists" in the sense that they participated in the intricately ritualized and animist world conceived and ordered by this lore, and all were as well involved in the common effort of subsistence.

Speaking some years later of his own discovery of the Pueblo Indians during a year-long visit at Santa Fe in 1919, federal Bureau of Indian Affairs chief John Collier expressed wonder at the tribal communities that in this manner engendered "earth loyalties and human loyalties, amid a context of beauty which suffused the life of the whole group." The crucial societal element, he reemphasized, lay in the "power of art—of the life-making art," a regime under which "no art-form exists for itself alone," but "painting, pottery, weaving, music, dance, poetry, drama, are each and all, in their main intent, vehicles of the tribal will." Modern America had much to learn from these aesthetic-symbiotic traditionalist communities, Collier believed, reiterating sentiments shared by Hewett, Austin, and many other regionalists hoping to find a solution to the interwar cultural crisis: "We—I mean our white world in this century—are a shattered race—psychically, religiously, socially, esthetically shattered, dismembered, directionless. . . . Our understanding of art, of work, of pleasure, of the values of life, and even our world-view may be somewhat influenced if we will pay attention to them." Austin thought that she saw the promise of the "poetic orgy" already at work in certain tendencies of modern poetry. "Although we have not yet achieved the communality into which the Amerind has entered by easy evolution," she wrote, "there is evident straining toward it in the work of such men as Masters, Frost and Sandburg." In fact, she wrote, "all our recent poetic literature" seemed to be "touched with a profound nostalgia for those happy states of reconciliation with the Allness through group communion, which it is the business of poetry to promote." Yet as vital and promising as Indian culture might seem, it was also true, as Hewett noted sadly, that the invasion of America by Europeans had "speedily made a pathetic wreck of its patiently evolved civilization," and that "this first great experiment in the evolution of human society in America is at an end." The times now called for preservation and understanding, a "problem of artist and poet, as well as of historian and scientist." Because modern America had developed largely from "a process of selection from the attainments of other peoples," it was essential to "avail ourselves eagerly of this which came from our own soil." Hewett paused finally to plead on behalf of the "native American race": "Are its sacred fires permanently quenched, or can the flames of the spirit that produced the temples of Central America and Mexico, the dramatic ceremonies of the Indians of the plains, the architectural wonders of the ancient Pueblos and cliff-dwellers be revived? If so, the gain to the Occidental world will be priceless."[15]

It did fall to others—novelists, poets, historians—to assess what exactly might be gained culturally from the "native American race," and to elucidate the concrete implications for modern individuals seeking to appropriate, to immerse themselves in, the way of life of integrated Indian communities, or the remnants of them that still persisted. Three *subregions* became the main loci for these researches: Hewett's and Austin's plateauland of the Pueblo and Navajo tribes in northern New Mexico and northeastern Arizona; the high plains home of the Sioux reservations, stretching across Nebraska and South Dakota and Montana; and the former Indian Territory of eastern Oklahoma, final destination for the Five Civilized Tribes and numerous others forced to migrate from the East and the West in previous decades. Everywhere there prevailed Hewett's sentiments that Native American traditions existed in the present-day as threatened and tenuous survivals, and that preservation was paramount.

At Taos and Santa Fe such efforts were reflected in the styles utilized at the art colonies and in the revival of ancient pueblo festival days; they took organizational form as well in the Indian Arts Fund and the Museum of New Mexico. Northward, in the Siouxan subregion of the Midwest and Northwest, the task of preservation fell primarily to Neihardt and to fellow Nebraska writer Mari Sandoz. Sandoz had grown up in the old Indian country of the Niobrara River, on the Sand Hills frontier south of the Pine Ridge Reservation straddling the Nebraska–South Dakota border. In 1930, when she set out in a Model T with a fellow researcher to interview the remaining Sioux and Cheyenne chiefs, headmen, and medicine men still living in the area, what she found were some very palpable "survivals":

Every time I go to the Sioux reservations I see fewer of the old aristocrats, fewer of the lean old meat-eaters who made fortitude the *wakan* tree of their existence through the tribulation of vanishing hunting grounds, whiskey traders and forked-tongue treaty makers, even to starvation. Soon (Ah, this is about the only topic on this earth that can bring a mist to my eyes) soon they will all be gone. . . . It is not comforting to know that their kind will never walk this earth again.[16]

Sandoz told H. L. Mencken a few years after these trips that her concern was "that something more than a few moth-eaten war-bonnets and scalps should be preserved of this magnificent people." Joseph Brandt, founder of the University of Oklahoma Press and a leader with B. A. Botkin of the regionalist circle in Oklahoma, agreed that preservation efforts must move beyond mere museum building—they must dovetail with the larger project of cultural reconstruction. He himself envisioned an "American Institute of Indian Civilization" to be established in Oklahoma, "the logical center of Indian research in America." Besides housing a museum and hosting conferences, the institute would, he hoped, "offer courses in the Indian languages, in Indian history, in Indian civilization, in Indian art." Fundamentally, Brandt declared, its purpose would be to treat Indian civilization "as, for example, we treat Greek and Roman civilization."[17]

If Native American cultures were to be used by artists and intellectuals as classical culture had been since the Renaissance—as an adversary culture, as a social model—then it was essential to appreciate, as poet Lew Sarett warned in 1928, that "there are profundities in Indian thought, Indian character, Indian religion," profundities that could not "be captured by any dilletante in Indian matters":

> No man can really "get" the Indian, or write of him, unless there is a lot of Indian inside him—unless he has lived life in the wilderness, in the environment of the Indian, and with Indians; and unless there is enough of the crass and elemental—as well as the pantheistically spiritual—in his own emotions and intellectual processes to enable him to understand the Indian.

Sarett shook his head, surmising: "Nearly all the stuff I've seen is surface work, artificial, or sentimental, or tourist-flavored." Sarett's comments pointed to a greater problem, moreover, a problem for the sincere and serious student of Indian culture—the difficulties of appropriation that any body of integrated traditionalism (and, in this case, a non-Western variety) posed for the possessor of modern disenchanted self-consciousness ("disenchanted" in a Weberian sense).[18] How might the modern artist or intellectual relate himself or herself, as Mary Austin had attempted in earlier years, to "the strange secret life of the tribe"? How might a mind socialized and educated to stand in rational and critical regard toward its own culture jettison its skepticism and engage itself with the assumptions of an often-mystical holistic worldview? How, in more basic (and modernist) terms, could an individual subjectivity find an objective ground for itself in the world?

The career of John Joseph Mathews provides a telling illustration of the dilemma. Mathews was an Americanized, mixed-blood Osage Indian born and raised on the tribal reservation in northeastern Oklahoma. He graduated from the state university with a degree in geology in 1914, spent the war abroad in Europe on duty with the Signal Corps, attended Oxford for three years thereafter, spent another year at the University of Geneva, and, over the next several years, did some aimless roaming around Europe and North Africa, all of it financed by reservation oil strikes that made the Osage very wealthy even as their traditional way of life was being undermined. One day, a chance confrontation with nomadic tribesmen in an African desert reminded Mathews of Osage warriors he had seen in his youth. "So, I came back," he recalled some time later. "Then, I started talking with the old men." Fellow Oxford graduate Joseph Brandt persuaded Mathews to write a historical account of Osage assimilation for the university press's new "Civilization of the American Indian" series. And it was during the writing of *Wah'Kon-Tah: The Osage and the White Man's Road* (1932)—eventually a very successful Book-of-the-Month Club selection—that Mathews underwent the painful process of trying to reclaim his "Indianness" from the slough of bohemianism, pop culture, and his own "Europeanization," as he revealed in this 1930 letter to his mentor, historian Stanley Vestal:

> I have just spent the week . . . among a few flaming youths of my acquaintance. . . . They have lost their charm, those posing darlings of the post-war decade. . . . They have led their elders into broader views of life perhaps, but they themselves are lost, poor little disillusioned nitwits. . . . Legs, sex, orgies, speed, alcohol, abnormalities, exaggerated frankness, and flitting around the candle of lust, have lost their thrill; they have become flat and stingless and the devotees are stupefied and listless. . . .
>
>   It may be that I shall turn to . . . Wahkanda, the Great Spirit, since the Greek gods have been of little aid, in fact turning from me. . . . To Wahkanda, I think I shall turn as soon as I learn enough Osage. I shall address him thus. . . . Oh Wahkanda, drive into my soul the spirit of the prairie which gave birth to mine own people. . . . Purge my heart and mind Oh Wahkanda of the phantasies of civilization, and fill the void with the things of the earth. . . . Oh Wahkanda, Intatsa, the wanderer is returned; the seeker after strange gods is meek before you.

Somewhat embarrassed at the end of the prayer, Mathews closed: "Writing such drivel has relieved the pressure, and I feel better. It is gratifying to be able to give vent to crazy thoughts sometimes."[19]

If an individual like Mathews, who had been socialized into tribal ways before his Americanization, found his relationship to Native American traditions to be problematic, how then might someone like Oliver La Farge, descended from a multigenerational New York–Rhode Island family, hope to comprehend them with any sincerity and sensitivity? La Farge's training as an anthropologist, his instruction in the anthropological paradigm of culture, served him well. But, most importantly, La Farge came to realize that the solution to the modernist-traditionalist dilemma—the solution which Mathews, writing his tribal history, resorted to, and which many other regionalists discovered as well—lay in art. La Farge gave this view extended explication in his novel *Laughing Boy* (1929), the story of a Americanized Navajo woman, Slim Girl, who wishes to renew herself in her tribe's customs and traditions, to regain the "trail of beauty." To accomplish this end, she marries Laughing Boy, a consummate Navajo, a warrior, horse racer, and master craftsman, who is wonderfully innocent of the white people's world; he becomes her "Slayer of Enemy Gods." Slim Girl—educated in American schools, kept woman of a white rancher—believes that she possesses "the secret of how to prevent American knowledge from doing harm," that she can make it "serve a good purpose." Using money given to her by the rancher, she sets up housekeeping along strictly traditional lines for herself and Laughing Boy. "Knowing that something of the true substance was forever lost to her," La Farge comments, "she surrounded herself as much as possible with the trappings of Navajo-ism. . . . In a sentimental way, she played at believing her people's religion." Yet La Farge also makes clear that Slim Girl's attempt at recovering the "trail of beauty" is largely successful. Her plan, her "design" for their life together, is that they will support themselves by selling fine crafts to other Navajo as well as American tourists. She knows that the key to her reentry into traditionalism hinges on her acquisition of handicraft skills under the tutelage of Laughing Boy. Her first efforts at weaving blankets are primitive and childish; later, however, as their "house of happiness" emerges around them, as she and Laughing Boy become "two parts who together made a whole," Slim Girl too develops into a master, her intricate and subtle designs deeply personal yet composed of the most customary patterns. The fundamental and continuous socialization process that every Navajo undergoes, La Farge argues, is thus essentially aesthetic in nature; Laughing Boy, for one, spends considerable time "thinking about a design for his life."[20] The collective living tradition of "the People" provides the materials and motifs to be learned by the practitioner of a tribal art; the self-expressive praxis of a handicraft, of lore, of "medicine-making" draws and enfolds the individual into the greater life of the tribe.

The painstaking "trail of beauty" followed by Slim Girl furnishes an analogy for the path to traditionalism attempted by the more or less thoroughly modern *Indian subregionalist* members of the larger interwar movement. Very often personal confrontation with and immersion in a native culture was part of the process—field trips, interviews with "old ones," participation in dances and ceremonies, instruction in art and craft-making techniques. Mary Austin, for example, occasionally went up into the New Mexican mountain villages where Indian–Hispanic Penitente sects lived to see and perhaps join in their demanding rituals. "I have done everything myself except lash myself and carry a cross," she told another would-be amateur Penitente in 1930. And one summer day during that same year, Mari Sandoz stood on a grassy wind-blown bluff above the Little Bighorn River in Montana. "There were many, many long silences on this trip, heavy silences, especially upon Custer's Battlefield," she recalled to an editor for whom she had written an article on Crazy Horse. "Here it seemed that I had stalked very close to the spirit of this fierce, handsome, brown-haired war chief of the Oglalas." And John Neihardt, hoping for an interview with the elderly Sioux medicine man Black Elk, arrived at South Dakota's Pine Ridge Reservation a few months after Sandoz visited: "We had a big feast and danced awhile with the Oglalas. I bought a Holstein bull and the Indians slaughtered it in the old-time manner for the occasion. I even ate raw liver with the old warriors, hot from the Holstein bull. I must say I didn't relish it." Nevertheless, the Oglalas adopted Neihardt into the tribe and gave him the name "Flaming Rainbow."[21]

Yet such excursions aside, it was primarily through their *art* that regionalists strove to neutralize one of the "acids of modernity," individualistic self-consciousness, and to establish real contact with totalistic folk communities. Rather than an anthropological study, carefully defined and categorized, La Farge wrote a novel, *Laughing Boy*, a love story, an allegorical tale of reverse assimilation, richly informed by anthropological insights. Casting these insights (and a not-so-subtle commentary on contemporary Native American policy) in fictional form allowed him to re-create the whole Navajo world of which they were abstracted elements. The imaginative fusion of narrative, setting, and characterization bound him to that world at something beyond the rational and scientific level; he was able to enter it fully with the whole of his personality. His art, in short, emerged as an effort to integrate him with the body of Navajo culture and tradition. Neihardt in 1931 articulated this experience of integration, his own sense (as he told "Uncle" Black Elk) that he was peculiarly suited as "somebody with the right feeling and understanding" to write the "great history" of the Sioux people:

A strange thing happened often while I was talking with Black Elk. Over and over he seemed to be quoting from my poems, and sometimes I quoted my stuff to him, which when translated into Sioux could not retain much of their literary character, but the old man immediately recognized the ideas as his own. There was very often an uncanny merging of consciousness between the old fellow and myself and I felt it and remembered it.[22]

Contemplating her own "great history" of the Plains tribes, Mari Sandoz concluded that a grand opera would be most appropriate for capturing the "race-mood" that Neihardt had tried to grasp with the epic poetry of the *Cycle of the West*. "All the violence, ferocity, humor, courtesy, generosity, poise and tragedy" of the Plains Indians needed for their expression a Wagnerian operatic synthesis of the arts, to communicate not merely the factual and historical, but the heroic and mythic. The proposed opera would never be written, but Sandoz became her own librettist of sorts when she wrote *Crazy Horse: Strange Man of the Oglalas* (1942), combining biographical, historical, and fictional techniques for the proper effect. Mathews's *Wah'Kon-Tah* was a book very much like Sandoz's, lying somewhere between fiction and history, attaining it seemed a greater truth, a greater fidelity, a felt sense of the past missed by the academic, positivist historian. Certainly this approach enabled Mathews to relive the life, and dissolution, of his tribe, as this pain-filled passage about the coming of the oil industry reveals:

> The derricks stood black against the red of sunset and where they were thickest, little towns grew among the hills and valleys like excrescences. . . . When these little towns were abandoned after the great frenzy, they became the first desolation on the rolling prairie; the first smirch to kill the happiness that the prairie at all seasons inspired. Around them was death and blatant squalor; pieces of rusted pipe, tin cans glinting in the sun, papers imprisoned in tall weeds, old tires and tin hulks of castaway automobiles. . . . Around all the grass worn down and killed, showing the brown rocks and the sterile earth.[23]

Through *Wah'Kon-Tah* and subsequent works, Mathews reentered the Osage world via the "trail of beauty" in a very literal sense. Ultimately, he was elected to the tribal council and, in the latter 1930s, helped to found and organize the tribal museum.

Mathews's appropriation of Osage culture, like that of Sandoz and the Oglalas, seemed possible because of the very blurring of methodological lines— histories with invented dialogue, vivid imagery, and metaphors—that became common in regionalist writings. When Joseph Brandt launched the University of Oklahoma Press on a "strictly regional program" in 1928, he realized early that it would mean a departure from the publication of "purely academic" books. He intended to steer the press beyond "the Scylla of esotericism and the Charybdis of the unutterably dull pot-boilers of bored professors." The evocative portrayal of the regional culture of Oklahoma and the greater Southwest not only meant an escape from those "deadly embraces of the clerical-minded scholar," but it also made possible a total enrichment of the cultural life of the state, region, and nation: if eminently readable, the "printed page," stated the press's imprimatur, became "everyman's university."[24] A regional consciousness thus was nurtured; a sense of place and a regional folk heritage, their vestiges fast disappearing, were disseminated, perpetuated, and re-affirmed. The appropriation of regional traditions, in short, required that they be apprehended as a lived reality, and such apprehension demanded the imme-diacy and drama of fiction, of poetry, and of other art forms that engaged not only the intellect but all the senses and emotions—only in this way could the experience of a self-encompassing culture be re-created. The *region* itself, as an organicist construct, as a complex congeries of myths, cultures, and tradi-tions, demanded the organicist approach—conceptualization as a "world"—which only art could provide.

In this self-conscious embrace of the aesthetic as the means to construct (or reconstruct) reality, and in their revolt against excessive subjectivity, their critique of abstraction, and their quest for a unified sensibility, regionalists like La Farge, Sandoz, and Mathews may in a general sense be considered modernists. Such a generalization, however, does not sit easily on the great diversity of individuals engaged in the regionalist cultural project, inside or outside the Indian subregions. In fact, they may be more neatly characterized by their differentiation from other important manifestants of modernism—most significantly, by their very appropriation of folk-Indian tradition and the natural environment as aesthetic and ethical source materials. A number of prominent modernists (such as T. S. Eliot), it is true, looked to traditionalism as a ground for their art, but usually this traditionalism was pressed into the service of a highly "esoteric" and formalistic aesthetic theory and technique. Although the regionalist movement did have its share of avant-gardists (fel-low travelers Faulkner and O'Keeffe, for example), it departed from the more aesthetically and substantively extreme forms of modernism by its avowal of a social art, a democratic culture to encompass Eliot and "Everyman." Beyond this aspiration, but part and parcel with it, regionalists advocated a literal reconstruction of modern society along folk-regional lines. If this utopian desire to effect an actual integration of the modern and the traditional by aesthetic, technological, political, and other means limited the extremity of re-gionalist artistic experimentation, it was because regionalism was not merely an artistic creed—it was also a nascent ideology.[25]

Certainly, regionalism was not the only cultural or political movement of the interwar years to have these high expectations. The Bauhaus movement, for example, had as one of its goals (in Walter Gropius's words) to "embrace architecture and sculpture and painting in one unity," to effect a marriage of art and industry in a way not dissimilar from the "integration of utility and beauty" that Hewett and others admired in folk-Indian cultures. But the Bauhaus school was predicated on a liberating antitraditional pursuit of absolute form, an aesthetic well-suited to the latest machine production yet repugnant to the sensibilities of most regionalists, who wanted their art and architecture to acknowledge "earth loyalties and human loyalties" (as John Collier put it). Pointedly, when Aldous Huxley made a fictional visit to the Pueblo mesa country through his characters Bernard and Lenina in *Brave New World* (1932), he concurred with the admiring analysis of Collier and the other Indian subregionalists that such "loyalties" nurtured an existence that was "wonderfully intimate," constitutive of social bonds of "great intensity of feeling." To his two ironically bewildered protagonists, fresh from Huxley's dystopian caricature of the regimented yet atomized, machine-modeled, world-turned-upside-down of modern civilization, the Pueblo tribes' traditional life of marriage, family, and religion was "absolutely mad"—"as though," Bernard remarks, "we were living on different planets, in different centuries." Significantly, however, in a new preface for an edition of the novel published years later, Huxley lamented that he had not given one of his characters, the Savage, some choice of existence alternative to the "insane life in Utopia, or the life of a primitive in an Indian village." Huxley's regret, and the suggestive comparison to Bauhaus, thus beg a crucial question: how then were the prescriptions of the sort of small-scale, communitarian, aesthetic-symbiotic, preindustrial Indian societies conceptualized by Austin and Hewett to be applied in a modern, urbanized, technologically advanced, continent-sized country like the United States? In a more general sense, how could the cultural project of regionalism be translated into a program of cultural transformation, a regionalist politics? The answers to this question explored during the 1920s phase of the project were tentative, partial, and somewhat unexamined at best. Nevertheless, all lines of inquiry seemed to converge on some form of *civic religion*—a self-conscious and "systematic" effort to reassert moral community by instilling, as Hartley Alexander phrased it, a "reverence for high traditions": a modern "poetic orgy."[26]

Yet the central question remained as to how such a civic religion might be established. One distinguished resident of the Taos colony, D. H. Lawrence, explored exactly this issue in his novel *The Plumed Serpent* (1926), choosing as his setting Old Mexico, with its Indian majority population. At the time still caught in the throes of a three-decades-long revolution, Mexico attracted many members of the Santa Fe–Taos regionalist wing, including Lawrence and his wife Frieda, as well as Mary Austin, Mabel Dodge Luhan, and Witter

Bynner, all of them (like Austin) fascinated by the "immense cultural activities going on up and down the great central plateau." There Diego Rivera and a cohort of revolutionary artists, under government auspices, were attempting to transpose traditional Indian values and motifs into the secular purposes of a mass democratic movement—a program very suggestive to the promoters of Native American culture from the north. Lawrence, however, was no democrat (at least in the liberal sense of the word), and his fictional vision of a modern folk political movement conjured instead the frightening scenario of the second coming of an ancient Mexican god, Quetzalcoatl, through the messianic leadership of Ramon—"the living Quetzalcoatl"—and his lieutenant Cipriano; together, they hope to make "the religion of Quetzalcoatl the national religion of the Republic." The two men invent elaborate and impressive ceremonies to recruit the "degenerate mob" of their all-too-modern countrymen into the faith and thereby restore them to their long-lost traditionalist "manhood." Their "Indian consciousness" was in this way to be released from under "the stagnant water of the white man's Dead Sea consciousness," and they would be united through "a renewal of the old, terrible bond of the blood-unison of man," by which "the blood of the individual" was to be "given back to the great blood-being, the god, the nation, the tribe." Lawrence posed this revived totalistic folk community against the pall of what he variously called "Americanisation" and "the modern spirit," which to his mind were blotting out the earthy soul of Mexico. America connoted "democracy" and "materialism," both of which were (in the often-mystical language of the novel) "negations" and death to the Indian soul. The negative freedom or "liberty" celebrated by a now-disavowed postwar liberal order was, Ramon remarks, "a rotten old wine-skin. It won't hold one's wine of inspiration or passion any more." White people, Lawrence asserted, had "conquered the lower worlds of metal and energy," but "becoming soulless," merely "whizz around in machines, circling the void of their own emptiness."[27]

Much of this criticism was standard fare for the 1920s. So too was Lawrence's radical and somewhat prescient solution to the modern malaise, chillingly evocative of a totalitarian regime (images of the armies of Quetzalcoatl, dressed in blue and white serapes, fanning out through the countryside), beginning to show itself on the European horizon. Yet Lawrence himself was ambivalent about the implications of his scenario; and in fact this ambivalence, and not the pontifications and ritual chants of Ramon, comprises the center of the novel, through the character of Kate, a young worldly and world-weary Irishwoman attracted to the two high priests of the Plumed Serpent. She is the stand-in for any number of intellectuals, regionalists (like Mathews) included, who had grown disenchanted with the 1920s—the jazz, the avant-garde, the bohemianism, the Bolshevism, the consumerism, all of it:

Ah, how tired it made Kate feel; the hopelessness, the ugliness, the cynicism, the emptiness. She felt she could cry aloud, for the unknown gods to put the magic back into her life, and to save her from the dry-rot of the world's sterility. . . . She had seen Ramon Carrasco, and Cipriano. And they were men. She would believe in them. Anything, anything rather than this sterility of nothingness which was the world, and into which her life was drifting.

Ramon and Cipriano want to recruit Kate for this very reason: she represents to them the rootless modern "New Woman." From Kate's own perspective (during enthusiastic moments, at least), the ultimate goal of the religion of Quetzalcoatl promises "a new conception of human life, that will arise from the fusion of the old blood-and-vertebrate consciousness with the white man's present mental-spiritual consciousness"—"the sinking of both beings, into a new being." This transfigurative fusion, however, is also what repels her from the faith. Although she eventually "marries" Cipriano, Kate (Lawrence writes) "had always looked upon her blood as absolutely her own, her individual own." But if the requirements of the new folk religion were "the blood is one blood," then were she to embrace it fully "it meant a strange, marginless death of her individual self"—"something aboriginal and tribal, and almost worse than death to the white individual."[28] Kate does not resolve this dilemma, and by the end of the novel it becomes clear that she can never resolve it; she must remain in the margins (of understanding, of sincere belief), grasping at whatever fulfillment she might gain from the communalism of an organic self-enfolding culture, yet retaining the integrity—and isolation—of critical individualistic selfhood.

As Lawrence shows, there was appropriable cultural potency enough even at the margins of Indian tribalism. While Ramon's movement gathers momentum and "strange baptisms" take place in the sea and a "scarlet and black tower of Huitzilopochtli" rises on the shore, "the whole country was thrilling with a new thing, with a release of new energy," Lawrence comments. "But there was a sense of violence and crudity in it all, a touch of horror"—born out of the fervor of the recently regenerate. Undoubtedly, with these frightening scenes of the new national religion in action, and with his portrayal of Kate's mixed revulsion toward it, Lawrence put forward a rare realistic and corrective picture of the dark side of existence within an integrated Indian community, rare amid all the contemporary regionalist utopian eulogizing about such a way of life. This discourse was filled with descriptive terms like *democratic*, *republican*, and *personal freedom*, but in actuality tribal life could in some ways be oppressive—the price of *intimacy* and *integration*, as some of the Indian subregionalists were gradually to discover. Oliver La Farge, for example, was taken aback by the methods of social organization he observed at the Santo Domingo and Jemez pueblos near Santa Fe, which he reported to John Collier in 1934: "In these two conservative pueblos, we meet the extreme of rigidity, with a ruthless suppression of minorities and a considerable use of punishment . . . to enforce the will of the governing group"; their "present system of self-government," he concluded, was in definite need of "liberalization." Clark Wissler, observing from the more clinical distance of the Museum of Natural History, was even less sentimental; as he later wrote in his book *Indians of the United States* (1940), "Finally, an Indian community was a human group: a few were lazy, some stupid, some immoral, some quarrelsome, some grasping and tyrannical, some intelligent, some thrifty and some industrious."[29]

In truth, regionalists—engaged in the task of cultural reconstruction—took what they needed from Native American civilization, mythicizing it, to some extent, where necessary. From their vantage in the "margins" they thought that they had discovered a communitarianism without coercion, a communitarianism of individual expressiveness—this was to be the model for a regionalist civic religion. Yet for all their paeans to organicism, they remained basically committed to liberal individualism. As even the sometimes extreme Neihardt was forced to qualify himself, "I am by nature socialistic, believing that the only real values are social values after all," and that "the individual counts only as he contributes to and furthers the social process, *or the reverse*" (italics mine). Lawrence's fictive cultlike mass political movement, and the real-life versions of it soon to erupt on behalf of the *Volk* and the *patria*, were hardly the type of civic religion that regionalists were groping toward. "If folklore can provide the patterns of the fascist," editor T. M. Pearce of the *New Mexico Quarterly* later wrote, "it can also provide the patterns of other traditions." And the folklore of the American Indian, he believed, was "a folklore of human values and social democracy."[30]

Regionalists wanted not a new cult, but a new culture; not an outright fusion of the primitive and the modern, but an infusion of the one into the other, drawing on a selective set of social and ethical lessons gleaned from the insights of regionalist art. These "lessons"—historicist, sociological, and philosophical—constituted the "vital significance," to quote Neihardt, of what the Indian subregions of the Southwest, Midwest, and Northwest "had to offer" the country culturally: "good models for us," Pearce wrote, "good medicine for the American tribe." The aesthetic-rooted "affective group mindedness" of the Indian village furnished a powerful example of noncoercive positive freedom, supplying a long-standing void in the abstract and (to the 1920s mind) anarchic liberal order. Further, the Indians' "sense of the *sacra* of the soil," together with their subordination of technology to larger social purposes, indicated ways in which humans might live lightly on the landscape, ways to be emulated if not concretely then at least analogically—again, fulfilling the shortcomings of a political culture that seemed prostrate before the Machine, unable to control the "frenzied development" that was effacing places like Mathews's Osage country.[31]

These articles of the regionalist civic religion, "human loyalties" and "earth loyalties," were to be disseminated not by a messiah or a demagogue (Ezra Pound's prince as artist), but by a more modest version of the "poetic orgy." The symbolic monumentalism of Goodhue and Alexander's Nebraska capitol, the epic poetry of Neihardt, the "trail of beauty" explored by Hewett and Austin and La Farge—through proselytizers like these, the values, styles, and traditions of Indian life were to be woven into the greater fabric of regional culture and purveyed by presses, magazines, arts societies, festivals, university courses, museums, and other organs of cultural transmission. If the mission of these educative institutions were less ambitious than the creation of a "new being" (or a new *reich*), their goal was nevertheless intentionally transformative: to contribute to the molding of a new kind of citizen, a citizen more conscious and respectful of the history and environment and diverse cultures of his or her locality, more tradition-grounded and community-minded, and less rootlessly mobile and blindly self-interested. Joseph Brandt staged one such effort at regionalist "aesthetic education" in 1934, when he organized a statewide "Centennial of Publishing" celebration in Oklahoma to mark the publication of an obscure century-old pamphlet in the Creek Indian language. Although most Oklahomans considered the state's still-brief history to have begun with white settlement in 1889, Brandt reminded them in a press release that "civilization, as we know it, was curiously brought to Oklahoma by Indians" several decades earlier. It was a theme emphasized again and again during the centennial's week-long observance, not only in newspapers, but also in sermons, on radio broadcasts, among school assemblies and civic groups, and in a proclamation by the governor. "Oklahoma has just passed through what is perhaps the last vestige of 'pioneer' pains" (the Dust Bowl), as Brandt explained his motivations. "It is settling down. It is ready to take whatever pride there is in age."[32]

Regionalists in many of the states encompassed by the Indian subregions were thus to cultivate an "art consciousness" of their Native American heritages during the 1920s and 1930s, to mitigate the effects of the Americanism represented by rugged individualism and pioneer-inspired "frenzied development." Their recourse was to an as yet embryonic and alternative Americanism, an Americanism not of self-annihilating nationalism or mindless racialism or anarchic individualism, but instead, an Americanism conceived as "a process of selection from the attainments of other peoples," to return to Edgar

Hewett's words. By 1930, the conception of regional culture emerging in the minds of artists and intellectuals throughout the Greater West was, in essence, dedicated to an inclusive and organic pluralism. Because they "came from our own soil," the Indian peoples of the United States exerted a particularly powerful influence on the regionalist movement as it grappled with the problem of "reforesting" America's "cultural territory"; regionalists looked to them for whatever wisdom they might have gained over all the long centuries of "humanizing" the American continent. Yet fundamentally, this act of "looking to" the Indian was to be of as much significance as any pearls they might find. In their eyes, the bison and maize and tribal sayings carved into the balustrades, the chiefs tooled on the senate chamber doors, the thunderbirds high on the dome—these were the true "prophetic conclusion" to the text of the "history and symbolism of political freedom" that adorned the Nebraska capitol, temple of the new regionalist civic religion.[33]

3

The Re-Discovery
of America

The Regionalist Movement and
the Search for the American Folk

Everything comes out of the dirt—everything;
everything comes out of the people, the everyday
people, the people as you find them and leave them:
not university people, not F.F.V. people: people,
people, just people!
—Walt Whitman, frontispiece to B. A. Botkin, ed.,
Folk-Say: A Regional Miscellany (1929)

"So this was regionalism, flourishing on the meanest capital, surviving stubbornly, and brilliant," observed John
Crowe Ransom in his 1934 essay, "The Aesthetic of Regionalism," describing a scene he had witnessed from a
train traveling eastward out of Albuquerque the previous
summer. During his stay in New Mexico he had made, he
wrote, "two acquisitions." The first was this "bright
and charming" and suggestive rail-side scene of Pueblo
tribespeople threshing grain in their villages, living "as
they always have lived." The second acquisition was a
story, which told of a local tribe that had for years rejected
offers of government aid despite drought and poor har-
vests:

> The chief knew that, while Indians compose in the
> mass a strong race, there are always weak-headed
> Indians [who would take the money and] buy white
> men's goods with it to import into the tribal life and
> corrupt it, that Indians are apt to set an inordinate
> value upon highly-coloured articles sold in the white
> ten-cent stores, which are less than trash when com-
> pared with the beautiful ornaments which Indian

weavers, potters, and jewelers make; that Indian bucks fancy white
men's shirts, which are unworthy of them; and that they are apt to part
with anything in order to secure alarm-clocks.

On scene and story, Ransom "regaled himself with certain reflections," which
he took back with him to the South: refusing the white man's money, "the chief
must have looked with apprehension upon importations in general, knowing
that a culture will decline and fall when the people grow out of liking their
own native products"; the wise chief held firmly to the principle, Ransom
declared, that "the aesthetic values are as serious as the economic ones, and as
governing."[1]

Significantly, these "reflections" of Ransom's on the "regionalism" of New
Mexico came to him less as revelations than as confirmations of what he, a
self-described "philosophical regionalist," had already discovered among the
white yeoman folk culture of his personal "concrete or particular regionalism:
an Upper South variety." As such, the significance of these reflections—and
that of the literal and figurative interpretations he gave to his interregional
travels—exemplify some larger tendencies emerging among many other artists and intellectuals outside the Indian subregions during the 1920s and early
1930s, above all, the parallel recovery of the cultures of the European American and African American folk for the purposes of cultural reconstruction. The
focus shifts therefore (to return to our original organizing image) up the steps,
from the buffalo-carven balustrades to the panel of the Pioneers and the
building-girdling bas-relief story of freedom; up the dome, from the thunderbirds to the Sower whose "harvest is the fulfilled commonwealth." Immediately, however, Ransom's story of the gravely imperiled if stubbornly surviving Pueblos must also call into question Goodhue's (and Ransom's own)
kind of monumentalized and mythic representations not only of the Indians
but, more acutely, of the pioneer folk as well. For if the "noble specimen" of
the Pueblo acclaimed by "every white traveller" (in Ransom's words) were in
actuality susceptible to the corruption of ten-cent stores and alarm clocks—
the "white men's" Progress—how might the cultures of the present-day
American folk themselves be faring under the forces of modernization? It was
precisely this issue that was to become the object of considerable regionalist
critical scrutiny during the late 1920s and early 1930s, even as the movement
began to loosely gather itself *as* a self-conscious national movement, well
shown by Ransom's summer in New Mexico and his participation as something of a Southern Agrarian ambassador to the First New Mexico Round
Table on Southwest Literature (1933).[2]

Indeed, in 1930, B. A. Botkin had posed that central problematic question in
the second volume of his *Folk-Say* anthology as the subject for a movement-

defining symposium, "Toward a Rationale of the Folk and Regionalism": "What (or who) is (or are) the 'folk' in America?" The answer was crucial, because the folk lay at the very heart of the concept of regional culture, defined this way by Botkin himself in 1929: "the traditional forces of custom, belief, locality, and speech which within a region constitute the peculiar disposition and expressiveness of a people, considered as a composite of racial and geographic influence and a component of national culture."[3] By almost any definition of "folkness"—definitions that usually hinged on oral tradition, handicrafts, and intimacy with specific environments—most regionalists assumed (with the Indian subregionalists) that contemporary Native Americans fulfilled all requirements. Many too believed (heeding *The New Negro*, perhaps, or drawing conclusions based often on familiar racial stereotypes, turned now to more positive social ends) that rural African Americans had evolved a distinctive folk culture, due to their long confinement in the South. Thus, not surprisingly, the issue of the survival of folkness in historical and modern America tended to focus primarily on European settlers and their descendants, those very people whom the writers of the earlier Midwestern renaissance had despairingly depicted as the twilight of the older America, waning into the all-too-modern vapidity of the present. Yet as the efforts of the Indian subregionalists reveal, the business of the emergent national regional renaissance was not despair but reconstruction, and so there developed a set of complimentary and, in some respects, competing analyses, all engaged in the task of conceptualizing the nature of America's cultural development, and all attempting to find a *positive* answer to that essential question, rephrased once more: How in Babbitt's America did folk culture persist—in living practitioners, as tenuous survivals, as literary tradition, as myth?

The critics, historians, folklorists, and sociologists seeking to recover an indigenous America were nevertheless impelled by much the same sense of urgency that had spurred the Indian subregionalists, and Ransom's wise chief, to their task: the sense (reinforced by their own generational experience of the world war "breaking the world in two," as Cather wrote) that this "earlier, basic" America, or what was left of it, was passing irrevocably away. Exacerbating and shaping the personal dimensions of this confrontation with cultural dispersion, the shared witnessing of disruptive change and decline (ranch country converted to resorts, plantations taken by weeds, city greenery crushed under skyscrapers), there was abroad during the 1920s ample intellectual justification for pessimism and alarm—in Henry Adams's "law of acceleration," in Frederick Jackson Turner's jeremiad on the closed frontier, in Oswald Spengler's universalist cyclical history. When regionalists came to write their own histories, they therefore often took on a decidedly *catastrophist* strain: narratives in which whole cultures "disperse" and "deliquesce," and once-vital traditions end up on "rubbish heaps." And just as the emblematic panel of the Pioneers (who brought with them "Anglo-Saxon institutions, and infused in these the whole tradition of the civilization of Europe") was given a singularly prominent place on Goodhue's capitol—mirroring its prominence in the national mythology—so too did the regionalist search for folkness come to focus on the role that the pioneer played in America's cultural development as either agent or victim of catastrophism, consciously and unconsciously preserving, abandoning, adapting, or inventing ways of living in the vacuum of the frontier, and changing the "history and symbolism of political freedom" from a biblical, classical, and European story to an American one.[4] For regionalists, the pioneer thus embodied the idea of culture as *process, evolutionary* process, from the static monistic organicism of Europe to the vibrant multiplicity of America, for example, or from an old oppressive order to a new, liberated one, or, in the view of the most catastrophist-minded, from culture to culturelessness.

The 1920s and 1930s have long been noteworthy for encompassing a sustained and occasionally acrimonious intellectual debate over the predominant Turnerian interpretation of this process, around which both believers and detractors revolved. In most of its essential features, this debate constituted a groping theoretical search for the origins, nature, and durability of American folk-regional cultures. Among those with catastrophist leanings—particularly Mumford, Van Wyck Brooks, Waldo Frank, Vernon Parrington, and, somewhat more ambivalently, Turner himself—a commonly sketched general model of the country's cultural development had begun to take shape (with, as will be seen, variations) by the mid- to late 1920s. That model may, for brevity's sake, be summarized in these terms: the pioneers at the earlier, frontier stages of a region's history were closest to the soil and its influences, furthest from an increasingly distinctive and "standardizing" urban-industrial life-style (and consequently at this moment most folklike), yet also, paradoxically, working most fervently for the progress that would carry them away from the former and toward the latter. Never a settled peasantry (with a few isolated exceptions) in the usual sense of the word, the folk in America existed historically always at some point along this modernizing, and imperiling, continuum. In the history of every region, however, certain moments of *equilibrium* occur along this continuum, when modernizing tendencies are balanced temporarily by folkness consciously and unconsciously invoked: first, the crucial frontier stage, when pioneers adapt or *root down* the culture they bring with them to the environment they encounter; next, a rural-pastoral stage, in which folk elements are preserved in a more long-lived and settled balance of man and landscape; then, as folk-regional societies differentiate into more complex stages of modernization, and folk-cultural elements are threatened with dissolution, self-conscious efforts to conserve them emerge, either as a political strain of sectionalism or as the art of regionalism (sometimes, but not always, concurrent developments). Thereafter, modernization complete, its folkish socioeconomic basis largely "standardized," nationalized, out of existence, a regional culture may live on only as a mythical if not stereotyped sectional-regional identity, as a regionalist artistic corpus, or as a few scant and scattered folkish survivals, to be remembered, or forgotten.

Lewis Mumford and his New York circle, which included Brooks and Frank, possessed perhaps the darkest and most catastrophic vision of how American cultural history had played itself out through these stages of regional culture, differentiating outward from older to younger regions of the country. In their scenario, the older America, the America where Frank's holistic "mystic tradition" and Mumford's New England village enjoyed a "lingering afterglow"—an evanescent equilibrium point on the Turnerian spectrum— terminated abruptly with the Civil War and the ensuing frenzy of urban-industrialization, which brought about the "death-spasm of all the Sections, of all our pasts," as Frank wrote, concluding: "America emerged from it without sectionalisms, without organic past at all. It was swept to a flat atomic form-lessness." Beyond the town limits of the antebellum New England village (where any number of great souls were born, "prefiguring in the imagination" a folk-regional culture teetering against a gathering modernity) or outside the walls of various other cultural cloisters scattered across the continent (Frank's "re-discovered" Fourierists, French Jesuits, Spanish Friars, and others), the historical folk, or any qualities of folkness, were little seen by the dark 1920s catastrophist works of Mumford's circle.[5]

Instead, according to their widely influential critique of the pioneer, the "epic march of the covered wagon" out across time and space into the Ohio Valley, the Mississippi Valley, and the vast country west of the Missouri was a death march of culture, "leaving behind it deserted villages, bleak cities, depleted soils," and any number of "sick and exhausted souls." Centering their attention on the post–Civil War period, the Mumfordians placed the pioneer squarely at the far unfolkish and modern end of the Turnerian spectrum, conceiving him as the "lustful" agent of a triumphant capitalist ethos, "the ultimate human atom," the "individual anarchic man," as Frank put it, "a barbarian," a "fragmentary self" who was "truly alone, truly without contact with an organic whole." The "pioneer spirit" repudiated completely the "old heritages," as Harold Stearns had observed in the *Civilization* volume, and pioneer life (especially in the dreary Midwest) produced "no folk-music, no folk-art, no folk-poetry, or next to none, to express it, to console it," or so argued Brooks in *The Ordeal of Mark Twain* (1920). In this book, Brooks then traced the cultural dissolution further, through the Gilded Age and beyond, when the utterly self-interested pioneer mind-set eventuated in a "general levelling down" of all those fragmentary individuals into a conformist pseudo-community or "social cult" dedicated to the "worship of success," to the sacredness of the pursuit of wealth, in the agrarian and mineral-rich West as well as the industrial East. As Brooks concluded in his own *Civilization* essay, the "heritage of pioneering" for the twentieth century was an empty "business regime," with its "burden of isolation, nervous strain, excessive work." The bequest of the frontier epoch to modern America, the Mumford group argued, was the abstract, rootless, repressed, cultureless world of Babbittry itself. To reform this world, to transform it, they sought to recover what little remained in the 1920s as "essential links" to the lost world of the Golden Day, which shone all the brighter given the bleakness of the interim (when the "promise of regionalism" was "exterminated"). Among these essential links were a "great line," a nascent regionalist literary tradition represented in the works of Emerson, Whitman, Thoreau; and, for Mumford especially, a few glimpses of the old village life of New England in places like the "indigenous community" of his friend and fellow planner Benton MacKaye at Shirley Center, Massachusetts—the remnants of the rooted communitarian world of the Golden Day, the world the pioneer spirit had left behind, and dispersed.[6]

As this scenario implies, the Mumford group's catastrophist conceptualization of American history could and did inadvertently undercut its own efforts to establish contact with a usable past, a "capturable America" (as Frank wrote), and by 1930 and thereafter, its members increasingly found themselves qualifying and backing away from the stark implications of their earlier interpretation, which was less than inspiring culturally or politically. In point of fact, many years later, Mumford for one admitted that his circle's cultural critique was "so relentless, so unsparing, so persistently negative that it was often grossly unjust, as I was in my ruthless denigration of the saving virtues of the . . . Pioneer." To be sure, there were some contemporary defenders of frontier life eager to point out the extremity of the Mumford circle's "theories," the most prominent among them being, of course, Western historian Bernard DeVoto, who began a famous decade-long literary feud with the Mumford group, and Brooks specifically, with the publication of his book *Mark Twain's America* in 1932. "A critical theory is a notion which may be converted to the assault of what one dislikes," DeVoto wrote, perhaps the first to point to the role of the pioneer for "Messrs. Frank, Brooks, and Mumford" as a somewhat caricatured catchall device of social criticism. Unfortunately, DeVoto countered, exhibiting the modernist-regionalist distrust of abstraction ("Simplifications are dangerous"), "the frontiersmen neglected to behave according to the theories."[7] DeVoto in fact was more correct in this assertion than he knew. Other regionalist writers in the late 1920s and early 1930s

(DeVoto included), seeking to conceive less catastrophic and more optimistic renditions of regional-national history, were also to grasp only a part of an ambiguous frontier past, as the regionalist movement as a whole began to grapple with the complex problem of how cultures change and evolve.

Southern sociologist Rupert Vance offered an initial and somewhat more sophisticated "theory" in the "Heritage of Pioneering" section of his *Human Geography of the South* (1932). Describing some of the "saving virtues" of the pioneer, Vance noted pointedly that "the frontier was not all individualism and competition in exploitation of the wilderness"; rather, "out of family and kinship groupings, out of the very hardships and crude contacts of the pioneer belts grew spontaneous associations and methods of cooperation." It was exactly these kinds of "saving virtues"—the folk characteristics that pioneers displayed at special moments along that modernizing continuum of development, moments as short as a generation (becoming shorter as the twentieth century neared), when culture and place melded, community flourished, a "yeomanry" emerged—that other interwar artists and intellectuals sought in turn to recover as their own usable pasts, tracing back the histories of regions in the South and West beyond New England, back from a mechanized, standardized present to a more humane and heroic past. In the West especially, that area settled in "the forty years that lay between the California Gold Rush of '49 and the Oklahoma Land Rush of '89" (as Parrington put it), these efforts at recovery were often "pioneering" attempts to "prefigure" a folk culture "in the imagination," to conceive it as art. Mari Sandoz, for instance, in *Old Jules* (1935), a fictionalized biography of her father, depicted not an "individual anarchic man" but instead (for all his personal faults) a man who envisioned the hard 1880s Niobrara frontier as "his home and around him a community of his countrymen and other homeseekers, refugees from oppression and poverty, intermingled in peace and contentment." And Lynn Riggs, the folk playwright who was part of the Oklahoma regionalist circle of Brandt and Botkin, recalled in 1929 his favorite setting, the territorial Oklahoma of only "thirty years ago": "a vanished era . . . an era a little more golden than the present one; a time when people were easier, warmer, happier in the environment they had created. Song flourished. There were the usual human anguishes, of course. But there was *wholeness* in the people, there was great endurance." Sadly, by his own time, Riggs lamented, all these folkish qualities had been "banished forever" by "our radios and autos."[8]

As Vance's model suggests, the Mumfordians with their "pioneer as proto-Babbitt" concept and these Western regionalists with their "pioneer as folk" construct were both grasping opposite sides of the same process of modernization. In the years after the Civil War particularly, localized and previously self-sufficient rural communities in the South and isolated frontier areas of the

West were incorporated into the system of a growing national and international cash-crop economy, and around the turn of the century, into an increasingly integrated national market of goods and services as well. It was a process driven by the requirements of survival (especially for the tenant farmers of the devastated and impoverished South), by hopes for mobility, and, additionally, by plain and simple greed; by homesteaders as well as speculators, and by homesteaders who were speculators; by understandable human desires for convenience and comfort (handicrafts abandoned for mail order), and—like Ransom's "weak-headed" Indians—by thoughtless confidence in Progress (victrolas replacing heirloom fiddles). Vernon Parrington described these changes in terms of "an America that was passing," of an inexorable "drift towards consolidation": "The machine would reach into the remotest villages to disrupt the traditional domestic economy, and the division of labor would substitute for the versatile frontiersman the specialized factory-hand. A new urban psychology would displace the old agrarian one."[9]

Parrington, in fact, attempted to go beyond the Mumfordians and the Westerners and combine the opposing sides of this passing folk America within a single line of analysis. Yet in the end he was only able to produce another catastrophist scheme, the product of his own irreconcilably splayed historical consciousness. His effort provides nonetheless another important case study in the groping regionalist search for the American folk. From a staunch Turnerian, neo-Jeffersonian perspective, but also, looking back disappointedly from the 1920s "Babbitt warren" that his native Midwest had become, Parrington constructed a modernization scenario every bit as dark as Mumford's or Frank's, perceiving not one but two catastrophes responsible for the folk-destroying tendency of "consolidation." First, there was the Civil War, which "swept out on the rubbish heap" the "old philosophies" of "natural rights . . . equalitarian democracy," and "local home rule"—the great legacies of the eighteenth-century physiocratic-republican frontier—meanwhile throwing the "coercive powers of a centralizing state into the hands of the new industrialism." As if signaling this break in history, the organizing "regional minds" conceit in the first two volumes of his mammoth study of American political culture, *Main Currents in American Thought* (1927, 1930), disappears suddenly in the uncompleted and fragmentary third, with one exception: Parrington's own "Middle Border," where, as he himself witnessed in the Populist Kansas of the 1890s, only the "western farmers," possessed of the "psychology of the frontier," remained as the "last stumbling block," the "last stronghold," the "last refuge" against an "encompassing industrialism" that portended Leviathan—last because it was the *last* frontier. Recounting their defeat, and the end of the frontier (the second catastrophe), where the "influence of diffuse landholding" had nurtured the "psychology of democratic individualism," instructing pioneers in "democratic sympathies and democratic economics," Parrington manifested his despair—his Jeffersonian faith fractured by a present-day America in which men have become "automata"—with double-visioned flashovers to the Mumfordian frontier, where the folk are revealed to be collaborators in their own undoing:

A scattered agricultural people, steeped in particularistic jealousies and suspicious of centralization, was to be transformed into an urbanized factory people, rootless, migratory, drawn to the job as by a magnet. It was to come about the more easily because the American farmer had never been a land-loving peasant, rooted to the soil and thriving only in daily contact with familiar acres. He had long been half middle-class, accounting unearned increment the most profitable crop, and buying and selling land as if it were calico. And in consequence the vigorous individualism that had sprung from frontier conditions decayed with the passing of the frontier, and those who had lost in the gamble of preemption and exploitation were added to the growing multitude of the proletariet. It was from such materials, supplemented by a vast influx of immigrants, that was fashioned the America we know today with its standardized life, its machine culture, its mass psychology—an America to which Jefferson and Jackson and Lincoln would be strangers.

It was, Parrington sighed, a "discouraging essay."[10]

If he thus had some difficulty forecasting an "ampler democratic future" from this catastrophist "reexamination of the American past," Parrington stubbornly held tight to his belief that "Jeffersonian democracy still offers hope." He had his "great line"—those like Crèvecoeur, Jefferson, Taylor, and all the others who had fashioned the frontier experience into an ideology. And in less despondent and more defiant moments, he could mentally resegregate the "spirit of Babbitt" away from the folk in the "producing hinterland," confining it to a separate space in parasitical "cheap and pretentious county-seats" and commercial capitals (the old regionalist trick of projection to ward off imperiling change), and thereby preserve pure an image of agricultural America "where the old-fashioned, kindly, neighborly, wholesome, democratic virtues" still hung on. Yet there were other, more sophisticated ways than this put forward in the 1920s and early 1930s to conceptualize the modernizing folk, ways that avoided the polemical one-sidedness, the despairing flip-flops, and the other incoherences of the catastrophism of Mumford and Parrington. Such models had to pull together the "pioneer as proto-Babbitt" and the "pioneer as folk" to capture the whole complicated process of "the America that was passing" along the Turnerian continuum, to depict an American folk that was both agent *and* victim of modernization. They had to explain, in short, ambiguous post–Civil War plains-frontier worlds like that of O. E. Rölvaag's *Giants in the Earth* (1927), where peasant immigrants "discarded the names of their fathers" for new American ones, scoffed at talk of old country superstitions ("We're through with all that troll business over in Norway"), destroyed other settlers' claim-landmarks to secure the best land for themselves, but also, responded with horror at the thought of new American names ("soon they would be discarding other sacred things"), beamed with pride when a son was born with a caul, and founded a school that served variously as "primary school and grammar school, as language school—in both Norwegian and English—and religious school," as a "debating society . . . a singing school, a coffee party, or a social centre"—a community institution which "bound subtly and inseparably together the few souls who lived out there in the wilderness."[11]

Bernard DeVoto and folklorist-critic Constance Rourke, each in his or her own independent scholarly search for a "native American" literary tradition, put forward one possible noncatastrophist historical scenario under which folk culture might have persisted in the context of the frontier's chaotic dynamism. To them, "the frontier," as DeVoto asserted in *Mark Twain's America*, far from being a death march of culture, "was a passageway down which came all of America—all its conditions, histories, and castes." Although Rourke's own scenario of historical change, outlined in her influential *American Humor* (1931), is framed in Mumfordian terms of "continual forces of dispersal" pulling America apart (she had some personal and interpretive dealings with the Mumford group, unlike DeVoto), and although it is sited on a Turnerian frontier under the action of which "vestiges of remembrance brought from the older countries quickly disappeared," Rourke's scheme argued that these dwindling vestiges of traditionalism were soon supplanted by a rich indigenous "comic tradition." More central to the emerging regionalist disavowal of catastrophism ("I'm rather distinctly a regionalist," she told H. G. Merriam in 1933), Rourke emphasized that this new tradition itself emerged from and reflected the "common life" of the Jacksonian frontier and "created fresh bonds, a new unity" as it "*marched with the forces of dispersal*" (italics mine). These forces had resulted (she acknowledged) in the constant breaking of "the fabric of local traditions" and the "short length" of memory in a mobile population, "mostly of a single generation." Rourke nevertheless hoped to shift the focus of scholarly attention away from the "great lines" and toward the folk themselves as cocreators of art and culture, by portraying a highly nomadic people "seeking the illusive goal of unity and the resting-place of a tradition" through the interpretation of their own "deeply-possessed native experience—the pioneer experience." DeVoto, for his part, lauded Rourke's path-breaking work and elaborated his own discovery of this "folk art," this "literature of oral anecdote," in a sweeping and poetic passage that he flung in the face of the catastrophist "theorists":

> By camp fires on the shores of lakes and rivers or on the plains, among the forests, or under the shadows of peaks; by the fires that blazed in skin tents, log lean-tos and cabins, sod huts, and trading posts; in the taverns, stores, groggeries, and meetinghouses of the frontier continent; on the decks of rafts, scows, flatboats, broadhorns, and steamboats—wherever frontiersmen met for conversation, this literature flourished.

It was, he concluded, "the frontier examining itself, recording itself, and entertaining itself. It is a native literature of America."[12]

In addition to this repudiation of the catastrophists' cultureless frontier, regionalists could also take heart from the further conclusions of DeVoto and Rourke: not only did frontier folk art constitute a "literature" in itself, a "deeply grounded regional expression" (in Rourke's words), but many nineteenth-century American literary masters had already availed themselves of it as a source material for high art, profoundly enriching the "great lines" into which moderns might link themselves. Referring to the works of Twain, DeVoto proclaimed that "they are the humor of the frontier in its greatest incandescence, realizing its fullest scope and expressing its qualities on the level of genius. In them an American civilization sums up its experience; they are the climax of a literary tradition." Rourke, in turn, developed a similar point more explicitly in the direction of the interwar project for cultural reconstruction, of the socially integrative function of high-cultural appropriation of folklore. Writers such as Poe, Hawthorne, Melville, Whitman, and Twain, she believed, had tapped into the body of frontier lore (made everricher as the nation marched to the Pacific) and consequently, over the nineteenth century, "a homogeneous world of the imagination" was created, in which "popular fancies and those of genius were loosely knit together" into something of a "common consciousness," despite the fact that "every large force in the nation seemed set against this effort." Thus, the tradition of deliberate artistic efforts to "recapture" the "vanishing American scene" was also part of the reason that culture was altogether a hardier, more durable growth than the catastrophists assumed. "The ellipses created by migration and change may never be filled," Rourke concluded only penultimately; "much of the past is now gone forever." And yet, she wrote in an epilogue on the postfrontier fate of her comic tradition in the twentieth century, hinting broadly to contemporary artists looking for material, "popular fantasies in familiar patterns still exist in abundant strength in America."[13]

Within the field of literary criticism, both DeVoto and Rourke by these means supplied a needed corrective to catastrophism with their conceptualization of a culture carried along with the mobile, modernizing—but not *too* modern—plain folk, a culture all their own, sturdy enough to make the rough trip west. So also did they evade the postfrontier barrier that wrecked the democratic political economies of Parrington and many other Turnerians, because they accepted more calmly a world in which the frontier continued to live on only as literature and legend. It had been made legendary even in its own time.

Yet in another respect, as perhaps Rölvaag's novelization of immigrant pioneer life suggests, Rourke's explicit and DeVoto's implicit Turnerian assumptions of a rapid exceptionalistic frontier-nurtured break between American culture and its European antecedents did their "native" folkloristic interpretive scheme a disservice. The immigrant frontiers dramatized by Rölvaag, Cather, and others portray much less clean a break than the physiocratic-republican myth assumes. The wealth of traditionalism—languages, stories, songs, dances, superstitions, recipes, religions, costumes, architectures— brought to America during three centuries of European and African settlement comprised a folk legacy fully as significant as the frontier experiences which were, it was widely believed, the essential naturalizing process, the process by which, as the émigré and eagerly would-be Anglo-American Crè-vecoeur had put it, "Europeans become . . . Americans." Indeed, at the opposite extreme from the view advanced by Rourke and DeVoto, folklorist Alexander Haggerty Krappe went so far as to claim that "there exists no such thing as American folklore, but only European (or African, or Far Eastern) folklore on the American continent," because "'folk' cannot be transplanted by colonization and centuries are required for a renewed growth of traditions on the new and hence thoroughly uncongenial soil." A more plausible scenario of folk cultural history, falling somewhere between those raised by Krappe and Rourke, was argued by B. A. Botkin, one that recognized the "European connection" and roots of American folklore but also posited that a transformative "independent development" took place as well—"that, in the very process of transplanting, these imported cultures and traditions have undergone changes that make them a new creation."[14] In any case, this folklore of hyphenated Americans, product of the arrival (during the nineteenth century especially) of succeeding waves of Europeans displaced out of ancient villages and agricultural districts by political upheaval, economic crises, land pressure, and industrialization in their home countries, bringing with them whatever caches of old customs they themselves had managed to salvage, must and did greatly complicate any myths of Americanizing frontiers and any models of inexorable catastrophist modernization.

The immigrant pioneer, yearning for New World opportunities yet bearing a carefully packed trunk of Old World habits and heirlooms, lay at the end of one of the many trails which regionalists followed during the interwar years in their search for an American folk. Most of these trails were *historicist*—they led *backward*, beyond the present of "radios and autos," back to the far end of the Turnerian continuum, encountering along the way not only the immigrant folk but also the greedy boomer, the independent freeholder, the liberated individualist, the community-building family man or woman, and all the other pioneer types who dwelled in the various frontier discourses of the regionalist movement. Yet clearly, no one interpretive scheme conceived during these years satisfactorily captured all the ambiguities of cultural change, or the diverse welter of cultural inputs, that went into the making of the American folk; at best, each offered a different vantage on a complicated, and processive, whole. Perhaps Texas historian Walter Prescott Webb wrote most wisely, at the end of *The Great Plains* (1931)—his study of the painstaking "adjustments and modifications" undergone by the "cultural complexes" ("weapons, tools, law, and literature") that settlers brought with them from the wooded humid East to the dry treeless West, or, more abstractly, his study of a culture rooting to a *place*—when he concluded that "here one must view the white man and his culture as a dynamic thing. . . . The new and the old, innovation and survival, dwell there side by side."[15]

This same commonsensical and evenhanded Webb, seven years earlier, had organized a protest by Western writers and historians over the "vicious" review of a fellow Westerner's work appearing in an Eastern magazine, a review that amounted to "an attack on all the cattlemen and all the pioneers of the West," Webb believed. It had called the pioneers (not without reason) "gaunt, homely, hungry" and described their life (rather accurately) as "hard, even to sordidness." Webb (who grew up on the frontier, and did not enjoy it at the time) would have none of this, however, because, like many of his regionalist counterparts, his own historical definition of the folk was inter-penetrated by myth. The pains at which the searchers for the American folk were often put in order to find a usable past underscore the essential *myth-making* dimension of their cultural project, a tendency that they shared with the Indian subregionalists. The quiet antebellum New England of the "well-balanced adjustment of farm and factory," but also, the New England of shoe manufacturers, railroads, state banks, cotton mills, and the Colt Arms Company; the "golden" Oklahoma territorial era when "song flourished" and there was "a wholeness in the people," but also, the era when those individuals who were not engaged in a land-grabbing frenzy were already being ground down into tenancy; the frontier-inspired "comic tradition" as the basis for a "common consciousness" in the Gilded Age, but also, the frontier Indian war as one of the period's bases for cultural consensus—if Mumford, Riggs, or Rourke (as examples) had developed Parrington's odd interpretive double-vision, disenchanted realist fidelity to history-threatening myths still unrelinquished, these would have been their ambiguous tableaux of the folk. As it was, myth filled in for, and caused, the historical incoherences, shortcomings, and blind spots of their folk-modernization scenarios. Yet myth also provided regionalist folk historiography with interpretive frameworks, with, above all, moral vision and coherence. It shaped rhetoric and narrative: Hartley Alexander's monumentally sculpted pioneer panel, for instance, and Edgar Hewett's "republican" Indian societies, and La Farge's noncoercive socializational "trail of beauty"; Parrington's and Rourke's Turnerian frontiers (where the folk magically became democrats, and Americans); and Mumford's catastrophism (the "extermination" of regionalism after the Golden Day a transposed "fall from the golden age," to be redeemed in a new regionalist world)—all were molded by myth. It was the rare regionalist who, like Mari Sandoz, could look largely unmythicized history almost full in the face (with only one eye, in her case— the other had been blinded during her ungolden frontier childhood by a Niobrara blizzard), seeing a father who heroically battled cattle barons yet terrorized his own family, a beloved home state that nurtured Populists yet harbored fascists—and *still* find herself a usable past. But even the tough-minded Sandoz in the end took artistic refuge within the legendary world of Crazy Horse.[16]

Myths are not "fairy tales," make-believe constructs debunked by "true" life. They are instead ordered, value-laden symbols and narratives, communally shared and transmitted, that interpret an irrational world and provide guideposts for action within it. Myths have concrete existence *in* history, but only in partially realized, problematized form. Art, religion, and politics abstract myths from history and seek to shape history's course according to their ideals. Regionalism, simultaneously an art and a religion, recovered the folk from the past as pure myth: the "high traditions" of the regionalist civic religion. This "myth-making" recovery was, for many regionalists involved, a self-conscious procedure of cultural reconstruction. As Mumford wrote, "We live in an age that has still to create or re-create its symbols." Donald Davidson, at the opposite end of the political spectrum, agreed: "Myths must undergo reanimation, or we must have new ones." Yet the folk historiography authored by regionalists, their definition of the folk, was not *purely* myth; they also recovered the folk as imperiled myth, or history.[17] In their various partial pictures of the modernizing folk (the pioneers), regionalists gave expression to a tension between pure reified myth (the belief that one's ideals have or have had concrete existence) and imperiled myth (the understanding that they are and have been, at best, only partially realized). Along that axis of tension lay the spawning ground of regionalist politics (ideology—the urge that one's ideals *should* have concrete existence).

The regionalist civic religion was one "program" born of this emerging mythic-historical political consciousness: the recognition of the *absence* of communitarian ideals in the modern era and the use of social art to fill that gaping moral vacuum. In seeking to explain, to understand the absence of folk communitarianism, moreover, regionalists entered the realm of history. Revealed as imperiled or problematized myth, the historical folk were shown to be agents in their own modernization, discarding folk qualities on the road to becoming Babbitts; the rootless, automatalike "sons of the pioneers" were thus ripe for the proselytizers of the regionalist civic religion. In addition, the historical folk were shown to have been stripped of their folkness, victimized, by impersonal forces of socioeconomic change; the preservation of folk ideals from this kind of "imperilment" would require programs of economic, social, and political reform, or so regionalists came to recognize over the course of the 1920s and early 1930s. This politicization of the regionalist movement in the direction of basic, brass-tacks issues was to take shape as a gradual and multiplex process at best, even after the Great Depression and the New Deal placed reform in the center of the movement's agenda. For depending on their grasp, their differentiation, of myth and history, regionalists were to assume several possible degrees and paths of politicization. Some remained largely apolitical antiquarians, lolling the mythic past over their palates and occasionally cursing a disenchanted present. Others put out calls for old-fashioned remedies to restore the golden world that was lost (and that, in fact, had never been). And still others underwent a slow maturation not unlike Webb's, only partially under way at the publication of *The Great Plains*: a gradual maturing movement away from mythicizing (taking offense at insults to cherished traditions) and into history (understanding how cultures change)—though the break was rarely complete—and developing over the years a more and more critical sensibility, a politicized sensibility, as the regionalist witnessed his or her myths betrayed (that is, having little or no or diminishing concrete existence) in the present or in the past and sought ways to realize them or to find alternatives. Rather than "old-fashioned remedies" (city dwellers back to the land), or the impossible utopianism of contemporary demagogues (South American frontiers, Share Our Wealth), or capitulationist surface measures to maintain the status quo (the anticompetitive codes of the New Deal's National Recovery Administration), many of the more "mature" were to seek a balance between the modern and the traditional, and thoroughgoing modern means for this realization—the compelling if elusive programmatic ground of regional-social planning.

All of these diverse and divergent political responses still lay largely in the future when the regionalist movement began assembling itself in the mid- to late 1920s, conceiving the folk liturgy of the civic religion. Yet even then one of the essential preconditions for politicization had upwelled with the gathering regional renaissance: the discovery, as the Indian subregionalists had found, that living folk and folkways were still abroad in twentieth-century America. The folk were not merely agents or victims of modernization, but, as DeVoto, Rölvaag, Rourke, and Webb indicated (and Ransom's wise chief exemplified), they were also preservers of their own folkness, or at least treasured individual elements of it. B. A. Botkin took this "corrective" of catastrophism one logical step further, elaborating into a full-fledged theory Rourke's assertion that folk cultures "still exist in abundant strength in America." Far more than the catastrophists, and even more than Rourke, Botkin believed that folk culture not only survived into a modern context, it persisted as a living, richly evolving worldview. "The folk," he wrote, "lies not only in the past but also in the present and so forms a link to the future." There was, in his estimation, not "one folk but as many folk cultures as there are regional, racial, and industrial groups" (of the latter, especially, such neo-producerists as coal miners, lumberjacks, and oil-field workers), and "folk-*say*"—his revised, anti-catastrophist variation on "folk*lore*," connoting the continually unfolding oral traditions of today—embodied their interpretations of the world.[18] The folk did not, as it were, wait around passively to be imperiled or recovered, but rather, as Rourke and others had perceived of the historical folk, they were active conservers and creators of their own culture.

Rupert Vance, in *Human Geography*, incorporated this survivalism explicitly into his dualistic conception of the frontier (economic individualism balanced by cooperative associationism), observing that "cultural change has never been so uniform that some parts of our culture were not left behind in the transition." Some folk-frontier elements, he argued, could persist along the Turnerian continuum, as Turner himself had posited—elements like "memories, traditions, an inherited attitude toward life." The postfrontier South of the 1930s, Vance wrote, was a case in point: "In the South today it can safely be said that no flavor is stronger than that imparted by the frontier," a flavor which lived on especially at "self-sufficing . . . isolated farmsteads in the open country," where folkish illiteracy lingered as did "folkways" of "mutual aid" and "hospitality." Willa Cather too, in *O Pioneers!*, depicted another of these postfrontier folk "afterglows," the hyphenated-American "rich French farming country" near Alexandra's home, thriving even though "the shaggy coat of the prairie has vanished forever" and the spaces of the Nebraska Divide have been geometrized into "a vast checkerboard" of fields, where "telephone wires hum along the white roads, which always run at right angles":

The French Church, properly the Church of Sainte-Agnes, stood upon a hill. The high, narrow, red-brick building, with its tall steeple and steep roof, could be seen for miles across the wheatfields, though the little town of Sainte-Agnes was completely hidden away at the foot of the hill. The church looked powerful and triumphant there on its eminence, so high above the rest of the landscape, with miles of warm color lying at its feet, and by its position and setting it reminded one of some of the churches built long ago in the wheat-lands of middle France.[19]

Such survivals meant that the regionalist cultural project's recovery of the folk was not exclusively a mythologizing or historicist enterprise; it was also a task for sociologists, anthropologists, folklorists, journalists, and photographers. Not surprisingly though, mythmaking was encouraged by survivals— as is clearly displayed in Botkin's whole concept of folk-say, or in Cather's golden description—because regionalists seemed able even yet to perceive, even yet to make contact with, the vestiges of their idealized worlds. When these hopes were shorn by disenchanting historical understanding, and by the widespread sense of cultural dissolution, they added poignancy and urgency to preservation efforts, and put an edge on the emergent regionalist politics.

Recognizing the folk as imperiled, vanishingly so, collectors went into the countryside, joining Sandoz, Neihardt, Austin, and other Indian subregionalists out in the field, looking for landscapes like the ones Vance and Cather painted, obscure places, backwaters, anywhere there were people with old songs, or crafts, or stories, or memories—the attenuated remnants of the older America. The self-described "ballad hunter," John A. Lomax, had begun his own lifelong, nationwide, "half-million mile" search before the Great War, recording first the efforts of "Ediphone-shy cowboy singers" in the back of Southwestern saloons and later, in the 1930s, with the help of his son Alan, the "songs of the Negro common people" living in Southern delta towns, lumber camps, plantations, and penitentiaries ("our best field"). Meanwhile, sociologist Howard Odum spent the mid-1920s taking down the words of a "Black Ulysses," John Wesley ("Left-Wing") Gordon, who worked on a road crew in Chapel Hill and had endless tales of his own wanderings and of the travails of his slave and African ancestors. During the latter part of the decade, Botkin himself combed through rural eastern Oklahoma gathering "play-party" songs, while Texas folklorist J. Frank Dobie roamed around the backcountries of West Texas, northern Mexico, and New Mexico, listening to any number of old-timers—cowhands and vaqueros who could remember the trail-drive days, desert rats with legends of hidden Spanish treasure. And Arkansas folklorist Vance Randolph came across what he believed to be a full-fledged

"American survival of primitive society" still existing, uncorrupted, in the isolated Ozark Mountains of his home state. One of these "real hillfolk" is pictured opposite the title page of Randolph's 1931 study, *The Ozarks*: an elderly bewhiskered man, wearing wide galluses, powder horn suspended by string from his neck, an ancient squirrel gun in his hands; "Old Ways Are Best," the caption reads. "There are not many real Americans left now, and we do not understand them any more," Randolph observed. "The Ozark hill-billy is a genuine American—that is why he seems so alien to most tourists. In a sense it is true that the American people are making their last stand in the wilderness, and it is here, if anywhere, that we must go to meet our contemporary ancestors in the flesh."[20]

Together with their Indian subregionalist counterparts, many of these searchers for the American folk conceptualized (and mythicized) the life lived by their past and "contemporary ancestors" as fundamentally aesthetic-symbiotic. Recalling his own confrontation with the Indians of New Mexico during the summer of 1933, John Crowe Ransom made this common tendency explicit in his essay on "The Aesthetic of Regionalism." Generalizing from an admiration for the "regionalism" of the Pueblo tribes, he noted that "as economic patterns become perfected and easy, they cease to be merely economic and become gradually aesthetic"; tools, dwellings, and other "manufactured things" become "ornamental, which in a subtle sense means natural." In sum, he wrote, the "economic actions" of the folk "become also their arts"—qualities he had already defined in a 1928 essay on "his concrete or particular regionalism" of the white Southern folk. Their folk arts, he had written, were "arts of living" and were as well "community arts, in which every class of society could participate after its kind." The Southern folk lived a "seasoned provincial life" which was "fully adapted to its natural environment," and which as a consequence was "stable, or hereditable." Enfolded by this larger communal and environmental context, the folkish individual related himself to nature by identifying with "a spot of ground," which for him "carries a good deal of meaning," Ransom believed, and which he tilled "not too hurriedly and not too mechanically," but rather observed in it "the infinitude and contingency of nature." In this manner his life acquired "its philosophical and even its cosmical consciousness"—a sense of organic wholeness.[21]

Numerous other regionalists might have elaborated Ransom's definitions, each according to his or her own myths. The "Oklahoma folk of thirty years ago," Botkin's friend Lynn Riggs told an interviewer of the sources for his play *Green Grow the Lilacs* (1929), "talked poetry without any conscious effort to make beautiful language"; truly, "they all had something of the actor in them," making "a definite effort . . . to dramatize their meaning and their personality." Similarly, the Negro folk, according to Howard Odum in *The Negro and His Songs* (1925), were each individually integrated by communal art, the "primitive" and "elemental" and "pleasure-giving" qualities of their songs, he surmised, appealing "strongly to the Negro's entire being," to his "whole nature." This vivid, colorful language of the folk, in Riggs's essentially Emersonian interpretation, stemmed from their "personal relationship to things," causing the corresponding "images in [their] speech" to have "an emotional existence and reality" not to be found in modern "sophisticated daily speech." Symbiotically bound to "natural facts" through language, the folk thus shared a world ordered by communal lore—"charms, signs, and omens," as Agrarian Andrew Lytle characterized the lore of the Southern yeomanry, lore which was used to "understand and predict natural phenomena," for example, and which therefore guided agricultural work. Many of the community activities of the yeomanry's "neighborhood culture," he added, activities such as "play-parties . . . ice-cream socials, old-time singings . . . political picnics and barbeques, and barn dances," were rooted in "traditions brought from Scotland and England" still unself-consciously "practiced by the plain people." Similarly, the "social songs of the Negro," Odum observed, encompassed and reflected all aspects of his "daily life and experience," an experience that was "part and parcel of the epic of the Negro come from Africa to America"—and the same might be said of the integrative culture of any American folk group. The "relation of the singer to his environment . . . home life and morals . . . social habits and ideals"—all were embodied in folk songs that were in themselves "testimonials of the creative ability and esthetic sense of the Negro"—like Riggs's "actors," individually expressive within an integrative culture. Even the "motion of work," Odum posited, "calls forth" a song, while "the song, in turn, strengthens the movements of the workers" who were engaged in "communal work": the folkish unity of beauty and utility, achieved also in folk handicrafts.[22]

The American folk—as living practitioners, as tenuous survivals, as literary tradition, as myth—thus conjoined with the Indians in the regionalist mind to provide evocative "home-loving, earth-loving" lessons in communitarianism. This was what regionalists, engaged in their reconstructive project, "needed" from them. Yet the European-rooted folk in America, especially those of English or Scotch-Irish descent, were conceptually endowed with an additional set of normative qualities not to be found, or not strongly pronounced, it seemed, in the "strange secret life of the tribe": Parrington's "psychology of democratic individualism," a neo-republican counterweight of natural rights and antiauthoritarianism that supplied the regionalist ethos with stronger principles of individualism and consensual community than those to be experienced, as Lawrence's Kate learned, in the expressive aes-

thetic regimes of holistic Indian societies. The neo-Jeffersonian invocation of
that republican watchword, "independence," resounded throughout regionalist discourse on the folk. "The typical Ozark hillman can never be enslaved by
anybody," Vance Randolph avowed. "He is almost insanely jealous of his
independence and personal liberty, and will fight to the death in defense of
whatever he happens to regard as his rights. The mountaineer may be poor
and illiterate and shiftless, but he is a free man." Up at the top end of the social
scale, Agrarian Stark Young's Southern planters in *So Red the Rose* (1934)
held much the same sentiments: "Independence is almost a definition of a
man," one character declares hotly, "else I have failed to understand what a
man is and what a state is!" The basis of that independence was, above all, a
life on the self-sufficient freehold, which homesteader Per Hansa in Rölvaag's
Giants in the Earth describes to his wife as "this kingdom of ours"—"and
no . . . king is going to come around and tell me what I have to do about it,
either!" He is struck with a vision of a decentralized society of freeholders like
himself stretching from the Dakota Territory across the plains "neighbor to
neighbor, clear out to the Rocky Mountains!" But there was greater individualistic freedom than this to be had further back along the Turnerian continuum, flourishing on the libertarian frontier of Dobie's "unfenced world,"
where the vaqueros roamed, and Neihardt's *Mountain Men*, and where "the
land belonged to anybody and everybody and so the man who would go to the
trouble and work to fence off a piece of it and say 'This is mine' was crazy"—
thus did the myth lay claim even to Faulkner's tough mind. This recurring
utopian conceptualization of a noncoercive "free disorder," as Dobie characterized it, a veritable state of nature in which republicanism itself might seem
oppressive, stood as perhaps the consummate emblem of regionalist estrangement from modernity: all, all of it erased in mythicized worlds where there
were only man and landscape and nothing more.[23]

Yet as regionalists of the postfrontier world well knew, the America of the
interwar years was far removed from this "unfenced world," progressing, it
seemed, at an ever-accelerating rate away from it, and marching toward the
modern end of Turner's continuum. Randolph, for one, observed how time
was pressing on his Ozarkers, imperiling them, because of an "invasion of
outside interests": "Great corporations are taking their timber and their
water-power, and their neglected little farms are fast falling into alien and
more efficient hands." The Ozark hillbilly, he concluded with resignation,
"must inevitably go the way of all primitive people who stand in the way of
economic progress."[24]

Other regionalists were not so resigned, however. "The artist is in revolt,
the intellectual is in revolt, the conscience of America is in revolt," Parrington
proclaimed. The discovery of folkway survivals and "contemporary ances-

tors" like the Ozarkers reinforced the sense that the older America was without doubt making its "last stand" during the interwar years, out in the Arkansas "wilderness" and (to invoke planner Benton MacKaye's metaphor) in the "wilderness of civilization"—"the America we know today," as Parrington defined it, "with its standardized life, its machine culture, its mass psychology." Breaking trails through this new kind of wilderness, searching past and present for the American folk, regionalists during the 1920s and 1930s were to be confronted with all manner of its tragic and monstrous denizens, inhabitants of chaotic modernity—Babbitts, phantom publics, share-croppers, communists, Okies, fascists, demagogues, monopolists, Nazis: the old gallus-wearing Ozarker, who " 'don't take no orders from nobody,' " would indeed have found them "alien." As the regionalist movement began coalescing across provincial America in the late 1920s, organizing itself, formulating definitions, issuing manifestos, and, like Rölvaag's frontier schoolhouse, binding "subtly and inseparably together the few souls who lived out there in the wilderness," its participants thus came to realize that "reforestation" must be carried out not only in America's "spiritual territory" but, as the depression was to make crystal clear, in its *social* territory as well.[25]

With their Indian subregionalist counterparts, the recoverers of the American folk attempted in vivid and methodologically blurred fiction, histories, and literary studies to take on "their [the folk's] voice, which is now his own," as Botkin later described the hoped-for integrative aesthetic interchange among modern author, "universal" material, and audience. For some, like the more apolitical Bernard DeVoto, such an interchange (which he termed "history by synechdoche") merely contributed to a more realistic and penetrating technique, better history writing, a greater art. But many regionalists would embrace the larger *ideological* possibilities implied by DeVoto's methodology, which equipped him (as he later wrote in *The Year of Decision*) to convey a "story in such a way that the reader may realize the far western frontier experience, which is part of our cultural inheritance, as personal experience." For the proselytizing artist himself, Botkin asserted, this creative, communicative experience must entail some manner of politicization (as DeVoto himself eventually learned), because it meant "becoming detached"—and critical—"with regard to his civilization, and becoming activized with regard to theirs," the life of the folk. Directed into the project of the civic religion, such individual efforts would instill, it was believed, an "art consciousness" of place and tradition in the citizenry, to stop them from discarding folkness. And to stop them from discarding the folk as well, the new "art" of regional-social planning, constraining rampant "economic progress" between the twin imperatives of "human loyalties" and "earth loyalties," would create a safe haven for folkness in the modern world. Guided by ethical and aesthetic considerations rather than the profit drive of the "great corporations" and others with "efficient hands," the planners would propose far different developmental uses for resources like the timber and waterpower and "little neglected farms" of Randolph's Ozarkers.[26]

To say that in this reforestation of culture and civilization the regionalist movement faced a daunting task would be a gross understatement. In 1929, Parrington wrote shamefacedly that "we have fallen so low that our faith in justice, progress, the potentialities of human nature, the excellence of democracy, is stricken with pernicious anemia." Parrington died suddenly in 1929, just as the movement was getting well under way, yet his stoic Jeffersonianism sets the tone, lays the scene, tells what was at stake, in a passage from the opening chapter of the unfinished third part of *Main Currents*. Although the passage actually concerns the titanic cultural and political forces aligning themselves to do battle during the Great Barbeque of the post–Civil War era, it serves equally as a description of the forces gathering for battle again on the eve of the Great Depression, the one side greatly diminished and the other tremendously stronger, but the battle rejoined, nevertheless. It was the regionalist equivalent of Dos Passos's "all right we are two nations":

> Two diverse worlds lay on the map of continental America. Facing in opposite directions and holding different faiths, they would not travel together easily or take comfort from the yoke that joined them. Agricultural America, behind which lay two and a half centuries of experience, was a decentralized world, democratic, individualistic, suspicious; industrial America, behind which lay only half a dozen decades of bustling experiment, was a centralizing world, capitalistic, feudal, ambitious. The one was a decaying order, the other a rising, and between them would be friction till one or the other had become master.

In *I'll Take My Stand* (1930), Agrarian Andrew Lytle issued the call to action. "Throw out the radio and take down the fiddle from the wall," he advised the imperiled folk. Then, defying the "acids of modernity," he intoned: ". . . let them hold to their agrarian fragments and bind them together, for reconstructed fragments are better than a strange newness which does not belong."[27]

Waldo Frank articulated one vision of what cultural form these "reconstructed fragments" might assume in his work, *The Re-Discovery of America* (1929). It was a fragile, plaintive vision. The book may in fact be read as nothing less than a synthesis of the utopian aspirations of many interwar cultural radicals. A former editor of the avant-garde *Seven Arts* magazine, an admirer of Walt Whitman (patron saint of the regionalist movement), and a student of the culture of America *Hispana*, Frank prefaced his vision with an obligatory and broad-ranging denunciation of the contemporary "reign of Power," which, he believed, attempted to regularize the chaotic "mechanical Jungle" of modern life through a coercive set of external "censors"—"the shell of business, law, and state." Such "regimentation," he declared in the same vein as Mumford, was the necessary result of "a people not yet able to live by its own spirit," broken free from the "deliquescence" of an older European organic regime but yet to achieve a newer, indigenous one. The blueprint for this cultural reconstruction, Frank argued, must perforce be drafted by the artist, because the work of art was "a particular constructed body from which is to be derived the *experience* of unity between the self and what is not the self," the "simplest as well as the ultimate expression of wholeness." In their role as "creators of concepts, of values, of art," artists were what Frank awkwardly termed "organic understanders," and he concluded: "From the experience of their experience"—the poetic orgy—"America may achieve an ethos which . . . can alone give us laws and institutions that are not modern censors, since they will express our modern inward nature."[28]

Frank agreed with the Santa Fe–Taos circle that the "native cultures of Maya and Pueblo" were evocative models for this organicist ethos, encompassing a wealth of traditional materials. So too did he look with interest to "our Southern brothers," especially "the best painters of Mexico and Peru," who had "absorbed their classic Amerindian forms, mastered the technic of modern Paris, shared the experience of the native, and welded the life of all these forces into a contemporary plastic action." Frank looked to the European-American "mystic tradition" as well, a tradition which had arisen "from the consciousness of the whole of man and of God" and which instilled a "sense of self as a focus of the Whole." All of these folk traditions, he believed, constituted a "*capturable* America," an appropriable America, the "germinal seed" of which promised "here, in our transfiguring sky, in our new earth, in our new race" to give birth to a new culture, a "new Whole." But this "new Whole," Frank carefully prophesied, must not issue in an enforced uniformity of "suppressions" and "excisions" (the *reich*) or the dull unconscious unity of the "herd" (Babbitt's America). Rather, the noncoercive, democratic path to Van Wyck Brooks's "social ideal" must be grounded in the acknowledgment that "our chaos is a variety, wondrously rich, of needs, potentials, natures, values." To resolve and order this chaos "without loss of the variety that makes it"—tellingly, Frank chose an aesthetic term—"would mean to *symphonise* it" (italics his): "to understand and to be conscious of the worlds whirling within our chaos." Led by a vanguard of artistic "organic understanders," Americans would become "a conscious people, a varied and integral people, the symphonic nation in whom all selves and all visions adumbrate to Wholeness."[29]

Thus did Frank conceptualize the Americanism of organic, inclusive pluralism slowly and vaguely dawning in the regionalist mind: the "symphonising"
or aesthetic integration of a *people* (a favorite word of Whitman's, and of
Frank's, and a word to gain increasing resonance during the 1930s) brought to
a consciousness of themselves through the social art of the regionalist cultural
project, which wove them into traditions and conceived them as cultures. It
was this "reforested territory," alternative to the fascist, communist, and
corporatist futures looming already by the early 1930s, that regionalists began
traveling toward during the 1920s, rediscovering folk remedies for an ailing
civilization. The "worlds whirling within our chaos" were the regions of
America.

It was a fragile, plaintive vision.

4 I'll Take My Stand

The Regionalist Revolt
against Modern America

"Why, we're territory folks. We ort to hang
together. . . . Whut's the United States? It's jist a
furrin' country to me."
—Aunt Eller, in Lynn Riggs, *Green Grow the Lilacs*

When John Crowe Ransom, early in the collaboration that
eventually produced the *I'll Take My Stand* manifesto,
agreed with Allen Tate that poets are "not merely the
expression, they are also the prophets and teachers of
their compatriots," he was careful to preface his statement with the qualification "to some extent." He wondered whether Tate attached "too much importance to the
principle of a community between the poet and his public?
Very fine thing if possible," Ransom averred. But, he
stressed, "poets can't wait on that. . . . Poetry comes out
spontaneously, not after looking to see if the times are
ripe." Yet the times *were* ripe for regionalism. In 1931—
the year that Pearl Buck's *The Good Earth* ("We must get
back to the land!") became a national best-seller—the
poet AE (George William Russell), emissary from the
Irish Revival, undertook a six-month tour of the United
States. He lectured at many locations, metropolitan and
provincial—Chicago, Detroit, Seattle, and Los Angeles, as well as Lincoln, Missoula, Columbia, and Baton
Rouge—speaking over radio networks and in front of
university crowds, farmers conventions, local chambers
of commerce, and tiny literary societies. Everywhere he
spoke on the interrelationship of the movement to revive
Irish folklore with Ireland's struggle for independence
from Great Britain. And everywhere he preached the
gospel of the rural "cooperative community" that he had
been spreading for much of his career and would continue

to preach, even as adviser to Henry Wallace and Franklin Roosevelt, until his death in 1935.[1]

His themes were simple, ominous, and inspirational. The United States, he worried to his audiences, though still in its "national childhood," was showing "symptoms of premature decay," threatened by "the same disease from which classic Italy perished," the decline of its rural life. ("Rest assured, our father, rest assured. The land is not to be sold," Americans heard Wang Lung's soft city-bred and traitorous sons tell their dying father in the tragic denouement of *The Good Earth*.) "The country is the fountain of the life and health of a race," AE declared in a message "To Some American Economists," echoing Virgil. "Our civilisations are a nightmare, a bad dream," he believed. "They grow meaner and meaner as they grow more urbanised." To reawaken the Western world was thus the essential task of the age, and there could be only one solution. "Truly the creation of a rural civilisation is the greatest need of our time," he wrote. It was "necessary for the creation of citizens, for the building up of a noble national life, that the social order should be so organized that [the] sense of interdependence will be constantly felt." Drawing his audiences into the vision, AE soared: "Is not the return of man to a natural life on the earth a great enough idea to inspire humanity? Is not the idea of a civilisation amid the green trees and fields under the smokeless sky alluring?" The task fell peculiarly to Americans rather than to Europeans: "They have the energy of young races, and where we are tired they are fresh." Quoting Whitman, AE called on America to fulfill his nationalistic "boast":

Have the elder races halted? Do they droop and end their lesson wearied over there beyond the seas?

We take up the burden and the lesson and the task eternal, pioneers, O pioneers!

"Your task," AE concluded, "is to truly democratise civilization and its agencies, to spread in widest commonalty culture, comfort, intelligence, and happiness. . . . I might say to the American nation, Will you do the work your race set out to do?" ("Then a voice cried out in him, a voice deeper than love cried out in him for his land," the American nation read of hero Wang Lung in the hopeful *catastasis* of *The Good Earth*, before its sad *catastrophe*:

And he heard it above every other voice in his life and he tore off the long robe he wore and he stripped off his velvet shoes and his white stockings and he rolled his trousers to his knees and he stood forth robust and eager and he shouted,

"Where is the hoe and where is the plow? And where is the seed for the wheat planting? Come, Ching, my friend—come—call the men—I go out to the land!"[2])

If the attendance levels at AE's lectures and the sales of Buck's book were thus any gauge, it was not unreasonable for regionalists to believe that, modern and imperiled though Americans be, there might exist a receptive public for their own proselytizing efforts. Undoubtedly, in 1931 the sympathetic hearing that AE's or Buck's utterances received might be explained by national reaction against Jazz Age excess, a yearning for simpler days (Wang Lung stripping off his fake finery) as Americans witnessed a hollow postwar prosperity collapse before their very eyes. "The revulsion from a materialism that soured upon our tongues seems to be driving many of us to an appreciation of the tall figures in our national growth," Mari Sandoz observed in 1932. "I find that many of my acquaintances who three years ago talked only of bridge scores, Packards, and freakish interior decoration now ask to hear about the things I've always pursued."[3]

Yet the regionalist revolt was also an artistic and intellectual expression of larger cultural tensions "in the air" throughout the interwar period, tensions often characterized as urban-rural conflict—the "two nations" of America— growing out of a culmination of the decades-long continental drift of values from producerism to consumerism, from Christianity to secularism, from the participatory to the bureaucratic, from the local to the national. Indeed, as a generation born in a rural world but growing old in an urban one, contemporary Americans (not unlike the "weak-headed Indians" described by Ransom) had already spent much of the 1920s taking backward glances. Prohibition, the Scopes Monkey Trial, the 1928 presidential race, the 1924 immigration laws, the Republican ascendancy, Henry Ford's Greenfield Village, the Ku Klux Klan, the 1928 gubernatorial victory of Huey Long, Rockefeller's Williamsburg, the Nonpartisan League—all had constituencies, audiences, or visitors clinging confusedly, swearing allegiance to, wistfully remembering, an older America. The sometimes ugly social and political dimensions assumed by these reaffirmations of faith were a measure of siege mentality, of a stern, labor-centered, patriarchal, white, family-oriented, God-fearing mind-set unable to understand why automobiles, radios, working women, picture shows, credit buying, membership organizations, home appliances, and factory jobs were causing its world to atomize. It was all right there in the Lynds' study of *Middletown* (1929): "A citizen has one foot on the relatively solid ground of established institutional habits and the other fast to an escalator erratically moving in several directions at a bewildering variety of speeds." If Middletown tended to "bear down harder on the relatively solid ground," the Lynds reasoned, "it is simply exhibiting the reluctance of changing habitual ways common to men everywhere."[4]

In "bearing down" on a solidity that social and cultural change was making more and more illusory, Middletowners around the nation—particularly as Klansmen, nativists, drys, or fundamentalists—had often to resort to intrusive legislation, coercive vigilance, even violence to make their myths come true. And what myths: a "100% Americanism" that sought simultaneously to legitimize a racially and ethnically pure moral conformity, rooted in a nineteenth-century village life-style, together with the God-given right of every man to the unimpeded self-interested pursuit of wealth. "Been mighty change since I been born. Change where I been but ain't change me," Odum's Left-Wing Gordon thinks wishfully, and the white Middletowners on the other side of the tracks held much the same attitude. The incoherence of their myths, their tenuosity—folk clannishness warped by a bourgeois ethos— were more than compensated for by the fervency of their believers, by the political and economic power backing them, propping them up, forcibly giving "concrete existence" to updated versions of worlds like the one that reigned before Gordon's ancestors were sprung from the slave quarters. Imposing "law and order" as best they could, Middletowners North and South spent much of the 1920s uneasily patrolling their myths' perimeters, even as their daughters, kept stylish by caste-conscious parents, turned into brazen "flappers," or as the "coloreds," lured by jobs at white-owned factories, moved into town and got a little uppity. Thus does the occasional heavy-handedness of the 100 percent Americans become understandable: they were seeking scapegoats, "explanations" for change, lashing out at a strange new America made more imperturbable by their own collaboration in it. When the "strange newness" of life in this polyglot and hedonistic America became too much for one such 100 percent American, ex-Oklahoma congressman William H. ("Alfalfa Bill") Murray, he resorted to perhaps the ultimate solution in myth protection, and maybe, the only one: lighting out in the mid-1920s for the frontier territory of Bolivia, South America with a boatload of colonists, hoping to establish there a farming community in which "the ten commandments are given as the foundation of all laws" and the individual could "strive to maintain the virtues of an American citizen" and "avoid the vices and errors of other races"—besides making a prosperous life for himself. The colony venture failed after a few years (the hardy neo-pioneers "began to 'crave the bright lights of America' even before we landed," their leader later fumed), but when Murray returned to his home state in 1929, he was promptly elected governor.[5] The imperiled "100 percent older America" had a following.

The border dividing the mainstream adherents of this "abusable past" and the cultural rebels of the regionalist movement, whose own myths *tended* to undergird a political orientation of social pluralism and economic communitarianism, was more blurred and fluid than one might first assume. Together, they were twin but divergent expressions of urban-rural conflict. At the very least, they shared an iconography: the small town, the family farm, the clapboard church, the wilderness-frontier, and the cowboy figure, to name a few. There were, moreover, some regionalists who, despite their differences with 100 percent Americans over such matters as economic organization, concurred with them that these were icons of a white man's country (the racists of the Southern Agrarian circle, for example, or more inadvertently, Hartley Alexander with his preeminently "Anglo-Saxon" march of liberty). Conversely, and more promisingly for prospects of regionalist cultural reconstruction, the remnants of folk culture and republican ideals might still exist in unexamined contradiction within the mentality of 100 percent Americans, the ignored subversively egalitarian and organicist flip side of their hard-hearted beliefs. Neo-republicanism was an essential component of Murray's hodgepodge worldview, for instance—folk imperilment in a nutshell. His utopian colony was not merely to be a lily-white enclave or a good investment; it was also to be a community of independent freeholders, living close to the land, bound together by the "tried principles of cooperation and mutual helpfulness." And what persisted in Murray as half of a deeply divided mind lingered to a lesser degree in many other Americans of the interwar years (like his voters) as a sort of cultural scar tissue—an accumulation of carefully selected warm rural childhood memories perhaps, or maybe something they had read in a sentimental novel, or experienced on a family trip in the countryside, or seen in the clichés of a movie—scar tissue that ached whenever they acknowledged that their 100 percent American myths had wrought a world far from perfect. As George Babbitt (in Sinclair Lewis's description) thinks to himself after leaving "with melancholy" the "last suburb of Zenith"—Zenith with its rat race, its insincere back-slapping good fellowship, its pall of domesticity—riding on a train to a Maine wilderness vacation:

All the way north he pictured the Maine guides: simple and strong and daring, jolly as they played stud-poker in their unceiled shack, wise in woodcraft as they tramped the forest and shot the rapids. He particularly remembered Joe Paradise, half Yankee, half Indian. If he could but take up a backwoods claim with a man like Joe, work hard with his hands, be free and noisy in a flannel shirt, and never come back to this dull decency! . . . Honestly! Why *not*? Really *live*. . . . He longed for it, admitted that he longed for it, then almost believed that he was going to do it. . . . "Moccasins—six-gun—frontier town—gamblers—sleep under the stars—be a regular man, with he-men like Joe Paradise—gosh!"[6]

At such moments, such points of consciousness, when the average Middle-towner began to feel that his or her myths were (as the term goes) dysfunc-tional, issuing at best in a soul-corroding "dull decency," at worst in the economic disaster of the depression, when that person then tried to look beyond them for an alternative set of meanings—these were moments that explain AE's and Buck's popularity, and moments that the regionalist civic religion could instigate and cultivate to bring about "conversions" to *their* vision of the older America, and of its "reforested" future.

"Ours is an age of taking root, of the resulting conflict and compromise, within a locality, of varied racial stocks and opposing orders of civilization," B. A. Botkin commented in the manifesto introducing his new folklore anthology, *Folk-Say* (1929—one of the first works issued under the "strictly regional program" of Joseph Brandt's new Oklahoma University Press). In the midst of that "conflict and compromise," Botkin perceived "certain strategic centers and areas of pressure" forming: "in the South, as a result of the battle of industrialism and the soil . . . ; in the Spanish and Indian Southwest, as a result of the clash of ancient and modern cultures; and in various frontier states like Oklahoma, as a result of the death-struggle of pioneering and the small-town conventions of Main Street, Rotary, Babbittry, and the public schools." At these "strategic centers," practitioners of the "New Regionalism," which had "its feet on the ground and its hands in the soil," were developing "a true historical sense," a "new feeling for locality"—the alternative myths of the civic religion. These developments were both symptomatic and ameliorative of the "genuine need of taking root, of finding solidarity and unity in identify-ing oneself with the community." Botkin had fulfilled that need in himself when, in preceding years, he had begun to conceive Oklahoma "as literary ma-terial." Thereafter, he had attempted to "make Oklahoma culture-conscious and Oklahoma-conscious (a twofold pioneering)." As he told Henry Nash Smith, "First there were my students to mold, and then some public opinion in the University and the state of my adoption." Writing in Smith's 1929 *South-west Review* symposium on "Regional Culture in the Southwest," Botkin outlined the means, what he later called "the business of the regional renais-sance": "Museums, galleries, publishing houses, magazines, historical, folk-lore, and poetry societies, art colonies, theaters, symphony orchestras, text-books, and courses in Southwestern art and civilization." These were, in fact, the means by which John G. Neihardt's Midwestern "art consciousness" could be achieved; and they were, more broadly, the path to Smith's vision of an

American "whose life moves harmoniously within a conception of the family, a government, a religion, an art organically related"—"a spiritual whole essentially related to this continent."[7]

The Southern Agrarians, whose *I'll Take My Stand* manifesto was to have the widest national impact, were strongly in accord with their counterparts to the west. As Donald Davidson wrote of his circle, "I believe we are all trying to formulate . . . some kind of *modus vivendi* for Southern Americans." An institutionalized "poetic orgy" would be essential to that task, he asserted; their manifesto should be considered "only a prefertory, not in any sense a final work." Davidson pitched the larger plan to Tate in early 1929: not only "a Fugitive Press," but also "a fully financed Southern magazine, openly provincial; associated with this magazine, a publishing house of a distinct sort; and associated with the whole enterprise, a chain of bookstores, to serve as a distributing medium." The bookstore chain never materialized, but across the South other organs of the scheme had already been put into place. W. T. Couch had launched the University of North Carolina Press on its own "strictly regional program" the year before, and James Southal Wilson with Stringfellow Barr had already gained the *Virginia Quarterly Review* some national prominence. Yet although each of these new institutions was in its own way seeking a "*modus vivendi* for Southern Americans," it was by industrially and ideologically accommodationist routes not necessarily to the liking of antiliberal Agrarians like Davidson or John Gould Fletcher, or even of the less conservative Westerners. In point of fact, during the period leading up to the publication of *I'll Take My Stand*, the Agrarians' private pronouncements on the urgency of establishing a new civic religion were more fervent than those of the most mystically minded Indian subregionalists. Not only did they have a long-standing regional "tradition of traditionalism" to defend (and *transcend*—the Old South "slough of sentimentality") as well as the Confederate hero cult to live up to (already a civic religion of sorts), they had also the whole progressive New South creed, a kind of Dixie Babbittry fed to them steadily and insistently since childhood, to repudiate.[8]

The most extreme expression of "the genuine need of taking root" came from the very "uprooted" Fletcher, who believed that "art must essentially be a social product," and who called for "a new spiritual communism, in the Medieval plan . . . adapted to modern conditions." Some version of such a religion, Ransom agreed, was "the only effective defense against Progress." More concretely, Davidson saw the Agrarians' task as one of erecting a cultural rampart around a "doctrine of provincialism," renewing "a certain sort of sectional consciousness and drawing separate groups of Southern thought together" to act as "a counter-influence and check to megalopolitanism." It was a task which could not end with the "prefertory" manifesto they were writing, as he told Ransom in 1929: "I have constantly felt . . . that our ideas had too much life in them to be merely cast upon the winds of publication in the vague hope that they might like seeds sprout somewhere; and I have always wished for the possibilities of action, believing that the time calls for a mixture of poets and philosophers in affairs." Davidson was convinced that the times were ripe to "commit ourselves to a definite 'movement' ": it was the only way that "something might be done to save the South from civilization." Announcing that "the South has an important part to play, if she will, in such a counter-revolution," Ransom, in an article for *Harper's* during the same year, broadened the plan for action beyond the South: "she may pool her own stakes with the stakes of other minority groups in the Union which are circumstanced similarly," like the "Western agrarian party," with whom the South had "much community of interest," and others "scattered here and there . . . with the same general attitude," such as "sociologists, educators, artists, religionists, and ancient New England townships," all of whom would join the resistance against "the powerful acid of the Great Progressive Principle." The "unifying effective bond between these geographically diverse elements" was quite simple and "clean-cut," Ransom claimed: "that the rural life of America must be defended, and the world made safe for the farmers." The "Articles of an Agrarian Restoration," a draft statement of principles by Ransom and his circle, outlined the gathering movement's immediate "practical program": "For the most part, we would disseminate a doctrine."[9]

Thus, to borrow from Ransom, regionalists were "not merely the expression," they were also to be "the prophets and teachers of their compatriots," an "organized leadership toward a usable culture," as Henry Nash Smith put it: a would-be vanguard.[10] As noted earlier, many of them had grown up in and subsequently spent their careers within the America of bourgeois 100 percent Americanism. But their education by the "acids of modernity" (literally, by a body of liberating, self-consciousness engendering knowledge, and figuratively, by the experience of cultural crisis) put them at odds with the myths that their compatriots, except at moments of acute crisis, accepted unconsciously as the way of things. Regionalists—whose educated understanding was shaped not only by myth but also by history, social science, psychology— were estranged from those conventional myths as a more or less permanent condition. Yet the break was rarely complete: witness the residual racism of Donald Davidson and some of the Agrarians. Most regionalists, however, began at least to question their racialist upbringing, lost their conventional religious faith, and rejected bourgeois business-as-usual—the "spiritual secession." Casting about from this uprooted condition (as Mary Austin had), they sought out, or discovered accidentally, the "alternative pieties" latent

within the imperiled traditions of the regional culture around them, backward
from the present along the Turnerian continuum, or out among the survivals.

"It is imperative that we *sink*," fellow traveler William Carlos Williams
wrote in the climactic chapter of his own attempt to find an indigenous tradition, *In the American Grain* (1925). It was imperative because, he believed,
"the primitive destiny of the land is obscure" and it had been "obscured further
by a field of unrelated culture stuccoed upon it that has made that destiny more
difficult than ever to determine." For regionalists, this obscuring "field of
unrelated culture" was multilayered: not only the bankrupt know-nothingism
of 100 percent Americans, but also the prettified genteel culture that to them
passed as high culture; the more extreme forms of the modernist mind-set,
which, in radically dissolving all the assumptions of the conventional American
mind, had unfortunately dissolved the concept of culture itself; and the "wilderness of civilization," countenanced by the 100 percent American's self-
interest, along with its most insidious outgrowth, mass culture, which was
merely pseudoculture, and which the moralizing didacticism of the genteel
tradition had been helpless to counteract. "Whitman had to come from under,"
Williams reminded his readers. "All have to come from under and through a
dead layer." The artist "wants to have the feet of his understanding on the
ground, his ground, *the* ground, the only ground that he knows, that which *is*
under his feet"—Williams might have been describing any number of regionalists. He continued: "I speak of aesthetic satisfaction. This want, in America,
can only be filled by knowledge, a poetic knowledge, of that ground." The
route to the American folk thus lay along the same self-immersing "trail of
beauty" that the Indian subregionalists had discovered.[11] Recovering (that is,
mythicizing) folk-regional traditions through art, regionalists would be supplied with roots, faith, a sense of place: what George Babbitt was searching for.

John T. Frederick, editor of the Iowa-based *Midland* magazine, wrote
something of a melodramatic parable depicting the "making of a regionalist"
in his 1925 novel, *Green Bush*, a tale of reverse assimilation into rural life very
much the white American counterpart to La Farge's *Laughing Boy*. Frank
Thompson, budding young scholar, freshly graduated from the study of Balzac
and Rodin, postpones his graduate work and returns to his home village of
Green Bush, in northern Michigan, to take charge of his (suddenly deceased)
father's country newspaper and farm. Making the rounds and meeting his
subscribers, he receives "for the first time" since childhood "a real glimpse of
the folk of the soil," as Frederick comments. "Dimly," on those initial excursions—Thompson reflects of one farmer—"he sensed what a man must feel
who had lived for thirty years between that hill and stream, and who had given
half his lifetime to the clearing and tilling of those fields and the care of that

orchard. 'He is rooted,' Frank thought, 'rooted like a tree.'" Later, drinking
in a panorama of the town at twilight (he pauses constantly to admire vistas),
Thompson realizes from his daily interaction with the villagers that "under-
neath this beauty crept ignorance and bigotry, petty jealousy, and spite and
greed." Yet "he felt somehow that the closeness of Lake and sky and wilderness set these things all in their right proportion"—the regional "ground"
under the "dead layer." Eventually, Thompson meets and marries Rose, the
daughter of a local farmer, who helps him to see that it was "easier to live nobly
here," that "he loved the Lake and the wilderness, and that he belonged to
them." Flouting his mother's bourgeois ambitions for him, he further postpones his brilliant academic career and decides to remain in Green Bush and
run the family farm and newspaper. In retaliation, his mother sells his patri-
mony (to a man whom Frederick unfortunately named "Finchburg"—another
of those 100 percent American residues).[12]

Uprooted, Thompson and Rose are forced to go to the city to make a living,
where, among the "hurrying thousands," they are "caught and impaled in a
huge and torturing trap," sitting "listless and unresponsive while they ate
their supper at some noisy cafeteria, and watched a motion picture, or the
varied numbers of a vaudeville performance." But when Thompson's mother
dies, he and Rose use her remorseful bequest to purchase a new farm near
Green Bush, and he resumes his job as country editor. Rose's family builds
them a new barn and house where, on their first night, they fall asleep
"warmed by the emotion bred . . . by hundreds of generations of home-loving,
earth-loving men and women." Still waffling about his academic future (a mentor keeps urging his return to Ann Arbor), Thompson throws himself into the
"first plowing of the new land," and that settles the matter. He experiences
"earth and the plow: an exultant sense of kinship with elemental things,"
becoming "a child of the earth"—the trivial existence of a scholar could not
possibly compare with it. There was, additionally, the "quiet pleasure of
dealing with the life of the community" to be had at his editor's desk. As the
story closes, Thompson has taken to using his father's old horse and buggy,
even though he owns a car. He tells his mentor that "perhaps before I die I
shall find something to say about this country here: it may be a monograph on
the crayfish or an ode to the wood-thrush." As he once told Rose, "It's a world
in little. That's the fascination of it to me—everything is so close and clear—
one can see it all. Talk about a *Comedie Humaine!*"[13]

So too with literal melodramatic strokes did Frederick depict in miniature
many of the larger tendencies of the regionalist cultural revolt. Just as Thompson rejects the academic life to maintain his contact with "elemental things,"
regionalists disavowed classical and Anglicized aesthetic criteria, all the morally and aesthetically correct genteel interpretations and methodologies that

pervaded academic historical writing, all "imported" scholarly categories that
tended to abstract culture, as *Frontier* magazine editor H. G. Merriam put it,
from the "soil it is growing in." They sought, as Williams wrote of his own
purposes in *American Grain*, "to re-name the things seen, now lost in chaos of
borrowed titles, many of them inappropriate, under which the true character
lies hid." There, at the reified core of meaning, lay the regional "ground,"
the "strange phosphorous of the life" which, captured in art and conveyed
through the regionalist civic religion, was essential to the task of cultural
reconstruction.[14]

Sitting lonely by a lake in northern Wisconsin during the late 1920s, Lew
Sarett, a minor poet with major resentments, articulated a few of them to
sympathetic listeners scattered across provincial America. In 1927 he sent a
harangue to H. G. Merriam, who at that moment was launching the *Frontier*
as a "magazine of the Northwest":

> You know the correct literary posture today, the literary vogue, outlook,
> manner. It is the development of a sophisticated jazz age. It is singularly
> metropolitan in origin and sign; it is urban and urbane, sophisticated and
> sour, blase and bored. Its creed is one of negatives from first to last; its
> few hints of affirmations center in Freud and Jung, in a pseudo-scientific
> psychology, in Watson and his behaviourism and mechanism. It is hard,
> cold, cruel, and malicious. It is the product of a decadent period.
>
> Can you imagine a writer who affects—or succumbs to—metropolitan
> ennui, sophistication, cynicism, a writer far removed from the elemental
> earth and its people, a writer subscribing to a creed of negations . . . can
> you imagine such a writer capturing the beauty, power, significance of
> Montana, the West? of the wild earth? of its people robust and rugged,
> whose loves and hates are spontaneous and naive and honest and bloody—
> and as true as the dirt under their feet? Can such a writer understand—let
> alone capture—a land and a people that say "yes!" to life—whatever
> bitterness may come—and whose day after day is full of affirmations . . . ?
> . . . It can't be done.
>
> At any rate, I think what I have said will bear thinking about—
> especially in Montana—in any state west of the Mississippi—any state
> courageous enough to do its own thinking and to go its own way, whatever
> pathological and neurotic New York may decree.[15]

The mid- to late 1920s were an era of many such manifestos, public and
private. They manifested the continuing ramifications of the cultural revolt
begun in the prewar period; in some quarters, they called for a revolt against
that revolt. "Not in Greenwich Village dirt or Mid-west loam or European

mold" but in "our own rocky soil" would Northwestern culture find its roots, declared Merriam in the inaugural issue of the *Frontier*. He considered these words from the lead editorial "something like the platform of a political party." The masthead of that first issue and subsequent numbers displayed a quote from Thoreau: "The frontiers are not east or west, north or south, but wherever a man fronts a fact." Art, wrote Merriam, elaborating, "if it is worth anything at all, must be a sincere expression of real life." Its cultivation therefore required the rejection of Eastern genteel cultural productions— "tea party poetry and skylark verelets"—which were "uncourageous, unindigenous . . . spiritually imitative and too uninspired." Equally inappropriate was the "crazy sophistication that is running through the East" and "eating the heart out of Eastern writing." Merriam wished that these modernist styles, with all of their repugnant assumptions (as outlined by the disgusted Sarett), would "get drowned in the Mississippi." Both the creaky genteel canon and the emerging "orthodoxy" of modernism represented cultural "importations" in relation to life as it was lived in the Northwest, serving only to obscure and alienate, not to interpret, make meaningful. "Culture to me is not and can never be an importation," Merriam told Carey McWilliams in 1930. "It is not a 'taking on' process primarily. Culture is a 'growing out' process; it is nourished by the soil it is growing in." To stave off the useless and worse-than-useless cultural influences of the East necessitated that the *Frontier* try "desperately hard to be a really sectional magazine—provincial, even." Just as new magazines of the prewar revolt like the *Seven Arts* or the *Little Review* had provided an outlet for alternatives to the dominant literary methodologies of their own time, so too would the editors of the *Frontier* remain "open-minded about literary form," Merriam announced. "We do not believe that all possible forms have been found." His hope was that these new forms would emerge from the *Frontier*'s "pioneer endeavour to gather indigenous Northwest material"—as would perhaps some measure of "spiritual growth" for the region as a whole.[16]

What Merriam wanted to accomplish for Montana and the Northwest John G. Neihardt desired for all the regions of the United States. During the same year that his counterpart in Missoula was launching his new literary magazine, Neihardt in St. Louis was contacting prominent writers nationwide on behalf of an "All-America Movement"—among them, Hartley Alexander ("I agree heartily with the whole program") and Carl Sandburg ("you can put me on the board of advisors"). To Mary Austin, he wrote:

> To attempt to fuse our various sectional cultures, such as they are, into a common national culture would be idiotic. Even if it were possible to do so by some magical process, the result would be fatal to every culture. It is

precisely the very obvious attempt to standardize us in keeping with the prejudices of a single commercially powerful section that we oppose. What we want to emphasize is the vital significance of what each section has to offer.

Merriam agreed. "We need a restatement . . . of culture," a "fresh restatement" in terms "of modern days," of "democracy," he told a writers conference at the University of Montana in 1931. Merriam framed his own "spiritual secession" in these terms: "If culture means following the leads of conniseurs [sic], I resist it stock, barrel, and lock. If culture means pretense, unwavering social conformity, the use of fashionable words and the wearing of fashionable clothes, I spurn it contemptuously." More generally, he swore, "if culture means a levelling to a likeness I am a foe of culture and of every influence that develops it. If culture means a loss of individuality, I am its implacable foe and enlist myself among its enemies enthusiastically."[17] Merriam was describing his personal experience of the manifold dimensions of the centralized cultural dominion of megalopolis, which in the regionalist geography was known by various ill-defined polemical labels: sometimes it was "the North," sometimes, "the East," and sometimes, "the Northeast"; least often it was called "New England" and most often, "New York." The precision that regionalists lacked in targeting their resentment (the general direction was clear enough, the industrial "core" to their "periphery") they made up in its intensity. And although other issues were to divide the movement, they converged on this central strategy: to bolt collectively out of the traces of this hegemonic regime and scatter into diversity, creating multitudinous new and decentralizing axes of cultural life.

There were any number of manifestations of these axes "in the making" during the interwar years. Solon J. Buck, president of the Mississippi Valley Historical Association, wondered aloud before its annual meeting in 1923 "why our courses in American history should contain so much of the local history of New England and Virginia and so little of the history of our own states." Lew Sarett told Merriam "emphatically" in 1927 that "those of us who are striving to capture . . . provincial life should develop our own medium, our own standards and forms. We should not for an instant turn our eyes to the East, to New York, to the bearded New England poets. . . . We've got to be true to our own soil, our own thinking, our own people." Carey McWilliams stated more emphatically in his 1930 *Southwest Review* essay, "Young Man, Stay West," that "'New York is not America.' It is a vile place to live—costly, vulgar, crowded, polyglot"—and "not only unrelated to, but actually contemptuous of, the land west of Hoboken. New York knows more of Paris and London than it does of the Middle West." Most extremely, Thomas Hart Benton would have none of New York's imported modernist art or its alien Marxist politics, rejecting them along with all the other "factors inimical to an indigenous art— colonialism, highbrowism, the make-believes and snobberies of the wealthy circles"—and joining with fellow painters Grant Wood and John Steuart Curry to represent instead "a home-grown, grass-roots artistry which damned 'fur-rin' influence and which knew nothing about and which cared nothing for the traditions of art as cultivated city snobs, dudes and *ass*thetes knew them." Bernard DeVoto, in retrospect from 1943, asserted his own revolt more flatly: "I have set myself to oppose the ideas, concepts, theories, sentiments, and superstitions of the official literature of the United States between the two wars."[18]

DeVoto and Benton protested too much, of course, as did most other region-alists who revolted against modernist forms and styles yet shared (as revealed in the Indian subregionalists) a number of the characteristics of the modernist mind-set. The basic affinity of their antigenteel rhetoric and project with that of an arch-modernist like William Carlos Williams, one of the architects of the modern poetry Neihardt objected to, was telling; so also was Benton's own earlier training in the latest techniques of Paris and the lessons learned from him by his protégé, Jackson Pollack. But even as regionalists joined "official" modernists (like the *Partisan Review* cosmopolitans) in their pursuit of an integrated culture and sensibility, they diverged from the modernist tendency which might seek that integration only via the individual artistic act *in itself*, created as a momentary point of order—of "ground"—and (in effect, if not intent) largely a personal and subjective point that was opaque and difficult for most readers or viewers. (The *Partisan Review* cosmopolitans, despite their Marxist credentials, were noteworthy in their disdain for the "popular" and "populist.") In contrast to this heinous "privatism of modernism, its ground-ing in an exaggerated individualism," Benton in later years vowed, the re-gionalist aim was "to set up a people's art."[19]

Regionalists thus attempted to make a democratic politics out of the essen-tially modernist faith in the ordering, integrative "power of art." B. A. Botkin, in fact, developed exactly this argument in an essay entitled "The Folk and the Individual: Their Creative Reciprocity." The goal of the folk artist, he urged, must be to gain a sense of "corporate anonymity," which (given its sinister connotations) he quickly defined as not "extinction but extension and integration of personality, through identification with audience and complete submergence in his materials" (Austin's "poetic orgy"). Once the artist had turned "himself inside out culturally," living inwardly (if not literally) the "life of the people"—what Carey McWilliams in his damn-praising evaluation of *The New Regionalism* (1930) called "the will to be naive"—he "assimilated folk consciousness," or "attuned" him- or herself to "symbolism in general and to the group's particular set of symbols." This "symbol-mindedness," Botkin wrote in classic modernist terms, "is the ending of the separation between the subjective and the objective, both forms of separation . . . being characteristic of modern man." For when the subjectivist, relativist mind of the modernist confronted the folk traditions of regional culture, Botkin thought wishfully, it would discover the "universal," the "eternal, universal human values" that were "rooted in the provincial." This is, to be sure, what Frederick's character Thompson discovers at Green Bush: "elemental things," a "world in little" where "one can see it all."[20] Botkin never doubted in this analysis the existence of the folk group's "symbols" as a collective, "objective" ground, nor did most regionalists. They staked their cultural reconstruction project on it and, in the final analysis, their attempt to formulate regionalism into a full-fledged ideology.

Botkin's argument itself also indicates that, in terms of formal criticism and critical theory, there was something more to the regionalist cultural revolt than the carping and swiping of a Thomas Hart Benton or a Lew Sarett. By the late 1930s, a number of the Southern Agrarians went on to develop the very influential New Criticism out of their own regionalist anti-industrial, antiscientific assumptions. But more immediate to the task of revolt, several folklorists—including Botkin, Constance Rourke, and J. Frank Dobie— sought to respond to and revise the orthodox genteel corpus of literary theory and historiography, with the all-important end, in their minds, of "creating taste" (as Botkin wrote) among critics and public alike for folk-regional art. This aspect of the cultural project was an essential dimension of the civic religion's "aesthetic education," because an "appreciation" of folk motifs was a prerequisite for their appropriation and, therefore, for the operation of their integrative "power." Yet more directly, this very "education" in folk culture was necessary to legitimize it in the eyes of academics and artists as both a source for art and as art in its own right. For although the culture of American Indians, despite its primitiveness, possessed something of an "exotic" élan (attracting salon-frequenting luminaries like Lawrence, Huxley, and Luhan), the culture of the American folk (certainly that of poor rural blacks and whites) was most decidedly considered "low" by the genteel guardians of taste and refinement—this at a time when even "American literature" as an entity separate from the canon of "English literature" was not yet commonly recognized. (A case in point: John and Alan Lomax, in the preface of one of their massive folk song collections published some years later, felt obliged to instruct their readers, "Do not 'sing down' to the songs.")[21]

As cultural critics, Botkin, Rourke, and Dobie therefore hoped to establish the "essential identity of lore and literature" (in Botkin's words), an identity that inherently and purposefully undermined the assumptions of genteel cultural hierarchy. Botkin himself, for example, in the manifesto introducing the 1929 edition of *Folk-Say*, retained the language of hierarchy as a rhetorical strategy to demonstrate the hollowness of genteel culture "in its estrangement from the folk." During "every age," he wrote, "literature moves on two levels—that of the folk and that of culture." The difference between them was a difference between "oral, or unwritten, and written tradition" and, if "culture literature" ever became too estranged (Merriam's "tea party poetry and skylark verelets"), a difference between "living and dead language." At such times (like the present), "culture literature" acquired an "artificial vocabulary," which Botkin, quoting AE's co-Revivalist, W. B. Yeats, characterized as "'the substitution of phrases nearly as impersonal as algebra for words and rhythms varying from man to man.'" Whenever "culture literature" becomes rarefied to this degree, Botkin argued, it must "return to the lower level of the folk" to be "strengthened and revitalized" by "the source of all art in the wonder and faith that are also the mother of religion."[22]

Dobie, too, conceived folklore as "fallow . . . literary material," spending much of the 1920s "collecting the legends of Texas and the Southwest for the Irvings, the Whittiers, the Longfellows" sure to come in the region's future, yet he carried Botkin's line of argument to its more radical conclusion: why concern oneself with "culture literature" if "folk literature" was an art, a more authentic and living art, in itself? When historians studied folk culture, their abstract analytic categories and "ethnological palaver" obscured its essential felt organic experience (as La Farge, Mathews, Neihardt, Brandt, and others in the Indian subregions recognized, loosening their methodologies accordingly). Dobie cited the case of the folk songs of a decrepit street singer he had once heard: "The colleges and universities are full of Ph.D's who could write historical learned sounding monographs on 'Utah Carl' and 'Little Joe Wrangler'—but who is going to make that woman vivid and alive and preserve the peculiar wail and emphasis she gave her dolorous songs?" In a 1924 essay "To Justify Interest in Legends," Dobie took the argument further: "These legends express a social background and often even better than authenticated history—often reveal the mind, the metaphor, and the *mores* of the common people"—above all, the "strange phosphorous" mythicized life that they lived in the mind of the regionalist. If he had his preference, Dobie would simply collect together this "veritable Iliad" with no encumbering analysis, preserve the legends from modernizing dispersal, and, as Rourke wrote of similar nineteenth-century preservation efforts, "make of them a treasure-house." If the conveyor of lore had any function, Dobie wrote of his own "autobiography" of vaquero John Young, it was to "help the reader to imagine what those old days in the brush were like," to re-create the experience of the heroic "fenceless world" of the frontier. The artist-scholar's role was, in sum, to act as the unintrusive "organic understander" convening the "poetic orgy" to disseminate the "truly Homeric" [Dobie's adjective] myth-laden and integrative folk ideals of the regionalist civic religion.[23]

For Dobie, it was enough to collect and to share with his readers a folk-regional culture "unalloyed," as he discovered it, thus strongly undercutting cultural hierarchy and the rootlessness that devolved from it. Constance Rourke agreed with him that "literary appropriation" should not "be hastened," but rather, through leveling efforts such as his, "the imaginative folk-life of our short past could gradually become a free possession, with the chance that its persistent patterns of thought and feeling and form would eventually flow into natural use." If "the literary critic, the student-scholar really joined in these undertakings," she wrote, "something like a full perception of our culture or cultures might follow"—genteel hierarchy would be replaced by a pluralistic vision. If the "social critic" joined in as well, "the many coherences of folk-life might be seen to possess lasting social values"—the normative mythic lessons provided by the civic religion of regionalism. At bottom, what Rourke was pointing to with this scenario of writers and critics and scholars "joining in" the life of the folk was the creation of a truly democratic culture, a contemporary yet more thoroughgoing renaissance of that "homogeneous world of the imagination" which she had perceived in the nineteenth century, when "popular fancies and those of genius" had been "loosely knit together." Grounded in the folk-regional cultures of America, Santayana's disdained "polite and conventional American mind" would regain its "basis in American life." And Van Wyck Brooks's high-brow/low-brow dichotomy would fuse together into a regionalist version of his hoped-for unitary "social ideal": the Americanism of organic, inclusive pluralism.[24]

For Botkin, this aesthetically enacted organic coalescence of culture was the democratic essence of his concept of folk-say. The "cultural flowering of the Negro," reflected in such movements as the Harlem Renaissance, well represented folk-say in action, he believed: an active cultural life of the "Here and Now" that was "bursting the barriers of repression," expressing ("saying") itself "from under" (as Williams wrote) despite its confinement by the class and racist myths of cultural hierarchy and 100 percent Americanism. Such were the liberating expectations of the makers of the regional renaissance, once "art [had] thus come to function in American life," as Thomas Hart Benton put it. "Let your American environment . . . be your inspiration, American public meaning your purpose," he recalled of the sentiments of the more self-conscious social artists and muralists. Solon Buck, standing before the assembled representatives of state and local historical societies from the nation's interior, charged them with similar "purposeful work": "to carry the gospel of salvation through a knowledge of the past to all who are capable of receiving it"—and not just any past, but "the history of the people . . . based upon a study of them in their local communities." Just as Joseph Brandt later tried to put the means of mass communications in the service of the poetic orgy, so also did Buck tell the delegates to spread the gospel with books and magazines that "will appeal to the general reader," with articles in local newspapers, with automobile history tours, with lectures to clubs and groups, and even with "radio broadcasting." The implicit modern-day critique of Benton's integrating "people's art," instilling an "art consciousness" of communal myths and traditions in the citizenry, would in this manner be given realist (yet populist) sinews of "historical mindedness or the critical spirit" essential to life in a democracy. By all of these means, the liturgy of the regionalist civic religion would bring modern Americans to an understanding, as Carey McWilliams affirmed, "that life does not have to be a mad, scrambling, roaring confusion."[25]

George Babbitt, riding the train out of Zenith, dreams of escaping from this kind of life. On his arrival in the Maine wilderness, however, he encounters Joe Paradise, who yearns only to "go down to Tinker's Falls and open a swell shoe store." Sinclair Lewis watches Babbitt return to Zenith a stillborn "child of the earth":

> Vast is the power of cities to reclaim the wanderer. More than mountains or the shore-devouring sea, a city retains its character, imperturbable, cynical, holding behind apparent changes its essential purpose. Though Babbitt had deserted his family and dwelt with Joe Paradise in the wilderness, though he had become a liberal, though he had been quite sure . . . that neither he nor the city would ever be the same again, ten days after his return he could not believe that he had ever been away.

Babbitt thus arrives at the modern dead end of the Turnerian continuum, where lay the mass cultural "world without a country," the Spenglerian "world-city," and "Leviathan"—all contiguous features in the emerging regionalist geography of the "wilderness of civilization," another of the rhetorical layers of their revolt against modern America. Just how imperiling they believed these modern forces to be is revealed in an apt image conveyed to Botkin by poet and folklorist Percy MacKaye, who described the *Folk-Say* annual—despite all "liberating" and "integrative" expectations of a "renaissance" of folk-regional culture and tradition—as "a pioneer's log fire, amid the mechanized wilderness of our Today," a flicker of coherence within the "mad, scrambling, roaring confusion."[26] From the perspective of the older America, those forces were as unprecedented as they seemed (in Lewis's depiction) unstoppable, and the "geography" of mass culture and megalopolis that regionalists and others began charting in the late 1920s represented an attempt both to criticize and comprehend their operation and, perhaps, to find ways of "conquering" them on behalf of regional "re-settlement" and "reforestation."

The Lynds' Middletown—Muncie, Indiana, of their native Middle West— was a prospering settlement in that ungodly new-fangled wilderness, and to make their survey of it, to gauge the state of the American folk in the year 1925 with the "objectivity and perspective with which we view 'savage' peoples," the Lynds found a normative "baseline against which to project the culture of today": backward along Turner's spectrum to the year 1890, when the city was still a "placid county seat" and "the young Goliath, Industry, was still a neighborly sort of fellow," and crafts like glassblowing were practiced by "a hand process that had come down largely unchanged from the early Egyptians" and "the speed and rhythm of the work were set by the human organism." In 1925, the Lynds noted, that entire glassblowing process "occurred without intervention of the human hand," the craft of which the bottle-blowing machines had made "as obsolete as the stone ax." During the 1890s, a natural gas boom had begun the transformation of the placid county seat into a "manufacturing city," a fate which Middletown shared with "hundreds of American communities" over the intervening thirty-five years, when the industrial revolution "descended upon villages and towns, metamorphosing them into a thing of Rotary Clubs, central trade councils, and Chamber of Commerce contests for 'bigger and better' cities"—the 100 percent American world with its "standardizing and fusing . . . pattern of loyalties" that Babbitt could not escape:

> Every aspect of Middletown's life has felt something of this same tendency: standardized process in industry; nationally advertised products used, eaten, worn in Middletown homes; standardized curriculum, textbooks, teachers in the schools; the very play-time of the people running into certain molds, with national movie films, nationally edited magazines, and standardized music.[27]

Meanwhile, regional planner Benton MacKaye, with the fellow-traveling Lynds another of the surveyors in this "wilderness of monotonous, standardized, mechanized uniformity," took his own measurements from a different part of the continent—atop Mount Monadnock in New England, tracing in *The New Exploration* (1928) the pattern of changes by which industrialism had there "descended upon villages and towns, metamorphosing them." Calibrating from the "colonial village culture . . . still near at hand" in his hometown of Shirley Center, "An Indigenous Community," MacKaye made an ominous discovery: the "chief significance" of the new wilderness was that "it is a wilderness which '*flows*.' We are invested not merely by a wilderness of civilization," he concluded, "but by an invasion of civilization . . . the metropolitan invasion." High above New England, he first traced the flow outward from the Boston Basin, where the process began with the effacement of old, intimate Boston Town; then he showed how it crept with "finger-like projections, glacier-wise," beyond the city limits, "obliterating such rural and village environment" as stood in its path. Next the stream of metropolitanism ran "along the railways and motor roads back through the hinterland"—so MacKaye continued, unrolling the map—where "little centers of metropolitanism in the Main Street towns and around the numerous gasoline stations" erupted as excrescences. Finally, he observed, "here and there" an invading tendril of civilization often "crawls up some mountain summit and obliterates a strategic particle of the primeval environment"—turning Joe Paradise into a shoe salesman.[28]

"Rootless, aimless," and "profoundly disharmonized," as MacKaye characterized it, metropolitanism was "a world without a country," a culture "made to echo the intonations of industry," infinitely expansive because of its fundamental artificiality and machine-reproducibility. In fact, the disruptive flow of civilization into the resistant but overpowered realm of the indigenous, MacKaye noticed, was occurring "not alone in America, but on every other continent" and especially in Western Europe, where artists and intellectuals were making their own surveys of the damage. Approaching San Francisco on an evening ferry during his tour of America, AE watched the city emerge from the waterline "like a city out of the Arabian Nights all glittering with rose and golden and silvery lights, and I said I am getting into Paradise," he afterward told friends in Ireland. "Then as I came closer I knew the jewelled lights were passionate appeals to smoke particular brands of cigarettes or to eat particular brands of tinned fruits." So too did Europeans across the Atlantic similarly shift their perceptions of America during the interwar years—far from being the home of the "children of the earth" depicted in Crèvecoeur's time, America now became synonymous with the mass-acculturating "world without a country" that threatened to engulf them, as it had engulfed Middletown, in a standardizing modern perversion of "the process by which Europeans become . . . Americans." As the British critic F. R. Leavis observed in his gloomy *Mass Civilisation and Minority Culture* (1930), "To this someone will reply that Middletown is America and not England. But the same processes are at work in England and the western world generally, and at an acceleration. It is a commonplace that we are being Americanised." A fellow British conservative, C. E. M. Joad, recorded the aftermath of the process in *The Horrors of the Countryside* (1931). "What, under modern conditions, is the country walker to do?" he wondered. Americanization had led to the "murder

of solitude" and the mass "uglification" and "destruction of the English countryside" by "British robots" seeking "the pleasures of mechanical men." They
were becoming just like Americans, Joad asserted—America, "where the
application of machinery to life has proceeded furthest" and "the lack of
individuality is most marked": "Americans dress alike, look alike, talk alike
and think alike." He sighed, acknowledging, "My generation is a survivor
from a world rapidly growing obsolete, a generation which, having known the
beauty that was England's, cries out to see it pass."[29]

Europeans like Leavis and Joad had been wringing their hands over the leveling tendencies of Americanization at least since the time of Alexis de Tocque-
ville; conservatives worried particularly about its effects on divinely ordained
and financially profitable social hierarchies. Yet regionalists in America, democrats all, joined with their interwar European counterparts in "crying out"
against this current guise of the process, with all of its standardizing and
centralizing consequences—the economic dimension of what Allen Tate called
"that all-destroying abstraction, America." Their folk-regional America was a
counterdefinition aimed at the very America which Joad deplored. AE's faith
that it would fall to Americans to lead Europe out of the "wilderness of
civilization" and into the land of democracy was inspired, perhaps, by the
Whitmanesque promise that he still perceived latent in the vast spaces of the
national landscape. "The size of the country is appalling," he wrote back home
with admiration. "You start on a ride and the fields go away to infinity and the
sense of vastness is impressive." But regionalists well knew that this sense of
ungovernable distance was illusory, that the "flow" of mass cultural Americanization was "murdering solitude" in America as well, and that the sheer
space of Dobie's now-fenced "unfenced world" was no protection. The anony-
mous pursuits which John T. Frederick's characters Thompson and Rose list-
lessly engaged in during their exile in the big city among the "hurrying thousands" could just as conveniently have been pursued in a less-romanticized
Green Bush. As Waldo Frank observed, to the farmer "motor, telephone,
radio, and word and picture of the press are as natural . . . as tree or cow."
Neihardt elaborated: "I hate to say it . . . but the 'small town' . . . is an urban
superstition, a mere literary convention. The 'small town' disappeared with
the coming of the automobile, the movie, the phonograph, the widely circu-
lated newspapers and magazines. It may be that there is a small town here and
there in out of the way places; but I'm sure they must be scarce."[30]

Buried under the dead layer of genteel culture, or confined to the shacks and
slums at the bottom of the 100 percent Americans' socioeconomic hierarchy, or
hidden away within their confused modern minds, folk culture could at least
survive in obscurity. But the tremendous expansion of mass culture during the
1920s (by the end of which eighty million people were going weekly to the

movies, and one-third of the national population was listening to *Amos 'n' Andy* on the radio) meant the end of obscurity and the end of folk culture, of *culture* itself, as regionalists understood the word. Some of them, it is true, did recognize the possible benefits of the urbanization of the countryside by the new instruments of mass communication. Lewis Mumford, for example, noted in 1931 that "the unique advantages of the metropolis" might be lost now that "its concerts may be heard over the radio or reproduced on the phonograph, when its art exhibitions may travel safely, when, in fact, most of its values are reproducible elsewhere—if they are worth the effort." Often they were not, however; often, these values were conveyed by "appeals to smoke particular brands of cigarettes" rather than cosmopolitan "concerts" or "art exhibitions." And even over the radio or over at the county museum, such high-brow fare had at best a limited audience, whereas *Amos 'n' Andy* had a listenership encompassing many socioeconomic levels. Yet perhaps this ability of mass culture to appeal broadly to a wide range of Americans, speaking to them generically, but also universally, embodied its own culturally reconstructive promise. Seen in this light, Waldo Frank's observations on mass culture—"millionaire and mill-hand read the *Saturday Evening Post . . .* the shop-girl of Paterson or Pueblo follows the styles of the Park Avenue hostess"—might be interpreted as the announcement of the common democratic culture that the regionalist movement so fervently pursued.[31]

But Frank and the regionalists, implicitly and explicitly, saw that there were crucial distinctions to be made between the culture of the mass and the culture of the folk. To them, mass culture was a socially atomizing caricature of the organicism promised by folk-say—the distinction between *conformity* and *community*. Their mythicized visions of Indians and folk depicted societies in which "all are artists," as Edgar Hewett believed, "artists" who participated in "living arts" that were also "community arts" (in Ransom's words), lore-enchanted worlds where nature, religion, art, work, play, and ritual intermingled. Displaced out of this way of living by the metropolitan "flood," or "weak-headedly" seduced away from it by the "mistress of our outreaching yet befuddled senses" (MacKaye's images)—the comforts, conveniences, thrills, and other advantages of modern urban living—Americans had, voluntarily and involuntarily, struck a fool's bargain. The machine order that made this existence possible might mean "freedom from primitive industry and raw-boned nature," as MacKaye wrote, but it thereby "built you in from the earth itself, cemented you away from any contact with the ground," as Willa Cather's Neighbour Rosicky mused. Having lost this contact, city dwellers lost the "shared stream" of the timeless "rhythmic stimuli" arising in an intimately understood natural environment that Mary Austin saw as the basis of the Indians' "common urge toward communality." Modern Americans lived instead in the "world without a country," which was, as MacKaye surmised, a "transient and ever-changing environment," constantly remade according to the dictates of efficiency, profit, or fashion. Thus, relating to machines rather than to nature, they lost the animist lore and the "cosmical consciousness" that came from constant exposure to "the infinitude and contingency of nature." Because, as the Agrarians declared, "there is no full-blooded aesthetic experience, and consequently, no creative art to record this experience, that does not rest emotionally on the love of nature," the modern American was transformed (as Andrew Lytle wrote of a fully applianced farmwife) "from a creator in a fixed culture to an assistant to machines."[32]

And not merely an "assistant"—the Lynds came across this editorial statement in a Middletown newspaper: "The American citizen's first importance to his country is no longer that of citizen but that of consumer." The social and political ramifications of consumerism, the act of *consumption*—in sharp contrast to the "creative ability and esthetic sense of the Negro" and other folk, the people themselves making their own culture—were what made mass culture so "insidious" to the regionalist mind. As the central force shaping the protean "world without a country," consumption—over and above the artificial urban environment itself—dissolved "earth-loyalties," because it encouraged work to be conducted for abstract profit alone rather than for the satisfactions of producerist craft, conducted "not too hurriedly and not too mechanically." Seeking only cash to buy goods, Americans cared less and less how hurried or mechanical their work was, or even whether they owned their means of living: the cash was the thing. They therefore lost not only their shared aesthetic, religious, and social ties to the land, but also the self-sufficient economic existence which found its basis there and the independent political life consequent from it. "To be a landless man was to be a wage-earner, a slave, all your life," Neighbour Rosicky reflected; "to have nothing, to be nothing."[33]

Rootless now, adrift in the "world without a country," the remaining communitarian bonds and folk cultural remnants of indigenous America were short work for the metropolitan flood swelling in the cities and overflowing into rural byways. Unlike the "orderly, integrated racial life" of American Indians, Middletown after 1890 split into "not just two worlds," the working class and the business class, but into "a multitude." As the Lynds remarked, "Small worlds of all sorts are forever forming, shifting, and dissolving." Automobility (each family with its own car), telecommunications (no need for talking face-to-face), impersonal economic exchange (few made their own products), fickle and thrill-hungry leisure in abundance (forever looking for something new and exciting)—these were among the acids responsible. Seeking to find meaning in this flux, Middletowners became perpetual joiners, trying to forge new organizational loyalties according to special interests. *Still* segmented, they, the Babbitts, sought to bolt these loyalties together crudely with the myths of 100 percent Americanism and with class allegiances sealed by the badges of consumption. But as "consumers" rather than "citizens," it was difficult to roust the faithful out of their houses when *Amos 'n' Andy* were on; political life thus declined, only occasionally lashing out on behalf of law and order. And consumption itself proved to be a slippery new "ground" as well. Not only did it exacerbate competition for status among members of the same "set," each trying to keep up with endless fashion changes and innovations (like Babbitt's "rich" new alarm clock—"socially it was almost as creditable as buying expensive cord tires")—but also, as Frank perceived, the badges of the better sort, going into mass and cheapening production, were continually finding their way down to the lower orders, creating a more and more un-differentiated society. That was the paradox of Middletowns everywhere: tending toward the "social isolation" of a "multitude" of worlds, especially the private spaces of fully applianced homes and cars, they were also conformist and standardized, as Middletowners attempted to give some order to all those worlds, and increasingly to do so with the only culture they had at hand, 100 percent Americanism itself waning from indifference: the mass-produced cul-ture that someone else had made for them, had made for no one in particular, molding "not living men but the simulacra of men," as Vernon Parrington described the phantomlike characters in Sinclair Lewis's fiction, "only shells from which the life has departed, without faith or hope or creative energy, not even aware that they are dead." The Lynds include testimony from ghosts speaking out of this dire imperilment:

"We ain't got neighbors any more."

"My friends and I see each other most at each other's houses and at the five-and-ten-cent store—generally when we go to the store."

"I like this new way of living in a neighborhood where you can be friendly with people but not intimate and dependent."[34]

The estrangement from nature, the loss of economic and political indepen-dence, and the atomization of community life perpetrated at the local level by the "metropolitan invasion" constituted what Parrington—in a chapter titled "Disintegration and Reintegration"—called "the imperious subjection of the individual to a standardizing order." The adjective *imperious* was carefully chosen, because to complete their survey of the "wilderness of civilization," regionalists had to travel upstream along the metropolitan flow, away from rural areas and little provincial cities like Middletown or Zenith and toward those larger metropolises that had come to "dwarf the country" like Chicago, which as early as the 1890s already (in Parrington's words) "bestrode the Middle Border like a colossus." Benton MacKaye, for one, "visualized" the relationship between the "hinterland" and the "great metropolis" as a two-way flow: the metropolis not only "invaded" the "realm of the indigenous," it also looted it. "Traffic streams" of raw materials flowed out of the countryside, "the realm of the soil, the ores, the forests, the water-power forces," and into the maws of urban plants and factories. Thus both upstream and downstream along the metropolitan flow, according to the regionalist scenario, *power*, imperious power, the "drift towards consolidation," traveled in one direction only—toward the plutocracies of the great metropolises. "Consolidation," in brute terms, often meant outright ownership of vast reserves of raw material out in the "colonial" lands of the West and the South. At the very least, consolidation meant the subordination of those regions within a system in which finished goods and services were exchanged for unprocessed natural resources. Worse still, the regulation of this national system required the "coercive powers of a centralizing state," as Parrington wrote—guidance by experts, vaster and vaster federal bureaucracies, in short, "a political leviathan too big and too complex for popular control." And part and parcel of the "standardizing order," it was in the great metropolises as well that culture, now also a commodity to be shipped out and consumed, was manufactured by "the paid agents of standardized institutions," as J. Frank Dobie called them.[35] In Chicago, Los Angeles, and, above all, New York City (dwarfing even the others) resided the radio networks, the movie studios, the big publishing houses, the record companies, the Madison Avenue agencies, and many of the factories for gadgetry like Babbitt's "nationally advertised and quantitatively produced" alarm clock. Thus was power, standardizing, consolidating, *nationalizing* power, drawn not merely into metropolitan but into *megalopolitan* concentrations.

Much of the regionalist critique of the "wilderness of civilization" was later to be honed sharper by the fierce politics of the depression. But during the late 1920s and early 1930s, an already deep sense of crisis was for many members of the movement crystallized, and their critical understanding quickened, by the appearance of Oswald Spengler's *The Decline of the West* (1926). "*World-city and provinces*—the two basic ideas of every civilization," which Spengler discovered in his examination of "whole millenniums of historical world-forms," seemed to be realizing themselves even in the exceptionalistic spaces of America, as the end point of the Turnerian continuum intersected with the negatively sloping curve of the Spenglerian history cycle:

The stone Colossus "Cosmopolis" stands at the end of the life's course of every great Culture. The Culture-man whom the land has spiritually formed is seized and possessed by his own creation, the City, and is made into its creature, its executive organ, and finally its victim. . . . In place of a world, there is *a city, a point*, in which the whole life of broad regions is collecting while the rest dries up. In place of a type-true people, born of and grown on the soil, there is a new sort of nomad, cohering unstably in fluid masses, the parasitical city-dweller, traditionless, utterly matter-of-fact, religionless, clever, unfruitful.

Paris, London, Berlin, New York—these were the world cities where the culture of the West was dying, becoming *civilization*. Regionalists, in revolt against that civilization, could not and would not follow Spengler any farther down his declining curve of history, however. Democracy and the "dictature of money," he posited, were both foundational elements of civilization in the world city. But "through money, democracy becomes its own destroyer," because the "dictature of money" was inevitably broken by the "coming of Caesarism"—"a high tradition and an ambition of strong families that finds its satisfaction not in the heaping-up of riches but in the tasks of true rulership." At the bottom end of history's curve, "no power that can confront money is left but this one." In the end, Spengler concluded with ominous ambiguity, "money is overthrown and abolished only by blood."[36]

Regionalists offered the West an alternative vision of the future. Benton MacKaye foresaw a "gradually awakening common mind"—the regional renaissance—gathering itself as part of the "twofold residence" of the "human" or "indigenous" realm in America, the other repository embodied "in the actual territory and landscape of a large portion of the country itself." Recasting and extending Parrington's image of "two worlds" in irrepressible conflict, he argued that this "human realm" was poised for "the great struggle of the immediate future," between "man himself and man's machine," between "Metropolitan America and Indigenous America," between "the aggressive mechanized portion of Western European society . . . and the indigenous portion of every society invaded." Beyond the pressing issues of cultural revolt most immediately engaged in this struggle, a number of regionalists worked further to "visualize" (MacKaye's term) the contours of the reconstructed, regionalized Western world that might emerge from it.[37] One of the most important and influential of these visualizations came, unintentionally but appropriately, from Frederick Jackson Turner, in a pair of his essays, *Sections and Nation* (1922) and *The Significance of the Section in American History* (1925)—unintentionally, because he considered himself to be writing history rather than projecting large-scale social transformation, and appropriately, because the "section" represented to him the sole hope for the survival of democracy beyond the end point of his modernization continuum, where the climactic "great struggle" was now under way.

Borrowing from Josiah Royce's definition of the "province," Turner conceived the section as "'any one part of a national domain which is geographically and socially sufficiently unified to have a true consciousness of its own ideals and customs and to possess a sense of its distinction from other parts of the country.'" Because America was "not a uniform surface," Turner believed, "but a kind of checkerboard of differing environments" into which a diversity of "migrating stocks" had settled, the result had been the creation of a number of such "differing societies in the different sections." America had, in other words, "become a nation comparable to all Europe in area, with settled geographic provinces which equal great European nations," but with this all-important, exceptionalistic distinction: America's federalist structure, its national political parties, and its national legislative bodies gave range to all this "sectional complexity and interplay" yet held the country together as a "union of potential nations" by "substituting discussion and concession and compromised legislation" for "the use of force" (with only one large historic failure). The linchpin of this noncoercive system was, according to Turner, "statesmanship," the ability to reconcile disputants through persuasiveness, to make one's ideals, one's vision of the national future, compelling and attractive to all concerned. In a liberal-democratic "federation of sections," he concluded, it was the only peaceful and diversity-respecting way to "bring the different regions together in a common policy."[38]

Turner had his own vision of the future, a "national vision" in which each section would "find its place in a worthy house" and a vision that he shared with many regionalists around the country—Botkin, for example, with his definition of regional culture as "a component of national culture," or Neihardt, for whom national culture was additive, a sum of the "vital significance of what each section has to offer." The provinces of America, Turner wrote, were encompassed by a national framework: "a common historical inheritance, a common set of institutions, a common law . . . a common language," and, more generally, common "American ideals." Yet if Americans were "members of one body," it was and must be a "varied body," Turner reasoned. In contrast to the "deadly uniformity" of the "nationally advertised and quantitatively produced" world without a country, or the "mob psychology" of mindlessly patriotic 100 percent Americanism, the section provided a site on which the sovereign individual might experience community locally and therefore concretely, sharing with fellow citizens "climate, geography, soils . . . economic interests," and, above all, "inherited ideals" and other "spiritual factors." Given the inherent uniqueness of each of these "differing societies," the significance of the sections for America *as a whole*, as a "symphonic nation" integrating citizen and community, localism and nationalism, became clear:

> [T]he sections serve as restraints upon a deadly uniformity. They are breakwaters against overwhelming surges of national emotions. They are fields for experiment in the growth of different types of society, political institutions, and ideals. They constitute an impelling force for progress along the diagonal of contending varieties; they issue a challenge to each section to prove the virtue of its own culture; and they cross-fertilize each other. They promote that reasonable competition and cooperation which is the way of a richer life.[39]

Rather than the mechanical standardization of Leavis's dreaded process of Americanization, the promise of the New World for the Old was embodied in this visualization by Turner and others of the centuries-long "dispersion of Europe" into a decentralized multiplicity of democratically symphonized indigenous regional cultures. This was "the significance of the section in *European* history," the fruition of the ongoing American experiment launched by Europeans, and from which Europe might redeem its own future. Turner, writing in the mid-1920s, offered them this vision of the "Americanism of organic, inclusive pluralism," a veritable "League of Sections," as an alternative for their dangerously hollow League of Nations. "We shall continue to present to our sister continent of Europe the underlying ideas of America as a better way of solving difficulties," he ended in an exceptionalistic tone. In fact, during the 1930s other regionalists would invoke much the same idea of a "continental federation of sections" as they witnessed the rapid dissolution of the league under the waters of "overwhelming surges of national emotions." And by the early 1940s, they would again look to "a vast and varied Union of unlike sections" as the basis for a *pax Americana*, even as the Europeans fulfilled John Gould Fletcher's 1924 prophesy that a failure to reconstruct "the religious impulse inherent in human life" (he pinned his own hopes on the regionalist civic religion) would bring about "a disaster to which the last war will appear childsplay."[40]

As events revealed, America was to save Western Europe not with a vision of a regionalized pluralist utopia, but with the national mobilization of its vast industrial power. Certainly, for many in the regionalist movement, Turner's mythicized conception of the "symphonic nation"—which he by turns saw as a long-standing though often-disharmonized historical reality—had still to be realized at home. If America were an exceptionalistic realm, as AE reassured them, a place where such possibilities might yet be created, it was also a "sister continent" to Europe in its Spenglerian "premature decay," a land drifting into the consolidation of megalopolitanism and Leviathan, a country

where citizens had become consumers. The onset of the Great Depression—
the complacency of Americans shattered, the "metropolitan invasion" glutted
and stalled—was to give regionalists a brief "moment" in which to build at
least a few ideological sod houses of AE's "rural civilization" out in the modern
wilderness, for it was only through some version of AE's vision, they believed,
that Turner's (and Waldo Frank's) had any chance of realization. But the futile
and rather pathetic regionalist exhortation of a Europe "between wars" was
to indicate the magnitude of the domestic difficulties confronting even a partial
fulfillment of the "task eternal." How were regionalists to convince Americans
to forego *Amos 'n' Andy* and "take down the fiddle from the wall," or to reflect
on the sculpted "history and symbolism of political freedom" adorning Goodhue's capitol? How were they to prevail against the "Great Progressive Principle" and all of the "imperious" powers entrenched in ever "bigger and better"
cities? How were they to contend with an all-too-quickly resurgent 100 percent Americanism, any number of would-be Caesars at its head?[41] How, finally,
were they to compete with suddenly popular "furrin" doctrines that did not
shrink from the coercive means necessary to bring about their own versions of
utopia? Against all of these adversaries the regionalist cultural project as it
entered the 1930s could pose only the aesthetically integrating folk-regional
communitarian and libertarian liturgy of their new civic religion—myths and
ideals made sublime, beautiful, and compelling—could pose, in short, only
persuasiveness, which was the way of a democratic culture.

In trying to accomplish the "task eternal," the regionalist movement as a
whole, however, had something more at its political disposal than mass democratic "aesthetic education." It had the *science* of regionalism (albeit a "science" of a peculiar variety), practiced by experts who conceived the region not
just as the seat of culture, myth, and tradition, but as the most fundamental
geographic framework for human society. Converging with the Indian subregionalist and American folk-regionalist participants of the cultural project
(and in some cases, sharing membership in that project) were the regional
sociologists and planners, those who spent much of the 1920s and early 1930s
developing techniques and designs for the "symphonious environment," as
MacKaye termed it, of the coming "symphonic nation." If, MacKaye wrote,
"indigenous America" was "under invasion by the iron glacier" of metropolitanism, spreading "out along the highways from each metropolis, large
and small—out of New York and out of 'Zenith'"—if regional "indigenous innate 'culture'" (the "world of intrinsic human values") was thus being "overtaken by metropolitan intrusive 'civilization'" to the extent that "Spengler's
winter" seemed to have arrived, then that invasion could and must be "met—

and dyked" by regional planning. Planning meant for him and for others "the remolding of the Metropolitan America in its contact with the Indigenous America." More specifically, it was "a scientific charting and picturing of the thing (whether logging railroad or communal center) which man desires and which the eternal forces [of nature] will permit." The industrial revolution, MacKaye argued, could be remade through a new "vision of its workings" to "direct its titanic powers to a prompt achievement of true freedom" and an "equable cultural climate." Unequivocally, at the crisis juncture where the postfrontier end point of the Turnerian continuum met Spengler's awful sine curve, MacKaye and the planners—among them, Rupert Vance, Howard Odum, and Lewis Mumford—proclaimed that "we have reached a new frontier of the journey of history," a time when America might burst beyond the folkless dead end of a frontierless world, and when the inevitable negative slope of the historical cycle might be redirected upward into utopian exponentiality.[42]

Citing Patrick Geddes, one of the scientific godfathers of regionalism, Rupert Vance in *Human Geography of the South* called for "a frank acceptance of the Utopian approach to regional planning," enacted through a two-pronged strategy: first, "a survey of the region-as-is," followed by "a blue print of the region as it can be reconstructed." The regional survey, he wrote, was "a matter of science, cartographic, geographic, descriptive, statistical," while the regional plan was "a matter of applied science, technology, and engineering." Yet the "science" of regionalism as the planners practiced it was not abstract science-as-usual. Just as participants in the cultural project were forced to cross methodological and disciplinary lines in order to achieve a complete and organic depiction of regional cultures—the "whole round of life," as Walter Prescott Webb put it—so also did regional planners look literally to the *organism* of nature for their own analytic models and analogies. Their regional approach was, moreover, a synthesis, more than a synthesis, of the prewar utilitarian conservationism of the Gifford Pinchot school (MacKaye himself was a wayward disciple of Pinchot's Forest Service), a school that emphasized the inventorying of natural resources for future sustainable, multiple-use exploitation. Regionalists appropriated and transcended as well the mystical single-issue preservationism of John Muir, concerned solely with saving a few patches of wilderness from an otherwise unreformed, engorging industrial economy. Vance, for example, in his *Human Geography* survey of the South, incorporated many of the insights of ecology for a fuller understanding not merely of natural systems but of regional "cultural complexes" (the folkish "region-as-is/was" recovered by the regionalist cultural project and the urban-industrial civilization that the regionalists repudiated) in relation to both the "physiographic region" (the geologic substructure) and the "region of the organic complex" (local flora, fauna, and climate). To Vance's mind, "the legitimate approach to human geography" lay "not in a detached study of the social significance" of each of these "geographic elements" in isolation, but rather in "an analysis of interconnected wholes." Indeed, after examining the interaction of culture and nature in the American South over the entire Turnerian spectrum, Vance concluded (with another regionalist godfather, conservationist George Perkins Marsh) that "the region which begins as a great complex of physical forces ends by being so re-shaped by the human groups which occupy it that it emerges as a cultural product."[43]

In this notion lay the analytic power of the concept of the region, and its utopian promise as well. For if the physiographic-organic regional complex were malleable according to a specific cultural complex, then the "adequacy" of various cultural complexes might be adjudged from the degree to which they worked symbiotically within parameters set by the local equilibriums of nature, the success of their adaptation being revealed by the cultural region's long-term stability and quality of life. The organic range of the regional survey's measurements, Vance asserted, was by this method "'destined to review all the sociological theories that speculate about some sort of abstract man,'" especially the capitalist, nature-conquering "economic man" of classical economics still enshrined by the creed of 100 percent Americanism. The testing of such inadequate cultural complexes—"the heedless rush pell-mell into an unplanned and chaotic industrialism"—inevitably pointed the way to the "region-as-it-can-be," because together with evidences of cultural failure surveyors obtained a thorough ecological knowledge of "regional resources and processes." Armed with these catalogs of potential regions, Vance and other planners in the South and around the nation hoped to "erect thereon a competent civilization," which to avoid the pitfalls of the thoughtless exploitation of the "metropolitan invasion" must, they believed, be "a thing of conscious group direction," of "social mastery." The cultural complexes of man, if they were to achieve the symbiosis of the ecological "climax community," must become merely one among the multiplex communities inhabiting the regional environment, with conservation substituted for get-rich-quick exploitation, with diversification replacing monocultural economies, and, striking at the roots of these problems, with prudent programmatic development spreading "in widest commonalty culture, comfort, intelligence, and happiness," correcting the imbalances of colonialism and plutocracy.[44] Shaped by an ecological consciousness, regional planning thus unfolded in the interwar years as an American version of social democracy.

Yet the still-emerging science of ecology was not the only source for the organicist sensibility of regional planners, nor was it the primary wellspring of their social-democratic political orientation. Certain of them shared more than the regional landscape with the members of the cultural project—they shared also the folk-mimetic techniques of regionalist art and the "capturable America" of folk values and traditions. Backward in time along the Turnerian continuum, with the intervening and obscuring layers of metropolitanism peeled away, the regional planner found in folk culture a historicist laboratory. On the frontier, for example, Vance discovered "the culture patterns of a complex civilization pruned and trimmed . . . to fit nature, open and undisguised," patterns surely valuable to those seeking symbiotic techniques of region building. Tracing the modernization of these regional "culture patterns" into the present, Vance's colleague at the University of North Carolina and director of its Institute for Research in Social Science, Howard Odum, assumed in fact that the "four generations of Southern Americans" portrayed in his work *An American Epoch* (1930) "comprehended every known element in the architecture of modern civilization":

> In these four generations were peculiarly reflected collective pictures descriptive of American reality, rich in power, range, and contrast, shaped and proportioned by strong backgrounds whose unfolding episodes were vivid with the quiver of life. Here were epic and tragic materials of history and literature alongside measurable elements for the scientific study of human society. Here were illuminating materials for the better understanding of American life through the study of regional situations and folk society . . . a sweeping American development reminiscent of universal culture.

To grasp the "epic and tragic" as well as the "scientific" data of folk-regional societies required not merely an organicist but an *aestheticized* sensibility, as Odum's odd hybrid *American Epoch* itself "peculiarly reflected." His "portrait" of the evolving South intermixed emblematic fictional characters, narrative history, and statistics, becoming at times so overwhelmed with the complexity of the region that it resorted to lists, with an almost stream-of-consciousness effect—such as these "social episodes in the Negro scene": "church meetings and picnics . . . church suppers and socials . . . country and village dances . . . corn shuckings and quiltings . . . courting and quarreling . . . Christmas and holiday gatherings . . . lodge and fraternal events . . . men, women and children dressed in Sunday best . . . high spirits and serious business. . . ." Finally, Odum threw up his hands: "Pictures and pictures. The South not one South but many"; it became a refrain—"*The* South, yet many Souths."[45] An aestheticized science, parallel to the "felt history" of regionalist historians like Sandoz, Mathews, DeVoto, and Dobie, was needed to capture such ambiguity. Not only did such an approach uncover intricate relationships in the human-physiographic-organic regional complex, it also revealed the "paradoxes," "contradictions," and "diversity" in folk-regional cultural complexes, qualities that might be missed with a more neatly categorized but more blindly abstract methodology. Certainly, in Odum's later and more strictly positivist sociological works, like *Southern Regions of the United States* (1936), the cartographic and demographic indices with which he hoped to depict the "many Souths" of Southern society multiplied into several hundred pages.

Beyond its usefulness in the portraiture of the regional survey, in the revelation of regional problems and potentialities, the aesthetic approach served a more crucial role in the larger task of social reconstruction. The practitioners of the "odd hybrid" science of regional planning relied on it for much the same reasons that regionalist artists did: to gain self-conscious access into the "universal culture" of the folk, the "intrinsic human values," the myths, and the traditions of indigenous America—and not just an appreciation of them, but a "folk-saying" appropriation, a fusion of scientific instrumentalities with the timeless lessons of integrative folkways. Aptly, the first meeting of the Regional Planning Association of America (RPAA) in 1923 took place at the Hudson Guild Farm in rural New Jersey, a "vacation habitat" for the relief of urban working-class members of a New York settlement house, yet also, on that particular April Saturday, the site for the monthly square dance, which was a long-observed tradition of local farmers. As Lewis Mumford described the symbolic scene:

> The local carpenter was the caller. We "outsiders" were allowed to join in; but alas! we stumbled and fumbled our way through the rounds of the first dance, helplessly laughing at our own awkwardness. But the old fiddler was properly outraged by our behavior. In the middle of the second dance he stopped playing, held up his hand, and called us to order. "You city folk seem to think this dancin' is fun. Well, it ain't. If you can't get down to business, clear off the floor!"
>
> That just rebuke sobered us up; even better, it improved our manners by making us readier to take our country neighbors and their lingering folkways seriously. From then on country dancing became part of our weekend conference programs—we even met for it on occasion in the city.

Through such contacts with "contemporary ancestors," Mumford and his fellow RPAA members (among them, Clarence Stein and Henry Wright) obtained insight into and reinforced their mythicization of the "fine provincial culture" embodied by the "communities that were planted on the seaboard and up the river valleys during the seventeenth and eighteenth centuries" and that had achieved "a full efflourescence" in the 1850s. Inspired as well by a lengthy correspondence with AE, Mumford proposed (as he wrote in the 1925 manifesto of the RPAA) to "give to the whole continent that stable, well-balanced, settled, [and] cultivated life." In the remnants of the "'all-roundness' of [that] colonial community living," MacKaye claimed in his own manifesto, *The New Exploration*, "I have myself taken part personally since the 1880's"; he marveled at how the New England village's "structural symmetry" was integral with its "cultural symmetry"—"physical, intellectual, artistic." It inspired his utopian definition of "the goal of living," one that he shared with regionalists movementwide—to transform modern America into an aesthetic society, seated in a multiplex "quiltwork" of regional communities: "we seek constantly to diminish the sphere of animal toil and to widen that of art; so that finally work and art and recreation and living will all be one." Regional planning, MacKaye argued, was "the effort to arrange the environment in such a fashion that this goal may be effectively and eagerly pursued."[46]

The "science" of regionalism, needless to say, made no claims to positivist value–neutrality; it was a science with an agenda, a science that was aestheticized and ethicized, a *folk science*—like the art of folk-say, an attempted fusion of the modern with the traditional. But to "arrange the environment" in order to achieve the regionalist "goal of living" would require a "folk engineering" as well, and to this purpose, MacKaye, Mumford, and other regional planners extended their mimesis of integrative folk culture even further, beyond the philosophy of planning to the actual techniques of regional reconstruction. Folk handicrafts united a respect for the integrity of raw materials (such factors as grain, texture, and durability) with a reverence for tradition, the stringencies of utility, a desire for beauty, and the urge for personal expressiveness—and it was essentially in the manner of a handicraft that regional planners proposed to shape the human and natural environments of the region.

Evocatively synthesizing and transcending his own conservationist-preservationist training, MacKaye, for one, envisioned that the region consisted of three "elemental environments": primeval, rural/communal, and urban/cosmopolitan; these three inherently belonged "to the soil and the human mind in contrast to the intrusive influence of the metropolis which does 'not belong.'" The job of the regionalist "engineer," he believed, was "not to 'plan' but to *reveal*" how "man's psychologic needs" could be met in the "complete and rounded external world" of these elemental environments—like a good craftsman, "to seek the innate design of forces higher than our limited powers." Equally important, according to MacKaye, the regional plan must be a community project. The civil engineer in designing such structures as a railroad switchback must be "integrated into a plan" that was the "product of the 'composite mind'" of several types of engineers, hydrologists, agricultural-ists, and city planners—not just because the complexity of the region required it, but because each of the three spheres was "a basic natural resource in man's development, and depletion in any one of them means a corresponding deple-tion in man's life": "the primeval is the environment of man's contact with nature; the rural (or communal) is the environment of fundamental human relations; the urban (or cosmopolitan) is the communal sphere compounded." The goal, in sum, was a modern replication of the "structural symmetry" and "cultural symmetry" built into the design of the New England town. To fulfill this goal, MacKaye, along with such "wilderness managers" as Aldo Leopold, focused primarily on the preservation of the primeval environment. His ef-forts produced one of the great achievements of the interwar regionalist movement—the Appalachian Trail, begun in the 1920s and completed in 1937, stretching two thousand miles from Maine to Georgia. Yet despite this accom-plishment, MacKaye still insisted that the Appalachian Trail and similar wil-derness areas could only be considered a partial first step, a system of pri-meval mountaintop "dykes and levees" intended to "form the indigenous base for controlling the metropolitan invasion" and, more essentially, to provide a basic foundation for the development of indigenous America. If "the funda-mental world of man's needs as a cultured being" were to be fully realized, and a symmetrical mode of living established, then the other two indigenous elemental environments must also receive cultivation.[47]

Down at the southern end of the Appalachian Trail, Vance, Odum, and a number of regional planners in fact took as their own "primary gigantic task" (as Vance described it) the rejuvenation of the South's "prematurely deca-dent" rural-communal environment, an environment encompassing millions of impoverished small farmers, tenants, and sharecroppers. "The mold in which the South is to be fashioned," Vance declared in 1932, "is only now being laid." And it was to be laid, Odum projected, by "modern scientific technique and education." In his *Human Geography*, Vance outlined some of the possi-bilities for "the reorganization of Southern agriculture": "intensive cultiva-tion" and crop rotation; diversification of the farm "to produce not only feed for stock" but also "food for family"; mechanization, especially, the cotton picker; "commodity cooperatives to regulate and stabilize the marketing of farm products"; and rural electrification via the "integrating" and unifying "region builder" of "super-power." Odum voiced the fear that these and other engines of progress might drive the region in the direction of "a cheap and snappy abundance in place of the values which were manifestly inherent in the South." Both he and Vance, though, were confident (on the eve of the New Deal) that regional planning would "seek to conserve certain regional values" and alongside the technical expert "find a place for the artist and the theorist."

To make the program of regional education and reform effective while conserving folk culture would necessitate, Vance suggested, "an adaptation of what we may call the technique of folk revival to the southern scene"—"after the same manner certain Victorian intellectuals, [John] Ruskin, [Charles] Kingsley, and [William] Morris, attempted to give tone and direction to the English laboring classes" or contemporaries such as George Russell (AE) sought to reorganize Irish agriculture by inspiring a "love of native place and native folk." Undertaking development within a framework of the "cultural ideals" of its long-standing rural tradition, the South, Vance wrote, might "finally attain many of the advantages of contemporary industrialization without suffering its accompanying deficiencies and maladjustments." Above all, it "need not produce the metropolis," but instead, with a yeomanry-oriented program of decentralization, "a large number of small cities" could be dispersed over the region—thus did the total vision of the Southern planners unfold—furnishing the markets essential to agricultural diversification and resulting in "a better balanced town and country relation."[48]

Looking outward to the rural-communal and primeval realms from his megalopolitan vantage in New York City, Lewis Mumford called this process of urban dispersal and rural-urban balance the "Fourth Migration," the dismantling of metropolitanism that must culminate and transfigure the previous three migratory flows of America that had occurred along the Turnerian continuum, first out to the frontier, then later back to the "factory town," and most recently to the "financial metropolis." Regional planning, he proclaimed in his 1925 manifesto, "asks not how wide an area can be brought under the aegis of the metropolis, but how the population and civic facilities can be distributed so as to promote and stimulate a vivid, creative life throughout a whole region." Yet regionalism had a further "civic objective" as well, he wrote: "it aims equally at ruralizing the stony wastes of our cities," at constructing the beautified, humanly scaled, green-belted "garden-city." Thus would MacKaye's three elemental environments be synthesized for all the citizenry by a new "seat of life and culture, urban in its advantages, permanently rural in its situation"—in all ways, "a higher type of civilization than that which has created our present conjested centers." The actual configuration of life in this new regional civilization, and the answers to the rhetorical questions posed at the end of the 1925 manifesto ("Regionalism or superconjestion? . . . Will man learn to master his man-made environment," or will he, mastered, "find himself without any purposes other than those of the Machine?") Mumford proceeded to visualize over the course of the next decade, with a more profound elaboration and application of "folk engineering" principles, bringing them together in *Technics and Civilization* (1934) as the prophesy of a deliberate "assimilation of the Machine" to the purposes of an organic order. "The pinnacles of handicraft art set a standard that the machine must constantly hold before it," he noted preliminarily. Yet the advent of the automated "basic production" now characteristic of the industrialized, mass-cultural metropolis was potentially *liberating*; because "as our basic production becomes more impersonal and routinized," Mumford asserted, "our subsidiary production"—the handicraft arts in which the regional civilization would thoroughly school the individual, and which the new leisure would allow him or her to enjoy as an "amateur"—"may well become more personal, more experimental, and more individualized." Thus would be established, Mumford soared, "a state in which creation will be a common fact in all experience," in which "no group will be denied . . . their share in the cultural life of the community." This "socialized creation," rooted in a freedom from necessity made possible by modern automation, represented an enormous step beyond the hard (if fulfilling) life of Hewett's Indian citizen-artists, or Lytle's yeoman-creators, for whom lore and handicrafts were harnessed as the means to mere subsistence. In the "higher type of civilization" that Mumford envisioned, the regionalist utopia of the folk was to be melded with the industrial utopia of abundance.[49]

Pictures and pictures, Odum might say. Pictures of the past, pictures of the present, pictures of the future of the folk in America—these were what the members of the regionalist movement had arrived at by the middle of the interwar period, the depression-era "moment" of national self-examination now opening before them: pictures born of odd hybrid ideological combinations of history and myth, social consciousness and art, sociology and ethics, science and utopianism. With these "pictures," these conceptualizations of aesthetically integrated societies, regionalists would attempt to redefine and reenergize American political culture, made moribund by the Great War, by the broken confidence of Progressivism, by the acids of modernity. Their task was to advance the nation beyond the feudalisms and anarchies of the laissez-faire "wilderness of civilization" and toward the positive freedoms and communitarianism of social democracy. But how their doctrinaire visions and plans might be turned into concrete reform programs remained the central question, the question that was to be settled in the 1930s. Although MacKaye, Vance, Odum, and Mumford all conceptually converged at a common regionalized rural-urban "middle ground," their original departures from (respectively) divergent conservationist-preservationist, agricultural, and metropolitan problem areas were, as MacKaye warned, ill-boding: given the interconnectedness of the "tangle" of modernity, what was needed was a regionwide, if not a nationwide, comprehensive assault. Even in an age tending toward Leviathan and phantom publics, no such assault, expensive and revolutionary as it must be, could begin without the considerable political momentum of a public mandate: and this the crisis of the depression would provide. As MacKaye remarked of the hoped-for democratic culture of regionalism (folk and artist, folk and planner joining together), "The point may be made that the technician unsupported by the people and a public consciousness is a head without a body, and that the public at large, unguided by technical advice, is a body without a head." Mandates are ephemeral entities, however, and what Vance predicted of an early depression-era project in the South for cotton price stabilization was relevant as well to the larger prospects for regionalist reform as a whole: "The greatest obstacle it will meet, and one that it may not overcome, is the apathy, the hopelessness, the ignorance, the inertia of its devotees, ossified in a routine beyond which they cannot see."[50]

Vance was, nevertheless, optimistic. In the fall and winter of 1931–32, popular agitation by some of the "inarticulate, unresponsive agrarian folk" on behalf of the multistate cotton stabilization drive—"the first gropings toward policies of regional control and direction"—seemed to him to signify that "regionalism in the South has finally reared its head as a folk movement." Truly, he declared, "if anyone rises to say that the common man of the South is not ready for regionalism and regional planning on the grand scale here is his answer." Unfortunately, a further encumbrance to regionalist reform, as he saw it, was that "political leadership notoriously lags far behind technical and scientific leadership." The regionalist civic religion therefore had a critical role to play in the effort to "rally a genuine regional movement." As Vance wrote of the "nostalgia for the old South" disseminated by the Southern Agrarian wing of the cultural project, "It has all the latent potency of a slogan, a catchword, a flag." Ultimately, the poetic orgy of the civic religion—the "gradually awakening common mind" arousing the grassroots, galvanizing artists and intellectuals, and prodding politicians—would be essential to sustain the moral force and vision of the regionalist movement (if its lessons could be heard above the cacophony of all those other contending voices). For as MacKaye wondered of "weakling man": "Can he, through sufficient understanding of his acquired powers, guide a triumphant means toward achieving some real and ultimate end and not merely in attaining further *means*?"[51] Such was the great peril of life in the modern disenchanted world of the twentieth century—that history would lose its myths, and art its social function, and sociology its ethical thrust, and science its utopian impulse, and the folk their folkness. To reverse this culture-corroding tendency—that was the "great struggle" which regionalists fought in the years between the wars. Willing themselves to be naive, they proposed to reforest, to reenchant the world: to build not merely quaint, impractical, old-fashioned ideological sod houses out in the "wilderness of civilization," but to resettle there, bringing with them a "higher type of civilization"—to build there garden cities.

Part Two

It Has Happened Here

5 Hidden History

The Great Depression,
the Ideology of Regionalism,
and the Crisis of American
Exceptionalism

A folk song is what's wrong and how to fix it, or it
could be whose hungry and where their mouth is, or
whose out of work and where the job is or whose broke
and where the money is or whose carrying a gun and
where the peace is—that's folk lore and folks made it
up because they seen that the politicians couldn't find
nothing to fix or nobody to feed or give a job of work.
We don't aim to hurt you or scare you when we get to
feeling sorta folksy and make up some folk lore, we're
a doing all we can to make it easy on you.
—Woody Guthrie to Alan Lomax, September 19, 1940

"The capitol tower stood straight and tall over the shim-
mering, dusty heat of the flat prairie town," Mari Sandoz
began "Mist and the Tall White Tower" (1936), a short
story depicting the cultural and psychological despair experienced by many of the down-and-out during the depression years. Throughout the work, she undercuts eulo-
gies to Bertram Goodhue's civic cathedral (her apartment
in Lincoln had a view of it) with a narrative that points not
to "that reverence for high traditions which it is the office
of public monuments to inspire," but to an ominous disintegration of meaning, to anomie:

> Alone it pierced the sky—timeless, enduring, a
> fluted shaft of stone and gleaming windows rising
> high from its broad base on terraced lawns to the
> banding of blue thunderbirds. Upon the gilded dome

the sower plodded his dark and solitary way, scattering his futile seed over the July plain, aloof from the sweating, heat-exhausted humanity barred from the grass by day guards.

In other of her works of the 1930s, Sandoz would explore the full political implications of the Sower's "futile seed," of the guards banning the people from their own house of state. In those works—*Old Jules, Slogum House, Capital City*—the characters would be fired by passion and ideology, by "the real issue, the eternal conflict of the small man against the big." But in "Mist," there are no nightmare scenarios of fascists in the heartland of America. Instead, there is an even bleaker story, a story of the world in dissolution, told through the character of thirteen-year-old Irvy Snell, who has come to Lincoln to see "the most beautiful building in the world" and to find the schoolteacher who once inspired him with her talk of its "covenant eternal as the rainbow in the sky."[1]

Irvy, uprooted and dispossessed, like "a fluff of seed from the old cottonwood at home," is something of a stock figure of depression-era fiction, and of the depression itself. According to the story, Irvy's father, having lost the family farm, hanged himself in a barn. Irvy was consequently left alone with his grandmother (one of the original homesteaders in the county) until she was forced by social workers to move off of her own farm and into an old folks' home in town, as Sandoz recounts, leaving Irvy with a cruel man who rented and abused his grandmother's once-admired property. Now having fled the four hundred miles eastward to Lincoln, where he vaguely hopes that "everything would come right" once he locates his teacher and the "beautiful building," Irvy spends the first night on the lawn of the capitol among other rootless and impoverished people, sleeping fretfully between dreams filled with images of decay.[2] If he were Tom Joad, on arising the next morning, he would come to an epiphany about the brotherhood of man; if he were a character in any number of proletarian novels, he might be caught in the cross fire of a violent strike and sacrifice his innocence to the Cause of Labor. But instead, in Sandoz's dark scenario, on arising the next morning, Irvy goes in search of his beloved teacher . . . and fails to find her.

"Not knowing where to go," Sandoz writes, he returns to the capitol and "almost without intention" enters it, walking in with a tour of schoolchildren. The previous night, he had been awakened from his dreams on the lawn by a potentially inspirational "sudden flood of light that poured over the wide tier of stone steps leading to the main entrance," illuminating "the panel over the wide doorway, a panel of pioneers" pushing "hopefully, bravely toward the West." In Irvy, however, it aroused only the thought that the epic in which his grandmother had participated was "long ago, more than fifty years ago, and the good times were long gone." And earlier that morning, he had watched a group of ragamuffin boys standing before "one of the great carven buffaloes" on the massive balustrades. "Arise with the dawn / Bathe in the morning sun," one of them had read from the Indian ceremonial inscriptions. But rather than a sense of renewal, the saying evoked this embittered response from one of the youths: "'Arise, it ought to read, Arise and go away before the day guards come, And take your filthy carcass with you.'" Another of the boys, Irvy watching, had then "spit upon the buffalo" and made "an obscene gesture."[3]

Irvy had been "angry and offended" at the time, but now inside the "most beautiful capitol in the world" he feels "bewildered" by it all. Rather than educating him with the "history and symbolism of political freedom," the building's overwhelming aesthetic presence empties him out: "Head tipped back, he forgot everything that was behind him, and before," Sandoz asserts. His main impressions are of colors, and light, and meaningless if pleasing figures in the mosaics; one symbolic grouping appears only to be "a circle of slim, friendly women with clasped hands." Irvy then happens on a funeral in the rotunda (a "sweet sickish smell . . . strong in his nose"), the casket holding a man "he had never seen in the papers" yet who was privileged with a service in the capitol and "truckloads of flowers," whereas there had been "only a painted box for his father, with not one flower, not one." When Sandoz notes that "a bitterness came to the boy's tongue," the expectation is that here, at last, political consciousness will begin; when Irvy stumbles into an elevator and rides it upward in the great tower to "Memorial Hall, the Hall of Heroes" under the dome, an epiphany seems in the offing. But there amid the monumental black marble he perceives only a "silent emptiness" of "lonesomeness and death." Wandering outside onto a stone parapet, the thunderbirds and the Sower looming above him, Irvy sees no heart-swelling vista of the Nebraska landscape below, such as he used to from a hill overlooking the family farms. Here, he stares into a blotting fog: "The whole world was gone, fallen away, even as his father had dropped his hard life like a slack string." But in the nothingness he senses a "great and good aloneness . . . a rest and a forgetting" and unconsciously climbs up on the sloping outer wall of the parapet, allowing himself to slide down toward the comforting mist. Suddenly the fog parts, not enough to reveal an inspiriting scene but merely a fragment of it, "the ridge of a black roof" far beneath him, jolting Irvy into the realization that he is about to fall several hundred feet. Out of pure instinct he scrambles back over the parapet wall and crawls into the tower; he "lay there shaking," as the story ends, "his wet cheek against the black marble of the Hall of Heroes."[4]

Sandoz's allegory provides an impressionistic gauge of the severity of the Great Depression, a sense of the hopelessness of its darkest days, when mere survival could be counted heroic. The story also furnishes a glimpse into the void of belief and direction gaping within many ordinary people whose most cherished myths—the promise of the frontier and mobility, the solidity of democratic principles—appeared to have collapsed. Sandoz further suggests, significantly, that the unfocused despair and resentment embodied by Irvy and the gang of homeless boys, or by extension most Americans, could be either apolitical or, potentially, prepolitical. She implies that a short fuse existed among the down-and-out yet leaves ambiguous whether their politicization (or the failure thereof) will manifest itself as a further descent into Irvy's kind of personal paralysis, as a class-fired populist renewal of democracy, as a disintegration into anarchy, or, possibly, as a darker turn toward home-grown dictatorship. The "mist" of the title represents the collapse of meaning, and it also enshrouds the future. It is the pall of apprehension that fell over America during the Great Depression, the most severe national crisis since the Civil War.

The story can therefore be read as a description of the "moment" in which the regionalist movement might exercise its would-be "leadership towards a usable culture," the moment when the American dream was thrown into doubt, and when many people, like Irvy, were searching for cultural and political guidance. As B. A. Botkin noted at the time, the "economic crisis" seemed paradoxically to have given the regionalist movement "significance, direction, and even motivation." This curious mind-set of utopian aspiration mingled with general foreboding emerged among many in the movement, and it was well displayed in a 1934 essay written by Howard Odum, making "The Case for Regional-National Social Planning." Odum surveyed the range of possible undesirable futures lying ahead of America: "general chaos . . . violent revolution . . . a new and increased dominance of corporate business . . . dictatorship. . . ." The final possibility was the "most vividly discussed in the United States," he wrote, because it was widely assumed that "in the failure of 'recovery' or of a better planned and ordered democracy would inhere the strength of fascism or its equivalent."[5]

There were undoubtedly good reasons for the regionalist vanguard to be obsessed with such possibilities. Only a year before, in 1933, the efforts of another vanguard a world away—begun during the 1920s as a fringe movement in provincial Bavaria—had convinced German voters to repudiate the "leaderless democracy" of the utterly discredited Weimar system in favor of the "National Socialist order and discipline" represented in "the Fuhrer, the Prophet, the Fighter," Adolf Hitler. ("For us in Germany, especially, parliamentary democracy is a foreign body," the Prophet later remarked. "It is not native to us, and does not belong to our tradition.") And in the same year, cadres of yet another variety, rejecting the capitalist chaos of the 1920s New Economic Policy, were fanning out into the Russian countryside, redoubling their attempt to establish a collectivized and "dekulakized" agriculture against stiff peasant resistance. ("Throw your bourgeois humanitarianism out of the window and act like Bolsheviks worthy of Comrade Stalin," the cadres were exhorted. "You must assume your duties . . . without wimpering, without any rotten liberalism"; *"Don't be afraid of taking extreme measures. . . .* Comrade Stalin expects it of you.") As these shadows lengthened across the world, regionalists watched with further dismay when a resurgent 100 percent Americanism began to take equally sinister antidemocratic turns at home. Cumulatively, the overlapping economic and political crises of the 1930s were important contextual precipitants spurring the urgent and ill-fated attempts of their fragile project to establish a new ideology, their "heroic efforts" (in Odum's words) "to conserve for the nation as much as possible of the Jeffersonian democracy of the simple rural culture to which will be added the building of a still greater democracy for the vast, complex, urban, and industrial America of the future."[6]

But for those like Botkin who hoped to provide cultural leadership toward this future, Sandoz's fictional depiction of an uninspired confrontation with Goodhue's symbol-laden building must also be seen as something of a caveat, a caveat that in the end proved to be all too accurate. By the mid-1930s, in fact, the more theoretically minded among regionalists were already beginning to perceive some of the limits of their cultural radicalism, quite aware that despite several years of "heroic efforts," they had not as yet instilled an "art consciousness" in their intended audience or nurtured in it a noticeable amount of "spiritual growth"—growth away from the failed industrial-capitalist system and toward the regionalist utopia. Surveying the degree of progress as of late 1934, Botkin was forced to conclude that regionalism had "failed to make itself felt as a vital and practical force in the whole of American life." It had, he surmised, "still to demonstrate its value as a way of living or even a successful literary program."[7]

Yet as was true of most regionalists during the dismal and exhilarating early 1930s, it was hard to cool Botkin's fervor. If his analysis was less than encouraging, it was merely prefatory to a new plan of action put forward in "Regionalism: The Next Step" and subsequent articles, in which he called for a redoubling of the "creative activity of writers, readers, editors, publishers, critics, and teachers" to foster "a regional public for regional art." The doctrine of regionalism remained, he asserted, a "symbol of decentralization" and a "rallying-point for bankrupt cultural and creative energies" pitted against "metropolitan and industrial standardization and centralization," its proselytizers more than ever determined to break the megalopolitan "stranglehold on the life of the hinterland." But more importantly, Botkin went on to argue that in light of the movement's undeniable lack of transformative impact, the "next step" for regionalists, moving beyond the first-stage "ground-clearing and spadework" of "proving that there are regional and folk cultures," must also involve a "mingling" of "native with cosmopolitan and proletarian influences." He was frank: since the onset of the depression, the "class struggle" particularly had "loomed larger as a theme for literature and an issue in criticism," making regionalism seem "a romantic, nostalgic, and anachronistic escape." An appropriative "mingling" to overcome this deficiency, however, did not mean a full embrace of social scientific analytic categories, or "experimental 'advance guard'" artistic techniques, or doctrinaire political creeds like Marxism—far from it. What was most essential was a more presentist orientation, a more "realistic" approach, as he later elaborated: "if regionalists understood contemporary social realities they would see and record the changes in their regional life and, conversely, in order to see and record these changes they would have to understand contemporary life." In short, regionalists must desist from their tendency to deal in pure myth and redirect their efforts toward a confrontation with problematized myth—toward *history*, past and present—"to integrate past and present."[8] Such a redirection, he implied (and in other essays demonstrated with his own use of anthropology), could be accomplished by the disenchanting tools of social science and cultural modernism. But "ideology" was yet more crucial to it, for therein the sinews of power structures were revealed to explain why folk-regional myths were not only problematized (existing in partially realized form) but also, more pointedly, imperiled (threatened with extinction). The redirection, the next step, must, in other words, emerge as a process of politicization.

"Mythology," Botkin made clear, was itself crucial to this process, "not only as a conserver," he wrote, "but as a selector and integrator of cultural values." In "Mist," Sandoz showed an individual consciousness "dispossessed" from communal myths; Irvy confronts history as pure irrational flux. An ideology such as Marxism could be an "organizer" of this flux. But implicit in Botkin's personal arm's-length flirtation with Marxism (to emerge later in the decade) was a critique of its abstractness and its reductiveness, tendencies that could themselves act as imperiling forces. In a paper read at the communist-dominated Second American Writers' Congress of 1937, he argued that regionalism performed "valuable functions for both society and literature," because by creatively engaging regional cultures with their "'slow accretions of folk elements,'" elements that embodied the "'humble influences of place and kinship and common emotion'" (quoting Constance Rourke), it promoted "a sense of basic human relationships." (In contrast, the contemporaneous "application" of Marxist principles taking place in the provinces of the Soviet Union necessitated that cadres "eradicate the economic and cultural anachronisms of the nationalities"—as one policy statement put it—peasant econo-

mies, village ties, languages, churches, all the folkish obstacles to the industrialized national homogeneity conceived in the Five-Year plans.) The equally
abstract liberalism to which most other regionalists adhered seemed to be in
need of a similar grounding in folk-regional myths and traditions—this was to
be the essence of the hoped-for revitalization of American political culture. As
Botkin noted in his 1934 analysis of writers like Erskine Caldwell who were
"interested in a regionalism of . . . the 'masses' as well as the 'folk'": "Refusing to be taken in wholly by ideology or mythology, they are striving, rather,
for a fusion of the two." Drawing on a "native tradition that is at once
provincial and cosmopolitan, social and individual," as well as "contemporary
and realistic," Botkin insisted, the "motifs, images, symbols, slogans, and
idioms" of regionalism could thus instill the polity with "regional, class, and
other forms of collective consciousness." As an educative "interpreter of social
thought," shaping it around the concrete through the power of art, regionalism could, he believed, assist national "integration and re-orientation by
helping us to understand and respect one another, and by showing the failure
and breakdown of old patterns and the growth of and hope for new ones"—
hope for the Irvys of America.[9]

When Botkin confessed his as yet unrealized aspiration of making regionalism "a vital and practical force in the whole of American life," he was expressing the desire that it might become a new national ideology—an impulse which
he shared with many others around the country. In essence, when he wrote of
the role of regionalism in conserving, selecting, integrating, and interpreting
"cultural values" and "social thought," he was describing the complex process
by which an ideology is created.[10] This process was initiated, as it always is,
out of a perception of cultural crisis, the interwar crisis when regional-national
myths seemed threatened with extinction and a period in which other ideologies, and liberalism particularly, seemed unable to provide social coherence—ideologies arise for precisely this purpose. During the 1930s, there was
a groping search by regionalists through the cultural materials at hand, the
received ideologies and traditions (including the tenuous remains of republicanism, utopian socialism, and Populism), for the instrumentalities, institutions, analytic constructs, and other politically useful means necessary to
bring their regional myths and ideals to concrete realization—which is the
goal of an ideology. This congeries of older political inheritances and contemporary elements they would then synthesize, transmute, and systematize into
a novel formulation, the ideology proper. The individuals engaged in this
search converged on it from a diversity of intellectual and political orientations, many of them self-described "liberals," "radicals," or, by turns, "conservatives," and because all of them hoped to find a new ideological home in
regionalism—alternative to liberalism, communism, or fascism—it meant

that the process of the movement's self-definition, especially at the programmatic level, would necessarily be a divisive and contentious one. Yet just as
there were broad common tendencies within the assumptions motivating the
cultural project of the regional renaissance (conceptions of folk, targets of
criticism, suggested remedies)—those shared ideas and beliefs that made the
regionalist movement a *movement*—so too did the politicization of regionalism, its more formal and purposeful construction as a new national ideology,
coalesce around certain widely held themes, particularly themes articulating a
crisis and critique of American exceptionalism.

As Botkin suggested, the "first stage" involved in the creation of an ideology
is the task of mythmaking, the task that preoccupied regionalists especially
during the 1920s and early 1930s, when as participants in the renaissance they
conceived their visions of folk-Indian, noncoercive, aesthetic-symbiotic societies. Mythmaking is, in fact, the first stage of ideologization not in a merely
preliminary sense but constitutes an ideology's foundation. Myths interpret
the world, provide meaning to people, and, through their function in an
ideology, prescribe behavior and legitimate power. But myths in themselves,
especially those mined from previous historical contexts (the "older America")
by the conservative sensibility of regionalists, possess little or no political
potency unless they can be made "contemporary and realistic," as Botkin put
it; doing so is the job of an ideology. Regionalists became politicized, at varying
rates and degrees, when they witnessed the hegemony of megalopolitanism
and 100 percent Americanism apparently dysfunctioning in the empty materialism of the 1920s and meeting its catastrophic comeuppance, at the cost of
widespread apprehension and hardship, during the depression years. The shift
in consciousness was as Botkin described it: from an apolitical estrangement,
an "escape" into a mythic past (as well as a utopian future, in the case of the
planners), toward a confrontation with history, with "contemporary social
realities," armed and guided by those myths. The crisis demanded leadership
and action. By the middle of the decade certainly, politicization, in all manner of
directions, was everywhere proceeding apace. Even J. Frank Dobie, one of the
most antiquarian of all regionalists ("The object of humanistic folklorists is not
to destroy myths . . . but to foster them!"), found himself "becoming a
contemporary with myself," as he told Walter Prescott Webb in 1937:

My sympathy for a past that is now as remote as the "university" pre-
sided over by Socrates has blinded me to almost everything going on in
the modern world; rather, it has prejudiced me against it so that I was
indifferent to understanding it. At one time I thought I would emulate
Charles Lamb: "Hang posterity; I will write for antiquity." For the last

four or five years, however, I have been finding that philosophy utterly inadequate.[11]

In this shift by regionalists toward a presentist orientation, their chronicling of the "failure and breakdown of old patterns and the growth of and hope for new ones" took on an ideological "charge," a charge reflected in the analytic frameworks and methodologies and in the very style and tone of their works. This ideological charge was directed toward *delegitimizing* the socioeconomic system that had brought America to ruin, and indicated as well (often allegorically, obliquely) the possible programmatic ways to national salvation. The urge to understand "contemporary social realities" in order to "see and record the changes in their regional life" (in Botkin's words) manifested itself as presentist and sometimes polemical history, as social or cultural criticism, and as "socially conscious" and iconoclastic art, all presenting variations on a basic theme of imperilment: the evil of the current socioeconomic order in its degradation of the last bedraggled remnants of the folk, who, despite their plight, yet embodied the humane values by which America might redeem itself.

Through this thematic scenario, the attack on the industrial system largely generalized or implicit in the conceptualizations of the folk put forward in the cultural critiques and manifestos of the late 1920s and early 1930s—the alienation from nature, the loss of economic and political independence, the atomization of community life—became more explicit, more clearly and provocatively defined, as all the cultural wreckage left in the wake of capitalist expansion was conveyed now in a charged language of power, oppression, exploitation, and acculturation. Newly employed categories of race and class, psychological, anthropological, and historical models, and economic and sociological indices all tended to raise the rhetorical key of regionalist works during the depression "moment," when it seemed the powers that be might at last be forced to yield before a public sufficiently aroused, its consciousness raised, by images of the system's worst victims—for the public was now itself a victim. To this end, regionalists ideologically reconfigured, sharpened to a critical point, the iconography of folk and rural life latent in mainstream political culture and still evocative even for city dwellers of the period, not a few of whom were but one generation removed from the farm and small town. In these "contemporary and realistic" studies and portrayals, the nation might come to see (the assumption among regionalists seemed to be) how threatened was this last repository of virtue, of the "real America." The goal of this task of delegitimation was to lay bare the vectors of power underlying the regnant corporate-megalopolitan order, to reveal this "geography of power" to the public as something alien and immoral (from the standpoint of "true" folk-regional values) which persisted primarily because of sheer power, and thus, most importantly, to persuade them of its onerousness, as something that must be "thrown off." Yet the regionalist rhetorical fulcrum must also push delegitimation further, to convince the public that the people themselves were also implicated with the powers that be, that their own behavior and beliefs— pursuing wealth, discarding folkness—had brought America into its current crisis. To accomplish this far more difficult feat, regionalist cultural radicals reappraised and rewrote some of the most basic myth-historical narratives underlying the cultural, political, and economic framework of modern America; in fact, they turned those narratives against that framework by what was often an agonizing process of realist disenchantment. Regionalists usually shared at least some of the myths they were now revealing to be hypocritical smokescreens, and they had to endure the loss, the consignment to the past (as Dobie did) of cherished folk-regional values they now knew in their more mature historical consciousness to be obsolete. As Thomas Wolfe remarked with typical overstatement, but appropriate tone: "With loathing, horror, shame, and anguish of the soul unspeakable—as well as with love—we've got to face the total horror of our self-betrayal, the way America has betrayed herself."[12]

Images of a postfrontier American wasteland (see Figure 5.1) did undoubtedly haunt the national mind during the 1930s, and it was by confronting the public with such images, images that called into question the *frontier myth*, the central narrative of the American dream of endless opportunity and mobility, that regionalists rested their primary hopes of delegitimizing the corporate-megalopolitan system. But as Wolfe's observation indicates, obtaining a critical distance from these most fundamental of myths and values involved emotional, psychological, and intellectual travails that even the "cultural radicals" of the regionalist movement, much less the average American, were often reluctant to undergo. In fact, through the interpretive and personal struggles of one reluctant regionalist cultural radical in particular, Dobie's colleague, Texas historian Walter Prescott Webb, the larger national trauma of the depression years may be read. Most importantly, Webb's attempts to move beyond regional-national myths reveal the *limits* of that trauma, the limits beyond which Webb himself was "loathe" to look, and against which other, more tough-minded and radicalized regionalists pushed hard, seeking to persuade and shame mainstream Americans beyond, but ultimately to no avail. As events revealed, if that trauma had erupted during the "moment" of

Figure 5.1 Photograph and caption (by M. L. Wilson and Ray Bowden) from *An American Exodus* (1939 edition), "Dust Bowl" chapter, p. 98: " 'Every deserted homestead shack is the key to some unwritten story that strikes deep.' Oldham County, Texas Panhandle. June 1938." (Photograph by Dorothea Lange, courtesy of the Dorothea Lange Collection, The City of Oakland, The Oakland Museum, 1993)

the depression and its no-growth "mature economy," when the American dream seemed suddenly (to Webb and many others) to have come to an end, it merely kindled the public's desire not for an alternative way of life, but to have the dream back again.

Over a number of painful years, however, regionalists like Webb came to recognize that it could never come back on the same terms it had once been pursued. Developing in *The Great Plains* (1931) and subsequent works a history of the influence of abundance and especially, natural abundance, on the national character and on the health of democracy, Webb was to see in ominous developments since the closing of the frontier the shape of an America where there was *not* "room for everybody," as Crèvecoeur had eulogized from the early New York frontier, contemplating a virgin continent which was then, it seemed, barely tapped. A century and a half later, contemplating instead the

possibility that the New World might be declining into an Old World configuration of power from which its abundance had always promised liberation, Webb
wrote in *Divided We Stand: The Crisis of a Frontierless Democracy* (1937):

> For nearly three centuries America drank deep of the potent wine of the
> frontier, a wine which produced exhilarating experiences of freedom,
> adventure, and boundless opportunity. It was a long, gay evening, but
> now America must face the morning after with its headache, moody
> introspection, and pathetic glance at an empty bottle wherein only the
> tantalizing odor of the wine remains.[13]

Writing from under the "pall of apprehension" generated by this sense of disintegrating exceptionalism, other regionalist cultural radicals, less enamored
of the American dream than Webb, would begin to question whether America
in the past or in the present had *ever* offered "everybody" freedom and
opportunity, and, furthermore, whether the American dream was worth the
price of emptying the bottle of the continent. Taking the measure of that price
in drunken Indians, shiftless sharecroppers, and white-trash migrants, they
began to write the "unwritten story" of frontier and postfrontier America.

Webb himself was, to be sure, an unlikely cultural radical in many regards:
product of a self-perceived rags-to-riches rise out of a Texas homestead to a
professorship at the state university (with visiting positions during the 1930s
and early 1940s at Harvard, Oxford, and the University of London), investor
in local Austin-area real estate, owner of the Friday Mountain Ranch, prominent member of the Town-and-Gown Club—all in all, he was a solid citizen.
Yet over the course of this classic American story of mobility he had also
acquired the store of memory and experience that made him a regionalist:
glimpses of an older cooperative economy in the rural environs and small
towns of Stephens County, "where there were no classes and few social
distinctions," and in the assistance he received from a distant benefactor
("there is no such word as fail, in the lexicon of youth," he was told); exposure
to populist radicalism during a brief period when "practically the entire community became socialistic" and held "encampments, bringing in speakers . . .
to harangue at the government and berate the capitalists"; remembrance of
the words of old-timers who were themselves "full of memories and eloquent
in relating them to small boys"—"Indian fighters, buffalo hunters, trail-
drivers, half-reformed outlaws, and Oklahoma boomers"; and, "lurking in
every motte and hollow" of his childhood world, the "red ghosts" of the
dreaded Comanche, "so recently departed." In sum, he later wrote, "there I
touched the hem of the garment of the real frontier," of the "whole Great
Plains in microcosm," the regional site of the heavily mythologized (in both
scholarly and popular works) national archetypes of frontier existence—the

Cattle Kingdom and the sod-house, dug-out settlement of the prairie–high plains frontier that superseded it in the vast interior of the country from Texas to North Dakota. There, most essentially, Webb had also the regionalist experience of cultural dissolution: "It seemed that I was in on the tag end of all the frontier life . . . and was to be in on the very end of homesteading, of having land fresh from the hand of God."[14]

As such a phrase should make clear, Webb was never really able to relinquish much of the national mythology that he learned from the Texas frontier (from the *closing* Texas frontier, the true "ghost" which haunted him) and from his personal mobility out of that setting. "What a century the nineteenth was, when any boy who was willing to pay the price could go anyplace he desired," he wrote (and was still writing as late as 1945) of the amazingly short period it took to settle Crèvecoeur's limitless vista. Because of the abundance of free land "fresh from the hand of God," that price (according to the frontier myth codified by Frederick Jackson Turner and given perhaps its last seminal expression by Webb) had been "exceptionally" low. Unlike the Old World, where the little man could become socially mobile only by waging class war on entrenched social hierarchies, and where whole nations must conquer others to improve their lot, America (so went the myth) had been blessed with a bountiful and practically empty "wilderness"—the key euphemism. Webb's *The Great Plains* was on one level a chronicle of the pinnacle of the great age of producerist expansion into this wilderness, of the Cattle Kingdom, which had arisen for a short and vibrant period on the vast decentralized range commons of the Plains to do business "magnificently" and heroically: "Hot days in the branding pen with bawling calves and the smell of burned hair and flesh on the wind!" Webb marveled. "Men in boots and big hats, with the accompaniment of jingling spurs and frisky horses. Camp cook and horse wrangler! Profanity and huge appetites!" Arriving soon after the cowboys in the march of Progress—so Webb continued his mythicized narrative—were the homesteaders, men like his own father and neighbors, who had become "landowners by the simple process of fencing land and living on it." He noted: "Without the frontier, all of them could not have owned homes, and none of them could have become very prosperous." But each received his freehold, joining in the "free and unlimited appropriation of national wealth" (as he wrote in *Divided We Stand*) that fostered individualism, equality, and, ultimately, democracy. Webb praised the "wise and far-seeing" Thomas Jefferson, who, in Crèvecoeur's time, had early "realized that only the frontier could make democracy secure in America." Looking out at "almost a continent" that beckoned from the West, Jefferson had "wanted to acquire it all, even to the Pacific, as a field of expansion for the democratic system," as an empire for liberty.[15]

In recounting the history of the spread of this empire into the environment of the Plains, Webb's *The Great Plains* was, more pointedly, an analysis of the processes by which a regional culture was created. The work was an attempt to reassert some sense of regional distinctiveness during the 1920s era of mass cultural standardization (of which Webb's fellow Texans, like most Americans, were happy and unworried consumers in the interwar years) that was effacing whatever was still left of the heroic Cattle Kingdom and sod-house frontiers. In 1924 cowboy-turned-writer Andy Adams, on hearing of Webb's nascent project to make Texas thus "conscious of her past," perceived with perhaps inadvertent insight its place in the emerging liturgy of the regionalist civic religion: "You have the material at your door. The material in your capital building rested in a rock quarry near, until an architect designed it, and the structure arose, conforming to the lines of beauty, from dormant material." Mythologizing, Webb shaped that material to prove that the West was not "a mere extension of things Eastern." He argued in his famous vision/thesis that on the rainfall line coinciding roughly with the ninety-eighth meridian lay an "institutional *fault*" beyond which "ways of life and of living changed." The "cultural complexes" ("weapons, tools, law, and literature") developed over two centuries of pioneering in the humid, wooded East were, when "carried across it . . . either broken and remade or else greatly altered" by contact with the Indians and by the necessities of a radically new environment—"level, timberless, semi-arid." The settlement of the Great Plains had thereby inaugurated a "gigantic human experiment with an environment," resulting in "Western life and institutions" with a "singularly unique and elusive character." The Cattle Kingdom especially was "a world within itself, with a culture all its own, which, though of brief duration, was complete and self-satisfying"—a folkishly "*natural* economic and social order" (italics mine). There the "rarefied population" inhabiting the range commons was governed by the libertarian "code of the West," which demanded, Webb declared, "what Roosevelt called a square deal; it demanded fair play." According to its dictates, "men were all equal. Each was his own defender. His survival imposed upon him certain obligations which, if he were a man, he would accept." By this means "he not only attested his courage but implied that he was skilled in the art of living"—among the loose, noncoercive, and decentralized community of "tall figures" (as Sandoz called them) in this "world" on the Plains. In the broadest sense *The Great Plains* was, at bottom, Webb's attempt to reassert American exceptionalism, conceived in retreat now westward to the interior from Crèvecoeur's original declaration of it in the colonies (now corporatized), from Turner's in the Mississippi "Valley of Democracy" (now industrialized), to the " 'new phase of Aryan civilization' " (as he quoted John Wesley Powell) arising in the Plains region, "a new civilization unlike anything previously known to the Anglo-European-American experience." Here was the *new* New World, and the last abundant stronghold of the empire of liberty for a "brief duration" before "the forces of the Industrial Revolution began to modify and destroy it."[16]

If *The Great Plains* was therefore very much a work out of the 1920s mythmaking phase of the regionalist movement, Webb's *Divided We Stand*, as a tract written in six furious weeks, well signified the difficulties that he and other regionalists had in moving beyond their myths and developing an effective depression politics. Carrying the narrative forward into the "crisis" of the postfrontier, *closed* frontier era, he used many of the terms from *The Great Plains* notched now appropriately upward into a politicized key, a *sectional* key, to demonstrate the processes by which a regional culture, and the *new* New World, were being obliterated. For rather than the "unfenced world" of Dobie's vaquero, or Per Hansa's vision of homesteaders stretching "neighbor to neighbor, clear out to the Rocky Mountains," Webb and other Plains regionalists during the 1930s were confronted with the freehold empire rolled back by debt and dust, Sandoz's emblematic Irvy fleeing literally and figuratively *eastward* four hundred miles from home to hopelessness ("Eastward I go only by force," went Thoreau's axiom, "but westward I go free"). Watching the ranks of the unemployed mount into the millions, Webb argued in *Divided We Stand* (still in the mythic mode, as had so many before him and as did many contemporaries) that "the frontier was above all else an outlet, a safety valve when [social] pressure was too high" in the already-settled states of the union, allowing America (at least before the official closing in 1890) to escape "those serious problems that arise when a nation is closed tight within unexpanding boundaries"—particularly Old World class stratification and class conflict. His subsequent presentist depiction of this earlier, expansive America where there was "room for everybody" as having since become an "empty bottle" indicated his effort to move interpretively beyond myth to *history*. He was no longer living in the past but distinguishing it as *past* from present day. He admitted as much in an observation on Turnerian historians that was also a confession of sorts: "The historians have not yet seemed to realize that if the frontier was a dominant force until 1890, the absence of the frontier has been just as dominant since 1890. They have accepted the thesis that the frontier shaped American life, but they have not so readily accepted the corollary that the absence of the frontier must change the shape."[17]

The "shape" that Webb and they could "not so readily accept," the basic "plot" of the "unwritten story" that regionalists wrote in the 1930s, was the hierarchical and coercive Old World contours of power apparently emerging for the first time in an America (or in their consciousness?) that now seemed to have "turned back upon itself," like any blood-soaked and oppressive European country. As for most American artists and intellectuals, the depression "moment" forced regionalists to confront the issue not only of catastrophic impoverishment, but also of America's long-term, endemic poverty ("Among the people is a class commonly referred to as the poor," Webb noticed), as well as the sinews of monopolistic corporate power that the apparently bloated but actually hollow prosperity of the 1920s had kept hidden. Without the safety valve, Webb reasoned apprehensively, "danger arises when a few become very rich and many become very poor." And whether democracy could "survive these changes," he wrote, was the "paramount issue" and the one he proceeded to address for his audience.[18]

Despite the extremity of some of its rhetoric, Webb's consequent analysis of the "shape" of power in America was at once incisive and gingerly, limited by his reluctance to let go of some of the most basic myths undergirding American exceptionalism, and his home region. For the critique of *Divided We Stand* hinged not on concerns over an emerging lopsided and "divided" (polarized) hierarchy of classes in the New World—Webb's deepest worries notwithstanding—but, widening its scope so that class structure was no longer discernible, it centered on the development of a "feudal" relationship between the *sections*. "Just how united are these United States?" he asked at the outset, then went on to claim that there were "fault lines" that "divide the nation into distinct social and economic sections"—North, South, and West— "each with its own mores, ways of life, and culture complexes, which have thus far refused to be obliterated." Because the Northerners were "the masters of the Industrial Revolution," Webb argued, the "story of the sections since the Civil War" was the story of "how the North has extended its economic conquest over the other two sections, how it has drawn the bonds constantly tighter until it owns not only its own section but a controlling interest in the South and the West." (The writing of the tract was triggered after Supreme Court justices declared the New Deal's AAA farm subsidy programs, which were favorable to the West and the South, unconstitutional.) This issue of "control" was a key one for regionalists like Webb, who judged modernity from the myth-historicist perspective of states' rights Southern Democratic political culture, populist neo-republicanism, and the code of the West adhered to by the ranchers, small farmers, and townspeople of Texas. To be independent, to be one's own man socially, politically, and, most crucially, economically, was the chief virtue in this worldview. His was a cultural radicalism from the perspective of the old-fashioned, solid producerist citizen, viewing with dismay the development of a new consumer economy and mentality, lurking at their heart the "dominant force" of the postfrontier era, the "Modern American Corporation." Webb's delegitimizing rhetoric in *Divided We Stand* thus played directly on fears of the loss of individual control over livelihood and, by extension, loss of local and sectional "control" as well, for not only did his still-mythicizing mind assume the existence of these besieged communities of interests, but also such a depiction made the vectors of power more simple, more clear, and more stark:

> . . . I see people everywhere in chains. Wherever I turn in the South and the West I find people busily engaged in paying tribute to someone in the North. If I could paint a picture representing the general scene, it would be in the form of a great field stretching from Virginia to Florida westward to the Pacific and from Texas and California northward to Canada, an L-shaped region comprising nearly four-fifths of the country. Here millions of people would be playing a game with pennies, nickels, dimes, and dollars, rolling them northward and eastward where they are being stacked almost to the moon.[19]

Webb meant "chains" in both a metaphorical and a literal sense. The North (he wrote in a language of victimization) "raped the states of the South and the West of their natural resources," and its corporations monopolized the production of consumer goods and, increasingly and more visibly, the distribution and marketing of those goods. The spread of Northern-headquartered chain stores drained off sectional wealth, displaced the local "little independent merchant," and turned their employees into uniformed "vassals." Webb's elaborately developed analogy of dominance and subservience was (intentionally) to medieval feudalism, to the "growing fiefs of the feudal lords" of the North. Even the farmer was in thrall to them, "dependent where once he was free," a "retainer" of the tractor manufacturers, automobile dealers, gas stations, and feed companies. Deploring the overmechanized operation of a fictional farmer, Webb wrote: "Something fine has gone out of that farm, and that is the spirit of independence and self-sufficiency that was present when mules were pulling the plow and the colt that had not yet felt the collar was frolicking in the meadow. . . . Something fine has gone out of John Smith, something of the spirit of independence."[20]

This analysis of *Divided We Stand*, with its portrayal of the maldistribution of the nation's capital and industrial base, was compelling in many ways. Webb's concerns about the deleterious effects of economic "colonialism" and centralization were widely shared among regionalists ("you have come very, very near to the deepest things in me," fellow Texan J. Frank Dobie told Webb in the earlier-quoted letter confessing his political awakening), and the book even made the rounds of the Roosevelt administration. Yet in laying down this broadest grid of the regionalist geography of power, Webb's analysis was significant as much for what it evaded as for what it revealed. The sectional perspective, so to speak, allowed him to behold the mote of "feudalism" in his Northern brother's eye while missing the class-stratified beam in the eye of the other two regions, especially the South. "Simplifying" his analytic framework to the sectional level, Webb the solid citizen (and the devotee of a mythicized Stephens County frontier, "where there were no classes and few social distinctions") carefully picked his way around such disenchanting and explosive issues. Indeed, he seemed at times at least half conscious of the potency of a class analysis to dissolve the sectional communities of interest between rich and poor, the mythicized cultural bonds holding them together, that he posed against the North as "King of Things." Standing far back from the map, he circled around such issues nervously. The "farmers and laborers" of the North, he admitted at one point, "are in the same position as these same classes in the South and the West. That is to say, the division in society is horizontal in the North, separating people into upper and lower strata"—quickly widening his focus to the national scale, Webb then backed away from this locally touchy area—"but when we view the three sections together . . . we find the division is strikingly geographic. Practically all the people of the South and West belong with the Northern masses to the lower income group"—all fellow victims. And again, after conceding that "there are also poor" in the South and the West, Webb immediately retreated with the stipulation that "this is not a story of rich and poor, and how each became such. It is a simpler story: that the North as a section is rich, and becoming richer; the South and the West are poor, and becoming relatively poorer."[21]

Although acknowledging that this colonial configuration of power had arisen in the closed-frontier era, Webb's own allegiance to the frontier myth would not allow him to penetrate further conceptually into the "unwritten story" of the frontier and postfrontier world. He could not confront the consequences for exceptionalism, for the myth itself, of any more analogies and parallels between Old World and New. Certain destabilizing implications—not merely "conceptual," but political—necessarily devolved from a recognition of social stratification and other features of a European configuration of power in America, and especially from a recognition of it out in the virtuous and victimized provinces. President Roosevelt's adoption of the language of "economic royalism" during the so-called populist phase of the New Deal, when his administration pushed more thoroughgoing reforms against the opposition of big business, gives some hint of its potential potency. Yet large corporations were relatively safe targets for criticism during the depression; it was when other, equally exploitative vectors of power began to be traced back to their origins in the localities, and when those vectors were contextualized by cultural radicals from the perspective of "betrayed" folk-regional traditions, that the real delegitimizing "charge" latent in the rhetoric of a lost exceptionalism began to be released. Webb shrank from turning that charge against his fellow

Texans, because he could not bear to lose a worldview. Other regionalists, however, came to perceive all the social ills and unexceptional power structures which had been legitimated on behalf of frontier-inspired rugged individualism, mobility, and opportunity, and which had, ironically, developed precisely because of such blind sides. For a number of these more radical regionalists, leftward of the reluctant Webb, their realist examination of the postfrontier "empty bottle" of 1930s America would ramify throughout their conceptualization of national history and lead them to begin to question, and reconfigure, the meaning of the frontier myth itself. If Webb and others conceptualized, and shrank from the implications of, a *postexceptional* America— an America in decline from a freer, folkish frontier past—the realist members of the movement were to author a *nonexceptional* version of America's past, the "unwritten story" of an America that had never been "exceptional" in its degree of freedom, never possessed an easy abundance, never built a model society—though it had demolished more than one. Theirs would be not a conqueror's, but a victim's history of the United States, history viewed through the eyes of Indians, African Americans, and even the conquering European immigrants and their descendants who, while imposing the "empire for liberty" on these other American folk, "betrayed" and victimized their own kind as well, in ways that Webb could not (at first) accept.

Yet there was still another possible regionalist response to the contemporary specter of an unexceptional America (for "European" patterns of power were all in the definition), a conservative response more extreme and individually reassuring than the wavering Webb's, and, by turns, a reactionary response directed against the revelations that those other, radicalized regionalists were to make on the blind side of sectional values. If the delegitimizing rhetorical device of the "section as victim" might not only lay bare the broadest inequities of the corporate system but constitute as well an unconscious means of evading issues such as *local* class stratification, issues too bleak to confront for a neo-Jeffersonian democrat like the myth-blinkered Webb, it could also provide a more self-conscious way of obscuring social arrangements and power structures that one deliberately wanted left unseen and untampered with. A sectional analysis could be a way, in short, of rallying the locals emotionally and unreflectively around a flag of chauvinism directed against "outsiders" who seemed to threaten structures and values deemed basic to a regional way of life. Such "defensiveness," of course, had a long lineage in the South, but in the hands of a Donald Davidson (the foremost exponent of sectionalism during the 1930s) it was carried to new heights of analytic sophistication—sophisticated enough to reject the sunny social forecasts of New South Progress and, simultaneously, to depict blacks with ostensible objectivity as the regional wellspring of "devoted servants and social problems, cheap labor and hideous slums, an endless flow of folklore and anecdote, and eternal apprehension for the future." But when that essentially racist apprehension was pressured, as it was by regionalist sociology and some New Deal policies, Davidson's (and by extension, the Agrarian circle's) sectionalism could all too easily revert to its traditional function: preserving the South's class and racial caste system from "outside interference" and any real challenge whatsoever. As liberal University of North Carolina Press editor W. T. Couch observed:

> The Agrarian demand that Southern cultural differences, folk ways, and moral values be respected has all the earmarks of perfect amiability and reasonableness until you realize that lynching, and excessive homicide rates, and numerous other customs and habits equally reprehensible constitute a part of those things which the Agrarians wish to have respected. Of course, they deny this when cases are cited. But they are constantly harping on the disloyalty to the South of those who study these phenomena and attempt to find ways to correct or eliminate them.[22]

That epithet of disloyalty was the most reactionary dimension of a manifold sectionalist argument which aimed to delegitimize a broad range of social and economic change, and to do so by recourse to a parallel set of apprehensions bound up with American exceptionalism. Remarking on the fact that his own volume of prosectional essays, *The Attack on Leviathan* (1938), had originally been entitled *Divided We Stand*, Davidson told Webb that "it is mighty interesting, I think, that we hit on exactly the same watchword for exactly the same sort of fight." Certainly, Davidson's sectional viewpoint hinged like Webb's on a reluctance to question the "heroic tradition" of the frontier myth, of his own frontier Tennessee ancestors whom he had poetically eulogized in *The Tall Men.* Like Webb, Davidson believed that the "spirit of the Old Southwest"—"highly individualistic," connecting self-sufficiency and liberty "with free-hold of land" and requiring "that one defended one's own substance by one's own valor"—yet survived in the modern sectional culture of the South, but was besieged there by the forces of "Northeastern imperialism." As befitted his book's more strident and ominously allusive title, Davidson articulated the process of corporatization as a threat to a retreating exceptionalism in much more overt terms than Webb's:

> From the close of the Revolution to the present day the Northeast has had a strong tendency to look to contemporary Europe for its cue in economics, culture, and general philosophy, and to reject, as outmoded, many of the Americanisms which it once shared with other sections. But the South and the sections of the West have retained . . . a stubborn doubt of the merit of European importations.[23]

Davidson took his political bearings not only from the more moderate Jefferson but also from the writings of arch-agrarian John Taylor of Caroline and the secessionist John C. Calhoun ("These pages, rather than the pages of Karl Marx's Capital, would seem to be the proper guide for Americans who wish to interpret their history in the light of American conditions"). With this ammunition, Davidson showed his audience how "a free state . . . based on agrarianism" had been "converted into a servile state" through the machinations of an "aristocracy of credit, monopoly, and incorporation" that had arisen in Europe and had been operating in America since Alexander Hamilton's time, drawing all sections of the country under the dominion of the "consolidated industrial empire" of the Northeast until, finally, the nation "had become . . . far enmeshed in the European system." Jefferson had prophesied the consequences of this transformation, symptomatized most portentously in the spread of the "urban culture and ideology" that had "accompanied the steady infiltration of the Northeastern economy throughout the continent": "When we get piled upon one another in large cities, as in Europe," Jefferson wrote, "we shall become corrupt as in Europe, and go to eating one another as they do there."[24]

Yet while voicing genuine anxieties about a European pattern of power in the corporatized, urbanized New World, Davidson's further rhetorical purpose in raising the specter of lost exceptionalism was to stigmatize the efforts of "propagandists" such as Couch, Caldwell and Bourke-White, "the Harlan County visitors, the Scottsboro attorneys," and "the shock troops of Dayton and Gastonia," who, "on their missions of social justice," he complained, "asked no questions about the genius of place." The segregated South (segregation a key element of its "genius") was being victimized by the "tactics of distortion, abuse, polite tut-tutting, angry recrimination," and the "baser devices of journalistic lynching" which researchers and reformers were utilizing in their attempt to impose an alien northeastern-European uniformity on the whole of the nation—on what had always been a white man's country—"sternly [demanding] that the local arrangements be made to correspond with it, at whatever the cost" (see Figure 5.2). Davidson thus made clear to his fellow white Southerners what that cost might be: an "evil choice between Fascism and Communism" and the possibility of "a gross and inflated repetition of European disorders . . . in the Southern scene," what with "our predisposition to violence and our difficult racial situation." If this "situation" were not addressed according to "Southern principles," he warned, there was a grave risk of "falling into blind and violent divisions whose pent-up force will hurl us at each other's throats." We shall, Davidson concluded, "take to eating one another, as they do in Europe."[25]

Considered emblematically, the sectionalisms of the "culturally radical"

Figure 5.2 Photograph and caption from *You Have Seen
Their Faces*, p. 35: "Fairhope, Louisiana: 'Beat a dog and
he'll obey you. They say it's the same way with the
blacks.'" (Photograph by Margaret Bourke-White, courtesy of Life Magazine © Time Warner Inc. and the Margaret Bourke-White Collection, George Arents Research
Library, Syracuse University)

Webb and Davidson suggest the magnitude of the cultural and political inertia that was to confront the more reform-minded wings of the regionalist
movement at every turn. For every Webb who reluctantly acknowledged the
changed national circumstances of the closed frontier, there were a million
Western "rugged individuals" who believed they could continue plundering
natural (and human) resources as if the frontier still existed. For every Davidson who was willing to concede (at least rhetorically) that certain "local
arrangements . . . might well bear some mending," there was a section full of
Scottsboro jurors who would allow innocent blacks to be executed rather than
concede any flaws in those arrangements. These kinds of attitudes were
challenged no thanks to the postexceptional, sectionalist approach, which in
effect sealed off values attendant with the frontier myth in a lost but glorious
mythic past, yet thereby preserved that past as a repository of values legit-

imizing for a less historically conscious 100 percent American polity any number of contemporary "reprehensible . . . customs and habits" (as Couch had put it).

Instead, it was left to the more radical Indian subregionalists, Southern sociologists, and California socialists to build up an "Irresistible Force" of delegitimation against such "Immovable Bodies" (as Davidson termed them), taking the battle to the frontier myth wherever it persisted, past or present. Out in the Greater West, the historyless, limitless, future-oriented West, the main thrust of realist cultural radicalism assumed the form, aptly, of a revised frontier and postfrontier historical narrative, a "hidden history" (as Carey McWilliams called it) challenging many of the exceptionalist myths about the course of national expansion that Webb and his fellow solid citizens held dear. In the South, the tradition-bound, insular South, delegitimation efforts took most potent form as a sociological, realist "facing of absolute facts" (as Howard Odum wrote), with the goal of liberating the audience from social practices that had given rise to a very un-American configuration of power within the "most 'American' of all the regions." By these means, regionalists in the West and the South began to "gain in sharpness of focus" (in Paul Taylor's words) an understanding of who was victimizing whom in 1930s America, an understanding that necessarily problematized the sectional analyses of the Webbs and the Davidsons, complicating the regionalist geography of power, drawing the lines closer to home—and thereby making it more subversive. As Howard Odum determined about the prospects for "social justice" in the South, his words applicable to the other regions as well: "The evidence all indicates that it is not possible to make adjustments or work out solutions on any purely 'southern,' sectional basis, which logically would have in mind primarily the interests of the white South," the ruling whites.[26] Penetrating into remote corners of provincial America, to the other side of the mythic blind sides that preserved these "interests," regionalists acting on behalf of a *regional, pluralist* agenda would attempt to publicize and promote the "interests" of the myriad victims who dwelled there.

The regionalist "hidden history" of America—and its roll call of victims— began, fittingly enough, with the process of settlement and its consequences for the native tribes (see Figure 5.3). As an updated and classic restatement of the mythicized and blindsided account of this "simple process of fencing land and living on it," Webb's *The Great Plains* is a convenient foil. It was not that it provided an "untrue" version of Plains history, but rather that its account, like *Divided We Stand*'s of the contemporary world, was as significant for what it obscured as for what it revealed. Much of the book deals with the "obsta-

Figure 5.3 Photograph and caption (by Rupert Vance) from *An American Exodus*
(1939 edition), beginning of "Mid-Continent" chapter, p. 45: "Race for Claims at the
Opening of the Cherokee Outlet, 1893: 'Oklahoma was settled on the run by a white
pioneer yeomanry.'" (Photograph by P. A. Miller and Thomas Croft, courtesy of the
Archives and Manuscripts Division, Oklahoma Historical Society)

cles" that the "white pioneer yeomanry" encountered when they attempted
to settle the harsh environment of the Plains region, perhaps the most formidable being, in Webb's eyes, the "human barrier of untamed savagery" comprised by the Comanche and other tribes. Certainly they constituted, according to Webb, "the most effectual barrier ever set up by a native American
population against European invaders in a temperate zone," and by such
geographically and anthropologically inspired language he at times euphe-
mistically masked his own white Plainsman's bias—but at other points, as
above, it shone through the rhetoric of objectivity. Webb never fully considered the disenchanting implications for the frontier myth and its image of the
"low price" of New World abundance embodied in a conceptualization of the
Europeans as "invaders" or the Americans as "conquerors." The keystone of
this blind side was the equation of Indian domains with empty "wilderness,"
with "land fresh from the hand of God." On the Prairie Plains, Webb observed,
"the soil was ready for the plow, the land was rich, and the whole country was

converted almost instantly from wilderness to frontier farm home." There were no rocks to remove, no trees to clear, and—another element of the "wilderness"—"no Indians to fight or to fear." Other areas of the Plains region were not so fortunate: they needed irrigation, and there were a lot more Indians to clean out before land could be fenced, "frontier farm homes" erected—and not the relatively "civilized" Indians of the East, but (Webb wrote) Indians "more ferocious, implacable, and cruel than the other tribes." Occasionally, as noted, the cultural relativism borrowed from his readings in anthropology caused Webb to develop a curious double vision, critically distancing him from the "red ghosts" of his white Plainsman upbringing:

> To the white man, especially the Anglo-American, the Indian was primarily a warrior, a fighting man, an implacable foe. The Indian's economy of life, his philosophy, his soul, were secondary and of little concern. . . . It was only the Indian in war paint and feathers and on the warpath that ever gave the pioneer—the only one who faced the problem in a practical way—anything serious to think about; therefore, so far as the Indian goes, the historical problem comes down to the single issue of his ways in war—his methods and his weapons.[27]

Fundamentally, it was from this perspective, as a "problem" for the pioneers, as so many tree stumps to be removed from the path of the beneficent empire for liberty, that Webb the Anglo-American (like most Anglo-Americans) beheld the Indians.

The progress of the empire for liberty looked somewhat different from the Indians' side of the frontier, however, and it was from this perspective that a number of Indian subregionalists—namely, Angie Debo, John Joseph Mathews, and D'Arcy McNickle, all more "culturally radical" than Webb— wrote during the 1930s virtually a new narrative of American history. In this narrative, the *frontier* no longer had the meaning that decades of mythologizing had inflated it with. Instead, during this decade peculiarly obsessed by specters of conquest, oppression, conflict—in a word, *power*— the subregionalists strove to make Americans look beyond their blind side (Webb's blind side) at a "new frontier": not the advancing vanguard of civilization into untapped abundant wilderness, or of divine light into pagan darkness, but rather the invasion front of an alien and ruthless race into cherished homelands, establishing in its wake a regime dedicated to the Indians' cultural, social, political, and economic subjugation. It seemed, after all, that there had never been "room for everybody" in America, that land came not from God but fresh from the hands of the Indians, that people had therefore been "eating one another" in the New World for centuries. Working out of these revised assumptions, Debo, Mathews, and McNickle related stories and histories of frontier and postfrontier worlds previously hidden in the innocent narrative demanded by the American dream.

Debo dealt most directly and self-consciously with reconfiguring that narrative, specifically with its more sophisticated and self-critical academic explication in the Progressive history paradigm. Her own major work of the 1930s, *And Still the Waters Run: The Betrayal of the Five Civilized Tribes* (1940), whose publication was delayed several years by censorship attempts, shared with the Progressive corpus a focus on the economic dimension in American life, the issue also most front and center (and most highly charged) during the depression. And like the authors of that corpus (Frederick Jackson Turner, Vernon Parrington, Charles Beard, and John Hicks), Debo recognized the pervasiveness of conflict in history, the presence of class polarization, the oligarchic forces loosed by capitalism and industrialization, the endless battles waged by the democratic counterforces of reform and freedom. But unlike those Progressive authors with their upward-tending narratives, Debo watched American history unfold from the vanquished Indians' reverse perspective, from the other side of a cultural-racial line. In her ideologized treatment, and the fictional versions of Mathews and McNickle, social evolution does not cure all ills, and freedom does not win in the end.

Debo, like Webb, had grown up on the frontier, on one of the *last* homesteaders' frontiers, the central and western half of Oklahoma Territory opened to settlement by land run and lottery during the early 1890s. (Watching this final blank space on the map disappear, Frederick Jackson Turner delivered his famous paradigm-forging essay on the significance of the frontier at the 1893 Chicago World's Fair, where in one ceremony celebrating the triumph of civilization over savagery several Sioux chiefs—shipped in especially for the occasion—appeared on cue during the singing of "My Country 'Tis of Thee" and, as one choked-up correspondent wrote, "Nothing in the day's occurrences appealed to sympathetic patriotism so much as this fallen majesty filing out of sight . . . waving congratulations to cultured achievement and submissive admiration to a new world.") Many years later one of Turner's prized disciples from Harvard, Edward Everett Dale, became Debo's mentor at the University of Oklahoma. Dale's biography was almost identical to Webb's; if anything, he was even more steeped by experience in Western frontier life and fable: born in the same Cross Timbers region of Texas where Webb the ambitious farmboy grew up, he later became a range rider in the Panhandle, homesteaded in southwestern Oklahoma, and, while attending graduate school at Harvard, became a minor legend of sorts when he strapped on his six-gun to help out during the Boston police strike of 1919. But more crucially for Debo's revisionist project, Dale was also appointed in 1927 as one of a nine-member team directed by the Department of the Interior to conduct a comprehensive nationwide survey of the condition of the Indian. Given his background, the journey must have been eye-opening. Visiting ninety-five reservations, agencies, and communities over a seven-month period—including the Navajo plateaulands, the Santa Fe–Taos area pueblos, McNickle's Salish (Flathead) reserve, and the agencies dotting the defunct Indian Territory of eastern Oklahoma (the landscapes of Debo and Mathews)—Dale and the other survey contributors to the Meriam Report criticized the deplorable state of Indian living standards, health, and education, laying the groundwork for much reform that was to follow in the 1930s. Their own prescription for bettering the Indians' condition? Accelerated and more thoroughgoing institutional efforts to assimilate them as individual, full-fledged, productive citizens, for (the specialists believed) "any policy . . . based on the notion that they can or should be kept permanently isolated from other Americans is bound to fail"—"mingling is inevitable."[28]

Debo, with John Collier and the other Indian subregionalists engaged in reconceptualizing Native American and American history, dissented from this prescription—if not from its conclusion, at least from the policy it entailed and, most significantly, from the worldview it embodied. In an ironically toned 1931 graduate essay on her mentor's work (and, by extension, *his* mentor's), Debo wrote that "his philosophy may be summed up in the one word *Progress*." Dale's life, she observed, "reads like an American saga," paralleling "that of a Horatio Alger hero," his viewpoint "both in its breadth and limitations . . . the viewpoint of the American pioneer." Thus, for him, "imperialism" (Debo's earlier graduate work had been in diplomatic history at the University of Chicago), "if he thinks of it at all, is the march of civilization across the waste places of the earth." Yet just as Turner was haunted by the dwindling of freedom in a postfrontier world, the darker downward-sloping reflection of the upward-tending line of his vision of "social evolution through various stages from savagery to a complex industrial civilization," so too did Dale, the Dale of the Meriam Report, perceive the Indians caught in this process with a double vision. "The most significant thing in all Oklahoma history," he wrote in 1923, "has been the Indian occupation of this region . . . this great Indian country, a region larger than all New England." There "Anglo-Saxon greed and lust for land" had driven the "remnants of some sixty-five or seventy tribes" to the "last home that was left to them"; the most prominent among them, the Five Civilized Tribes, were forced out of their Southern homelands and onto the westward Trail of Tears by Donald Davidson's "Tall Men." For almost half a century, Dale marveled, the "great Indian territory was owned exclusively" by the various tribes "holding their lands in common and living under some form of tribal government." The highly sophisticated Five Civilized Tribes developed into "virtually independent nations," against the borders of which "waves of white settlement beat and surged" until, finally, the Indians were pulled completely into the stream of white history:

> [T]he barrier gave way and a flood of pioneer settlers came pouring in, peopling Oklahoma with a farming population whose society and methods of agriculture were primitive enough at first but which steadily advanced, making the region one of improved agriculture where in time grew up cities and towns and all the complex organizations of industrial and commercial life.

Displaying his odd double vision, a double vision which, like Vernon Parrington's of the sturdy republican yet proto-Babbitt pioneers, sprang out of the unraveling of the Turnerian paradigm, Dale concluded that "Oklahoma history is therefore but a part of a much larger history, that of the conquest and development of the American Wilderness"—the "great Indian country" merely "an attractive but little inhabited island of wilderness"— and the settlement of which was the "story of the evolution of civilization, of the development of society, of human progress."[29]

With the onset of the depression, the Turnerian paradigm (as Webb well realized) broke asunder on a Progress that seemed to have screeched to a halt: not a "Horatio Alger hero" but John Dos Passos's rootless and impoverished "Vag" became the representative American of the age. Occupying with a number of other regionalists the critical point at which Turner's rising time line suddenly intersected the declining curve of Spenglerian decay, Angie Debo looked backward along that curve to the period when the cultures of the "great Indian country" still flourished in their last refuge and began *And Still the Waters Run*—at Dale's suggestion. But while he was diffident about the ensuing "story" (perhaps unable to bear it), the story of "the process by which the land embraced by the old Indian Territory passed out of the possession of members of the Five Civilized Tribes . . . and came into the possession of the whites," Debo was outraged. The book was, on one level, a depression-era parable of the systematic exploitation of the powerless by the powerful, of the "common man" by "economic royalists." Taking advantage of the Dawes Act division of the tribal domains into individual allotments at the turn of the century, "grafters" following a "philosophy in which personal greed and public spirit were almost inextricably joined" had engaged in a wholesale "plunder of Indians," Debo argued. In their "speculative fever," she wrote with her constant undertone of controlled rage, in terms with resonances for post-Crash Americans, "if they could build their personal fortunes and create a great state by destroying the Indian, they would destroy him in the name of all that was selfish and all that was holy." This "gigantic blunder," she estimated, giving a rather different denouement to Oklahoma history and the "larger history" of which it was a part, "ended a hopeful experiment in Indian development, destroyed a unique civilization, and degraded thousands of individuals."[30]

In constructing this argument, Debo carried the theme of arbitrary and unconstrained power considerably further, elaborating in more direct and more charged language Dale's conception of the Indian domains as "independent nations," and joining Mathews and McNickle in their own near-catastrophist and antiexceptional renderings of assimilation. Each of the Five Civilized Tribes, she declared, engaging in some mythmaking of her own, "formed an intensely nationalistic small republic with distinctive customs and institutions." Each "found Christian teachings fitted to their own way of thought," and each "maintained a complete school system under its own administrative officials." Moreover, she asserted, with their "natural genius for politics . . . trained through countless generations in the proud democracy of primitive councils," each of the tribes "found their borrowed Anglo-American institutions in perfect harmony with their native development." Having thus successfully adapted to white ways according to their own terms, not surrendering but utilizing their own "natural gift for collective enterprise," the tribes were, for a period, "contented and prosperous." But unfortunately they were living under a system of communal ownership that "seemed actually sacrilegious to the individualistic and acquisitive white man." Debo quoted with little commentary, but with devastating irony (especially for a depression-era audience), a passage from a report written on the Cherokee by Senator Henry L. Dawes of Massachusetts, sponsor of the acculturative allotment policy, after an 1885 "visit of inspection" in the territory:

The Head Chief told us that there was not a family in that whole nation that had not a home of its own. There was not a pauper in that nation, and the nation did not owe a dollar. It built its own capital, in which we had this examination, and it built its schools and its hospitals. Yet the defect of the system was apparent. They have got as far as they can go, because they own their land in common. It is Henry George's system, and under that there is no enterprise to make your home any better than that of your neighbors. There is no selfishness, which is at the bottom of civilization. Till this people will consent to give up their lands, and divide them among their citizens so that each can own the land he cultivates, they will not make much more progress.

Thanks to Dawes and some "Eastern humanitarians" of "crusading motive," Debo proceeded to show, in the three decades after 1900 "these Indians, who had owned a region greater in area and potential wealth than many an American state, were almost stripped of their holdings and were rescued from starvation only through public charity." This "orgy of exploitation" came about, she argued, because the citizens of the "Indian republics" were "forced to accept the perilous gift of American citizenship and they were despoiled individually under the forms of existing law." The "simple but sufficient economy of the old Indian country," and the "perfect society" it supported (as one contemporary called it), thus made short work for the "restless energy of the invading whites," filling a new "wilderness," engaging in the "free and unlimited appropriation of national wealth" (as Webb had phrased it). Debo commented: "Such treatment of an independent people by a great imperial power would have aroused international condemnation," but in America the destruction of the tribes' national autonomy was considered "a matter of internal policy." The Turnerian paradigm and Webb's Anglo-American world-view were in this way reconfigured, inverted, subverted, in Debo's hands: with progress came decline; with assimilation, atomization; with "social evolu-tion," social degradation. In her view, the only "wilderness" existing in the beleaguered space of the Indian Territory was the wilderness that the white settlers brought with them—the "wilderness of civilization."[31]

The darker, antiexceptional connotations of the *empire* for liberty that Debo explored primarily at the economic and political level, equating assimilation not with Progress, but with power, Mathews and McNickle fictionally elabo-rated into morality plays about cultural imperilment. Seeking to delegitimize the myths underlying a blinkered 100 percent Americanism that saw the "wilderness of civilization" as the apex of civilization and characterized Indian culture in terms of "treachery" and "cranial measurements" (as Webb wrote), the two subregionalists found a potent fulcrum in a taboo subject: racism. There was a reason why Webb's pioneer had only seen the Indian "in feathers and warpaint and on the warpath"—he was defending his village and tribe against a race war launched for the subjugation, if not the annihilation, of his people. "He killed our brothers because they were not his brothers," a character in Mathews's novel *Sundown* (1934) observes simply, recalling the Indian wars of the nineteenth century.[32] Tapping into the still-volatile post-frontier reverberations of this usable past—for many of these prejudices and resentments still persisted as "contemporary social realities"—Mathews in his semiautobiographical work and McNickle in his own novel, *The Sur-rounded* (1936), not only probed the sensitive area of race directly, they also pressed racial categories into the service of a wider socioeconomic critique as a kind of rhetorical tar, sullying the "standardizing order" of modern America in all its dimensions, and obliterating all traces of an exceptional past or present.

With his depiction in *Sundown* of the oil-rich yet tortured life of a young mixed-blood named Challenge Windzer ("He shall be a challenge to the disinheritors of his people," his father declares at his birth bed), Mathews framed the assimilation of the Osage tribe, and the costs of modernization generally, in the stark terms of cultural-racial polarization played out through the self-destructive psychological drama of Challenge's mixed blood warring within him. From the perspective of his own reclaimed Indianness (the book was written in the months prior to Mathews's election to the Osage tribal council, where he became a staunch advocate for John Collier's policies to restore Indian autonomy), he portrayed a character whose Indianness had been excised by the racist-acculturative system of the Osages' conquerors, and who attempts his own reclamation but fails. Establishing his moral bearings in the *prefrontier* Indian Golden Age, and setting up as well a narrative of inevitable declension, Mathews begins the story with Chal's birth, when "the great god of the Osages was still dominant over the wild prairie and the blackjack hills." Chal enjoys there a relatively pastoral youth, despite the frontier-era division of the tribal reservation into allotments and the steady and finally explosive growth of his hometown after the discovery of oil. Back then, he later recalled, he rode his pony across the prairie and "found himself still talking with the birds and animals, and held regular conversation with the old pinto." He regarded the traditionalist full-bloods with awe, picturing them "standing there on the hills, aloof from all the hammering, the loud talking, the swearing, the shrieking of steel" taking place in the boomtowns. The whiteness he was taught at the agency school, and in the bustling streets of Kihekah, he had conceived as "continually playing a role," a role he was glad to escape from out on the prairie.[33]

But as the years of education in American schools finally took their toll, Chal eventually "moved with the new tempo as he grew taller," Mathews wrote. He begins to repress his Indianness, to try to conform to the emerging pseudoculture (and superego) of Babbittry, as revealed in his thoughts on the ruined landscape of white-built towns seen passing during a train trip:

Chal did not know the reason for this ugliness; this ugliness which white men seemed to produce. . . . He felt simply that these things were not beautiful. He would not have dared suggest his thoughts to anyone; it would have been like sacrilege and certainly unpatriotic. One believed in his country and his state, and accepted the heroics of the race for land in the new territory, and all the virtues of the Anglo-Saxon; the romantics and righteousness of their winning of the West, as taught by his history. He almost despised himself for the feeling deep within him which feebly remonstrated. He kept this feeling subdued; kept it from bubbling up into the placid waters of his consciousness, so that nothing would disturb those waters to keep them from reflecting the impressions that ought to be mirrored, if one were to remain in step. He certainly didn't want anyone to know that he was queer.

Chal's wealth gains him entry into a white fraternity at the state university, where he becomes even more concerned not "to call attention to the fact that most of his blood was of an uncivilized race like the Osages." In one particularly painful scene, he sees his reflection (dressed in evening clothes) and notices "a bronze face in black-and-white; the white making the bronze stand out." As Mathews noted, "he had often wished he weren't so bronze"—"if his face were only white." With this attitude, Chal is consequently drawn more and more deeply into the empty materialism of the white world. During the twenties, Mathews observed, "he did very little except ride around in his long, powerful red roadster . . . attended all the dances, and became a pretty fair pool player"—and drinking, always plenty of drinking.[34]

Yet the more white Chal becomes, the more his inner torment increases, at once stirred and embarrassed by tribal dances, and drawn to the old full-bloods yet ashamed of them. In a central scene, he is persuaded to join them in a cleansing sweat lodge, where one of the headmen ("using many words of which Chal had to guess the meaning") intones, "My son . . . this evil in your heart . . . cannot stay in your body forever." Although Chal was "happy and contented" during the lodge ceremony, he soon afterward comes to see its participants, including himself, as "silly" and "sentimental." Still torn, however, "he wasn't very happy after coming down to earth again." During an anticlimax, Chal roars off drunk and alone one night into the prairie, stops his car, and begins to dance by the side of the road, singing "one of the tribal songs of his people." He dances "wildly," then "frantically," but he "couldn't dance fast enough"—his whiteness had destroyed his Indianness beyond his capacity (aesthetic or otherwise) to redeem it. Mathews thus abandons Chal to his plight for rhetorical (and at bottom, political) reasons, leaving him in a poignant void between two fundamentally unreconcilable races and cultures. As the headman muses in the sweat lodge, speaking what amounted to an aesthetic-symbiotic critique of exceptionalism:

White man came out of ground across [the] sea. His thoughts are good across that sea. His houses are beautiful across that sea, I believe. He came out of earth across that sea, and his songs are beautiful there. But he did not come out of earth here. His houses are ugly here because they did not come out of this earth, and his songs and those things which he thinks, those things which he talks, are ugly here too.

European culture--Mathews translates to his depression-era readers—in dispersing across America and across modernity, had been transformed not into something exceptional but into something essentially alien to "human values," into something "evil." Some provision must be made to save the Indian cultures caught in its path, cultures being eroded and swept away by the "screeching mechanism of Progress." Mathews pleaded most plaintively in the voice of the old headman: "We must have time to keep our place on earth."[35]

Observing this postfrontier dispersal a thousand miles to the north in Montana, D'Arcy McNickle—like Mathews, a mixed-blood, of the Salish tribe, an Oxford graduate, previously a student at H. G. Merriam's University of Montana, and later a biographer of Oliver La Farge—made much the same plea in his carefully titled novel, *The Surrounded*. "They called that place Sniel-emen (Mountains of the Surrounded)," the book's frontispiece states, "because there they had been set upon and destroyed." Whereas Mathews personifies the destructive imperilment of assimilation (and in a more general sense, modernization) through Challenge's psychological struggle and racial confusion, McNickle externalizes the conflict, portraying it much more overtly and explosively as the incursion of racist and acculturative *power* into the once-pristine alpine homeland of the Salish. The postfrontier struggle to throw off or at least to escape from this power—represented particularly in the local Indian agency, Catholic mission school, and sheriff's office—begins to unfold after the return to the reservation of the main character, a young Americanized Spanish-Salish mixed-blood named Archilde Leon, who has been living out in the wider world. McNickle's presentist depiction of a pow-wow seen through Archilde's estranged eyes shows what a "pathetic wreck" the invading Americans had made of Salish culture: "It was a sad spectacle to watch. It was like looking on while cruel jokes were played on an old grandmother." Archilde likens the ceremony to a "low-class circus where people came to buy peanuts and look at freaks," the dances staged in a pavillion ("protruding above the roof of boughs . . . the American flag") that was "surrounded by selling booths decorated with bunting," where "the crowd was coaxed to buy 'ice col' pop' and 'strawberry ice cream' and to win a 'cute Frenchy doll' on the roulette wheel." In the midst of this "circus atmosphere," a proud and blind old chief, dancing, cries, "Let it be today as it was in old times!" But a "poetic orgy," it seemed, it was not.[36]

Published in the year that McNickle began a sixteen-year tenure at the Bureau of Indian Affairs, starting as an assistant to Commissioner Collier, the bulk of *The Surrounded* is devoted to an indictment of the white institutions that had brought the Salish to such a state, developed through two converging plot lines. The first concerns an emblematic and deadly confrontation during a hunting trip between the local game warden and Archilde, his mother, and his brother. "The woods seemed to be full of guardians of the peace," Archilde thinks sardonically as the warden interrogates them, and he notices how nervous his relatives had become, for whom "the Law was a threatening symbol." After a series of misread cues and innocent gestures, his brother is shot dead by the overly suspicious warden, who is then killed in retaliation by Archilde's mother (with a hatchet blow to the head). Through this allusion to the Indian wars, McNickle reveals them to his audience to be not the crusade of law and order making a savage frontier safe for decent people (as Webb and the mainstream myth would have it, portrayed repeatedly in western pulp and movies), but a struggle for power that the Indians lost, leaving them a conquered population subject to the laws of their occupiers, laws that were merely rationalizations of oppression. Indeed, despite mitigating circumstances, Archilde buries the warden's corpse and obscures the campsite, having no illusions about justice—only hanging—from the white courts. He spends the rest of the story living in dread of the local sheriff, Quigley, "a name that could frighten most Indians," for he was self-consciously a "sheriff out of the Old West," McNickle wrote, an "imperturbable rock" whose job was to keep the Salish in line: "It seemed that every time an Indian left the Reservation he almost certainly ran into the Sheriff and had to give an account of himself."[37]

At his mother's insistence, they bring the brother's body back home to be buried in the "special ground" of "the Fathers" running the mission, to whom she is known as "Faithful Catherine"; since the priests first arrived in the virgin territory of the Salish, she had always been the most fervent of believers.[38] McNickle thus begins to intertwine his depiction of the brute coercive power of the white legal system with a further critique of an institution equally if more subtly oppressive to Indians, the Christian church. Symbolically, Father Grepilloux, the local priest most like Willa Cather's kindly and tolerant Archbishop LaTour, dies coincidentally with Archilde's brother, taking his more humane and broad-minded tradition with him, and setting the stage for McNickle's examination of the problematic consequences of Christianization. Seen from the receiving end, he argues, it was not the triumph of goodness over sin, but the acculturative displacement of one creed by another, of one moral world by another, through force if necessary.

As McNickle relates in the second of the two plot lines, Archilde's wild and antsy young nephews, Mike and Narcisse, had earlier been deceived into attending the mission school—in effect, trapped there ("They were like animals brought to the zoo")—by their well-to-do and well-intentioned Spanish grandfather, Max Leon. Subsequently, Mike's spirit is broken by the priests in "a small room of unpleasant reputation," where he is subjected to physical abuse and psychological torture. The fear of God (or the Devil) instilled most crudely by these forced conversions and more insidiously by formal instruction, McNickle implies, was merely another means to instill social discipline and conformity. "The Indians who had been taught to understand sin," Max reflects over Father Grepilloux's grave, "one had to ask of them—were they saved or were they destroyed?" He extended this "blasphemous" line of thought, considering Grepilloux not only in his role as devoted proselytizer but also as "pathfinder," agent not only of God but also of Americanization: "Grepilloux had shown the way over the mountains and the world had followed at his heels"; now, "life and industry"—"the railroad . . . banks, stores, and farms"—"filled the valley from one end to the other." And yet, Max wonders of Progress and the Salish, "were they saved or were they destroyed? Bringing the outside world to them was not exactly like bringing heaven to them."[39]

McNickle's novel culminates in the attempts by Max Leon's Indian family (he himself dies unexpectedly) to free themselves from this imperiling American world, or, more directly, from the naked expression of its power, the racist-acculturative regime that rules the reservation. In the aftermath of the "battle" with the game warden, "Faithful Catherine" reexamines her faith, repudiates her baptism, and goes to the tribal leaders to submit herself to their punishment (a ceremonial whipping). With these acts, McNickle observes, "the old lady . . . completed her retreat from the world which had come to Sniel-emen," but he then proceeds to show (like Mathews) that for others this invidious reverse-perspective world of Progress was not so easily evaded. Still under suspicion for murder, Archilde must himself escape from the reservation system. Yet unlike Mathews's Challenge, Archilde had largely come to terms with his modernized self, his sad alienation from Indianness, and so he hopes to flee to Europe—from this inverted antiexceptional perspective, freedom lies in the Old World—to pursue his vocation as a musician; merely to "hide in the mountains . . . like an Indian" he at first rejects outright ("By God, no!"). The story, however, draws to its inevitable, unhappy conclusion, with Archilde forced into the role of oppressed Indian object-victim seized by the white power structure. His mother Catherine falls ill and dies, and despite her request that there be "No priest!," one appears to administer the last rites. Archilde believes that "it meant nothing," that "the power of the two sticks, the Somesh which Father Grepilloux had carried over the mountains, was dissolved." But when word arrives that he is to report to the Agent regarding the warden's murder, he realizes that while death might have freed his mother, "as for himself—he too belonged to the story of Sniel-emen." In a plot turn as old as American literature (or as old, at least, as Crèvecoeur's imaginative flight from oppressors—arisen now, astonishingly, in the New World—away into the wilderness, to the Indians), Archilde and his rather coarse and Americanized girlfriend Elise ride off into the mountains, joining the truant Mike and Narcisse who had already been living there by redemptive traditional ways for some time. Their mood is grim, though; as Archilde tells his ever-optimistic companion, "You can't run away nowadays, Elise," because (Mike and Narcisse know) "how much greater—how everlasting—was the world of priests and schools, the world which engulfed them": the postfrontier world. Finally, the sheriff, the Agent, and the posse do arrive, and in the confusion, Mike and Narcisse gallop away, farther down the trail ("loose in the mountains, like birds let out of a cage . . . like a pair of buffaloes turned out of the Government reserve"). The book ends with the Agent's words and a final unsubtle image:

> "Why those little fools! How far do they expect to get? . . . It's too damn bad you people never learn that you can't run away. It's pathetic—"

Archilde, saying nothing, extended his hands to be shackled.[40]

The unsubtle themes running throughout the works of the Indian subre-gionalists—the expropriation of the Five Civilized Tribes "under forms of existing law," the "ugliness" of white American culture and society (recalling the centrality of the aesthetic in the Indian's worldview as the means of social order), the rejection of "white heaven," the recourse to violent resistance and, finally, to exile—these themes sought to persuade the audience of the *illegitimacy* of white rule, to answer unambiguously Max Leon's question whether Indians had been "saved or destroyed" by the alien regime that arrived with the frontier. In answering this question from the Indians' van-tage of the frontier line, from beyond the ethnocentric blind side that con-cealed tragedies such as Challenge's or Archilde's, their works tended not only to undermine the myths of American exceptionalism, they made them appear irrelevant to any discussion of national history except *as* myth—a crucial critical (and political) breakthrough. Yet as the bleak denouement of McNickle's novel indicates, such a perception, common enough among Native Americans and their advocates, was relatively impotent to bring about liber-ating change unless there was a concomitant epiphany on the part of those who considered *themselves* to be "native Americans," and who patrolled and en-forced the values and institutions of the system predicated, however dysfunc-tionally and paradoxically, on those myths. The historicist and presentist revelation of this dysfunction and paradox—and necessarily, of further trag-edies unfolding behind still more blind sides—must therefore take place on the white side of the frontier line and outside the Indian subregions in the post-frontier "world which engulfed them."

It was this disenchanting task that the Southern sociologists and Califor-nia socialists undertook during the depression, when mainstream Americans were obliged to acknowledge (as they periodically are) that poor and op-

pressed people lived in their country. As the Indian subregionalists demonstrated, a pluralist perspective, tracing modern social and economic development through the hidden history of diverse neglected races and classes, was
essential to achieve a critical distance from the myths that "native Americans" like Webb and Davidson held dear. Yet equally important were the
"objective" tools of social science, which could measure the socioeconomic
"differentials" (as Howard Odum called them) between the American way of
life and life as it was actually lived by many of the folk of rural America. As
artists and intellectuals in the South and the West politicized beyond the
purely myth-constructed *region* of the regionalist civic religion (though continuing, like the Indian subregionalists, to take their ethical bearings from it)
and beyond too the inherently conservative politics of sectionalism (the region
uncritically, prejudicially championed), they arrived via the pluralist and objective approach at a politics of regionalism (the section become self-critical)
that viewed the region from a national if not global or *universal* "distance."
And what they came to discover from this distance were the relationships—
power relationships—that explained those "differentials" in terms—antiexceptional terms—that belied the frontier myth, revealing an empire for
liberty that had rewarded the conquerors of the American continent, and their
descendants, with more empire than liberty.[41]

Howard Odum, whose circle of North Carolina–trained social scientists were
in the forefront of such delegitimizing discoveries, paused at one point in the
six hundred pages of diffuse and generally diplomatic prose comprising his
Southern Regions of the United States (1936—issued by W. T. Couch's reformist University of North Carolina Press) to describe the nature and consequences of the South's "blindside" with uncharacteristic frankness. Because
of "continuing emphasis upon racial issues, Nordic superiority, and one hundred per cent Americanism," he wrote, "most of the prominent folk of industry and farm never recognized the poverty and suffering of the five million
tenant folk" (see Figure 5.4). There had never been any "authentic measure of
the South's economic actualities in which, through gradual, inevitable, logical
processes, millions of marginal folk, white and black, had in reality no semblance of equality of opportunity or even of living much above the subsistence
level." Much of *Southern Regions* was devoted to providing such an "authentic measure," using almost seven hundred statistical "indices of measurement
for regional culture," from "Amount and distribution of farm income" to
"Infant mortality and maternal mortality"; most of the indices showed the
South to be, comparatively, in the worst and lowest brackets in the nation.
There were the "differentials" *between* regions that provided evidence, Odum

Figure 5.4 Photograph and caption from *An American Exodus*, "Old South" chapter, p. 16: "Agricultural Ladder: 'The Committee's examination of the agricultural
ladder has indicated . . . an increasing tendency for the rungs of the ladder to become
bars—forcing imprisonment in a fixed social status from which it is increasingly difficult to escape.' President's Committee on Farm Tenancy. Georgia/1937." (Photograph by Dorothea Lange, courtesy of the Farm Security Administration, Prints and
Photographs Division, Library of Congress, LC-USF34-18030)

and his circle agreed, for the South as Webb's "colonial economy." But there
were also those highly disparate socioeconomic "differentials" *within* the
region, between races and classes (and, complicating the "portrait," among
twenty-seven subregions), that pointed to the emergence of configurations of
power which could only be explained, Odum asserted, by "the facing of absolute facts rather than substituting rationalizations which grow out of irrelevant comparisons or defense explanations of how things have come to be as

they are." By substituting the objective "new regionalism for the old section-alism," the "regional-national as opposed to the local-sectional emphasis," he and his counterparts—especially, Rupert Vance and Arthur F. Raper—proceeded to uncover the "gradual, inevitable, logical processes" of social change that would settle "the whole question of the place of large race and propertyless classes in a region theoretically the most democratic in its clamor for the rights of the common man."[42]

At the center of their historical and sociological analysis of this question—paradoxical only when seen from the poor white and black perspective of the South's blind side—lay the cotton economy, which since the antebellum days had been (in Odum's words) "a hard master over the whole human culture of the region." For decades several layers of myth and apology had kept obscure the hard facts of life forced on many Southerners by this economy, supported first by slavery (legitimated under the plantation myth of the Old South) and after the war, into the 1930s, built upon farm tenancy (a status justified with the New South's "agricultural ladder" model of mobility). Although the de-legitimizing critique that the regional sociologists brought to bear against the cotton economy was to focus primarily on the broken "agricultural ladder" and other hard facts of the contemporary tenancy and sharecropper system, it also necessarily encompassed a revision of Old South myth and history. The wide-spread assumption among Southern artists and intellectuals during the inter-war years was that the "cultural complexes inherited from the Old South," in Odum's words, continued to cast a "spell" or a "shadow" over the life of the modern South. The very concept of a unique and glorious antebellum civiliza-tion was central to the identity of the New South; like the heroic "unfenced world" of the West, it provided a repository of values and flattering self-images. "The plantation system," wrote its most famous (or infamous) mod-ern practitioner and apologist, Alexander Percy, "seems to me to offer as humane, just, self-respecting, and cheerful a method of earning a living as human beings are likely to devise." The sociologists themselves were not completely immune from the "spell" of the plantation myth, as Odum revealed in this description of some of its "distinctive and glamorous" qualities: "a setting of classical architecture, classical libraries, elegant furnishings, in the midst of groves and gardens and feudal settlements; dignity, polish, respect for form and amenities, pride of family, hospitality with merriment and conviv-iality abounding."[43]

Yet Odum and his colleagues realized that there was also a hidden history behind the antebellum plantation and its modern survivals. Even "if it had been what it was purported to be, which it was not," Odum qualified himself, the plantation began to reveal some very inglorious (and antiexceptional) features when the full social, economic, and political implications of its "feu-

dal" organization were framed from the perspective of the "victims" at the
bottom. As Rupert Vance reminded his audience about the pre–Civil War
years, "Slavery, it must be remembered, had come to be regarded by the
enlightened opinion of mankind as an abnormal industrial relationship." And
yet, Arthur Raper noted, there was "still an element of something not unakin
to slavery in the rich Delta plantations" as late as 1941. Other elements of the
plantation economy, past and present, were equally onerous and persistent,
such as the "concentration of large landholdings" and, "more disconcerting,"
the fact that "white tenants have entered the cotton system on even terms
with the ex-slaves." Thus, for all those who were enamored of the South's
romantic "feudal" past and sought to recapture it in the present, Raper had
this rejoinder: "The South's landless farmers constitute a veritable kingdom, a
kingdom of neglect and want." As Vance reflected of the "hard master"
reigning over that kingdom, the "shadows of slavery and the plantation,"
"The persistence of the pattern after sixty years is, therefore, no cause for
congratulation."[44]

The project of delegitimation undertaken by the Southern sociologists thus
assumed its first task: to persuade their audience that the emergence and
perpetuation of a "feudalistic" pattern of power in the South was not "peculiar" (and somehow inevitable) or "romantic," but antithetical to democratic
ideals, its persistence very much the product of ruling class self-interest. This
puncturing of the élan of the Cavalier South, the "yearning for the symbol of
the old plantation" (as Vance described it), they accomplished by embracing a
conceptualization of the antebellum period as essentially a *frontier* stage in the
region's development, particularly in the heavily mythologized Black Belt
subregion stretching through two hundred counties from Virginia to Texas.
There, they argued, rather than a settled, traditionalist aristocracy (as the
Old South "invented" itself), the plantation owners were preeminently men
on the make, their "large landholdings . . . bolstered," as Vance wrote, "by the
speculative and land grabbing activities of the frontier"—" 'buy more land
and grow more cotton to buy more Negroes, to grow more cotton to buy more
land . . .' and so on *ad infinitum*." Elaborating, Raper asserted in his book
Preface to Peasantry (1936) that "the plantation economy . . . rested upon a
reckless exploitation of natural resources"; the "traditional Black Belt planter
often moved his seat of operations from exhausted land to virgin soil." This
frontier interpretation of the Old South, to be sure, was not uncommon during
the depression, sensitized as artists and intellectuals were especially to the
economic dimension of behavior. One outgrowth of it was the depiction of the
planter as self-made *faux* aristocrat, which received its fullest explication, of
course, in William Faulkner's *Absalom, Absalom!* (whose Sutpen—born dirt
poor in remotest West Virginia—arrives in Mississippi with "wild niggers"

and architect in tow, carves "Sutpen's Hundred" out of the woods, and becomes "the biggest single landowner and cotton-planter in the county," acting
out thereafter "a role of arrogant ease and leisure"; nevertheless, Faulkner
showed, "his flowering was a forced blooming"). W. J. Cash, in his *The Mind of
the South* (1941), agreed: "How to account for the ruling class, then? Manifestly, for the great part, by the strong, the pushing, the ambitious, among
the old coon-hunting population of the backcountry. The frontier was their
predestined inheritance."[45]

The focus of the Southern sociologists, though, was not on the mask of
gentility itself (as was Faulkner's and Cash's), but on the coercive system of
power relations that lay behind it as another layer in the South's blind side.
Their recourse to a frontier interpretation of Southern history proved to have
a host of unmasking and delegitimizing consequences, most potently, the idea
that the "cultural complexes inherited from the Old South" represented, in
Odum's words, a "retarded frontier dominance." The present-day extractive
"colonial" cotton monoculture should be seen as both cause and symptom of
this crypto-frontier "immaturity." Its "reckless exploitation" and "waste,
actual and potential, of human and natural resources" served no higher purpose than to fill the pockets of landlords and creditors, who were not "disin-
terested" aristocrats but self-interested capitalists, and who were "pater-
nalistic" through no familial affect but only in the degree of control that they
exercised over the lives of laborers and tenants. "Upper-class whites too often
accept the differentials which they themselves enforce as proof of their own
superiority and inherent worth," Raper noted. By thus pointing to the essentially coercive and exploitative "arrested frontier pattern" of the Southern
economy, the Odum circle attempted, in sum, to reendow words like *aristocratic* and *feudalistic* with all the negative and antiexceptional connotations
that by rights they should have in a New World context, signifying not
romance and gentility, nor the sectional "communities of interests" that Webb
and Davidson assumed, but the "differentials" of a "stratified society," the
"stern class lines" of "social hierarchy."[46]

There was unavoidably the most fundamental differential of Southern society for the sociologists to consider as well in their delegitimizing project, the
"caste principle" of race, which had no necessary economic basis, superseding
even class divisions (see Figure 5.5). "As seen by whites," Raper wrote of the
antebellum period, and failed to show much change since then, "all Negroes
were at the bottom of the social hierarchy. Even the sorriest of poor whites
regarded himself as better than any Negro." Southern "liberals" of the 1930s
like the North Carolina sociologists often disappoint the modern reader with
regard to such racial issues, asking for every reform short of outright "social
equality"—a granting of civil rights, for example, or equalized funding for

Figure 5.5 Photograph and caption from *You Have Seen Their Faces*, p. 89: "Scotts, Arkansas: 'And so the fairy godmother in the storybook touched the little white girls with her wand and they were all turned into little princesses.'" (Photograph by Margaret Bourke-White, courtesy of Life Magazine © Time Warner Inc. and the Margaret Bourke-White Collection, George Arents Research Library, Syracuse University)

segregated facilities—and assuming (as another of Odum's colleagues, Guy B. Johnson, wrote) that "the races can go the whole way of political and civic equality without endangering their integrity." But just as often it is difficult to discern whether such rhetoric revealed some bedrock of racism or instead reflected a recognition of the facts of Southern political life. Odum, a longtime student of black folk culture and a leading member of the Council for Interracial Cooperation, argued the most radical of theoretical positions in *Southern Regions*, counting as a "major error" the assumption that "race was an entity in itself, a purely physical product rather than the result of long developed folk-regional culture," or that the "races were inherently different," or categorizable according to "superiority and inferiority." Nevertheless, his diffuse prose style, his (possibly studied) tendency to include a range of opinion, and perhaps more concretely his own potential political vulnerability as an institution head— all combined to soften the thrust of Odum's antiracist arguments.

Recognizing racism as "the region's hardest problem," he advocated a gradu-
alist reform program because, he declared (ostensibly in full political retreat),
"Manifestly, it is asking too much of a region to change over night the powerful
folkways of long generations."[47]

And yet, Odum and his circle clearly believed, there were other possible
ways to redress social problems stemming from this "Immovable Body" short
of a full frontal assault, as the more extreme and plainspoken Arthur Raper
argued (with Ira De A. Reid) in such works as *Sharecroppers All* (1941—
another of W. T. Couch's productions). Although he proclaimed flatly that "the
establishment of democracy in the South means the discarding of all differentials which reason cannot explain and justice cannot excuse," Raper knew the
intractability of "that foremost bugaboo of the South, 'social equality,'" and
seemed resigned to the fact that "any social program is certain of defeat if it
can be interpreted as promoting" such changes. It was therefore crucial to
follow the "simple principle" that "first things come first." For Raper, Odum,
and Vance this meant above all the *economic* differentials of the tenancy and
sharecropper system, under which "the plight of whites and blacks" were "as
one." Their hope, fundamentally—and it had been one of would-be reformers
in the South since the Populist days of the 1880s and 1890s—was that the
"common denominators in the disinheritance of the poorer whites and Negroes" (as Raper wrote) would override the factor of race prejudice and allow
them politically to "break the cake of custom which the gentility has argued
could not be broken because of natural antagonism between them." By overcoming the economic competitiveness exacerbated by the "traditional playing
of race against race," Raper noted, voicing the assumption of many in the
Odum camp, the common quest for "economic equality" might lead through
the back door, as it were, to more "wholesome relations between the races,"
something possible "only in a society where justice and opportunity are
real."[48]

The further delegitimizing task of the Southern sociologists lay then in
revealing the origin and nature of all the disinheriting "common denominators" that occurred not only behind the rhetoric of those who would "prove
that the South is still in the colonel-darky-mint-julep-horse-and-buggy days of
their grandparents," Raper observed sourly, but also on the blind side of
enterprising "bourbon Southerners" (often, like Alexander Percy, one and the
same) who boosted New South "Progress" and who—in Vance's estimation—
saw "no further than the interests of the credit institutions and large land-
holders." The Odum group became much preoccupied with demonstrating
that modernized "land concentration and the commercialized farming of the
cotton system" were a "chimera" (as Vance put it) from the standpoint of

"justice and opportunity." To this end, the recourse which they took to a frontier interpretation (and disenchanting revision) of the Cavalier South proved to be a weapon which could be doubly effective: for by depicting an "aristocratic" and "feudalistic" European configuration of power arisen on the Southern frontier, they exploded the frontier myth in precisely the antiexceptional ways that the reluctant Webb could not confront. This is not to say that they were unable to salvage from its problematized wreckage the neorepublican values that shaped their ideals of "justice and opportunity." The same Southern frontier that gave range to the Sutpens of the world was also, they believed, the site where flourished the nonslaveholding "independent free-holding yeomanry, living self-sufficient lives on family-sized farms." Yet it was from this normative baseline—still embodied in the present-day cryptofrontier "rural predominance" of Southern culture—that the Odum group wrote the frontier and postfrontier "hidden history" of the South, a narrative very much *antiexceptional* rather than *postexceptional* in its depiction of the quantity of freedom to be had in the New World, despite the presence of the antebellum Jeffersonian yeomanry.[49]

"The present-day exploitation of Americans one by another is nothing new," Raper wrote in *Sharecroppers All*. "When we look realistically at our past, we see that practices of exploitation have been continuous." First, "the Indians were dispossessed." Then, on the Old South frontier, the presence of slavery and planter hegemony spoiled the mythic picture. And in the postbellum, postfrontier period culminating in the 1930s, there was the specter of more and more of the would-be yeomanry entering the cotton system "on even terms with the ex-slaves." As Vance wrote, "A dread of tenancy . . . was brought from Europe by every stream of agrarian immigrants coming from semi-feudal backgrounds"; the "first tenure census of 1880," which showed "25 per cent tenancy, brought dismay to those who believed that America would pass beyond the land tenure conditions of the Old World"—by Vance's own time, that figure had increased to almost 60 percent in some areas of the South. Vance and his colleagues aimed to delegitimize the economy that had brought about those conditions by questioning and revealing as "chimerical" all the New South "rationalizations and defense mechanisms which the controllers of the plantation system have fabricated," most centrally, the unfulfilled promises of the "agricultural ladder" model of tenant mobility. In so doing, they attempted to strike at the very heart of the frontier myth and the American dream.[50]

Writing in the inaugural 1935 issue of the *Southern Review*, Vance observed that "the theories of tenancy so far developed in America are barely more than defenses of capitalistic agriculture." W. J. Spillman's famous "ladder" theory was, he argued, "the most able attempt to rationalize the system":

According to this theory the young and inexperienced farmer has to go through a series of progressive stages represented by the system of wage labor and tenancy in order to acquire the capital and experience necessary to farm ownership. Tenancy is thus a stage through which farmers climb rather than a status into which they fall.

In fact, the agricultural ladder was nothing less than a transposition of the classic mobility myth of the nineteenth century ("when any boy who was willing to pay the price could go anyplace he desired") into the context of the tenancy system: first one worked as laborer or apprentice, proving one's mettle, saving one's pennies, then, inevitably, one became an owner, an employer; the status of *employee* was always transitory. That one's life must follow this mythic narrative, that, at the very least, one's lot must constantly improve over time, was of course deeply ingrained in the American psyche. But as Odum, Vance, and Raper attempted to show, the ladder theory and this central narrative were "sharply challenged" by the "absolute facts" that the "new demography" revealed about farm tenancy. Vance, whose own father had been a less-than-prosperous farmer, cited the fact that "the percentage of tenants who are over 55 years old has been increasing for several decades" not only in the South but also at the national level. "There are now about 375,000 who . . . have struggled a lifetime towards ownership and in their old age possess no home of their own and no more security than when they started." Novelist Erskine Caldwell publicized the plight of one such individual for a wide audience in *Tobacco Road* (1932), a best-seller during the decade because of the absurd antics of the Lester family, certainly, yet also, perhaps, because Caldwell touched on something very chilling to depression-era Americans: the void of anomie that Sandoz's Irvy confronted and that gaped for Jeeter Lester and any other American whose life and livelihood were no longer moving through "progressive stages." As Caldwell wrote of Lester near the end of the novel, Lester who was now a tenant on land his grandfather had once owned:

> He had felt himself sink lower and lower, his condition fall further and further, year after year, until now his trust in God and the land was at the stage where further disappointment might easily cause him to lose his mind and reason. He still could not understand why he had nothing, and would never have anything, and there was no one who knew and who could tell him. It was the unsolved mystery of his life.[51]

Raper, writing in *Preface to Peasantry* (its frontispiece consisted of photographs of two actual and now elderly former slaves, as presiding spirits) offered one explanation: "The very life of the plantation system is threatened when tenants accumulate property, exhibit independence." Many observers remarked upon, and Caldwell turned to purposes of pointed humor, the improvidence, shiftlessness, and dependency of Southern poor whites and blacks. But to Raper these qualities were demanded by the operation of tenancy and all the other forms of agricultural labor useful to the plantation regime, and therein lay its insidiousness. Its victims, he wrote, "must be amenable to instructions, must live in the houses provided, must accept the merchant's and landlord's accounting, must remain landless." For many, the agricultural ladder, with its lesser ranks of status below outright ownership— "wage hands on the bottom, croppers on the next rung, renters on the third, and owners at the top"—was no means to become self-made men, Raper argued; rather, it perverted whole populations into individuals, black and white, who were "incapable of self-direction": these were "landless and defenseless men, without bank accounts, without commercial credit, without votes, and without friends in court getting themselves in debt to men who have bank accounts, commercial credit, influence with peace officers and court officials. By these very debts, they secure for themselves protection not unlike that which hovered about the slaves."[52]

Particularly heinous to Raper's neo-republicanism was the disfranchisement of tenants and sharecroppers. Because of the poll tax and other barriers, the Black Belt was the "backbone of the 'Solid South,'" where "almost no Negroes vote and where less than half the whites—frequently less than one fourth—go to the polls"; as a consequence, they had "no tradition of participation" in political affairs. Further underscoring for his audience such violations of basic American ideals, Raper devoted a section of his book to the process by which "The Negro Becomes a Landowner," showing that class-based white-black "common denominators" notwithstanding, racism affected the prospects of blacks in some very un-American ways. The black man who, during good years, was able to aspire to landownership in the Black Belt subregion must have a "white sponsor," he noted, a veritable *patron* to convince the higher levels of the social hierarchy that he was "acceptable" and "safe," that he "knows 'his place' and stays in it." The black individual's still "submerged status" thereby limited whatever "economic and cultural advantages" he might gain from ownership: "The Negro landowner is an independent Negro farmer rather than an independent farmer." This portrait of the ambitious black who nevertheless could not "go any place he desired" assumed the dimensions of a parable: fundamentally, what Raper was pointing to, for both blacks and whites caught in the tenant system, was the "increasing tendency for the rungs of the [agricultural] ladder to become bars" (as the 1937 government report phrased it), "forcing imprisonment in a fixed social status from which it is increasingly difficult to escape." What he was pointing to—and what the myth-clinging Webb had not been able to contemplate, what David-

Figure 5.6 Photograph and caption from *An American Exodus*, "Plantation Under the Machine" chapter, p. 35: "'They ain't nothin' but day labor. . . . Right smart empty houses on that place. . . . Heap of 'em go far places.' Mississippi Delta/1937." (Photograph by Dorothea Lange, courtesy of the Farm Security Administration, Prints and Photographs Division, Library of Congress, LC-USF34-17623)

son, invoking visions of a neo-slave revolt, wanted left alone, and what the ladder theory apologists obfuscated—was the antiexceptional social stratification of the "most 'American' of all the regions."[53]

Even as the Southern sociologists and others were describing its structure, the plantation system was changing before their very eyes, presenting them with the seeming paradox of institutions at once "immature" and "decadent," a "decay" that had accelerated during the 1920s and become catastrophic by the late 1930s and early 1940s (see Figure 5.6). Besides racial and other structural impediments to mobility, the freezing out of the various levels of the agricultural ladder into "stern class lines" was also symptomatic, the Odum group believed, of the problems of overproduction and low profitability that had long afflicted the South's "precarious" economy. "Why is cotton production not sufficiently profitable to afford Southerners a decent livelihood today?" Rupert Vance asked in a 1936 article on the "Old Cotton Belt." He enumerated a number of reasons: the decades-long incursion of the boll weevil, the fierce competition from the more efficient and mechanized cotton belt of the "new Southwest," and the "loss of world markets" attending the depression. Against this backdrop, the collapse of cotton prices in the late 1920s heralded a particularly ill-boding development marked by Raper in *Preface to Peasantry*: a "downward shift on the agricultural ladder" over the period 1927 to 1934, when the number of "croppers decreased and the wage hands and laborers increased, making this lowest tenure class the largest." In the Georgia counties he examined, this shift signified a definite loss of status, Raper decided. Because of rock-bottom prices, drought, eroded and depleted soil, and other obstacles to merely growing a crop to "share," there was "a distinct tendency for people who were poor in 1928 to be even poorer now."[54]

To make matters worse, the drop to the wage labor rung represented a greater loosening of ties to land and place than was true even for the generally peripatetic sharecropper class, for now, Raper found, "the planter can tell a wage hand at any time that he does not need his service, and the wage hand has no choice but to get out of the house which belongs to the planter." Undoubtedly, many nouveau wage hands and displaced croppers left of their own accord (as they had in the decades since the mills opened), heading to other plantations and to nearby towns and cities for temporary jobs, federal work relief, any available employment. At the same time, wage labor ranks everywhere were further swelled by an equally bodeful rural in-migration of people thrown out of mill and factory jobs. But rather than treating this influx as the hopeful harbinger of a "back-to-the-land" movement, Odum worried about the ensuing "spectacle of an already over-populated rural cotton South unable to absorb any of the stranded folk set free from city and industry." One despairing jobless man summed up the migrations to Dorothea Lange and Paul Taylor: "They come off the plantations 'cause they ain't got nothin' to do. . . . They come to town and they *still* got nothin to do." Another such dispossessed person, standing in the shade of a roadside billboard, remarked that "the country's in an uproar now"—and so it was during the depression. Odum and his circle were hard-pressed to chart the vast movements of impoverished people back and forth across the South and beyond, uncertain at first what shape the social structure was taking, but apprehensive about the swarming pool of laborers gathering down at the landless, homeless bottom of the tenure ladder.[55] If this metamorphosis might spell the end of farm tenancy in all its previous forms, it also might mean the breakdown of the agricultural ladder and even its limited chances for upward mobility. And thus, most dreadfully, it might mean that social stratification would persist in the rural South, but now, apparently, in a much more polarized and extreme configuration.

Throughout this confused period of "disintegrating feudalism" (as Raper termed it), the Odum group *was* able to trace for its audience one constant: the "exploitation of land and people" and the concentration of power in the hands of the planter "aristocracy" that had always characterized the frontier-inspired "hard master" of the cotton economy. As of 1935, Raper remarked with a certain bitterness, the "controllers of the plantations" were "better off than in recent years." It went without saying that "the plantations themselves have been under pressure—some have been abandoned," he wrote. Yet ironically, "many more have been held together by federal credit and subsidy." Few if any of the "landless farmers," in contrast, had "received any appreciable benefit from these federal expenditures." But programs to encourage production cuts had acted to "push workers off the best land," and overall (Raper concluded) "the New Deal's efforts to increase farm and industrial incomes" in the counties he surveyed had paradoxically "left many people without means of a livelihood"—rental benefits, ginning certificates, and most of the crop loan money went to the economic and political powers that be. All that was left to the former sharecroppers particularly was the "relief program," which was intended merely "to maintain creature-comfort standards."[56] The greater irony was that the planters took advantage of relief programs to curtail the "furnishing" system under which they had previously supported (and controlled) tenant and sharecropper families as their price for a guaranteed pool of labor. Now that the government was providing such basic maintenance, the planters could have their pick from the surplus wage day-labor pool, especially during peak-season harvesting periods.

Regarding the longer planting and cultivation period, on the other hand, new calculations came into play for them, and could at last come into play in the "backward" South, thanks to the indirect subsidy of relief and the web of price supports that protected what was still a thin profit margin: "From 30 to 50 percent of Delta farm labor must ultimately be replaced by machinery if plantations are to escape foreclosure," one experiment station bulletin advised as the best way to reduce production costs. But the cotton harvest yet required the delicate touch of the human hand and so, counseled the same bulletin, "Putting labor on a cash or day basis will increase its efficiency 50 to 100 percent." Writing from the perspective of "labor," Raper was appalled by the implications of these "progressive" improvements ("essential to farmers who expect to earn decent livings and fair returns on investments"), which seemed to signal both the hopelessness of permanent "technological unemployment"—in the end, *depopulating* the rural South—and, perhaps most bleakly, the very kind of "technological *employment*" that the farm mechanizers recommended. "The trend," Raper noticed as early as 1936, "is toward fewer agricultural workers and a lowering of tenure status." But worse, under this new regime, the would-be yeomanry—those who remained behind, their bond to the land ever more tenuous—would become mere appendages to machines. "Man is not a machine," Raper objected simply, and he warned:

> When centralized control and power-driven gadgets lead to an increase of propertylessness and dependency, mechanical efficiency is more than offset by social inefficiency. "But," says the incurable expansionist, "look at the American standard of living!" Yes, look at it. Look, too, at the forgotten folks and gullied fields, particularly in the South, and estimate how much it will cost America to restore the resources that have been wasted and reestablish the people who have been disinherited![57]

The final chapters of the delegitimizing regionalist hidden history of America, recounting fully the nightmarish and unexceptional emergence of the mechanized rural life that Raper, Vance, and Odum had begun to trace in the "time-lagging" South, were most appropriately written by a group of Western left liberal and socialist artists and intellectuals—Paul Taylor, Carey McWilliams, John Steinbeck, and others—who believed that they had seen the future (and in some regions, the past) of rural America, and it was California-style agribusiness (see Figure 5.7). "Industrialized agriculture has its fullest development in California," Berkeley economist Taylor wrote under *An American Exodus* photograph taken by his wife, Dorothea Lange, a photograph appearing in the "Last West" chapter wherein the logic of the organization of the book was revealed. "Old South . . . Plantation under the Machine . . . Midcontinent . . . Plains . . . Dust Bowl . . . Last West"—each part told the "unwritten story" of the "human erosion" that had occurred as the empire for liberty marched westward over the continent. Yet the narrative was by no means one of chronological or even linear progression—unless it was traced as greater and greater technological mastery over nature, from the "hoe culture" still used in the South to the omnipresent trucks and tractors of California. But this story line too was complicated by photographs of pneumatic-tired Farm-Alls "invading the Delta," as Raper had witnessed, and by ample documentary evidence (human figures stooping in the foreground, Caterpillar diesels behind) that the agribusinessmen of California also had much need for manual labor. Instead, the logic of the organization of *An American Exodus* was a reverse logic, as it were, a logic of the postfrontier world. It was a book best read from end to beginning: "For three centuries an ever-receding western frontier has drawn white men like a magnet," Taylor began the final chapter. "This tradition still draws distressed, dislodged, determined Americans to our last West, hard against the waters of the Pacific." Unfortunately, there they did not discover another *new* New World, retreated one final time

Figure 5.7 Photograph and caption from *An American Exodus*, "Last West" chapter, p. 91: "Gang labor and piece rates in an open-air food factory. near Calipatria, California/February 1939." (Photograph by Dorothea Lange, courtesy of the Farm Security Administration, Prints and Photographs Division, Library of Congress, LC-USF34-21050)

westward out of Webb's fallen Great Plains. Rather, they found to their despair that "settlement and mechanization have transformed our frontier. The land is already occupied, and men work upon it with machines as in factories, or at hand labor in gangs as in industry." The opening image of the book—a row of cotton bales, with the caption "The Empire of Cotton Now Stretches from the Atlantic to the Pacific"—was now comprehensible, as was the larger plan. "More and more," Taylor wrote in the last few pages, "the pattern of agriculture dominant in the West is spreading into the best cotton lands of the South," backflowing out of the closed California frontier *eastward* through the Empire of Cotton. Thus, fundamentally, Taylor and Lange's "study in human erosion" was a survey of an America that had "turned back upon itself."[58]

Before arriving in the South, the California pattern of large-scale mechanized farming, making its decades-long way backward across the country, had first encountered the Plains environment. It was from this region, in fact, the realm of the Dust Bowl, that reports about another "victim" of industrialization—nature itself—received their widest dissemination during the depression. The "waste of land and forests" (in Odum's words) and other forms of environmental damage, which were the corollary of "human erosion," had constituted an important subtheme in the delegitimizing efforts of the Odum group. As Raper wrote, "Soil depletion and human exploitation go hand in hand; they are the physical and social expression of the same philosophy"— "traditional Americanism is their common ancestor." Therefore, he posited, the "'dust bowl' in our new agricultural Southwest is a lineal descendent of the depleted and abandoned fields of our old agricultural South and East."[59]

Yet it was the disastrous coincidence of the multifold technological amplification of this exploitative mind-set—manifested by the huge "gang disk plows" of Southwestern "bonanza farming," driving the "hoe culture" of the South out of business—together with the ecologically volatile context of the High Plains subregion, which brought home to 1930s Americans the message of that "traditional Americanism's" bankruptcy in the most palpable way. In case the point of topsoil falling out over the Atlantic seaboard was lost on them, the chief interpreter of the Dust Bowl, botanist Paul Sears (a member of B. A. Botkin's Oklahoma circle), elaborated an ecological list of charges against the frontier myth in his book *Deserts on the March* (1935), the most widely read work issued during the decade by Joseph Brandt's University of Oklahoma Press. Written while dust storms were "obscuring the sun for days at a time," *Deserts on the March* stressed the essential alienness of an extractive, industrial relationship to the land and, not unrelatedly, disclosed an antiexceptional vision of American history. "Mile high, these gloomy curtains of dust are the proper backdrop for the tragedy that is on the boards," Sears mused, and he served warning: "The lustful march of the white race across the virgin continent, strewn with ruined forests, polluted streams, gullied fields, stained by the breaking of treaties and titanic greed, can no longer be disguised behind the camouflage which we call civilization." In delicate environments like the Great Plains, Sears argued, "man, maker of wilderness . . . no longer accepts, as living creatures before him have done, the pattern in which he finds himself, but has destroyed that pattern and from the wreck is attempting to create a new one. That of course is cataclysmic revolution." Balance and equilibrium were "demanded by nature," Sears reminded his audience. "If man destroys an old order he must take the consequences." Folk humorist Will Rogers, who was sympathetic with the general 1930s critique of the frontier myth, told an apprehensive nationwide radio audience what those consequences might be, the unexceptional consequences of the *new* New World brought to the Plains—and no doubt exacerbated their apprehensions:

My wife and daughter has [*sic*] just returned from a trip down in Egypt. . . . That was a great civilization, you see—buried in the blowing

sand. See? . . . And that's how every civilization since time began and the
whole world has been covered up. It's been this dust. . . . In years to come
the archeologist . . . will dig and find Claremore, Oklahoma, and people
will come there to the ruins and dig down and say, "Here lied a civilization." You know?[60]

Writing their own hidden history from behind the "lies" of civilization,
Taylor, McWilliams, Steinbeck, and the other regionalists located on the West
Coast were most interested in the social and political (rather than the natural
or apocalyptic) ramifications of the industrialized agriculture backing up out of
California and rolling across the southern United States, uprooting land and
folk. As Taylor revealed, they had good reason to be concerned with events
beyond their immediate locale: "The link between South and West literally is
human." By conservative estimate, "a full 300,000" refugees from the west-
ernmost margins of the Southern sharecropper system in Texas, Oklahoma,
Arkansas, and Missouri, and others from tenant farms on the High Plains, had
arrived in California between 1935 and 1939. "More than nine-tenths are
native American whites," Taylor emphasized, the remnants of the old yeomanry, the "distressed sons of the settlers."[61] Seeking to explain to their
readers the processes by which these would-be solid citizens had been dispossessed, Taylor and Steinbeck depicted a darkly unexceptional landscape
out of the America "turned back upon itself," a landscape pinioned between
the colonial corporate-megalopolitan power emanating from the East and the
brutal techniques of machine agriculture that had reached their apotheosis in
the Far West, each now brought to bear against its victims often with the
willing collaboration of the local powers that be.

In the "Plains" and "Dust Bowl" sections of *An American Exodus*, for
example, Taylor described what had happened to the yeomanry of Webb's
Great Plains in the years since the demise of the Cattle Kingdom. On the
Southern Plains of Texas particularly, there had emerged "a democracy as
evenly based as the surface of their land," where most "either owned their
farms or, more commonly, as tenants" much better off than the Deep South
variety, "they owned teams and tools, feed and seed." The "topography was
adapted to the most progressive methods of tillage," and thus they "adopted
the highest ratios of power per man" and "sought the largest amounts of land
per family." As late as 1925, the spirit of frontier expansion continued to reign
over the region, a point that Taylor emphasized by including a real estate
advertisement calling on all takers to "invest in 160 to 320 acres" of "fertile
soil" which would "truly bring you contentment, peace, and plenty" ("Does it
appeal to you? If so, get busy . . ."). But the 1930s brought drought and price
crashes, which meant foreclosure for the small owners and displacement for

the tenants, as well as a pattern of social relations that would have been familiar to Arthur Raper:

> Landlords in desperation who previously rented their land to tenants, and loan companies which have foreclosed, are taking over the operation of farms. Spurred by the necessity of cheaper costs of production and the desire to avoid sharing with tenants the cash payments under the agricultural adjustment program, they are shifting from operation by tenants to operation by wage labor employed by the day. And they are turning to mechanization. . . . Thus they reduce the human labor required and . . . enlarge the size of their farms by cutting one tenant family from the land where there were two before. . . . [Meanwhile] the displaced tenant, stripped of his farm and his property, is also stripped of his vote by the poll tax requirement of Texas. . . . [And] depopulation seems destined to be permanent.

Resorting to a rhetoric also familiar to other regionalists—the portentous emergence of an Old World configuration of power in the New—Taylor likened this process to "movements to enclose the common land" that had occurred in England "from the reigns of the Tudors to the nineteenth century," displacing generation after generation of English peasants. Anticipating the blind side that would keep its present-day parallel just as obscure, he concluded:

> In the long view of history, it has been adjudged by scholars that the economic effects of British enclosures were beneficial. Likewise scholars of the future may well take the view that mechanization on the plains enabled farmers to cut costs of production and to recapture a portion of the slipping export market. But the price of such progress in terms of social disorganization and human misery comes high on the plains, as it came high in sixteenth century Britain.[62]

Joining in the alternative regionalist "view of history," John Steinbeck depicted the "enclosure" of the American countryside in somewhat more modern "European" terms, yet the fact that such terms might find application in the national heartland implied equally grave consequences for exceptionalism. In one scene from *The Grapes of Wrath* (1939), he articulated an analysis of mechanized dispossession through the mouth of his recurrent Everyman character, speaking the odd congeries of ideas gleaned from "Paine, Marx, Jefferson, Lenin" that provided the novel's political bearings, a kind of folkish neo-republican labor theory of value. When men from the local bank arrive to evict "the tenants" from their foreclosed Southern-pattern farm ("the tenant system won't work any more"—"one man on a tractor can take the place of twelve or fourteen families"), the tenants cling to their land with perhaps more spiritual than sociological truth: "We were born on it, and we got killed on it, died on it. . . . That's what makes it ours—being born on it, working it, dying on it. That makes ownership, not a paper with numbers on it." When the men from the bank, and later the tractor driver employed by them, shrug their shoulders, a famous exchange ensues, as the vectors of power begin to reveal themselves and yet, pointedly, remain elusive:

We're sorry. It's not us. It's the monster. The bank isn't like a man.

Yes, but the bank is only made of men.

No, you're wrong there. . . . The bank is something more than men, I tell you. It's the monster. Men made it, but they can't control it.

. . . The driver [a local man] said, "Fellow was telling me the bank gets orders from the East. . . ."

"But where does it stop? Who can we shoot? I don't aim to starve to death before I kill the man that's starving me."

"I don't know. Maybe there's nobody to shoot. Maybe the thing isn't men at all. . . .

"I got to figure," the tenant said. "We all got to figure. There's some way to stop this. It's not like lightning or earthquakes. We've got a bad thing made by men, and by God that's something we can change."

Sensitized by Marx to the impersonal working of economic forces (which so "inhumanly" imperiled its victims), Steinbeck argued that in the America "turned back upon itself," *enclosing* itself, power had become systemic, all-pervasive; not only were its "owners" (who were also "owned" by it) remote and unaccountable, there was no haven from its operations. Inexorably, "raping methodically," he wrote, "the tractors"—moving like the alien harbingers of Benton MacKaye's "iron glacier" of megalopolitanism that they were— "came over the roads and into the fields . . . straight down the country, across the country, through fences, through dooryards. . . . They ignored hills and gulches, water courses, fences, houses"—and found and seized the little farm of the Joad family. The California pattern of agriculture thus arrived in the heartland. Steinbeck's rural Everyman, realizing his weak protests were of no avail, could see it coming: "We got to get off. A tractor and a superintendent. Like factories."[63]

Continuing relentlessly the "unwritten story that strikes deep"—"a half-million people moving over the country; a million more, restive to move; ten million more feeling the first nervousness"—Taylor and Steinbeck followed the "progress" of the Joads and "tens of thousands" of other refugees who, together with the dispossessed people of the Plains, were led by the folk urge of the frontier myth westward, hoping to find in the "Last West" of California "opportunity in terms of the old frontier," as Taylor wrote. There, the Okies and Arkies poured "into the agricultural sections seeking land," seeking the abundant Garden of the West, where "you can reach out anywhere and pick an orange," in the sinister refrain of *The Grapes of Wrath*. "For the South," Taylor observed, "the emigration of her people is like the escape of steam through a safety-valve." Sadly, however, that human steam was now being released into *postfrontier* America. Like McNickle's Archilde, the Joads and other migrants discover to their dismay when they roll into places with names like Imperial Valley "how much greater" was "the world which engulfed them," and why "you can't run away nowadays": "In California the old West is gone." And here the "unwritten story" of the modern West was taken up by Carey McWilliams, whose *Factories in the Field* (1939) told the "hidden history" of the state's agricultural "march toward industrialization." What he uncovered was that in California, the Old West had never been. "In no other state has farming so quickly lost its traditional character and become an established industry as in California," McWilliams wrote. "Today, 'farming' in its accepted sense can hardly be said to exist in the State." He set out his delegitimizing purpose: "Here, reads the fable"—retreated to its last space on the map—"life has always been easier and abundance an acknowledged historical fact." His "social history of California"—a "story of theft, fraud, violence, and exploitation"—was to be an "attempt to dispel a few of the illusions and to focus attention on certain unpleasant realities."[64]

McWilliams too, like many of his regionalist counterparts across the nation, expressed those "unpleasant realities" in the antiexceptional terms of European power structures arisen on American soil. For him, the connections between the New World and the Old were historically persistent and substantial. According to his depiction, on the California frontier—where native Americans squeezed out from land-pressured eastern regions might make their claim to the dream of landownership, and where immigrant peasants and proletarians were presumably transformed into American yeomen—the Turnerian homesteading period had been vanishingly short, almost nonexistent. When the would-be miners ("mostly Eastern and Middle Western farmers") who had come west during the Gold Rush of 1849 were "pushed out of the Mother Lode by a few mining barons" in the late 1850s, McWilliams recounted, they began "to look about for land." And "there was land to burn: untenanted, undeveloped, unoccupied"—39 million tillable acres. But just as the process of settlement got under way, the pioneers learned that "they were being excluded from the great farming empire that was California," in a manner similar to the "despoliation" of the Five Civilized Tribes recorded by

Angie Debo. "Under forms of existing law," in this case, Mexican land grants, wholesale fraud was committed during the 1850s and 1860s to dispossess settlers who had already taken occupancy of the California "wilderness." As McWilliams wrote: "The owner of the grant, usually by assignment from a Mexican settler who had sold an empire for little or nothing, would sit idly by while settlers entered upon the grant and made extensive improvements. He would then come forward with his grant, usually forged, ask for its confirmation [by the courts], and then evict the settlers." Most portentously for McWilliams, the use of the Mexican grants established the basic and unexceptional distribution of landownership, and therefore power, that would persist throughout California history. "Through the instrumentality of the Mexican land grants the colonial character of landownership in Spanish-California was carried-over, and actually extended, after the American occupation." For this reason, he concluded, it was possible to understand in the present day "why the valleys are made up of large feudal empires," subject to "feudalistic patterns of ownership and control."[65]

With the single exception of the "prophetic experiment" of the Kaweah Co-operative Colony, which flourished just long enough in the 1890s amid these "dynamics of centralization" to provide McWilliams with a usable utopian socialist past, the rest of California's rural history could be characterized, he argued, by "the most remarkable single circumstance" of "the unbroken continuity of control," not only over land but over "minority racial and other groups," which as farm laborers had been a part of agriculture there since the days of Henry George. If land "monopolization" had made California farmers (as McWilliams quoted George) "'lords as truly as ever were ribboned Dukes or belted Barons,'" it had turned the laborers into "'a kind of peasantry,'" or "peons," and worse. For, McWilliams wrote, "time has merely tightened the system of ownership and control and furthered the degradation of farm labor"—a degradation that he, as director of the state Immigration and Housing Office, had had ample opportunity to observe in his own time. The industrialization of farming techniques and organization had proceeded apace over the decades, from the giant, highly mechanized bonanza wheat ranches, which needed relatively few workers, to the development of the corporate fruit and vegetable farms (usually irrigated and therefore heavily capitalized), which, because of perishability factors, tended "to bridge the gap between country and city," bringing the processing factories and highways near the fields and requiring much intensive, unskilled, mobile, and, above all, cheap labor. In a chapter titled "The Pattern Is Cut," McWilliams described the resulting modern California pattern of rural life and used the unexceptional word that Raper had been searching for, the word that Davidson did not want spoken, and the word that Webb—and all of them—dreaded to contemplate:

The land is operated by processes which are essentially industrial in character. . . ; the "farm hand," celebrated in our American folklore, has been supplanted by an agricultural proletariat indistinguishable from our industrial proletariat; ownership is represented not by physical possession of the land, but by ownership of corporate stock; farm labor, no longer pastoral in character, punches a time clock, works at piece or hourly wage rates, and lives in a shack or company barracks, and lacks all contact with the real owners of the farm factory on which it is employed.[66]

Looking for a little piece of land on which to make a new home, the innocent Joads and many other Okies, Arkies, and Texicans were drawn into this system, "tens of thousands, across the country, hundreds of miles, up and down, from valley to valley, crop to crop, ranch to ranch" (as Taylor wrote; often their plight moved even economists and sociologists to uncustomary eloquence). Yet as McWilliams revealed, the Okie migrants were only the latest in a decades-long succession of races "run through the hopper" of California agribusiness. First the Chinese "coolies," then the Japanese, Filipinos, Hindustanis, blacks, and Mexicans—each group, coming to the land of opportunity, had immigrated into or been especially recruited for labor on the farms, and each had subsequently been discarded when they began to organize or when a cheaper alternative swelled a surplus. "The influx of drought-bowl refugees," though, had broken through the racist blind side that had hitherto preserved the exploitation. "These despised 'Okies' and 'Texicans,'" McWilliams observed, not without a certain irony, "were not another minority alien racial group (although they were treated as such) but American citizens," whose victimization at the hands of other white American citizens had "forced public recognition of an acute social problem . . . the evils of which have, of course, long been pointed out." This "recognition"—in which the "culturally radical" books, articles, and photographs of the California regionalists played no small part—had by 1939 already borne fruit, according to Taylor, in the establishment of "decent" government-sponsored camps for the migrants, such as the idyllic Weedpatch Camp appearing in *The Grapes of Wrath*. But Steinbeck, Taylor, and McWilliams well understood that people like the Joads were still obliged to go out of the camp into the "world which engulfed them" in order to continue to support themselves—still rootless, traveling "up and down, from valley to valley, crop to crop"—their plight begging that more fundamental issues be redressed. As Taylor wrote in *An American Exodus*:

In our concern over the visible and acute distress of dislocated people, we must not lose sight of the permanent farming organization which is being laid down. This grave question arises: After the sweep of mechanization, how shall our best lands be used—our southern plains, prairies, deltas, and our irrigated valleys of the West? Shall factory agriculture—our modern latifundia—prevail with its absentee owners, managers, day laborers, landless migrants, and recurrent strife? Or shall other patterns be sought for the relation of man to the land?[67]

During their various surveys of the transformations taking place in the nation's countryside, a number of regionalists discovered that the people themselves had begun to develop one such alternative "pattern" (of sorts)— ultimately, indeed, a fleeting pattern, spun out of the "moment" of the depression—a puny inertia against the driving forces of capital, marketplace, efficiency, and greed, but nevertheless a way of living on the land that would not require them to become wage laborers or migrants. Arthur Raper was among the first to report this pattern widely; he defined it as the rise of an American "peasantry." For him the word did not have altogether negative connotations, because what it described apparently indicated a desire by many to remain on the land, to till a farm or cultivate a crop that in some sense they could consider their own. "Among the uprooted workers themselves there has been and is an unmistakable strain toward self-support on the cheapest land," he wrote of his two Georgia Black Belt counties and other areas of the South. Carey McWilliams, tracing the march of the California pattern eastward in *Ill Fares the Land* (1942), saw much the same phenomenon out on the western edge of the sharecropper system among "The Joads at Home" in Oklahoma. There the "cheapest lands," he wrote, were "like magnets," attracting "ex-oil workers, ex-miners, and dispossessed farm owners and tenants who cannot get a foothold . . . in the better farming areas." It was, to be sure, not much of a life, both men agreed. The "cheapest lands" were also the "worst eroded lands"— "eroded cotton fields" on the outskirts of the large farms and plantations, "hillsides stripped of timber" out in the backcountry. Worse still, McWilliams observed, "the constant pressure of population" on these limited marginal areas was resulting in "ever-smaller units of farm operation," which, "in turn, accelerate the process of erosion." Out of this depleted ground the new peasantry coaxed something resembling a "self-sufficient farm economy," under which (according to Raper) they "produce little, sell little, buy little." And finally, "the people, in time, become badly 'eroded' themselves," McWilliams wrote, finishing Raper's thought, his tone becoming more and more grim. "They lack capital; they lack education and training; they lack medical care and attention." Meanwhile, "as the soil blows away or is washed away, the relation of the people to the land becomes increasingly tenuous."[68]

Probably these "eroded" peasants of depression-era America stayed on in such an unpromising situation because it was all that they knew (see

Figure 5.8 Photograph and caption from *You Have Seen Their Faces*, p. 171: "Hull, Georgia: 'Sometimes I feel like I've been on this place since the world began. Maybe I'll be here when everybody else has gone to heaven.'" (Photograph by Margaret Bourke-White, courtesy of the Estate of Margaret Bourke-White and the Margaret Bourke-White Collection, George Arents Research Library, Syracuse University)

Figure 5.8). Certainly they did know that there were worse alternatives—the migrant camps, the barracks of the latifundia, the rural relief "ghettos" near big cities, the shacks of the plantation, the unsteady government work, the urban bread lines, the mill towns with their company stores, the open road. Many who assumed peasant status had already tried some of these ways of "getting a living." That they would still look to the land, any piece of land, as a preferable means to earn a hard-scrabble subsistence might be explained by the sentiment Erskine Caldwell ascribed to the stubborn Jeeter Lester: an "inherited love of the land."[69] But to say instead that "it was all that they knew" is to invoke again the context of the interwar years as a crucial "moment" in the history of rural America and for America's image of itself. There had been a time in the nation's past, well within the living memory of 1930s contemporaries, when "rural" was no specifying modifier of "America." The regionalists' depiction of the urban industrialization of the countryside as a crisis of American exceptionalism, seen in this perspective, thus becomes understandable: they could not imagine (or dared not imagine) an America that was *not* predominantly rural.

Howard Odum's consternation over the broadest of population statistics is telling. In 1930, he noted, "of all the more than 120 million people in the United States less than one-fourth were rural farm population"; the total including rural villages was "less than 40 per cent." With postdepression and post–World War II hindsight, aware of the consequent depopulation of the countryside, the figures seem substantial. But to Odum already they signified "the complete surrender of the rural nation to that of an urban America." This kind of mind-set—tending sometimes to the apocalyptic, judging the illegitimacy of urban-industrial progress precisely in its tendency to destroy rural life—this mind-set was linked somehow to the decision of those evanescent "peasants" to remain and cling to the land for shelter from the forces of "human erosion," even as the land itself was disappearing from beneath them. For otherwise, regionalists and imperiled folk together would have to confront the fateful questions that Steinbeck's migrants had to answer as they prepared to make the trip from the homeplace out to California, trying to decide what could be loaded onto the truck, and what had to be left behind. They despair at how little they can take with them: family heirlooms must be abandoned, as must a familiar willow tree, and the very land outside the door. "How can we live without our lives?" they ask. "How will we know it's us without our past?"[70]

Lewis Mumford
(Photograph by Eric Schaal,
courtesy of Monmouth College)

Benton MacKaye
(Courtesy of Dartmouth
College Library)

Howard Odum
(Courtesy of Southern Histor-
ical Collection, University of
North Carolina at Chapel Hill)

Rupert Vance
(Courtesy of North Carolina Collection,
University of North Carolina at Chapel Hill)

Arthur Raper
(Courtesy of Southern
Historical Collection,
University of North
Carolina at Chapel Hill)

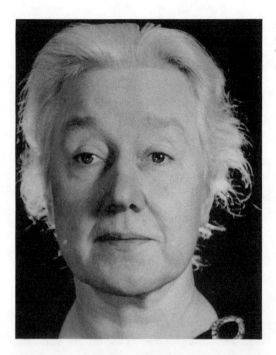

Constance Rourke
(Photograph by Helen K.
Taylor, courtesy of Vassar
College Library)

Walter Prescott Webb
(Courtesy of Eugene C. Barker
Texas History Center, Univer-
sity of Texas at Austin)

J. Frank Dobie
(Courtesy of Eugene C. Barker
Texas History Center, Univer-
sity of Texas at Austin)

Donald Davidson
(Courtesy of Photographic
Archives, Vanderbilt
University)

Allen Tate
(Courtesy of Photographic
Archives, Vanderbilt
University)

John Gould Fletcher
(Photograph by Fayetteville
Engraving, courtesy of General
Picture Collection, Special
Collections Division, Univer-
sity of Arkansas Libraries,
Fayetteville)

John Crowe Ransom
(Courtesy of Photographic
Archives, Vanderbilt
University)

Mari Sandoz
(Courtesy of University
of Nebraska Archives and
Special Collections)

Carey McWilliams
(Photograph by Will Connell,
courtesy of Will Connell, Jr.,
and the Department of Special
Collections, University
Research Library, UCLA)

Mary Austin
(Courtesy of Museum of
New Mexico, neg. no. 45221)

214

John Collier
(Courtesy of John Collier
Papers, Manuscripts and
Archives, Yale University
Library)

John G. Neihardt
(Courtesy of Hilda Neihardt
Petri and the John G. Neihardt
Papers, Western Historical
Manuscripts Collection,
University of Missouri-
Columbia)

Edgar L. Hewett
(Courtesy of Museum of
New Mexico, neg. no. 7365)

John Joseph Mathews
(Courtesy of Western History
Collection, University of
Oklahoma)

Angie Debo
(Courtesy of Western History
Collection, University of
Oklahoma)

Henry Nash Smith
(Courtesy of Elinor Lucas
Smith)

Joseph Brandt
(Courtesy of Western History
Collection, University of
Oklahoma)

B. A. Botkin (Photograph by Jack Delano, courtesy of University of Chicago Archives, University of Chicago Library)

W. T. Couch
(Courtesy of North Carolina
Collection, University of North
Carolina at Chapel Hill)

H. G. Merriam
(Courtesy of University
of Montana Archives,
Mansfield Library)

The Way Out(?)

Toward an Ideology of Regionalism

Contemporary history is filled with manifestations of man's hysterias and furies; with evidences of his daemonic capacity and inclination to break the harmonies of nature and defy the prudent canons of rational restraint. Yet no cumulation of contradictory evidence seems to disturb modern man's good opinion of himself . . . he continues to regard himself as harmless and virtuous. The question therefore arises how modern man arrived at, and by what means he maintains, an estimate of his virtue in such pathetic contradiction with the obvious facts of his history.
—Reinhold Niebuhr, *The Nature and Destiny of Man*

Most of the regionalists involved in delegitimizing the forces of "human erosion" that had brought the peasants and migrants to such straits *were* making some hard revisionist choices about the national past, choices with important ideological implications and, they believed, fateful consequences for American exceptionalism. For if they had shown that an exceptionalism rooted in the frontier myth was, at the very least, a postfrontier dead letter (as was the case with Walter Prescott Webb and Donald Davidson) or, at worst, always an exploitative illusion, they nevertheless had not given up on the *ideal* of exceptionalism itself. The further and central question which their cultural radicalism must resolve concerned the redefinition of what constituted that ideal, and already the usable pasts of the regionalist civic religion had provided a partial answer, in myths reclaimed from marginal places, imperiled folk, briefly effloresceing "kingdoms," and "golden days." But the regionalists' catastrophist anxieties over being "without our past" because of the demographic death of rural America—not only its growing depopulation, but also the megalopolitan abolition of the very distinction between city and countryside— fueled their sense of crisis, their sense that unless something were done soon to arrest and control the process of urban industrialization, all possibility for this second chance at exceptionalism might be gone. It was over this issue of "control," regionalists came to understand, that America must finally prove its exceptionality: the means, who would possess the means, and to what end—the basic questions of politics. And it was in answering these basic questions for themselves that regionalists had to begin to make the inevitable hard choices, the *political* choices, regarding their values, the values from the older, rural America: what part of those values must be sacrificed to realize any of them, even partially, in the modern disenchanted world, to reshape that world.

The questions which John Steinbeck's migrants asked before departure were undoubtedly analogous to those that the regionalists confronted. What, in effecting Lewis Mumford's "organic break" with the past, had to be consigned to the past, and what could be carried into modernity? Most regionalists were realist enough, historicist-minded enough (distinguishing past and present), to know that certain values, behaviors, and practices appropriate to a small-scale, rural, insular, homogeneous, low-technology political economy could not (and, many believed, in the case of such values as racism, should not) find applicability in the qualitatively different and exponentially more complex world of contemporary life. Conversely, regionalists were realistic enough in the presentist sense (individuals *of* their own time) to acknowledge that modernity could have its advantages in the realm of living standards and quality of life particularly, a concession underscored by their confrontation with the poverty of contemporary rural life, the amelioration of which depended largely on technological advances (electrification, sanitation, medicine). When pressed finally to articulate a vision of the future, most regionalists revealed that they objected not so much to the instrumentalities of modern life as to the configurations of power that had been allowed to develop around them, under cover of the blind sides of anachronistic social values like the exploitative frontier myth. Apprised by their revisionist examination of regional-national history of the disjunctions that could emerge between the ideal and real (shortfalls made up with admixtures of coercion and hegemonic control), regionalists—thus politicized—searched the older America for the integrating replacement values that would bring to actual fulfillment America's long-delayed promises of democracy, freedom, and opportunity for all. Like Steinbeck's folk migrants preparing to leave the homeplace, "They sat and looked at it and burned it into their memories"; then they departed. But

on the way to an unknown future they asked these questions of the forces
which had dispossessed them: "Is a tractor bad? Is the power that turns the
long furrows wrong?" American exceptionalism with all of its promises, Steinbeck and other regionalists were convinced, would be conditional upon the
nation's political response to the reply, the simple demand for *control*, that
these victims of modernity made to their own query: "If the tractor were ours
it would be good. . . . If our tractor turned the long furrows of our land, it
would be good."[1]

The difficult beginnings of this process of moving not only beyond myth
but beyond the delegitimizing regionalist historical critique—anchored by
myth—and toward a positive political doctrine (and finally, a concrete program) may be traced, once again, through the career of the reluctant cultural
radical, Walter Prescott Webb. It was Webb who, it may be recalled, nostalgi-
cally decried the use of a tractor by "Farmer Smith" while his mules stood
idle; and it was Webb who confessed to a correspondent about the postfrontier
era, "I am sure intellectually the future generations will adjust themselves,
but it is a little tough on those of us who are bowing out the old life." Just how
tough it could be was reflected in the interpretive lengths to which Webb
resorted in order to preserve the teetering frontier myth, the center of his
worldview, intact. Yet paradoxically, he did, in fact, "bow out the old life," and
his solution showed as well the final and logical culmination of the regionalist
sense of disintegrating exceptionalism.[2]

As was the case with Arthur Raper, Carey McWilliams, and the other
critics of the frontier myth, Webb's perception of the symptoms of a European
configuration of power in contemporary America ("feudalistic" sectionalism
and, more indirectly, class stratification) had raised them in his awareness as
historical forces. But unlike his fellow regionalists, he shrank from acknowledging them in the strained analysis of *Divided We Stand* for the very reason
that they threatened to call into question the sufficiency of the frontier myth as
historical or sociological interpretation and exceptionalism as historical reality. Thus it was no accident that in the same year (1937) which saw the
publication of *Divided We Stand*, Webb began sending out proposals for a new
book, a book on a far vaster scale than his previous works, a scale large enough
to save his worldview from complete dissolution:

I propose to make a study of the relation between Democracy and the
Frontier, as illustrated in Europe and the Americas. My tentative conclusion . . . is that democracy and its accompaniments of freedom and individualism, grows up spontaneously under frontier conditions—"in frontier countries or in countries of Europe that had colonial frontiers. . . ."

The crisis of democracy comes after the frontier is closed. . . . At this point, it would seem, democracy and its concomitants begin to be super-ceded by various types of controls, economic and governmental.[3]

Clearly, in contrast to the delegitimizing works of other regionalist cultural radicals, which tended to revise American history to resemble that of the Old World, Webb was hoping to accomplish quite the opposite. By interpretively "universalizing" the past influence of the frontier to include Europe, effacing the differences between the New World and the Old, he eliminated the conventional Old World historical narrative of endless imperial war, social hierarchy, revolution, and class conflict, creating in its place a new narrative in which America and Europe were *both* exceptional for a time, but now no longer. American history therefore did not have to be rewritten along Old World lines (and to Webb's mind could not be, if such distinctions had never been true). In effect, by these roundabout interpretive means, Webb was able to salvage the frontier myth *as history* from the midst of a disintegrating exceptionalism.

But it was, in the end, a Pyrrhic interpretive victory at best. Though it was preserved, *sealed off* in the past, conceptually, ethically pure, still the unique wellspring of "spontaneous" democracy and freedom, the "Great Frontier" (as Webb later was to call it) was nonetheless dead in the present, an "empty bottle," its influence not operative in the closed frontier world. At the same time, by more explicitly obliterating the distinctions between New World and Old than even the most fervent of the frontier myth's critics, Webb's "universal" history in fact brought about a final antiexceptional (in the strictly American use of the word) merging of not only the pasts of Europe and America, but their present and future fates as well. His new narrative carried both continents toward a contemporary "crisis of democracy," because (Webb told fellow ex-frontiersman E. E. Dale) "the closed frontier, not only in America, but in all the world, means that our type of democracy," rooted in a formerly easy and widespread abundance, "is near the end unless it is willing to make the radical readjustments that the situation requires." As he and other regionalists were all too aware, such "readjustments" to the crisis were already taking shape in "the European countries," which had "attempted to solve it by turning to dictatorship." The same possibility loomed in the postexceptional United States, Webb concluded, unless a "way out" for democracy could be found along "a high divide separating two great evils," on the right the "peril of corporate fascism," and on the left "the more radical forms of socialism," especially the collectivist "pit of communism."[4]

With this scenario, a scenario which, at bottom, created the context for a second chance at exceptionalism (or a renewed lease on it, in his unique post–Great Frontier version), Webb's rhetoric reverted somewhat incoherently back to the New World–Old World dichotomy wherein America might avoid the latest incarnations of European despotism. Yet this incoherence in his universal historical scheme, this break in the narrative of inevitably diminishing freedom, indicated that Webb had begun groping toward a postfrontier politics. "The closing of the frontier," he wrote, "brought democratic America to the first test of its ability to govern, to solve problems rather than to enjoy an escape from them." The subtext of this statement was the source of the break in history signaled by Webb's reversion to a New-Old rhetoric, a subtext that he himself pointed to: "Human nature has repeatedly blighted democracy in Europe, as surely as nature has, many times in the past, prevented titled nobility from arising in America."[5] This fundamentally republican concept had always been one of the pillars of exceptionalism: a man was not subject to the will of another if he owned his means of livelihood ("independence"), preeminently as landed property. Because America was blessed with natural abundance, all men there could be independent and free—there need be no struggle for power, as all men possessed the essential power, over himself. Even the ambitious man, the would-be ruler, could not exercise control over men so independent. And because Europe (in this standard version of the frontier myth) did not possess this natural abundance, men there could be subject to the whims of the man who owned their means of existence; to own themselves, they must seize those means from their owner, that is, engage in the struggle for power, or *politics*—a struggle that could be won and lost—as it had in fascist-communist Europe. Thus, now that the abundance of natural means had come to an end in America, men there too must rely on politics, rather than nature, to own the power over themselves; they could no longer "escape" into nature but must prove exceptionalism in the type of social configuration emergent from the complex clash of wills, ideals, and appetites (human natures) which constituted political life.

The "shape" of that postfrontier social configuration was readily discernible to Webb. From the noncoercive "unfenced world" of laissez-faire ("letting alone" those frontier-nurtured self-directed individuals), the nation had entered a world in which coercion was, apparently, unavoidable. "Business abandoned the principle of laissez-faire for that of monopoly," Webb wrote in a central passage of *Divided We Stand*; "the government is abandoning the principle of *laissez faire* with respect to the powers of monopoly and in behalf of the people." By "the government" Webb meant "the federal government," the collective national will, which was, he had to admit, "the only power that can handle" the corporate overlords. Given the necessity of regulation—that "men must unite to limit business that they may regain some measure of freedom"—the "crisis of democracy" which must be resolved in order to renew exceptionalism, Webb showed his readers, was multifold. First, the "feudal" power of the overlords must be reduced. To accomplish this, the "rugged individuals" who opposed all government "interference," whose frontier-era thinking yet persisted, must be persuaded to "compromise with the Government" or in their "resistance" they would "bring the whole structure down on the heads of us all," the frustrated, impoverished masses resorting possibly to "violent revolution." To prevent this eventuality, it was necessary to enact a national "policy for restoring to all sections and classes . . . a semblance of equal economic opportunity." Furthermore, if such a policy were to be enacted, it was just as essential that the people not exchange their "political rights for economic security"—"compromising" too much with the government—which would mean the "radical readjustment" of a European-modeled "authoritarian" state. "Tyranny is as hateful in one quarter as in another," Webb reminded his audience. "Oppression by business is as undesirable as oppression by government." In either case, "regimentation" would be the common plight.[6]

Such extreme pronouncements seemed to indicate that Webb, at heart, never believed that the "crisis of democracy" was resolvable toward a restored exceptionalism. As he told one correspondent, "I believe it does help to take an optimistic attitude towards the future even though you know it isn't justified." Still transfixed by the "unfenced world" of the Great Frontier, he could not abide the "readjustments" of state power that he knew to be essential to control the overlords of the great corporations or, those readjustments failing, the continuance of their power. "Democracy of the frontier type," he wrote—the type rooted in natural abundance—"must give way in both cases." If reforms were implemented, Webb reiterated to E. E. Dale, "then the question will be whether what we have is democracy. Certainly it will not be in the old usage of that term"—the libertarian frontier myth usage.[7] With this as his standard of freedom, he resigned himself to postfrontier public or private coercion in one form or another.

Yet perhaps *because* of his resignation, Webb in the last pages of *Divided We Stand* began to trace the outline, the barest glimmer, of a way out through a *regional* configuration of power, a way out that would fulfill all of his preconditions for a new exceptionalism and, somehow, not require the coerciveness he knew to be inevitable. "There is a way out," he insisted, "and the American people when informed will find it in the application of the 'good neighbor' policy at home"—"among the sections as among the nations." Moving away from Davidson's divisive sectionalism (the economic always loomed larger for Webb than the racial) and toward Howard Odum's pluralist regionalism, he argued that "like the body, the nation is one, and can survive only so long as each section performs its function without impoverishing the others and impairing their work." The key ingredient of this good neighbor policy was "cooperation," rather than coercion—at bottom, good will, "human nature." The "national industries, the corporations" headquartered in the North "have it within their power immediately . . . to mitigate the evils that their growth and expansion have produced," he believed. "They can now decentralize industry through electric power; they can co-operate more with the government, state and national, if they will." Most importantly, the coordination and formulation of this policy without resort to authoritarianism, and in a manner that would "preserve this democracy and save the spiritual values for the individual," would necessitate "a sustained and increasing interest of people in their government"—a grassroots upswell, the linchpin of Webb's and many a regionalist's scheme. As Webb asked rhetorically, "Is there a way out?," he himself replied: "The hope is bright for a positive answer only through" such an upswell, the assumption being that no policy could be coercive if the people not only consented to but also participated in its framing.[8]

But it was here, at this all-important juncture and others, that Webb's regionalist glimmer began to fade. "The problem," he wrote—in the era of the phantom public—"is to find the secret of sustaining such interest." The "solution of that problem," he argued with some circularity and vagueness, lay in the adoption of the policy for restoring equal opportunity itself. Meanwhile, the uncoerced "co-operation" of the "feudal lords" was in turn essential for that adoption. "The North, when informed," Webb wrote, revealing his own faith in the efficacy of cultural radicalism and not sounding entirely convinced himself, "will not allow its corporate greed and blind self-interest to ruin a great nation," either by refusing to cooperate or by being coerced into it by an authoritarian state. If by "ruin" one's definition centered, as did Webb's, on the constriction of liberties believed to have existed in an "unfenced world," the glimmer must fade further still. Webb's underlying fatalism thus becomes understandable. Over the years, he wrote three major books on the frontier, and all of them (except for *Divided We Stand*, with its glimmer of a way out) ended in the same manner: with the postfrontier, postexceptional onset of "regimentation." As he confessed, "I lean naturally to tragedy." His last important work, *The Great Frontier* (1951), produced like a pulled tooth fourteen years after his original proposal, traced the outline of that tragedy as world-historical principle. He called it the "Parabola of Individualism": "a biography of the individual from the time he appeared out of the folds of medieval institutions and made his way across the lovely valley of the frontier where he walked like a man until now when he is disappearing in the folds of modern corporate institutions."[9]

Despite the divergence of Webb (and his fellow apologists for the frontier myth, such as J. Frank Dobie) from the main thrust of the regionalist movement's delegitimizing frontier critique, his tortured attempt to find a political way out from the inexorable "regimentation" of modern corporate institutions, public and private, was nonetheless symptomatic of the movement as a whole. Like Webb's trajectory of the post–Great Frontier "tragedy," the bleak catalog of seemingly irresistible modernizing forces and the long roll call of victims generated by the Indian subregionalists, the Odum group, the Californians, and the Mumford circle (which, it should be remembered, originated the critique in the 1920s) meant that their historical revisionism tended as strongly toward the catastrophist as it did to the antiexceptional. Yet political action to transform those modernizing forces, to rehabilitate the victims (or their descendants) must begin, quite simply, with a belief in the possibility of change, of a way out. Webb himself developed a reformist politics out of an apparent "incoherence" in the inexorable logic of his universal historical narrative. What precisely this free random element represented, as well as its larger implications for regionalist politicization, can be seen with greater clarity in the more sophisticated and self-consciously constructed universal histories of Lewis Mumford, *Technics and Civilization* (1934) and *The Culture of Cities* (1938). If in these works Mumford's world-historical phases of development all but effaced the distinctions between New World and Old, they also provided him (the arch-catastrophist, as it were, of the 1920s) with the framework for a retreat from catastrophism and for a positive program not merely of reform but of utopian transformation.

Mumford's ambition in both books was not a small one: "to lay the ideological basis for a new order." His formulation, he wrote, would take into account "life as it was lived in the concrete," rather than life as it was now and historically had been "conceived as but a shadow of the prevailing myths and arrogant fantasies of the ruling classes—or the often no less shadowy fantasies of those who challenged them." To gain this concreteness, his revisionism stretched back a thousand years, dividing the "development of the machine and the machine civilization" into his famous "three successive but *over-lapping and inter-penetrating phases*: eotechnic [the economy of wind, wood, and water], paleotechnic [coal and iron], and neotechnic [electricity, light metals]." Mumford's complex narrative thus proceeded from the relatively humane, handicraft-dominated, highly creative eight-hundred-year eotechnic phase (still a "civilizing" survival in the modern era) through the briefer "disastrous interlude," the "upthrust into barbarism," of the industrializing paleotechnic period, which was marked by "the ultimate abysses" of a "quantitative conception of life, stimulated by the will-to-power and regulated only by the conflict of one power-unit—an individual, a class, a state—with another power-unit." In the modern Western world the comparatively "humaner technology" and yet-emerging social organization of neotechnic industry was now dominant, Mumford asserted hopefully, but "paleotechnic ideals"—what other regionalists

identified as the exploitative frontier mentality—still reigned as a "barbarizing influence," its potency multiplied by the ever greater power harnessed
with neotechnic machines and their "immense" possibilities for "good and
evil." If the outmoded "methods and habits of thought"—the "maggoty
corpse"—of the paleotechnic regime were not supplanted by the more appropriate "organic" ideology of a nascent "biotechnic" order, Mumford warned,
then "our relapse into barbarism will go on at a speed directly proportional to
the complication and refinement of our present technological inheritance."[10]

With fascism looming in Europe, Mumford recast this delegitimizing secularized jeremiad in *The Culture of Cities*, which was his attempt to "summa-
rize the course of city development and to correlate this with the rise and fall of
civilizations." And if the shape of the narrative remained the same (promise,
decline, prophesy), it was elaborated in terms less abstract, more dark, more
catastrophic. "The chief question before the Western World today," he wrote,
"is whether disintegration must be complete before a fresh start is made."
Eopolis (village order), Polis (associated villages), Metropolis (mother city),
Megalopolis (standardizing metropolis), Tyrannopolis (barbarizing megalopolis), and Nekropolis (sacked city of the dead)—by this "Cycle of Growth and
Decay" Mumford painted himself further into a deterministic corner. The
regnant megalopolitan stage, under which "the threat of widespread barbarism arises," was "the beginning of the decline," he postulated ("Representatives: Alexandria, third century B.C.; Rome, second century A.D.; Byzan-
tium, tenth century; Paris, eighteenth century; New York, early twentieth
century"). Judging from his metaphors, the modern megalopolis was already
a city of the dead in many ways—"a rootless world, removed from the sources
of life: a Plutonian world, in which living forms become frozen into metal." At
the same time, its "shapeless giantism" meant that "more and more power
gets into [the] hands of fewer and fewer people." Worse still, ominous symptoms of "the remaining downward movements of the cycle" were everywhere
in evidence, particularly in the "war-metropolis" that had been spawned
during the latter 1930s, the spread of its "architecture of imperialism" from
"Washington to Tokyo, from Berlin to Rome" representing "the maximum
possible assault upon the processes of civilization," inspiring a "collective
psychopathology" in the lumpen proletariat, bourgeoisie, and ruling classes
together. With the onset of this terminating stage, Mumford wrote, concluding his "Brief Outline of Hell," the city, which should be "man's greatest work
of art," became instead "an anti-civilizing agent: a non-city"—finally, after
inevitable war and famine, "a tomb for dying: sand sweeps over the ruins."[11]

At his point, however, Mumford not only concluded his catastrophist narrative, he went on to repudiate it in a manner which, like Webb's, was essential
for his politicization. "The end stage, over which Spengler gloated, is an

undeniable reality that has overtaken many civilizations," he conceded. "But one must not, like a Spengler . . . make the mistake of identifying the logical stages of a process, as discovered and systematized by intellectual analysis, with the living reality." This quintessentially modernist assertion—also underlying the regionalist impulse toward writing an antiabstractive "felt" (and mythicized) history—had important liberating implications: it was, in effect, a declaration of free will. Mumford elaborated:

> Social life has its own laws and rhythms: much remains hidden or irrational: much escapes empiric observation and still more escapes statistical analysis. All one can say with any surety is this: when a city has reached the megalopolitan stage, it is plainly on the downward path: it needs a terrific exertion of social force to overcome the inertia, to alter the direction of movement, to resist the immanent processes of disintegration.

But where there's life, there's hope, Mumford wrote: "But while there is life, there is the possibility of counter-movement, fresh growth." Just as Webb broke (or tried to break) with the deterministic Turnerian-republican scheme relating democracy with nature to assert human agency in history, a *political* way out (cooperation) by which Americans did not have to accompany post–Great Frontier Europe into totalitarianism, so too did Mumford stop his narrative to declare that at this point, *ideology*, the new ideology of regionalism, must intervene as a "counter-movement" to the paleotechnic-megalopolitan forces determining the shape of his historical cycle. And that intervention in history is what all ideologies claim for themselves: the ability to control historical change, to create meaning and order. As Mumford, revealing his own faith in cultural radicalism as a politics, wrote of the relationship between formal (written) ideology and the process of asserting control: "When all the other elements in social change are duly taken into account, the definition of the new framework itself becomes, not a piece of utopian wishfulness, but a decisive element in the whole process."[12]

Having shown with other regionalists the illegitimacy of the paleotechnic regime, uncovering with them its true nature, Mumford called on his now-enlightened audience "to cast off the dead form of the metropolitan order" and to build a new one. The "next step" in this process of intervening in history, he believed, echoing B. A. Botkin, "lies in contriving the political organization appropriate to this new task, and in working out, in concrete detail, the effective economic means"—the "way out." That this way out would lie through a "regional framework," that it was, in truth, the *only* way out to freedom, Mumford argued as well, again adopting a style of rhetoric common to all ideological discourse—that "ours is the only way": the "issues of war and peace, socialization or disorganization, culture or barbarism, rest in good part on our success in handling this problem." Such success, he made clear, would be judged in the final analysis on their avoidance of tendencies taking shape in contemporary Europe, which set the context of a second chance for exceptionalism. For despite his scrupulously antiexceptional narrative (America's differentiation from Europe is rarely if ever invoked in several hundred pages), events in Germany and Italy undoubtedly exercised a strong influence over his depiction of the final stages of the cycle of city development, especially the stage of Tyrannopolis. Mumford thus conceptualized the gathering world crisis as one pitting the regionalist project "to conceive and to germinate fresh forms of human culture" against the "stale cult of death that the fascists have erected." Moreover, although he and others could perceive ominous embryonic signs of Tyrannopolis in the United States, Mumford's modernist suspicion of pure intellectual constructs again provided him with a refuge from its catastrophic effects, and with an exceptional haven for his social values. Because society was "much less of a unity than we are compelled to conceive it" in language and thought, he argued, neither culture nor history formed "a consistent whole," a "solid laminated block." Therefore no civilization could be completely dominated by the pathology of world cities. "Even in the stage of Tyrannopolis," Mumford observed,

> there still remain regions and cities and villages with other memories, other backgrounds, other hopes. . . . In the heyday of the megalopolitan economy, such regional centers remain *partly outside the cycle* [italics mine]: some failure of enterprise, some lack of opportunity, or some sturdier sense of life-values keeps them from sharing the delusive growth and splendor of the metropolis.

With this recourse to an exceptionalism retreated into the provinces, "outside the cycle" even of universal history, Mumford demonstrated that—his own massive intellectual edifice notwithstanding—he too was "reluctant" to relinquish the surviving remnant of imperiled values yet embodied in such places as the little colonial New England village, from which he still was taking his ethical bearings as late as 1940. "The roots of a culture are deep," he posited and, politically, must posit, because the New England village was not merely a "remnant." It was, "veritably," a "saving remnant."[13]

Much the same tendencies may be traced in the works of the Indian subregionalists, the Odum group, and the Californians, who, despite their recognition that there had never been any "lovely valley of the frontier," were each still able to salvage some usable past from the greater "tragedy" of modernizing cultural imperilment and dispersion perpetrated on the "blind side" of the frontier mentality. So also did they rhetorically come to define a renewable exceptionalism in juxtaposition to the fascist specter arising in Europe and, it

seemed, already stalking the American landscape: thus the totalitarian overtones of D'Arcy McNickle's *The Surrounded*, the frequent comparisons that
even the understating Howard Odum made between the South and Nazi Germany, the pointed descriptions of California agribusiness practices by McWilliams as examples of "fascist control." And still another, most crucial pattern
emerges as well when Webb and Mumford (and their circles) are so gathered
together with their fellow regionalists from the South and the West: seeking to
contrive the "political organization" and "effective economic means" of the
regionalist way out, they departed from the "saving remnants" of aesthetic-
symbiotic folk values and converged via diverse programmatic routes (as will
be seen in the next chapter) at a common vision of noncoercive cooperative
community life. As Arthur Raper stated, mirroring Webb's stab at a postfrontier politics: "The South, along with the rest of the nation and the world, now
faces a choice between cooperation and coercion."[14]

Raper defined his terms in a significant way: "When the rank and file of the
people participate responsibly in community affairs, the basis of cooperation is
being laid; when they are inarticulate recipients of practices and policies which
they themselves do not determine, coercion is already at hand." Other members of the movement, sharing his assumptions, expanded on them. To reconstitute such a community life it was necessary to invoke the saving remnant of
folk culture that the people themselves yet possessed, "to understand and use
their genius for collective effort," bringing about a "revival of racial self-
consciousness through free consultation rather than arbitrary rulings," as
Angie Debo argued in the case of returning self-government to the Five
Civilized Tribes. Yet it was equally important to acknowledge, as Raper did,
and as the California socialists well knew, that "the political organization of a
people takes its character largely from the way they earn their living." The
"End of a Cycle" had arrived for the California pattern of industrialized
agriculture, McWilliams surmised, when it had drawn into its maw "American
citizens familiar with the usages of democracy." Forthwith "their struggle for
a decent life . . . may issue a new type of agricultural economy for the West and
for America"—a "collective" type. Paul Taylor and Dorothea Lange supplied
a summing mythic image of this regionalist cooperative vision: men in overalls
and women wearing gingham, sitting together in classic town-meeting style,
one from among them standing with hand raised in argument: "Beginnings of
Organization: Their tap-root to the land severed, they search with their
fellows where new roots may be sunk."[15]

It may be remembered that Webb—who as the reluctant cultural radical
was by no means notable for his realism —had been somewhat dubious about
the prospects for "increasing and sustaining" this mass democratic linchpin of
the regionalist ideology. Mumford, perhaps the most radical of the radicals,

and certainly the foremost theoretically, tried to explain in *The Culture of Cities* just how the phantom public was to be transubstantiated into an uncoerced grassroots polity. It was all a matter of "rational politics," he wrote, all too cognizant that quite the opposite variety seemed to be sweeping the world in the late 1930s. The alternative to this "tyrannical compulsion," according to Mumford, was not "unconditional 'freedom,'" as Webb's "rugged individuals" would have it, but rather "the systematic practice of rational discipline through education and co-operative service." Education was the true key to the regionalist way out, because it provided the noncoercive means—"persuasion and rational agreement"—by which "political power" was to be "rationally conditioned and successfully diffused" among the members of the cooperative community. Mumford agreed that "human conduct is full of irrational residues" (some would say more than mere "residues"), yet in his eyes that was all the more reason to "increase the area of rational judgements and rational political activity, and to divert or sublimate those forces which are inimical to co-operation." This unlikely task was possible only through the special kind of education embodied in the "regional survey," which in Mumford's literal formulation (other regionalists would concur that some such grounding was essential) entailed, as a first step, an exposure of the youth to all the "resources and activities" of a region "felt and lived through as concrete experiences," so that they might see their "personal lives as subject to the same processes." Next, and most centrally, would come a more rigorous *scientific* investigation by the students of the local soil, climate, geology, industry, and history—like many of his contemporaries, Mumford believed that science was the basis of a truly rational discourse; thus, "when science becomes an integral part of daily experience," he wrote, "the foundations for a common collective discipline can be laid." But there was one final element in this political education toward a noncoercive community life:

> What is needed for political life is not mere factual knowledge: for this by itself is inert: what is needed are those esthetic and mythic impulses which open up new activities and carve out new forms for construction and contemplation. When the landscape as a whole comes to mean to the community and the individual citizen what the single garden does to the individual lover of flowers, the regional survey will not merely be a mode of assimilating scientific knowledge: it will be a dynamic preparation for further activity.

That further activity, the "grand task of politics for the opening generation"— so Mumford exulted in this last important manifesto and theoretical work of the regionalist movement—was the "re-animation and re-building of regions, as deliberate works of collective art." Indeed, given that the "regional survey" education in communal experience, symbiosis, and the shared liturgy of aesthetic and mythic values was cumulatively directed toward the cooperative nullification of coercion, Mumford's true goal, and the goal of many other regionalists who shared his vision of regional community life, was clear. The grand task of politics for the opening generation was, ultimately, to *end* the struggle for power—to *abolish* politics: the task of utopia.[16]

Here it is necessary to reiterate that most regionalist artists and intellectuals, particularly individuals like Raper, McWilliams, Vance, and Debo, should not be considered "political infants." But to the extent that they held these kinds of aspirations, that they believed it possible, as John Gould Fletcher wrote, "to educate America with a principle alien to its whole historical development," many regionalists were to be in for a rather different kind of political education over the course of the 1930s—an education in mainstream politics-as-usual, wherein *power* was the key and the *irrational* arranged its configuration.[17] This "education" comprises the denouement of the story of the regionalist movement, the subject of our next chapters. Yet, as has already been intimated, regionalism did have its Cassandra, whose agonized prophesies about the fate of those utopian aspirations in the arena of politics-as-usual went unheeded by regionalist cultural radicals and ordinary Americans alike: Mari Sandoz. If Sandoz's cautionary tale of Irvy's visit to Goodhue's civic cathedral had cast doubt on the very efficacy of cultural radicalism, her subsequent fictive visits to the capitol, which was a central symbol for her, furnish a guide to the collective waning of regionalist hopes through the darkening political contexts of the depression and pre–World War II years, when more and more regionalists came to realize that they themselves had been Cassandras all along.

Sandoz's own qualification to be a Cassandra for the would-be ideology of regionalism was simple: of all regionalists, she probably had received the most extensive "education" in power politics-as-usual and, not unrelatedly, in the realities of America's abortive exceptionalism. Her consequent rather bleak view of the world, she once related, had led some communists of her acquaintance to call her a "defeatist," to which she wryly replied: "They might feel less hopeful too, if they lived in a midwestern state capital." Yet if her fellow regionalists might be said to fit Sandoz's description of those idealistic communist acquaintances—"all very learned intellectuals, given to abstract discussion and gifted with a great faith in the perfectibility of humanity towards citizenship in a Utopia"—it is also true that she herself remained an arch-populist throughout the 1930s, in spite of all that she had endured and witnessed.[18] True to type, hers was to be a stoic, fatalistic embrace of politics, a rearguard action against the coming of dystopia.

Just as fellow Plains dweller Webb's *The Great Plains* was "an autobiography with scholarly trimmings," very much a Texas-centered study of a huge and diverse region, Sandoz's own dark and disenchanted vision of the Plains frontier (and American mythology and politics in general), explored through several volumes, was equally a product of her upbringing in the harsh Niobrara country of northwestern Nebraska, which was far from any "lovely valley." Her "education" there readily explains why Sandoz took the theme of betrayed exceptionalism the furthest of any regional writer. In contrast to the "pure American stock . . . of English or Scotch and Scotch-Irish descent" that settled Webb's corner of the Plains, the Niobrara subregion was dominated by what he called "the foreign element"—Sandoz's people, "Newly Immigrated" Bohemians, Poles, and Swiss (like her own father, Jules Ami Sandoz), who together set for her a microcosmic context of European settlement in America. They lived a hard life there among the Sand Hills, nowhere more apparent than in the Sandoz household portrayed in *Old Jules* (1935), Sandoz's fictionalized biography of her father. Whereas the greatest frontier hardship little Walter Webb had to endure was his parents' (to whom he dedicated his "autobiography") making him do his daily chores, young Mari lost the sight in one eye herding cattle lost once during a blizzard. Moreover, from the age of three months until she was an almost fully grown slip of a girl, Sandoz was regularly beaten by her father (on that first occasion, as she wrote in a distancing third person, "he whipped the child until she lay blue and trembling as a terrorized small animal"). And yet, Sandoz paradoxically avowed, "My feeling for Old Jules was always one of intense admiration." She considered him the real-life mythic embodiment of the frontiersman, "a sort of Moses working the soil of his Promised Land," a pathfinder and claim locater who "had never failed his community. He fought drouth, cold, hunger, and loneliness for them. He brought them in as penniless homeseekers [and] helped them to stay."[19]

The process by which Jules and his immigrant community enacted the frontier myth provided a further important element in Sandoz's realist Niobrara political education. She and her family actually lived in the Cattle Kingdom that Webb the farmboy fantasized about and that the adult Webb depicted to be a folkish "natural institution adapted to its environment," a "kingdom" because of the vastness of its scale and its chivalriclike code. But the word could only have a more sinister connotation for Sandoz, whose family became deeply embroiled in the range wars that erupted when homesteaders arrived to supersede the cattlemen, in a setting not too far distant or different from the infamous Johnson County War of Wyoming. The Niobrara conflict loomed in her eyes as part of "the real issue, the eternal conflict of the small man against the big." Thus, in her depiction, when Jules as Moses led his oppressed Old World people into the Promised Land of the Niobrara, they discovered "the country and the court's in the hands of the cattleman already"— not Webb's *new* New World, where there was "room for everybody," but the same Old one of power and privilege they thought they had left behind. Her father, Sandoz observed, "had chosen to come to America, America the land of the free, to find that corruption followed upon the heels of the settlers as wolves once trailed the buffalo herds. One year of settlement and it had come" (much as McWilliams's homesteading ex-miners had found in California). As a character in *Old Jules* remarks: "This country will develop—in time. . . . But not until the ground is soaked in misery and in blood." After years of feuding with the powerful ranchers—eventually with success, but also with many losers on his own side—Jules (and Sandoz herself) had to agree with an immigrant neighbor who mused, "Empire crazy. . . . All empire crazy. England, France, Germany, Russia, America—all except *die Schweiz*. And there is no future there":

> That was it. No future, and here there was, but the country was in the hands of cattlemen, grafters, expansionists. "Bigger country, but not better."

> "No, nothing better."[20]

If Sandoz with her version of universal history in this manner broke down the distinctions between Old World and New World more explicitly and self-consciously even than most of her fellow critics of frontier myth exceptionalism, she nevertheless joined them in defining a second chance for exceptionalism in relation to the latest European-model tyranny, fascism. Sandoz, in fact, probably became concerned with such issues sooner than many of them—a not-surprising sensitivity, given her early experiences among the power- and land-hungry on the Plains. As early as 1932, she was writing of the "will-to-power" and the "Messiah complex" as central psychological and political categories. How these tendencies had been enacted historically or might in the future be enacted in an American context, and how they might (or might not) be overcome to achieve exceptionalism, became a personal obsession for Sandoz, confronted in two novels which she considered complementary, *Slogum House* (1937) and *Capital City* (1939). In her conceptualization, fascism and the "irrational" power-obsessed psychologies underlying it were by no means to be discerned as purely European phenomena. *Slogum House*, set on the corrupt and violent Niobrara frontier that Sandoz knew so well, tells the story of one ruthless "will-to-power individual," Gulla Slogum, who over the course of the narrative expands her ranch's holdings by whatever means necessary, including fraud, terror, and murder. Slogum House itself is an oppressive caricature of the mythicized and innocent frontier log cabin, featuring an upstairs brothel and secret passages that allow Gulla to spy on guests and family. There, as hapless homesteaders and power-broken ranchers are pushed off their land one by one, a map on her bedroom wall is sketched in to illustrate "the far reaches of the ambitions of Gulla." By the end of the novel "red boxes enclosing land mortgaged to Gulla, and red x's indicating land she owned, run by renters" were "all over the map," building the author's portrait of a landlord from a frontier to a postfrontier, depression-era climax, when Gulla anticipates grabbing still more foreclosed or abandoned land. "Hard winters," Sandoz observed, "make fat coyotes." As Donald Davidson feared, people did "eat one another" in America, and the frontier where there was presumably "room for everybody" thus provided a perfect delegitimizing setting to explore, in Sandoz's words, the "universal theme of a driving will-to-power and the means always employed in its fulfillment, whether the ambitious one be a Gulla Slogum, a Rockefeller, or a Hitler."[21]

The more central plot line directed toward finding the way out of this fallen world to a yet-to-be-realized exceptionalism—and revealing as well the direction of Sandoz's personal politicization—concerned the local opponents to Gulla's expansionist aims. Although brief references appear in the book to the frontier as a "safety valve" and a "poor man's heaven," the thrust of Sandoz's narrative demonstrates that, consciously or unconsciously, she had gone very far conceptually toward apprehending the frontier myth *as* myth rather than, like Webb and its apologists, conceiving it as objective reality. She was well on her way to a modernist conceptualization of history (such as Mumford's) in which culture—rather than fate, or Providence, or geography, or blind economic force—was the determinative factor in history. Although Raper, McWilliams, and others involved in the realist revision of regional-national history had made a similar breakthrough, Sandoz (or, at least, the voice Sandoz adopted in *Slogum House*) differed from them in the sense that the usable past which she salvaged from her own disenchanting exposure to life in the Promised Land was the frontier myth itself. She embodied this functional conceptualization in the character of claim locater Leo Platt, who (just as her father had) roams a corrupt and preempted landscape attempting to realize the ideals of the myth for the victims of Gulla's machinations. His accomplices for this task are not the "tall figures" of Western pulp but, instead, a somewhat unmythic group of surveyors and, on one particularly important mission to overturn the false claims of Gulla and others, "government inspectors and secret-servicemen."[22] To assist his fellow settlers, Platt spends more of his time in courthouses and the state legislature than in the Niobrara "wilderness," which in Sandoz's depiction becomes a rather litigious frontier. Mortgages, loans, foreclosures, lobbying, government investigations, congressional acts, and presidential orders—in a word, *politics*—appear just as significant as ax or plow in the opening of this "free" land; and those methods failing, there were also "politics by other means," such as gunplay and law enforcement. In short, Sandoz attempted to demonstrate that the frontier had never offered an exceptionalistic "escape from problems," as Webb insisted, but had itself always been the object of the struggle for power.

This conclusion, needless to say, would have come as no revelation to the Indian subregionalists, the Odum group, or the Californians, who expended much effort portraying the victims of such struggles in various frontier and postfrontier regional contexts. But Sandoz's narrative featured not just "villains" and "victims," it included "heroes" as well, heroes to show the "way out." Acting *politically* on behalf of the frontier myth, its promises of equality of opportunity and limitless mobility, Leo Platt seeks to create order out of the corrupt chaos brought on by Gulla's irrational self-interest. He acts *in history* to solve problems rather than (as Mark Twain wrote, to solve Huck's predicament) "lighting out for the Territory" to evade them (not possible in a postfrontier world in any case). The underlying theme of *Slogum House* was that America's chance at exceptionalism stemmed not from frontier abundance in itself but from the democratic institutions and traditions—rooted in many of the assumptions of the frontier myth *as* communal myth—through which struggles over that abundance were conducted and resolved, preeminently the "great Midwestern liberalism" of William Jennings Bryan, Robert La Follette, and George W. Norris.

This message was brought home most forcefully in the climactic moment of the book, when Sandoz joined her fellow regionalists in prescribing a mass democratic solution to the problems of an America "turned back upon itself," returning to Goodhue's civic cathedral on the dark eve of the New Deal. The grasping practices of Gulla and other landlords—banks, Eastern land companies—have dispossessed many farmers in Nebraska, but rather than take the despairing route of Irvy's father, they instead organize two thousand–strong under Leo Platt and march on the capitol in Lincoln. As Sandoz describes the scene, "They overran the wide grounds and jammed the steps of the ten-million-dollar capitol, paid for by the energy and frugality of these men and their kind. Now they had come demanding that their homes not be taken from them, their children turned out on the road." She watches while "those sunburnt, determined men stalk through the stone portals . . . under the pioneer panel commemorating the heroism of their fathers and mothers." And she notes: "Those who could still assert themselves would stop to spit into the fine brass cuspidors"—not derisively *on* the symbolic sculpture, as had the ragamuffin boys in her story "Mist and the Tall White Tower," but with respect for the order and proper process represented in the architecture, and at the same time declaring their ownership of the capitol over the "parasitic" officeholders who inhabit it. They continue into the building, "troop into the House chamber . . . pack the galleries," and "spread through the corridors almost two blocks long, the statehouse officials scurrying out of sight before this silent, dark-faced, desperate lot." Their spokesman, "in overalls and patched cowhide shoes," stands before "his lawmakers" and announces, "All we want is a fair shake," staring as he talks toward the rotunda of the tower "white and strong and high, the symbol of equality before the law." Not long after the rally, a character reflects on how the lands of the frontier had fallen into the possession of Eastern-dominated "mortgage holders and landlords." He sees his own small town as

> but one village in a great nation that was so short a time ago the land of promise, still the richest of all the world, and yet paralyzed, all activity halted except foreclosure and eviction and the lengthening of the lines of those who had no roof and no bread. Through the grey fog of his helplessness rose the words of Jeremiah: "And I brought you into a plentiful country, to eat the fruit thereof and the goodness thereof; but when ye entered, ye defiled my land, and made mine heritage an abomination."

Sandoz thus makes clear that the regenerative "way out" of that "abomination," just as many other regionalists had concluded, was mass political action; the agitation of the farmers has broken the national paralysis, showing democracy still to be healthy. They ask merely for a reprieve, a government-ordered two-year moratorium on foreclosures, a "fair shake" that will leave basic property relations undisturbed but will allow the people to retain the homesteads that are the foundation of their livelihood and their political virtue. Because of their pressure, the measure is passed—and proclaimed as though a new frontier had been discovered. Riding westward back to the Niobrara country, the same character who had recalled the verses from Jeremiah sings along the way a song of his immigrant *grossmutter*'s, "one she learned during the long weeks of her passage to the new land, a song of youth and hope and joy, *Amerika 's' ein schones Land*."[23]

That song had all too quickly died in Sandoz's throat as she bore witness to events following the inauguration of the New Deal, years marked by labor violence, the resurgence of reactionary forces, the failure of recovery, and the flagging of the very kind of limited New Deal–style stopgap reform measures that her fictive farmers had rallied behind. Significantly, in 1936, the year *before* the publication of *Slogum House*, she confessed to a friend that "it seems to me . . . the sun of mid-western liberalism has set," that "the great tradition of mid-western liberalism, the agricultural liberalism of the Bryans, the LaFollettes, the Manahans and the Norrisses, is dead." Thus in *Capital City* Sandoz reveals the reawakening at the (ironic) end of *Slogum House* to have been a false spring—the "small man" was still losing to the "big." Her chief teacher in this "agricultural liberalism" (other than her father Jules) had been historian John Hicks, who ended his *Populist Revolt* (1931) celebration of the "triumph of Populist principles," product of the last great uprising of the People, with an evaluative overview by turns naive, pathetic, and true:

> . . . in so far as political devices can insure it, the people now rule. . . . [On] the whole the acts of government have come to reflect fairly clearly the will of the people. Efforts to assert this newly won power in such a way as to crush the economic supremacy of the predatory few have also been numerous and not wholly unsuccessful. The gigantic corporations of to-day, dwarfing into insignificance the trusts of yesterday, are, in spite of their size, far more circumspect in their conduct than their predecessors. If in the last analysis "big business" controls, it is because it has public opinion on its side.

Reading over his own words, Hicks noted that, based as it was "upon an essen-tially individualistic philosophy . . . designed merely to insure for every man his right to 'get ahead' in the world," the "Populist type of reform" seemed to the modern radical "futile," as problems caused by yet-unregulated market forces and deep-seated maldistribution of wealth must inevitably and periodi-cally recrystallize. He conceded that "something more drastic is required": "It seems reasonable to suppose that progressivism itself must progress." San-doz, who traced the origins of *Capital City* to the university course she took with Hicks in 1930, quite agreed. And so she broke with the laissez-faire world of the frontier myth and with Leo Platt and the "great midwestern liberal-ism," which were too limited a step beyond it: "This is a new world that de-mands something more than a stubborn sitting upon the midden heaps of a vanished era and crying for its return." For "progressivism" to "progress," she believed, it must be broadened (toward pluralism), deepened (toward so-cial democracy), refabricated—just as in *Capital City* she remodeled Good-hue's civic cathedral, which could no longer contain her politics: Hartley Alex-ander's "Anglo-Saxon" bas-relief progress of freedom becomes "the Frieze of the Peoples of the World" supporting a "stone globe," with "the shoulders, the hands" of such groups as the "Negroes and Japanese and Jews bearing an equal share." And the principle of "equality before the law" is taken a "monu-mental" step further as well: a statue of Benjamin Franklin, namesake of Sandoz's fictionalized capital city (in the state of "Kanewa"), replaces a real-

life statue of Abraham Lincoln—and his long-exhausted free soil Republican
unionism—with these words of Franklin inscribed: "Private property . . . is
the creature of society and is subject to the calls of that society whenever its
necessities shall require it, even to its last farthing."[24]

It was at this point, in fact, that Sandoz's role as Cassandra became manifest, for even as she radicalized to confront these immovable bodies of American politics—racism, nationalism, and property rights—she recognized them
as immovable bodies. Much like Raper and Odum, she tended to shunt the
issues of racism and nativism together with the problem of class oppression,
believing as did many artists and intellectuals of the 1930s that the power
underlying 100 percent Americanism was primarily economic. The prominence she afforded the imaginary Franklin statue was in this sense premedi-
tated: its subversive inscription was made doubly so given Franklin's own
longtime status as an icon of generations of would-be "Horatio Alger heroes,"
drilled in the sayings of Poor Richard. Her purpose here was to begin to
undermine the sacrosanct notion of "man's inherent property rights," as a
"minister of the Trinity Church" in *Capital City* describes them. Sandoz
believed, with most other regionalists, that America's fixation on the sanctity
of individually owned property—from the freeholding republican farmer, to
the naturally acquisitive "economic man" of classical economics, to the conspicuous consumer of the American dream—had led to the emergence of the
very undemocratic European configurations of power that dominated modern
society. Webb, for one—otherwise typically vague on this explosive subject—
criticized particularly the Fourteenth Amendment–protected corporate "individuals" who found legitimacy for their feudalistic concentrations of wealth
under the same mythic rubric as the small farmer. But he reserved a further
measure of ire for those same small-farmer "rugged individuals" who resisted
all attempts at the regulation of the flow of capital and other "inviolable"
private spheres as *un-American*: "As individualists they stand, unorganized
and practically inarticulate, against the greatest organized forces of the world.
They furnish the best soil in which these organized forces can grow. They are
the manure at the roots of the corporate tree." In the eyes of many regionalists, the Populists, the Progressives, and now, apparently, the New Dealers as
well may have pruned the leaves, or at most, the limbs of entrenched property
interests (to continue Webb's metaphor), but the roots and main body of
corporate power had remained intact and had, to be sure, expanded over the
years (as Hicks indicated). Sandoz and most others in the movement—the
conservative Agrarians, with their Property State, were a notable exception—thus concluded that the "grand task of politics for the opening generation" must entail some radical redefinition of property relations. As Carey
McWilliams wrote of migratory labor reform, "The final solution will come

only when the present wasteful, vicious, undemocratic, and thoroughly anti-social system of agricultural ownership . . . is abolished." So too did Mumford well understand that his vision of transforming regions into "deliberate works of collective art" must be prefaced by a new pattern of property holding: "As long as individual ownership is regarded as sacred, the most important needs of the community may be balked. . . . By means of communal ownership, the land can be functionally apportioned with respect to the needs of communal life."[25]

But Sandoz understood better than most how reluctant Americans would be to "give up their last farthing" to the "community" or any other entity. Schooled in politics on the Niobrara, where ownership disputes had steeped the landscape "in misery and in blood," she knew that any radical attempt to budge this most immovable of immovable bodies was all too unlikely if it were predicated on noncoercive "persuasion and rational agreement." To break the grip of the "irrational residues" of self-interest, greed, and the will to power that fueled the capitalist economy would inevitably require, she feared, a "politics by other means." Her glib comments on the touching faith of her communist (and regionalist) acquaintances "in the perfectibility of humanity towards citizenship in a Utopia" were in sharp contrast to her own "defeatist" position. Nevertheless, she wrote, "We believe that human justice"—short of Utopia—"must be fought for, and we battle for it with the only weapon the priviliged interests really fear—organization of their exploited."[26]

Yet something held Sandoz back from embracing any of the more violently revolutionary varieties of Marxism (toward which her social analysis seemed headed). Her use of the statue of Franklin as a delegitimizing device indicated a desire to remain within the American radical reform tradition. She held out the hope-against-hope that the fight for human justice could be an electoral fight, that somewhere there was one more member of the dwindling Mid-western liberal tradition, a "bright young crusader" like her father Jules, or Leo Platt, or Billy Bryan, to engage now in some "grander task" than the old-style Populism, a hero to "expose" injustice to the people, readjust all social imbalances, establish a new order, "persuade" them toward a "way out." For Sandoz, that way out assumed a familiar shape. It was essential to realize, she wrote in *Capital City*, that "the large industrial centers are probably done; that in the future most of the factories will be in semi-rural setups, in small units, using electricity as power, the workers living on acreages and small farms; no more soot and slums, no more starvation from crop failure." The key to this future, she ended, "is in the middle west, with its still fertile soil and its cheap water power." But Sandoz was such a political being that she could not invoke this vision without immediately compassing it around with all of the obstacles in its path. She alluded to the "TVA fuss," which in her eyes was an effort to "detain the growth of public control, to sell it out, break it." She warned of the "industrialists" and their threat to co-opt the new electric power grid, and cautioned that "the fight will have to be won and rewon, next legislature, even this election." In the final analysis, she said through the voice of the activist Stephani (her fantasy self-personification in *Capital City*), public versus private control was "the means to freedom or slavery." Lewis Mumford, master theorist of regionalism, agreed: "Without the decisive control that rests with collective ownership . . . regional planning is an all but impossible task."[27]

And Sandoz, as Cassandra, knew that it was not going to happen, that there was "nobody with a chance" to make it happen (as she wrote), that some other scenario must unfold out of the American character as she had come to know it in the heartland. There it had shown itself to be nothing exceptional at all: only universal "human nature." Together with many other American artists and intellectuals witnessing the dark turn of events in the world of the late thirties and early forties, Sandoz had arrived by the writing of *Capital City* at a number of unsettling conclusions about human nature, some modern, some not so modern. Foremost in her mind was the "capacity and inclination," ancient and omnipresent, that Americans had been reminded of by Reinhold Niebuhr and by the rise of Adolf Hitler. Sandoz had first learned about these tendencies on the family homestead, where her own father had so often brutalized her: "In Jules, as in every man," she surmised, "there lurks something ready to destroy the finest in him as the frosts of the earth destroy her flowers." Sandoz devised a veritable form letter to reply to shocked matrons writing her their sympathy after reading the revelations of *Old Jules*:

> Here was a character who embodied not only his own strengths and weaknesses but those of all humanity . . . his struggles were universal struggles and his defeats at the hands of the environment and his own insufficiencies were those of mankind; his tenacious clinging to his dream the symbol of man's undying hope that over the next hill he will find the green pasture of his desire which he has never yet deserved.

The matrons' shock, Jules's tenacity—these were symptomatic of another much-discussed aspect of human nature that was also brought to the fore by the emergence of Nazi Germany, and perhaps not unrelated to the fashionability of Niebuhr's words: the aspect of self-deception. Its political ramifications were of the greatest moment, with Lippmann, Freud, Marx, Mannheim, and others providing a new (and largely, but appropriately, "European") vocabulary with which to discuss them—phantom public, mass delusion, false consciousness, collective psychopathology, the "mask" of "ideology" itself. Sandoz was well acquainted with manifestations of self-deception in Nebraska, given how her realist depictions of the frontier myth had been received there: if one's work displayed "any critical attitude at all toward society," she wrote, "[one] immediately becomes a dangerous fellow, with morbid and unAmerican ideas." Yet to re-create America as a deliberate work of collective art, Americans *must* relinquish the frontier myth; and they *must* live with the tragic history that regionalists had rewritten for them. Why this transformation would not ultimately occur was no better illustrated than by the tough-minded Sandoz herself, who could not always sustain her Cassandra's view of history, but who instead with her own self-delusive and compensatory feelings of "great admiration" for her frontiersman father ("his grasp upon a vision and his unfaltering pursuit of that vision places him among the exceptional") demonstrated that all-too-human capacity of "substituting," as Freud wrote, "a wish-fulfilment for some aspect of the world which is unbearable." Because she lived with something tragic and monstrous, Sandoz wrote of the young Mari, "from the time she could walk, she hid away, retreating into fancy."[28]

The climactic scenes of *Capital City* were, however, one occasion when Sandoz did steel herself to report to her outraged audience (the book prompted more than one death threat) what she had discovered about the American character, looking with her realist, frontier-blinded eye beyond the blind side of national mythology. "*Capital City* is my study of an organized society letting itself slip into fascism," she wrote simply. The scenario that Sandoz as Cassandra projected out of these insights was very much part of the mood of nightmarish possibility that was so "vividly discussed" among the politically thoughtful of the time, writing within the context of disintegrating exceptionalism—in Sinclair Lewis's *It Can't Happen Here* (1935), for example, and Walter V. T. Clark's *The Ox-Bow Incident* (1940). In her own work, Sandoz traced the closing off of the way out through the conceit of return after obsessive return to the symbolic sculpture and architecture of her refabricated version of Goodhue's civic cathedral, which in the Thermidor descending on the late 1930s are no longer the liturgical touchstones of moral and political community, but have become symbols of social conflict and division. She notes that the content of the "Frieze of the Peoples of the World" is not given "publicity" by the powers that be, and that the Franklin statue with its subversive inscription is deliberately kept hidden by landscaping and isolated (without sidewalks) from public accessibility and edification—a subtle censorship that is only a small indicator of the city's class, racial, ethnic, and religious polarizations, all signs of the advent of Mumford's "Tyrannopolis." Certainly, the capitol still has some power to inspire: Sandoz repeats in her later novel the climactic scene of *Slogum House*, with strikers in protest against an antipicketing law marching "into the capitol rotunda with its imported pillars of marble about them and high overhead the frieze of Peoples of the World";

they seek and win redress from the state supreme court. Yet in *Capital City* this is not the climax of the story, raising hopes of another "spring upon them"; rather, it is only a fleeting complication.[29]

Increasingly, the political life of Franklin is marked by the breakdown of the rule of law, the loss of community, and the substitution of force and intimidation as the means of social order—the extremes to which Americans were willing to go, Sandoz believed, to protect the sanctity of property and to keep from questioning their beliefs. Hired antiunion thugs, "Christian Crusaders," the Ku Klux Klan, and a local fascist group called the "Gold Shirts" (recruited from among upper-crust authoritarians and "Mist's" nihilistic ragamuffin boys) roam the cityscape and terrorize down-and-outers and their would-be organizers, bringing on political paralysis once again. Near the finale of the book, Sandoz's young idealistic protagonist (and descendant of one of the heroic town fathers), Hamm Rufer, looks sadly out on the tableau of a winter's night falling over the capitol tower, where the likelihood of sniper fire is one hallmark of the now-foreclosed second *political* chance for exceptionalism: "Down there, at its foot, was a statue of Franklin, heavy lids shading the tired eyes . . . and about him lay the grey, sooty snow of the capitol grounds, unbroken by any tracks except those of a timid cottontail that dared come out only with the cover of dusk."[30]

"Our people fled to America from oppression," the father of a Gold Shirt victim laments. "But now there is nowhere to go." As the down-and-outers sense the country's exceptionalism fading with the loss of freedom and opportunity, the "hope of their eyes . . . burned out," Sandoz wrote, carrying the story to its now inevitable conclusion—many real and fictive versions of it were occurring in the world of the 1930s. For such powerless and desperate people could be easy prey to men promising instant relief and rapid renewal, usually via anticonstitutional shortcuts that made them equally attractive to the powerful and well-to-do, those yearning for "social discipline." One such man appears in the emblematic political battleground of *Capital City*, Charley "America for Americans," "Thirty Dollars Every Thursday" Stetbettor— literally a snake-oil salesman. With the mainstream conservative and liberal vote split among several candidates, Stetbettor is elected governor. Thereafter, the final scene of the novel is again sited by Sandoz at the transfigured capitol: in a lot across the street, Gold Shirts charge a picket line; blows are exchanged, shots are fired; Hamm Rufer falls dead (his face "singularly untouched by life"). Meanwhile, Stetbettor—with "three heavy trucks of the national guards"—arrives to take office, and Goodhue's onetime civic cathedral acquires yet another set of meanings: a "long column" of "armed guardsmen," Sandoz closes, "marched to the capitol, left sentinels with rifles stationed at each side of the entrance, and passed in through the great bronze doors." After a pause, "from the wide window of the governor's suite," seen in twilight, "hung a new American flag."[31]

For her next and last major work, Sandoz sought refuge in a biography of the Sioux chief Crazy Horse that she had been contemplating for some years. She wrote furiously during the earliest and blackest months of World War II, when it seemed to her that "there was a great chance of Hitler's taking everything over." She had "plunged into" Crazy Horse, she later admitted, "because I believed it should be written and I had a good promise of [a] concentration camp [because] I had proved unwilling to 'cooperate' with the nazi boys, local and international." The work covered "the transitional period from the buffalo hunt to the walking plow, the boarding school, and the political agent," Sandoz told B. A. Botkin, and therefore, she added, "the whole thing has the inevitability of Greek tragedy"—"the characters are so helpless in it," trapped on the wrong side of the frontier myth. If with these worries about concentration camps and narratives of inevitability Sandoz well reflected the regionalist tendency toward the stoic, the tragic, the martyred—apparently, as will be seen, the occupational mind-set of most advocates for the older America—she seemed nevertheless to be groping for some different kind of hero in her story of the "Strange Man of Oglalas," a hero appropriate to the modern age. The mystic loner Crazy Horse and his band of warriors "tried to act with wisdom and foresight for their people," Sandoz wrote, but they "finally came to the place" in that modernizing and imperiling "transitional period" to Progress where "they saw that death with a bullet in the heart would have been preferable." Paradoxically, this bleak story, written as "felt" history, filled Sandoz with "a peculiar sense of physical power." As she described her emotions, "It seems I could go out and tear down a butte top and throw it into the next county, or blow the clouds from the sky. And nothing has ever broken my heart so."[32]

In the summer of 1956, two Walters sat together at the Bale of Hay Saloon in Virginia City, Montana, a former mining boomtown built when Jefferson's empire for liberty arrived in the Rockies on its way to the Pacific, the mines long ago played out but the town and saloon subsequently restored as an Old West tourist attraction: one was Walter Van Tilburg Clark, author of The Ox-Bow Incident, a novel chronicling the murder of innocents by a lawless mob, "a kind of American Naziism" (Clark said) set in nineteenth-century Nevada; the other was Walter Prescott Webb, older, wiser, sadder, there to interview Clark for an afterword to a new edition of the novel. "What I wanted to say was, 'It can happen here,'" Clark told Webb over a bottle, talking into the early morning. "It has happened here, in minor but sufficiently indicative

*ways, a great many times." Of the town Webb afterward observed that "a
wealthy man has done for Virginia City what Mr. Rockefeller did for Williamsburg, restoring the place to a semblance of what it was when it had a
reason for existing." Of Clark's novel, he concluded, with some admiration,
that it had "reversed the western formula, preserved the vitality of real life,
and proved that western men are pretty much like other men and that literature can be made of their folly."*[33]

Part Three

Pickett's Charge

7 The Grand Task of Politics

The Ideology of Regionalism and the Program for Utopia

> It is only by paying attention to the limitations of each region, and by allowing for the driving force of history, that we can make the earth come to terms with man's idola. This is perhaps the most difficult lesson that the eutopian must learn.
> —Lewis Mumford, *The Story of Utopias*

During a 1938–40 lecture tour of the United States, exiled German author Thomas Mann, retracing the provincial itinerary that the Irish poet AE had followed earlier in the decade, sought to allay any anxieties that had grown up around American exceptionalism. (Diary entry, November 27, 1937: "Spent the morning on the speech for America. Democratic idealism. Do I believe in it? Am I only adopting it as an intellectual role? In any case, it is well to remember this world.") The symbolism of Mann's arrival in America to seek refuge from events in Europe—this man who was to many the embodiment of the vanquished Weimar Republic and, indeed, German culture itself—was not lost on the capacity crowds to whom he predicted "The Coming Victory of Democracy." In fact, he called it to their attention: "It is my own intention to make my home in your country . . . because here, in contrast to the cultural fatigue and inclination to barbarism prevalent in the Old World, there exists a joyful respect for culture, a youthful sensitivity to its products. I feel that the hopes of all those who cherish democratic sentiments . . . must be concentrated on this country," because (he added in another lecture, "The Problem of Freedom") "of your youth and moral rigor, because the soul of this country is still close to the Biblical and the monumental." To "speak on democracy in America," Mann flattered audiences at stop after stop—Ann Arbor, Dubuque, Cincinnati, Salt Lake City, Tulsa, Dallas, and Lincoln (where Mari Sandoz, preparing *Capital City* for publication, heard him)—was to "carry owls to Athens," to bring "an article to a place where such things already exist in abundance." For, he told them rousingly, "I am in the classic land of democracy."[1]

Yet as a whole career spent chronicling the "swan song" of bourgeois culture might indicate, and as his self-detached diary entry confirms, Mann also had a more problematic and less comforting purpose in mind for his lecture tour than the mere promotion of 100 percent American patriotism and complacency. Democracy, he said, was a "spiritual and moral possession of which it would be dangerous to feel too secure and too confident." He warned his audiences that it was "not an assured possession, that it has enemies, that it is threatened from within and from without" even in America. He had known not the Sandozian fantasy but the all-too-horrific reality of its demise in Germany. To ensure its continued survival, a twofold task, he believed, was essential—"here it will be possible—here it *must* be possible." First, "the time has come for democracy to take stock of itself, for recollection and restatement and conscious consideration, in a word, for its renewal in thought and feeling." And second, Mann said, this spiritual renewal must take concrete programmatic form as a "social renewal": "*Social Democracy* is now the order of the day." The "salvation of democracy" lay in "this solution to the problem of freedom," a "socially established freedom, which rescues individual values by friendly and willing concessions to equality; through economic justice which ties all of democracy's children to it." This "reform of freedom" would be "something very different from the freedom that existed and could exist in the times of our fathers and grandfathers, the epoch of bourgeois liberalism," he postulated. "Now we need something different from 'laissez-faire, laissez-aller,'" for "the times of Manchesterism and of passive liberalism are gone forever." Mann declared that this social democratic solution to the "problem of freedom" could be achieved by a "human synthesis, a reasonable and just synthesis . . . between freedom and equality, individual and society, the person and the collectivity." In the end, he argued, the envisioned renewal would create a "communal spirit," a "national unity," and finally a "community of nations" that "eventually will abolish politics itself." He confessed:

> I am no sans-culotte, no Jacobin, no revolutionary—my whole being is that of a conservative; that is to say I stand by tradition. I am a man who regards it as his task in life to advance the German heritage, though with modern means and in the modern spirit. . . . We must not be afraid to

attempt a reform of freedom—in [this] conservative sense. I believe it to
be the duty of every thinking man to take an active part in this task—
which is tantamount to the preservation of culture.[2]

Mann was undoubtedly "bringing owls to Athens" when he issued this call
to action—it was precisely the task that regionalists had already been pursuing for a decade or more. During that period they had assembled the rudiments of a new national ideology, an ideology which sought both to preserve
and to transcend the culture of their fathers and grandfathers, and on the
successful implementation of which, they believed, rode the fate of national
exceptionalism and, therefore, the very existence of freedom and culture in
the world—or at least freedom and culture as they understood them. That this
implementation must "abolish politics" and create a new communitarian order
ultimately of global dimensions (as some in the movement projected) was also
part of the regionalist utopian vision. But just as they discovered through
their revisionist "hidden history" that the United States had never been the
"classic land of democracy" of Mann's preface, so too would regionalists with
their abortive attempts at establishing an American version of "Social Democracy" prove the rest of Mann's address to be more empty exhortation. They
would find that the "rudiments" of an ideology, as powerful and evocative as
these critiques and visions might be, were impotent without concrete expression in the requirements of modern politics—platforms, programs, candidates, organization, funding, lobbying, bureaucratic and other means of control. That regionalism was an ideology intended to do away with most of these
necessities meant, in the final analysis, that it was to be no ideology at all.
Instead, it would remain something apart from the world, kept pure of deal
cutters and "diabolical powers," maintaining the integrity of a doctrine in
many regards devastating to the assumptions undergirding the immovable
bodies of American society, but unable to move them—more fruitless exhortation itself: an "adversary culture," a jeremiad, a "utopia of escape," an elegy.
   Yet to all appearances, by the mid-1930s, regionalism may be seen to have
been functioning in many of the ways that an ideology is supposed to function.
It was, first of all, articulating and proselytizing a set of myths and ideals
through the individual and institutional media of the regionalist civic religion,
myths and ideals which, at least analogically, were intended to prescribe
personal and collective behavior. Regionalists were attempting in effect to
teach Americans about the necessity of community and symbiosis, the importance of diversity and tradition. These efforts "to take stock" of democracy, to
renew it in "thought and feeling" by means of "aesthetic education," reached
a culmination of sorts in the telling example of the National Folk Festival,
established in 1933. The organizer of the festival, Sarah Gertrude Knott

(executive director of the Dramatic League of St. Louis), enlisted the advice of a number of prominent regional artists and folklorists, including the North Carolina folk playwright Paul Green (festival chairman), Constance Rourke, Percy MacKaye, J. Frank Dobie, and B. A. Botkin. "We really want to make it 'by of and for the people,'" Knott informed Green and, bringing a few owls to Athens herself, further expanded on the festival's guiding philosophy to Botkin: "I am sure you will agree that the folk-lore idea is the very beginning of real Art in America. Most of our previous Art has been copied from that of the European countries, and executed by a select few. Our folk-lore idea is creative and open to the masses." A significant organizational complication immediately arose concerning the festival's program, however, a complication that quickly and aptly took on the dimensions of a pluralist fable: Whom to include in the celebration? or, as Knott put it, "What limit should we have?" As originally conceived, the first festival, to be convened in St. Louis, was to bring together almost exclusively "native" white American folk performers. Knott told Chairman Green:

> We plan to ask such groups as of course The Carolina Playmakers with some of your plays, The Santa Fe group, the Wisconsin Players, The famous Kiowa Indians . . . The Henry Ford Dearborn Dancers, The Cowboys from Texas, the Mountaineers with their songs and dances from the Ozarks, etc.

But Botkin, already in 1933 well on his way to developing a doctrine of folk-cultural pluralism, raised this question to Knott: "Do you intend to limit the festival to Anglo-American lore, including the Negro but excluding the Indian and foreign-language-groups?" Relating the question to Green, Knott wrote, "I don't want to limit it anymore than absolutely necessary. I want to include both the Indian and the Negro"—to which Green assented: "All the American folk arts both native and primitive should be represented in the Festival, and this includes white, black, and Indian." He added parenthetically, "If all the racial matters were handled with your usual tact there [sh]ould be no friction." Yet this broadened all-American program was all too soon called into question by the "foreign-language-groups"—"Since they are hearing of the Folk-Festival they are wanting to get in," Knott wrote Green, slightly exasperated. "I think it will be better to keep it American," she declared, but finally conceded that "those who will be here . . . might be interested in folk song or dances of other nations—It might help in appreciation of our own." In its fully developed form, the festival came to "include" such diverse performances as Louisiana Acadian music, Navajo craft making, Lithuanian harvest rituals, Scottish pipe ballads, West Virginian fiddle playing, Negro spirituals,

New England sea chanteys, Slavonic tamburitza songs, Spanish and Mexican folksinging, Pennsylvania German lore renditions, and Dunkard hymns.[3]

As the National Folk Festival grew and evolved over the decade, to hundreds of participants, with portions of the "pageant" broadcast nationally by NBC and CBS radio, minority racial and ethnic groups became an integral element of the program and of the "lesson" in democracy it was meant to convey. Not only was it true that "Every Section Contributes to America's Folkways," as the guide for one typical year (1938) stated, but also the "Songs and Music of Many Lands [Were] Woven Into U.S. Tradition":

> America is the largest and richest seed bed of folklore in the world. Into the texture of her civilization have been woven and is being woven the customs, the songs, the dances of many lands. Across her doorstep have poured the cultures, the attitudes and the patterns of thought native to almost every part of the globe.

Botkin, in an essay for the same guide entitled "The Function of a Folk Festival," made the propluralist argument more explicitly. America had in recent years found its diversity "menaced by aggressive nationalism and standardized mass culture," he wrote. But in response a "new social consciousness" had arisen, a "new feeling for cultural diversity and roots which succeeded the abortive 'melting pot' myth"—according to which immigrants became Americanized (discarding Old World customs and languages) by intermarriage and by their fervent climb up the ladder of opportunity. In contrast and dissent, the "new social consciousness" offered an antiethnocentric, *cultural* version of the myth that there was "room for everybody" in America. As President Roosevelt commented on the 1940 festival: "We have the best of man's past on which to draw, brought to us by our native folk and folk from all parts of the world. In binding these elements into a national fabric of beauty and strength, let us keep the original fibers intact." As a focus for these pluralizing tendencies, the folk festival had a crucial educative role to play, Botkin believed. "That it is . . . a good thing for the folk groups to participate, in so far as participation increases the self-awareness and self-respect of their communities and promotes mutual understanding and respect among groups . . . goes without saying." Then Botkin made the leap of faith and logic underlying cultural radicalism. "This heritage," he wrote, "must not be allowed to stop with the past or with a public performance. It must be allowed to grow and function as a liberating force for our art and society," creating the basis for "fuller and freer social participation" by all of the ethnic and racial groups involved: the grassroots upswell on which hinged so many regionalist political hopes. The national "integration and re-orientation" that was the goal of all the media of the regionalist civic religion—monumental architecture, regional magazines, public art, documentary photography, realist novels, epic poetry, sociological treatises—would thus be served.[4]

This hoped-for "integration and re-orientation" of the American polity around the values of the mythic folk liturgy would in fact signify the *legitimation* of the pluralized, democratized social structure and the decentralized configuration of power demanded by a regional civilization—another of the functions of an ideology toward which regionalism was apparently tending. To be legitimized, the ideals and modes of behavior proselytized by the civic religion must be seen by the polity to have a foundation in objective reality, in "Truth," in the "way of things." To this end, regionalists in their work resorted rhetorically to almost every category of truth available, with the exception, at least overtly, of the divine; doubtful to their secularized minds and to a secularized society, it was perceived to be no longer a politically useful category. Yet a residual belief in the existence of other "universals" strongly shaped the subtexts of truth underlying regionalist attempts at mass "persuasion," some of them very much a part of mainstream liberal political culture (from which most regionalists sprang), others indicatively diverging toward the justification of a new and alternative social order. Cultural relativists in their pluralist and inclusive extension of the choice of values beyond those prescribed by bourgeois society, most were not *moral* relativists, according to whom no single set of values could be socially agreed upon and enjoy legitimacy. In the same way that their aspiration of making regionalism a new national ideology had limited their artistic experimentalism to one "by of and for the people" (as Knott wrote), so also did regionalists in their search for a just "human synthesis" of values stop short of following out the logic of modernist cultural radicalism (Nietzsche's logic). "The breakup of coherent values systems has undermined the possibilities for unified action," Lewis Mumford acknowledged. "The values of Orthodox Christianity, of Protestantism, of individualistic humanism, of capitalism, of humanitarianism and libertarianism, have been weakened, not merely through conflict, but through internal erosion." Yet, he wrote, "one may confidently prophesy the emergence of a new system of values, which will displace the debris of these dying systems: a system shared, if not yet successfully formulated, by most men of good-will today."[5]

Many elements of the regionalist attempt to conceive this new system of values (the new order promised by every ideology or would-be ideology) were not so new. *Nature*, despite any number of modernist challenges to its presumed immutability and cognitive transparency (by Mach, Einstein, Whitehead, Heisenberg, and others) remained for many regionalists the primary universal, closely attended by the universal *Reason* which made its laws and relationships knowable, and which must therefore possess similarly incisive, ordering powers with regard to human nature and society. Surprisingly, for all of their modernist protestations against abstractionism and their insights into cultural relativism, most regionalists still built their positive political agendas at least partially on assumptions grounded in these two pillars of the Enlightenment. Most accepted, for example, assumptions of the essential goodness and rationality of human nature (in itself a premodernist category), as manifested by their adherance to political concepts rooted in Harringtonian and Lockean natural law—republican virtue and independence, consensual popular sovereignty, and liberal egalitarianism, to name a few—all central concepts of the regionalist political economy, and, as such, basic axioms, goods in themselves, which remained largely unexamined. And most regionalists (the sociologist and planner wings especially, the Agrarians excepted) strove to maintain the marriage between humane values and the social sciences, invoking the language and authority of *Science* (revealer of the universal operations of nature) as another way of legitimizing their vision of the good society, and thereby bucked the trend toward "value neutrality" that many social scientists were pursuing in their quest to formalize their fields as "hard" sciences. Eventually, regionalists (like Mari Sandoz) would find ample reasons for questioning their assumptions about human nature and science in events leading up to and culminating World War II—when their "will to be naive" would be broken. Yet there was, while the movement lasted, little in these legitimizing assumptions to distinguish regionalist cultural radicals from any random group of left-leaning New Deal liberals.

The rhetoric of regionalists was, however, constituted by further layers of legitimizing subtexts that did differentiate them ideologically from liberals (of both classical or "conservative" and "New Deal liberal" stripes, their primary rivals for power in America) and that implicitly proffered a critique of central liberal articles of faith. While it was true, for instance, that mainstream political discourse frequently resorted to argument by tradition, referring to the Founding Fathers, dead war heroes, the frontier myth, rural Jeffersonian iconography, and other elements of the national past in order to define Americanism (and un-Americanism), regionalists sited legitimacy in folk-regional counterdefinitions to most aspects of that tradition, counterdefinitions which reflected some fundamental disagreements and divergences with liberal thought. The virtue of "living close to the land" might find its way into the speeches of sentimental mainstream politicians, yet it did not have the centrality in their thinking that it had for regionalists. For them, the "wise" respect that the folk had for the processes of universal *Nature* explained the imitable stability and longevity of their traditional social arrangements, its interdependencies their interdependencies, because for regionalists nature was not a man-centered objective mechanism of fixed properties, formulas, and colliding particles, but a biocentric, organically enfolding, post-Enlightenment, post-Darwinian nature comprehensible only in terms of process, flow, and interconnectedness. Thus, to the regionalist mind, the "natural" and therefore "legitimate" society was an organism, rather than a collection of separate particles. This analogy was not the only universalist basis of their communitarianism, however. Their organicist social vision was also framed rhetorically in the light of the "simpler" and elemental truth of the social praxis of the folk itself, and in accordance with the authority of social thinkers and psychologists from Comte to Freud who posited a culturally and socially constructed individual rather than, like most liberals, an individually constituted society. All of these legitimizing devices—traditional/mythic, natural, and scientific (recall Lewis Mumford's "regional survey" method of education)—were mustered in the regionalist campaign to replace the abstractly atomic, "naturally" self-interested, and acquisitive "rugged individual" of the capitalist economy (countenanced by a well-intentioned liberal philosophy) with a new kind of citizen who recognized all the claims that the human and natural community made on him or her.

But it is essential to note the continued commitment to liberal individualism, to the nurturing of the individual personality, that regionalists retained even as they attempted to convert Americans to their vision of a communitarian social order. Looking for that "human synthesis" of which Mann spoke, most regionalists believed that they had found the solution not only for this tension in their thought but for others as well—their embrace of the rational and scientific with their modernist sense of irreducible reality, for example—in the integrative "power of art," as John Collier had termed it. In effect, *Beauty*, with its manifold connotations, comprised yet another basis for legitimizing the regionalist future. The beautiful evoked and corresponded to the patterns of nature, many regionalists assumed, patterns revealed by intuition and by science. Closing the dichotomy between an objectifying rationality and the complex world of nature, the beautiful was embodied in works of folk art and handicrafts, even whole landscapes, which were communally created and shared. Beauty fostered an *affective* and integrated personal experience between the individual and some greater whole beyond the self, bridging the alienated void between self and society. Beauty signified truth and therefore legitimacy (in this rather ancient but persistent sense) precisely because it corresponded to reality (not literally but emblematically) and because its motifs were agreed upon by the members of society, especially as they were formalized in collective rituals like the civic religion. For each individual member this truth was further validated by his or her own artistic practice, its craftsmanship, respecting the qualities of raw materials in themselves, proven by utility as well as aesthetic pleasure. Moreover, because there was for the folk (according to myth) little or no distinction between the artistic and the economic, the symbiotic relationships inherent in the strictures of beauty thus lent themselves to an economy that was superior—in terms of renewable growth, stability of living standards, and long-term efficiency—to modes of production that ignored such strictures. The guiding principle of the regional economy, as Mumford wrote, was not the capitalist "mine and move," but rather "stay and cultivate." Under the regime of beauty, no aspect of life, least of all the individual citizen, was to be treated as mere means, as migrants, sharecroppers, and industrial workers were when "run through the hopper" of capitalism. For the political corollary of the aesthetic appreciation of objects in themselves was, at bottom, a "socially-established freedom" (as Mann wrote), in which the singularity and uniqueness of each member of society was respected by all. In the final analysis, the legitimacy of the regional civilization, as of any social order (so proceeded regionalist thinking) could be validated only by the degree of freedom it afforded in its solution to the "problem of freedom."[6]

This fragile vision, and all the legitimizing subtexts buttressing it— *Tradition, Nature, Reason, Science,* and, again, *Beauty*—recurred in various forms throughout the discourse of regionalists as they assumed during the 1930s the final and most critical task in the formulation of an ideology: conceiving the social and political institutions and instrumentalities and, more immediately, designing the antecedent programs of reform, that could bring their utopia to concrete realization. At the outset, though, it would be more accurate to refer to their *utopias,* because only the most radical (the Mumford group, for example, and perhaps, the Indian subregionalists) embraced in a literal way a majority of the assumptions amplified and generalized above. Other groups and individuals retained somewhat more conventional ideological loyalties, hoping to ground freedom in some type of small property holding, for instance, and professing at least an ancillary role for the "power of art" as a seal of community (the Odum circle, Sandoz). Still other wings of the movement either repudiated certain (but not all) of the elements of the radical "case" for regionalism (such as the Agrarians) or advocated a somewhat different economic and political foundation on which to construct the decentralized regional configuration of power (the Californians). As this process of ideologization unfolded, the regionalist movement might be visualized as a set of intersecting subsets, all of which encompassed *some* of the mythic and legitimizing assumptions of the regional civilization, but each of which diverged from the others—along different programmatic paths particularly— according to the literalness (realizability) with which they construed such concepts as the "symphonic nation," their grasp of the operations of brass-tacks politics, and their own special agendas, which only the region could fulfill. To trace these divergences, these differing paths, is to discern the fragmented and *unfinished* condition in which regionalism, despite the glow of mythicizing, legitimizing, and (as recounted in Part II) delegitimizing activities undertaken on its behalf, remained. It is to trace through to the end the ultimate abortiveness of the movement.

This perception from hindsight was hardly prevalent during the mid- to late 1930s, when regionalists involved themselves most fervently in formulating programmatic solutions to the "problem of freedom." Despite the pall of apprehension spread by the depression and the rise of fascism, there was a common feeling of being part of momentous, even revolutionary events. "We are on one of the great 'watersheds of history,' looking back upon the individualistic past and forward to the sunrise of a new social conception," wrote John G. Neihardt in 1935, after completing the "Song of the Messiah" segment of his epic *Cycle of the West*. "Sometime, somewhere, somehow, the nation is accustomed to embark on new adventures and epochs," Howard Odum declared in *Southern Regions*; "the present is such a period." The conservative Agrarians too believed that "a reformation in America" was in the offing, as Herbert Agar wrote in their second manifesto, *Who Owns America?* (1936). And as late as 1940, marking the fifteenth anniversary of his own circle's original *Survey Graphic* planning manifesto, the yet-optimistic Mumford proclaimed: "This is one of those times in human history when only the dreamers will turn out to be the practical men. . . . We are laying down the foundations of a new stage in human culture."[7]

Mumford was reiterating the assertion of *The Culture of Cities* that an intellectual "definition of the new framework" of a regional civilization was "a decisive element in the whole process" of creating it, by implication treating his own essentially theoretical work as a crucial political act—another assumption that was widely shared in the crisis atmosphere of the times. Certainly few in Mumford's immediate group sought to dissuade him from this problematic view. Van Wyck Brooks praised *Cities* as a book "sure to work slowly as a ferment in vigorous minds and bring forth fruit all over the country"—"if we are saved from chaos, you will have had a pretty large hand in it." But surely Mumford and others were not exaggerating the importance of the need, as he wrote, "to educate citizens," the end of which was "to give them the tools of action, to make ready a background for action, and to suggest socially significant tasks to serve as goals for action." He well knew in the case of his circle's own "goals for action"—which, as noted, would require the overthrow of "sacred" private property—that "without such a broader cultural foundation, regional planning can have but minor political significance."[8] Yet clearly Mumford and most other regionalists had political aspirations for their doctrine beyond the lectern, debate circuit, and bookstore. Among those searching for avenues of political expression, there was some brave talk like that of Agrarian firebrand John Gould Fletcher's of "real physical force revolution," of launching third parties, of organizing youth movements, factory and farm unions, and consumer cooperatives (much as the more activist communists were attempting in the South, aiding the Scottsboro defendants and starting sharecropper unions). But the natural tendency among regionalist artists and intellectuals (many of whom were academics) was to make this task of education itself their movement's sole and primary "goal for action," rather than a preparatory stage. Unfortunately, this exclusive focus on a politics of cultural radicalism was both to encourage their politicization and, in a practical sense, to channel its energies into less-than-effective directions.

The justifications, seductions, and limitations of this movementwide tendency to rely on the all-sufficiency of a "program" of cultural production may be illustrated in the fortunes of the most well-known regionalist circle, the Southern Agrarians. In 1930, soon after the release of the widely reviewed *I'll Take My Stand*, Donald Davidson assured a critic of the book that "we represent principles that are looking for a party, and for men." He conceded that "we don't (at present) have an actual candidate for some office, and a platform for him to stand on"; the Agrarians' manifesto must be considered, he wrote, "hardly . . . more than a feeler" to find out who their friends and enemies were. Anticipating a further and immediate campaign of polemics to energize public opinion and bring good men flocking to the "Cause," the group planned (as John Crowe Ransom told Allen Tate) "to get us a press and go to hammering," and "to acquire a Tennessee county newspaper"—neither of which came to pass.[9] A lull settled over the Cause as it gradually became apparent that few were, in fact, flocking (or willing to finance a press or newspaper).

Given this obvious lack of progress, Davidson defined the political role of the Agrarians in these somewhat more limited terms to Allen Tate in 1932, and his words were applicable to any number of regionalists around the country:

We like to think of ourselves as crusaders; in our mind's eye, we can see ourselves doing a kind of Pickett's charge against industrial breastworks, only a *successful* charge this time. But we don't actually do the crusading. We merely trifle with the idea a little. And while we trifle with it, we neglect the other role in which we really can accomplish something. . . . We are, after all, writers before everything else—and only secondarily, if at all, cavalry commanders, orators, lobbyists, and ward-heelers [*sic*]. We ought to write then, and keep writing. . . . if our ideas are right, we shall in the end reach the people who can do the other needful things.

By 1933, an increasingly restive John Gould Fletcher, looking back on their one accomplishment, the original "Agrarian Symposium," complained to Frank Owsley that it would not "have any effect unless it is backed up with a definite political movement," and to this end he suggested the never-to-materialize "Grey-Jackets" youth organization. Still agitated, he worried aloud about the prospects of the Cause to Ransom who, concurring with Davidson, replied, "You are too quickly discouraged. You do not take the long view. You assume that nothing is being accomplished. You are quite wrong. . . . Publication anywhere is something."[10] In fact, judging from the volume of "publication" at least, the Agrarian wing did suddenly flare back to life in 1934, when it found an outlet in the fascist-leaning Seward Collins's *American Review*. The Agrarians also laid plans for another, more programmatically oriented symposium.

Allen Tate, writing Davidson about these plans in 1935, echoed B. A. Botkin's contemporaneous worries that the regionalist movement as a whole had "failed to make itself felt as a vital and practical force in . . . American life" and revealed his own growing frustration at years of effort without concrete political results: "We've got to put up or shut up. We can't go on writing our pleasant little laments for our own consumption. We've got to get into action or admit that we are licked. The whole agrarian movement has become a reproach. Of course, we can say privately that we don't care, but if we don't care what public opinion makes of us, why do we write for public opinion?" Typically though, despite his frustration, Tate meant "getting into action" not by the formation of a new party, or the financing of an Agrarian lobbyist, or even campaign work for favored mainstream candidates, but rather (like the nationally focused Botkin) a redoubled and more intensive literary "program" of making themselves "heard." But when the fruit of this program, *Who Owns America?*, appeared in 1936, it was to be the group's last collaborative effort; the Cause was already well on its way to breaking up. The erratic and extremist Fletcher had by then quit in disgust, the ablest economic thinker of the circle, H. C. Nixon, had moved on to pursue his more leftist brand of politics, and the others (Ransom, Tate, and Andrew Lytle) were shifting with little trouble to more "purely literary articles or historical specialties," as Donald Davidson, forced subsequently to "'carry the ball'" alone, noted several years later. "Don, you have a gift for persecution and martyrdom," Tate replied to his resentments in a 1942 letter. "You evidently believe that agrarianism was a failure." Although "the practical results of agrarianism have been slight," Tate admitted, "I think it was and *is* a very great success; but then"—he added, not quite accurately but with some self-mollification—"I never expected it to have any political influence." Agrarianism was therefore

to be seen as something other than a projected social and economic "reformation in America": "It is a reaffirmation of the humane tradition, and to reaffirm
that is an end in itself. Never fear: we shall be remembered when our snipers
are forgotten."[11]

By thus revising Agrarian history and seeking out the age-old consolation of
ignored writers—timeless tradition and posterity—Tate avoided having to
draw some unsettling conclusions about the efficacy of cultural radicalism as a
politics and the apparently peripheral role of the artist and intellectual in
American society. Indeed, given that the Agrarians were "writing . . . articles
to be read chiefly by ourselves," as Tate in 1935 had feared they were, a
central question was raised by the ebbing of their circle over the 1930s: why
did they persist in their belief in the "all-sufficiency" of cultural radicalism
despite their obvious lack of "political influence"?[12] This question was central
as well to the larger regionalist movement, which on this issue of "means"
shared much the same assumptions with the Agrarians, though pressing them
into the service of somewhat different reformist ends.

One important set of reasons for their persistence related simply to *whom*
the regionalists were. As artists and intellectuals and, more to the point, as
academics, it was in the realm of education rather than mass politicking that
they found their most comfortable and amenable roles—as proselytizers of the
regionalist civic religion, and as advisers and experts seeking to influence the
polity and the powerful. Cultural radicalism allowed regionalists to fulfill their
yearning for service, their desire that the practice of their vocation be publicly
useful. At the same time, in accordance with their libertarian predilections, it
was a politics that they could pursue with little or no sacrifice of individual
autonomy, the autonomy of the Emersonian social critic. As Ransom reminded
Fletcher, referring to the comparatively close-knit Agrarian circle, rather
than the much more sprawling larger movement: "We are not in a political
sense a group, and never can be; too many individuals, all up in years and
positions and advanced in different styles of individualism."[13] Conversely,
cultural radicalism also fulfilled certain psychological needs that devolved
from this way of intellectual life, constituting a further solution to the isolating
and paralyzing solipsistic tendencies of modern self-consciousness. For in
conceiving the writing of a history, the painting of a mural, or the compilation
of a sociological study as political acts, regionalists not only broke out of their
subjectivity by linking themselves (through reification) to the objective "universals" of nature and folk culture, they more immediately bridged the gap
between self and society by joining a community of individuals disseminating
those universals, engaging themselves as "educators" in the collective issues
and travails of the contemporary world. To become members of such a non-

coercive regime of "persuasion" was, moreover, part and parcel of the regionalist cultural project, which helps additionally to explain their ready adoption of this particular political style.

So beyond personal and professional reasons, the essential motivation for regionalists to persist in their adherence to a politics of persuasion lay in its centrality to their ideology. If an "aesthetic education" in regional myths, traditions, and environments were to be the basis of the regional community, its source of integration, then it was natural to assume that a program of such education was a sufficient plan of action to instigate that community. In other words, regionalists hoped to establish a noncoercive community life by noncoercive means, by a mass conversion of the polity, a reversal of modern imperilment. These were the only "means" that could establish their various utopias without the excessive coercion that would otherwise be necessary to move immovable bodies like private property. Certainly, this style of "politics by conversion," which was very much a politics to "abolish politics," had deep roots in the American reform tradition, reaching back to the abolitionists and other movements of the pre–Civil War years. Married to the confidence of the modernist sensibility in the "power of art," it proved to be a seductive vehicle for yet another American attempt at radical reform. "The people are, contrary to some opinions, open and eager to hear the truth," Howard Odum and many other regionalists convinced themselves. In the era of the "phantom public," they *had* to have faith that their audience could be both rational and participatory—otherwise, admitting the insufficiency of persuasion as the bond of social order, they would have to confront the raw mechanisms of power necessary to implement the radical restructuring of the national economy entailed by their vision of a "symphonic nation." The embrace of cultural radicalism by regionalists allowed them (most of them, at least, for a time) to evade such hard ideological issues. *I'll Take My Stand,* for example, "lacked constructive proposals to restrain and regulate industrialism" (as Fletcher himself observed), because to the degree that such works became programmatic, questions of power intruded into the vision, and it was the utopian purpose of regionalism to nullify power.[14] Possessing faith in the potency of persuasion, regionalists were lulled by the precepts of cultural radicalism into equating understanding with action, criticism with program—to sketch their visions of aesthetic-traditionalist societies, garden cities, symphonic nations, and symphonious environments seemed enough.

Yet it is also necessary to qualify such generalizations with reference again to the crisis-filled context within which regionalists were, and perceived themselves self-consciously to be, historical actors. During this period when the fictive totalitarian scenarios of *The Plumed Serpent* and *Brave New World* seemed to be coming nightmarishly true, regionalists did strive to formulate concrete programs (however evasively sketchy these might sometimes emerge) in order to achieve the delicate balancing acts necessary to reconcile the dilemmas of power which such artistic expositions depicted but left unresolved. Kate's intense yearning for integrated community life torn by her revulsion against any loss of individual expressiveness; the "third alternative" between utopian regimentation and primitive hardship that was the only "possibility of sanity"—regionalists could undoubtedly find solutions to these puzzles in their own "acts" of cultural radicalism, in their evocative literary, historiographic, and sociological "visions" of regional life in the past, present, and future.[15] Politicized, they felt compelled to advocate those solutions, to aspire to leadership and responsibility. But in the wake of mass culturalization, Sacco and Vanzetti, the Red Scare, the Great War, and under the contemporary specters of depression and a probably greater future war, theirs was a movement marked by certain distinctly modern, disenchanted tendencies, haunted by the curious undercurrent of foredoom born of antiperfectionist and antiexceptional insights like those of Mari Sandoz, which no amount of the "will to be naive" could completely erase. Out of this context of hope and gloom, fostered further by the mingled sense of cultural dissolution and boundless possibility instilled by the catastrophic pace of change of the interwar years, the psychology of the "way out" thus emerged: regionalists *must* persist in their efforts because the fate of the American experiment seemed to hang in the balance.

In *The Culture of Cities*, for example, Lewis Mumford described the fallen world from which must spring the mass democratic upswell of converts who alone could be led to the new Promised Land of the regional civilization—in terms few fellow regionalists would have quarreled with:

> At present . . . our metropolitanized populations throughout the world are both witless and wantless: true cannon-fodder, potential serfs for a new totalitarian feudalism, people whose imaginative lives are satiated by shadows, people whose voices are dimmed by loud-speakers, people whose will is capable of response only under mass stimuli and mass pressures, people whose personalities, instead of being represented by an integer, can be represented as but a fraction—one one-millionth of a voting crowd, a war-crowd, a drill-crowd.

From this darkly realist perception of the present, regionalists projected their utopian visions into a future in which power rested lightly on the polity, if at all. For Mumford and his circle, the way out from this unexceptional present was a noncoercive community constituted by "education" to "increase the area of political rationality and human control." He elaborated this conception of "rational politics" in view of its true function—to nullify power:

Instead of an external doctrinal unity, imposed by propaganda or authoritarian prescription, such a community will have a unity of background and a unity of approach that will not need external threats in order to preserve the necessary state of inner cohesion. . . . In this concrete sense— and not in any vague hope—education is the alternative to irrational and arbitrary compulsion.

This grassroots "alternative" provided the foundation for frameworks of radical reform envisioned by regionalist circles from across the political spectrum. Herbert Agar, in his loosely worded contribution to the conservative symposium *Who Owns America?*, asserted that there were "two prerequisites for peaceful reform" in America: "First, there must be a public whose deepest feelings are sympathetic to the reformation. Second, there must be a group of leaders capable of appealing to those feelings, of organizing them and giving them conscious form." Bear in mind, he wrote, that "our movement is a democratic movement, and democratic politicians cannot impose ideas upon the people from above. They can only implement ideas which have been clarified and accepted." This arousal and education of the public, Agar concluded, was the only manner by which the Agrarian program could be effected "without serious dislocation and without tyrannical interference on the part of the State." Similarly, Howard Odum, writing in *Southern Regions* on behalf of his group's more leftward agenda, cautioned that social planning, as he conceived it, must attempt "no utopian tasks superimposed through dictation." Effective democratic planning could come about only through what he foresaw as an "extraordinary effort in adult education, carrying to the people the power of both fact and thinking," which would in turn engender "a powerful regional motivation and also a spontaneous folk movement." By these means, he wrote, a noncoercive local-regional-national "equilibrium between individuation and socialization" might be achieved.[16]

Constructed on this noncoercive, persuasive footing, virtually every other element of the various programmatic expressions of the way out which regionalists formulated was directed (as Odum's concept of an equilibrium implied) toward dispersing political power and ending the struggle over abundance which had characterized America's not-so-exceptional history. From this broadly defined common ground, however, regionalists diverged along their particular and sometimes conflicting programmatic paths toward the "new stage in human culture," in ways that reflected the degree of their allegiance to the world of their fathers and grandfathers and their understanding of the nature and magnitude of the immovable bodies against which their advocacy must build up irresistible force. The social visions that emerged from this complex of "political choices," choices about which values should and should not be incorporated into the task of national recovery and reconstruction, reflected another of the reasons for the regionalists' "persistence" in their fragile project, despite the conspicuous failure (as the Agrarians were not alone to confront) of a "flocking" public to materialize: making those choices, regionalists, like any true believers, never subjected their own faith to the kind of incisive questioning that they directed toward the capitalist-megalopolitan order. For according to those visions, the "limitations of each region" (prejudices, bogeys, ingrained behaviors, fiefdoms large and small) might be ignored, or transcended by rational argument, or overcome with moral and emotional appeals; the "driving force of history"—perhaps time itself—might be stopped, or at the very least, made to conform to deliberate and conscious control; the struggle for power might cease to be a factor in human affairs; and civilization, "soaked in misery and in blood," might be made into a work of art. Even a cursory survey of the various regionalist "ways out" will reveal such assumptions at work and provide as well a preface for answering the further question of why the polity, during the most severe national crisis since the Civil War, failed to flock to the "flags" that the regionalist movement "hoisted" on their behalf.

One might begin this survey with the most grandiose scheme, the utopian vision of the Mumford circle, pointing the neotechnic-biotechnic way out from the barbarism of the paleotechnic regime. In a 1933 article, Benton MacKaye summarized much of this circle's previous work and many of its future programmatic dreams, speculating how he would sculpt America if given the chance to be "public works dictator." Of all the various wings of the movement, Mumford's was most cognizant that the future of America lay in the city rather than on the farm. The approach of the Mumford circle encompassed the entire "valley section," synthesizing urban planning with resource conservation and wilderness preservation. Using this approach, MacKaye envisioned for his audience a twofold plan of "civilization-building," the first part "physical," hinging on the control of the flow of water in the valley complexes, and the other "cultural," diking the flood of metropolitan growth. To this end, he wrote, the water-control plan would involve the "maintenance of forest cover" to renew and perpetuate watersheds and halt soil erosion; the development of large-scale "river regulation works," particularly levees, storage reservoirs, and hydroelectric dams; and the erection of far-ranging grids of "power lines" to distribute electricity widely to "smokeless factory and home." Yet this physical plan, MacKaye insisted, served mainly as the "base for the cultural portion," which was directed toward "the conservation of the basic settings (of wilderness, community, [rural] wayside) and their protection from the influx of the metropolitan slum." Such protection would demand an entirely new pattern for the transportation network and the closely related flow of urbanization. The "essence of this pattern" was "inaccessibility," MacKaye and other planners believed, and one of its key elements would be the "townless highway" or "freeway," which would have limited entrances and exits for automobiles and would otherwise be closed to any type of abutting construction along its path. The next step (each part of the design essential to the whole) would further this "living divorce of dwelling and transport"—the "townless highway" must connect "highwayless towns." The model community of Radburn, New Jersey (already constructed by the City Housing Corporation, builder of Mumford's Sunnyside Gardens home), was the prototype, a place consisting largely of cul-de-sacs to restrict traffic flow off main streets and of interlinked park areas traversable only by footpaths. MacKaye expanded the vision outward: "what the cul-de-sac is to the town of Radburn, my whole town would be to its surrounding region"—multicentered, extendable only within "fixed limits," encircled by "substantial open areas" that were themselves buttressed by the final crucial ingredient of the "cultural plan," an enriching backbone of primeval "forest wilderness." Implemented *in toto* not only regionally but nationally, MacKaye exhorted, these physical-cultural components of the new regional civilization were *the* alternative to the "flood" of the metropolitan slum and the "sprawling sea of suburbs" spewed out of megalopolis—an enfolding "environment of safety, beauty, and communal consciousness."[17]

There were as well other programmatic ways out from the America "turned back upon itself" proposed during the 1930s, particularly those formulated by the Odum group, the Agrarians, the Californians, the Indian subregionalists, and others hoping to bring about what H. C. Nixon called the "rural renaissance." This utopian reversal of the anti-Jeffersonian, antiexceptional impoverishment and depopulation of the countryside would require, most of them believed, a complete transformation in the class-rigidified rural economy, a veritable "decentralization in physical property," as Agrarian Frank Owsley put it. Two distinct visions of this decentralization—both, in actuality, calling for a redistribution if not an outright expropriation of land—emerged over the course of the decade. The first centered on the idea of "peasant proprietorship" (so labeled by Rupert Vance), which was argued most fervently by Owsley himself and his fellow Agrarians but also adhered to by the somewhat less enthusiastic Odum group ("There are strong signs of a rapprochement between Chapel Hill, North Carolina, and Nashville, Tennessee, as to policy and aims," John Crowe Ransom noted in 1934). Under this new tenure system, as many as 500,000 Southern black and white tenant families (a number often invoked) would be resettled on their own small parcels of inalienable land, where the growing of subsistence crops would be the first order of business and cash crops only secondary. This system could also provide, according to Owsley, a "permanent relief from permanent technological unemployment," a persistent worry of many in the 1930s, when some 10 million Americans seemed unable to find work regardless of improvements in the business cycle. Yet "peasant proprietorship," in its various forms, was to involve much more than mere subsistence or relief; as the Agrarians often protested to their critics, "we do not propose any literal restoration of the old civilization." The new owners would be schooled in soil rehabilitation and reforestation techniques; they would, moreover, engage in various cooperative enterprises (here the enthusiasm of the privatist Agrarians began to wane—although mention of cooperatism made its way into *Who Owns America?*—while the Odum group warmed to the task), including the "pooling of rural labor" for rehabilitation projects, the "pooling in county and/or community of heavier machinery for harvesting, threshing, storing, and processing farm products," as well as "special county unit plans for utilizing and developing forest and grass lands," as Odum projected. Clearly, technology would play an important role in the proprietary renaissance: both the Agrarians and Odum's circle built their versions on rural electrification and other means of bringing (in Ransom's words) the "comforts of the city" into the countryside, albeit on the countryside's folkish and decentralizing terms. The hoped-for "agricultural reorganization" was to furnish a basis "for decentralized industry, for village and community industries, for a large number of new smaller industries," Odum stated in no uncertain terms. The Agrarians too predicted that the system of "peasant proprietorship" could eventually light the way out from monopolistic corporatization, establishing in its wake (as Ransom wrote) "business on the small scale—many owners, little businesses."[18]

But for other regionalists in the South and the West, the necessities of industrialization, the force of tradition, and, above all, the demands of "social justice" seemed to require a somewhat different configuration for rural reconstruction, one tending away from the proprietary individualism of "many owners" and toward a full-fledged cooperatism and collectivism. Arthur Raper tentatively took this further step beyond the lingering neo-republican prejudices of the Odum group with his call for "democratic cooperative endeavor" in *Sharecroppers All*, and the erstwhile Agrarian H. C. Nixon made a more dramatic break from his *I'll Take My Stand* cocontributors in his own work, *Forty Acres and Steel Mules* (1938): "Mechanization of agriculture suggests large-scale operation, which, in turn, suggests farming by wealthy individuals, by corporations, or by cooperative enterprise," he wrote and, though qualifying his assertion with the stipulation that small ownership should continue with some crops, then went on to indicate the true way out by praising the "missionary zeal" of the managers of the experimental, interracial, and communally tilled Delta Cooperative Farm in Mississippi. Nixon sketched (and actually attempted to enact with the tenants on his own farm) his vision of the rural renaissance—a new regime of cooperative stores, sawmills, cotton gins, tractor pools, community centers, and "village workshops" to produce handicrafts for sale and goods for "home consumption," each village linked in "cooperation and common action" with "all the communities of a region." Meanwhile, writing from California, where the mechanization and industrial organization of agriculture had reached an apex, Paul Taylor and Carey Mc-Williams made the case for cooperatism, for an American version of collectivization, even more directly: "We do not believe . . . that more small subsistence farms afford suitable solution for those who are displaced from either agriculture or industry," Taylor wrote. The "advance of the machine" on the "modern latifundia" meant that "the collective principle is there," McWilliams declared; "large units of operation have been established, only they are being exploited by private interests for their own ends." Collectivization could thus be brought about by "merely a change in ownership" from the barons to the migrants. And so, in the future, these "large-scale corporate farms," Taylor projected at the end of *An American Exodus*, must and would have "working farmers for stockholders."[19]

For the Indian subregionalists, who were also projectors and participants in the rural renaissance, a similar change in ownership of Indian lands promised to inaugurate not only a "new stage in human culture," but also a restoration of ancient communal tenure, repudiating the alien individualistic system that had been imposed on the tribal landholding pattern along with all the other white evils that had attended it. This transformation would not entail a regressive "back to the blanket" movement, John Collier and his supporters were constantly forced to reiterate. As part of their rehabilitation from the deplorable conditions revealed in the Meriam Report, tribal members were to be given "technical training of all kinds," Oliver La Farge wrote in a 1936 defense of Collier's policies. He emphasized the importance of traditional "arts and crafts" and their sale as an additional source of income, an income sufficient "to buy the machine-age luxuries" that were "increasingly desired" on the reservations. Both La Farge and Collier largely rejected pessimistic depictions like that of John Crowe Ransom of such consumption as self-inflicted imperilment by unwary "weak-headed" Indians. "The possession of these machine age luxuries and conveniences," La Farge assured Collier in a report on the Pueblo tribes, "need be in no way destructive of Pueblo values." Any "reasonable policy" of assimilation, he wrote, must be so formulated to allow the tribes "to select desirable elements from the surrounding civilization, not in order to imitate white men, but in order to create a progressive, intelligent Indianism." The key to this reconstruction, as Collier argued fervently all decade long, was "decentralization":

> To decentralize the Indian services; to "integrate" them within the local areas; to unite the local Indian Service staffs with the local Indian people; *and to bring it about that the local areas, not Washington, shall shape the objectives, the programs and the projects of service*—this is the paramount necessity of Indian administration.

Although operating within "a continuing framework of Federal guardianship," this new system of "local self-government" and "community organization for self help" would include, La Farge hoped, a tribal council with sufficient autonomy "to protect and encourage native arts, traditions and religion." For an "intelligent, progressive Indianism" like that being developed for the Pueblos, he and Collier believed, must continue to nurture the integrative, "intimate relation of Pueblo art to the whole pattern" of the Indian "renaissance," the ancient noncoercive aesthetic-symbiotic pattern of "land, community, religion."[20]

Collier's and La Farge's hopes for a framework of federal decentralization reflected the widely shared desire among regionalists that the programmatic substructures underlying their various visions of social democracy would provide control without excessive compulsion. It was very much a mentality born out of the interwar perception of a crisis in liberalism—yet another of the reasons for their "persistence" in their ideologizing task. Regionalists had been witness to the "anemic" laissez-faire years of the corporate-dominated 1920s as well as the puritanical conformities of 100 percent Americanism; in the 1930s they confronted the resultant chaos of the depression at the same time that the New Deal was taking unprecedented regulatory measures and Europe was showing them an unthinkable way out via totalitarianism. Somewhere along these axes of anarchy and oppression must exist, regionalists assumed, that "dynamic equilibrium between individuation and socialization" of which Odum wrote—a nexus where universal and local values, justice and freedom, community and individualism, national interest and self-interest could all be reconciled. Like Collier and La Farge, most of them (even, for a brief time, the Agrarians) conceded that some form of federal intervention would be necessary to adjust and balance out this "equilibrium"; the oversight of nation-straddling concentrations of private corporate power would necessitate it, as would the enormous capital, infrastructural, and administrative needs of local and national economic recovery. Yet regionalists were equally concerned (again like the Indian subregionalists) about the manner in which this "inevitable coercive federalism" (as Odum referred to it) would come to bear on local communities and the individual citizen.[21] Out of these yearnings and concerns the abortive ideology of regionalism arose, seeking some way to mediate, to mitigate the enclosing matrices of private and public coercion that were otherwise inevitable and unavoidable.

Southwest Review editor Henry Nash Smith provides one example of a search for this regional equilibrium at work. In 1933 he confessed to Mary Austin, "I am discovering that I am not a liberal in the Roosevelt sense. I don't like the overtones of the NRA [National Recovery Administration]"—the corporate broker state—"yet I don't like the *I'll Take My Stand* unreconstructed attitude either"—sectionalist laissez-faire. "Maybe," he wrote, "there is a conservatism which we have been feeling for in our regionalism, and which is conservative only in its assertion of the value of some contact with the past and in its insistence upon some variety of individualism." Smith would "persist" in this search for much of the decade; in the end, his departure from both New Deal liberalism and classical liberalism led him to embrace, at least during the crisis-filled "moment" of the interwar years, the more "adequate political framework for Western Civilization" (as he wrote in 1942) that the Mumford group of regional planners had fabricated.[22]

Yet Smith's choice of words, that he was "feeling for" a middle way between corporatism and rampant individualism, was telling. Seeking their new "framework," regionalists solved many a social or political problem by recourse to "felt," organicist, and intuitive devices—unexamined poetic images (garden cities), metaphors (symphonic nation), and all manner of unlikely imaginative scenarios (rural renaissance) which were hallmarks of an unworldly utopian mind-set and a primary reason for the movement's abortiveness. The oxymoron "dynamic equilibrium" was a case in point. It recurred not only in Odum's works, but in Mumford's as well ("a region is characterized by . . . a state of dynamic equilibrium").[23] In the broadest sense, it was meant to signify an organic balancing of forces that, with every change, reasserted itself. As political theory, it connoted a pluralist yet communitarian order in which individual volition and expressiveness were still possible, whether that individual was a single citizen or an entire region. But programmatically, institutionally, the dynamic equilibrium, like many regionalist visions, proved difficult to translate from "vague hope" into the "concrete," even on paper.

"Plans that do not rise out of real situations, plans that ignore existing institutions, are of course futile: mere utopias of escape," Mumford wrote in *The Culture of Cities*. "But plans that neglect to formulate the potential creative forces, even though they are perhaps feeble at the moment of formulation, are equally futile." Mumford explicitly (and Odum implicitly) staked the establishment of the regional dynamic equilibrium on the "feeble" yet "potential creative force" of "communal education" by the regional survey itself. As a somewhat bemused W. T. Couch noted of the Odum circle's monographic works, "Out of their facts they seem to think that some irresistible truth will come of itself." Only with the assumption that a "conversion" of the polity had been brought about by this "irresistible truth" could Mumford, for example, seriously consider the rest of his own programmatic scenario to represent a possible "real situation." First would come the resolution of the "fundamental issue": the peaceful abolition of private property and the return of land to the "common stock," to "the community from which it was originally derived." As he commented, "This should be particularly easy in the United States; for here there are no immemorial privileges of ownership and residence . . . here the greater part of the continent was still *public land* up to a century ago." Once the "common ownership of land" was accomplished, the next stage would unfold: "decisive control" would be put "in the hands of responsible public administrators"—"geographers, sociologists . . . engineers"—who, "working for the common good," would "map out areas of cultivation, areas of mining, areas of urban settlement" and would create with their expertise—in close consultation with "the philosopher, the educator, the artist, the common man"—"a system of dressing and keeping the land as it must be dressed and kept for an advanced civilization." Thus proceeded Mumford's tenuous attempt to turn an oxymoron into a "politics." Every plan, he admitted, must undergo "a readaptation as it encounters the traditions, the conventions, the resistances, and sometimes the unexpected opportunities of actual life." He would not, in fact, *could* not, compromise his basic scenario, however: a plan "loses some of its efficacy as plan if it sacrifices, at the beginning, the clarity of the ideal by timidly anticipating all the qualifications and reductions that ideals are subject to in the course of their translation."[24]

As will be shown in the next chapter, certain programs of the disparate regionalist agenda did make their appropriated way into the political arena— regional planning, rural resettlement, and Indian tribal autonomy, to name a few. Yet unfortunately, by acquiescing in the liberal-democratic system, regionalists accepted the politics of the "strong and slow boring of hard boards" (as Max Weber had earlier characterized them in his essay "Politics as a Vocation"—the type of politics that the Nazis, implementing their dystopia, had promptly swept aside in his own country). The development of democratic instrumentalities to circumvent politics-as-usual—for therein lay the dead end of utopia—thus became a primary challenge for regionalists. But Rupert Vance's depiction of the 1931–32 Southern cotton stabilization drive as a hopeful first development in the effort to make regionalism a folk movement with a mass base of support—and therefore "a challenge to technicians, academic leaders, and agricultural extension workers whose thinking it outruns"—could have served as a cautionary tale. The drive, Vance noted, was "sponsored" by Huey Long, "a state governor who is both a folk product and a rabble rouser, a man who lives with his ear close to the ground"—and, it might be added, a man with a great deal more political savvy than the artists and intellectuals of the regionalist movement. He was more than willing to have truck with "diabolical powers" (as Weber put it), often playing fast and loose with the constitution of his home state. His political skills had availed him of the de facto governorship of Louisiana and a Senate seat in Washington, and were preparing a credible presidential bid. Long's efforts on behalf of cotton price stabilization, as one admiring observer reported, had made him "the idol of 95% of our people . . . the common people." Nevertheless, even with Huey Long's considerable powers of *persuasion* energizing it, this relatively simple "regional program" (as opposed to creating garden cities, merely a "cotton holiday" during which farmers would voluntarily forego planting in order to raise prices) was in Vance's words "thwarted . . . by our peculiar federal structure, our constitutional and legal commitments," and by what he somewhat mysteriously called "folk processes themselves"—probably short-term economic need, the greed of landlords, processors, and middlemen, and that cussed American individualism which regionalists were never quite certain how to accommodate, unwilling to suppress it, unable to overcome it, unsure how to "symphonize" it.[25]

"We will be beaten . . . as our fathers were," John Gould Fletcher had predicted of the "Cause" to Allen Tate as early as 1927, writing with the Civil War allusions of which the Agrarians were so fond. Yet despite these sentiments, few regionalists were as devoted to the Cause of regional America as was Fletcher. He once described himself as "more radical than the radicals," and confessed to Frank Owsley: "I realize I have got to die sometime, and the only damn thing I want to die for is the South." He would devote himself stoically to the reconstructive ends of the cultural project:

> Just because we haven't got a Virgin, or a God, should we stop trying to find one? I think not. If the whole of the present generation has to go to pot, and myself along with it, I don't propose to abandon my irrational hopes that humanity will somehow solve the problem, through art . . . of its own nature and destiny. I admit that I have no solution, but I am going to go on trying to find one.

Thus, in 1931, Fletcher was present at the first important national gathering of the movement, the University of Virginia Round-Table Conference on Regionalism, and over the years, he alone among all regionalists forged substantial personal and professional bonds with most of the disparate and otherwise largely isolated regionalist circles around the country—as a member of the Southern Agrarians, as a correspondent with Mumford and Van Wyck Brooks of the New York–New England wing, as a contributor to B. A.

Botkin's Southwestern journals and anthologies, and as a frequent visitor to the Indian subregion of Santa Fe–Taos (renewing his acquaintance with a landscape he had first explored in 1907 on an archeological expedition with Edgar Hewett). Even after his break in 1935 with the Agrarians over their lack of political action and lesser issues, he pursued into the late thirties the movement's "very hard and thankless task": "I am still working with faith in very little, except in trying to promote a regional consciousness in this country of ours." Earlier he had admitted to Lewis Mumford that "I frankly do not see any way out of the impasse that our mass civilization has got itself . . . than by means of a change in heart, a change in values"—but, he reminded Mumford and the rest of the movement, "such a change is the most difficult, if not impossible thing, that can be imposed on people." And so as the fragile, plaintive "programs" of the regionalist movement began to make their way into the political arena, becoming subject to "readaptation" as they encountered "the traditions, the conventions, the resistances, and sometimes the unexpected opportunities of actual life"—or were merely ignored—Fletcher's evaluation of his own activism at the Virginia conference, that first "official" political foray of the movement, assumed a larger meaning, almost a prescience, regarding the final fortunes of the regionalist movement *in* America: "Anyhow, many of those present knew that a certain flag had at least been hoisted . . . even if later on it might have to be hauled down again."[26]

8

Termination

The Regionalist Movement, the New Deal, and the Coming of World War II

Consider: consider my friend: the handful of intelligent
and sensitive and expressive people in the world need
each other's friendship and comradeship: we exist in a
jungle, surrounded by men, who like Odysseus' crew,
have had their manhood enchanted out of them: we
must keep our faith in each other, in order that we
keep our faith in the work we severally and collectively
are ordained to do. Whatever undermines our good
will is not merely grievous personally . . . but it
undermines the work we have in hand: civilizing the
jungle, fighting the hyenas, turning the swine back
into men again.
—Lewis Mumford to John Gould Fletcher,
     June 27, 1935

"It is important, at an early stage of the movement, that
we should arrive at a common meaning," Lewis Mumford
said to the delegates gathered at the 1931 University of
Virginia Round-Table Conference on Regionalism. Along
with John Gould Fletcher and a number of urban planners
and administrators (as well as a few politicians), H. C.
Nixon was there, corepresenting the Agrarians; Mumford's colleague Benton MacKaye was also in attendance,
and so was Howard Odum, up from Chapel Hill; Stringfellow Barr played host out of the editorial offices of the
Virginia Quarterly. There were no Westerners present,
although Mumford had invited B. A. Botkin to speak on
their behalf. Sending his regrets, Botkin promised to continue his efforts to "serve the end of that increased 'inter-

course and reciprocity' between regional centers upon which I have felt, as you, that the future of the movement depends."[1]

As these and similar avowals should attest, for more than a few participants, the regionalist *movement* was no mere historian's device, reconstructed from hindsight and defined by generational biographies or common intellectual problems and discourses. Regionalists themselves aspired self-consciously to become a movement: if the 1920s had been an era of manifestos, the 1930s were an era of conferences. Yet even in the early stage of their organizational efforts, many regionalists were all too cognizant of the disunity stemming from the inherent isolation and inward focus of the various regional centers and, most crucially, from the excessive individualism of the political style of cultural radicalism. Again, the example of Fletcher is instructive. If he stood out as a paragon of personal devotion and commitment, as well as representing with his wide-ranging national connections the politically essential " 'intercourse and reciprocity' " that the regionalist movement was never to attain, he also symbolized, paradoxically—with the fervency of his prejudices ("arid and bitter provincialism," Mumford called them) and the extremity of his prescriptions ("more radical than the radicals")—the very sources of divisiveness that were to preclude unity and abort chances for a common political agenda. Over the years, Fletcher by turns insulted the Mumford group ("you can say more than anyone else why New England is so played out nowadays," he told Van Wyck Brooks) and appalled them (Mumford labeled a Scottsboro apology by Fletcher "Fascism or Hitlerism"), while the other centers failed altogether to live up to his expectations: Botkin's final *Folk-Say* volume was, to his mind, "inspired by Moscow," and the "Santa Fe art and literary crowd" were "pretty dull . . . combining Greenwich Village artiness with feeble provinciality." In the end, even his Agrarian brethren failed the test of faith. "You are traitors to the cause you serve," he railed at Allen Tate and John Crowe Ransom in 1935; then he resigned—to go it, fittingly, alone. At times erratic and unstable, Fletcher nonetheless represented only the extreme of the "tendency toward disintegration" (as Donald Davidson noted of the Agrarians) that plagued not merely the various regionalist attempts at national organization, but the local circles as well. Thus, not surprisingly, Robert Penn Warren (another of Fletcher's Agrarian colleagues) observed not long after the *last* major regionalist gathering in 1935 at Baton Rouge: "The sporadic 'Conferences' and 'Congresses' of writers in different sections of this country . . . have tended to define differences of opinion rather than concord; certainly, no program or dogma has emerged." Consequently, "no political party stands behind the regional writer, in fact, no organization of any description."[2]

But the issue of organization, or the lack thereof, begs a more fundamental question: would it have made any difference in the fortunes of regionalism? The assumption was that (as Davidson wrote) "if our ideas are right, we shall in the end reach the people who can do the other needful things." Wielding whatever influence the force of their ideas and their own eminence could muster, an influence that must be more potent if unified, regionalist artists and intellectuals would guide and advise the powerful to enact their programs. (As will be seen, more than a few regionalists also sought a more directly engaged and participatory influence on 1930s reform agencies than that prescribed by Davidson.) Yet in defining "differences of opinion rather than concord" at their various meetings—and in other mediums—regionalists were doing more, much more, than squabbling and undercutting their chances for organization and influence. They were carrying on an internal debate, raising for themselves the "qualifications and reductions that ideals are subject to in the course of their translation" into actuality. As regionalists operating from divergent subsets of assumptions found that the *region* was not big enough to accommodate all of the different "frameworks" of civilization which they were "feeling for," they themselves began to trace the abortiveness of each other's programs and, painfully, to discard their own proposals as well.[3]

Some of the most cogent "qualifications" regarding the planning philosophy of the Mumford group and the Odum circle, for example, were voiced by the Agrarians, most incisively by Donald Davidson. His main targets were fellow Southerners in the Odum group, and his central criticism was that they did for a fact "eschew politics"—a puzzling function for a would-be ideology to seek to fulfill:

Apparently social planning means that everybody will stop fighting, cheating, and vituperating and be a good Christian. It is not dictatorially imposed but calls for "cooperative and coordinated design of, for, and by institutions and regions rather than by government alone through centralized autocracy." Seemingly that implies that social planning will be in large part voluntary and unofficial. . . . The thing will work amiably and flexibly. It will have as its principle "a working equilibrium in the whole culture process and function." It proposes not to tear down the old institutions forthwith, but to ease them painlessly through some orderly transitional process [that] . . . is going to be extra- or super-political and will be in [the] charge of social science.

Davidson's attack on planning, like Mari Sandoz's reluctant critique, was based on a less-than-optimistic conception of human nature. Conflict was built into human affairs, he assumed, and it could only be done away with by the harshest forms of oppression. Mumford seemed to anticipate this objection to his scenario, yet significantly his own qualification was added almost as an afterthought at the end of *The Culture of Cities*. "The student of utopias knows the weakness that lies in perfectionism," in "a harmony too absolute," now made "manifest in the new totalitarian states," he wrote; "what is lacking is a realization of the essential human need for disharmony and conflict." Typically, he saw conflict not as an unavoidable and necessary evil but largely as a further design element to be incorporated into the overall aesthetic milieu of his garden city—it would be "intellectually stimulating," "dramatic," and "vitalizing," he predicted.[4]

For Davidson and other Agrarians, the specter of a "super-political" rationalism thus so confident in its powers that it could choose consciously to constitute a "contrapuntal order" (or not to constitute one) was ominous, to say the least. As had conservatives since the days of Edmund Burke, he and his colleagues based their antiplanning arguments on a critique of Reason, bolstering it with their modernist rejection of abstractionism. Despite the planners' "Realist" protestations, Davidson contended, "statistical tables, sociological and economic," ignored "the folks behind the abstract ciphers." And because they did, the reforms that they indicated, if implemented, could only be "rigid and dictatorial." (As Burke wrote of an earlier group of radicals, "With them defects in wisdom are to be supplied by the plenitude of force.") John Gould Fletcher attacked Mumford's faith in science, the very basis of his antipolitical "rational politics," more directly. "One thing I am sure of," he wrote in a 1933 letter: *"that modern science is not going to help us to preserve our regionalism, as you seem to think.* . . . Because our regionalism depends on the individual and the community, whereas modern science depends on mass-technique." Mumford, of course, countered that the "organic plans" proselytized by his "regional survey" were designed to create the very "human synthesis" of science and humane values, rational control and local tradition, which the Agrarians declared to be antithetical. Yet Benton MacKaye's tongue-in-cheek fantasy of being made "public works dictator" could hardly have allayed their suspicions, and Mumford's revealing conclusion about overcoming the obstacles to planning in *The Culture of Cities* seemed also to agree with their worst fears: "Such success as totalitarian states have shown in their collective planning," he wrote, "has perhaps been due to their willingness to cleave at a blow the Gordian knot of historic resistances."[5]

It was not so much "historic resistances" as the "driving force of history" that qualified and reduced the plans of the would-be makers of the rural renaissance in the South and the West, as they themselves became all too aware. One of the earliest public airings of rural renaissance proposals, and their problematic aspects, occurred in 1930 during a debate between John Crowe Ransom and Stringfellow Barr, the onetime Agrarian recruit whose more liberal-leaning views precluded his contribution to *I'll Take My Stand*.

Significantly, the debate, which was held in Richmond, Virginia, before an audience of 3,500, was moderated by Sherwood Anderson, who in the rather changed interwar context of the cultural revolt had come almost full circle from his grim 1910s *Winesburg, Ohio* depiction of rural small-town life, announcing that he wanted to be "a worm in the apple of progress" and that he was "glad of the life on the farm and in small communities"—sentiments with which neither of the debaters would have disagreed. Regarding the topic at issue, "Shall the South Be Industrialized?," Ransom argued a rudimentary version of what would remain the Agrarian case, equating an adequately and therefore abhorrently coercive "regulated industrialism" with "Russian communism" ("it is offensive to our deepest political instincts to think of having to go socialist") and advocating (in Barr's accurate rephrasing) "a bloody shirt program [directed toward] inflaming the agricultural population of the South against the industrial carpetbaggers," a strategy which, Ransom agreed, "could be nasty and could be effective." Pointedly, Barr's criticism, articulated at the Richmond debate and in earlier private letters to the Agrarians, centered on the ludicrousness of the debate topic itself, sixty years into the New South era: "I am not much interested in a childish longing for the past," he said. "The South's problem is not whether it will adopt the machine, but how it will adopt it. . . . I personally regard the industrialization of the South as inevitable." Barr then came to the crux of the matter, for the Agrarians and for all of the other advocates of the rural renaissance: "I think the trouble with your position is that you think it is eight o'clock when it is some minutes past ten." In Richmond, Ransom could only rebut Barr with the other horn of the regionalist dilemma: "He talks of industrialism as an 'irresistible force.' I do not know how an 'irresistible force' can be 'regulated.'"[6]

In *Southern Regions*, Howard Odum provided some more precisely defined measures of just how late the hour was for the American folk. Even as he expressed the hope that the "frontier folk" of the Southeast and Southwest might offer "still a baseline from which to explore the possibility of a sort of 'recovery of the past' through projecting an American culture that might have been," he knew that certain "absolute facts" had to be faced:

For those who long easily "to recapture the past" for Jeffersonian agrarianism, it must be pointed out that . . . the task is not so simple in the modern complex America. Compared with the earlier days, there was, for instance, the Jeffersonian eastern America in which the farmer was the bulwark of democracy; and there is the wide regional variation in the agriculture of the 1930's which, all told, provides less than 13 per cent of the nation's income. There was Thomas Jefferson proclaiming "the mob of great cities add just so much to the support of pure government, as sores do to the strength of the human body," and there is the 1930 America with more than 60 per cent of its people living within metropolitan areas, with 96 such regions each boasting over 100,000 population, with a single metropolitan area having twice as many people in it as all of Jefferson's beloved domain. There was Thomas Jefferson admonishing "to let our workshops remain in Europe," and there is the new America with more than 37,000,000 or 76.2 per cent of all its working folk occupied in manufacturing, mechanical distribution, and social services.

Thus the vision of the rural renaissance began to fade. In a 1934 *Southwest Review* essay titled "The Dilemma of Agrarianism," Henry Nash Smith considered what would be required to reverse these long-term demographic and economic trends on behalf of a landed "economic and social independence" for displaced tenants and workers, as the Agrarians and the Odum group were proposing. "A contemporary Agrarianism," he discovered, would be "a matter of large-scale planning, centralized administration, and infringements upon the rights of a great many persons to order their own lives."[7]

Undoubtedly, it was in response to critics like Smith—"to clear up all the nonsense that has been said about us," as Allen Tate wrote—that the Agrarians issued their programmatic manifestos, *Who Owns America?* and "The Pillars of Agrarianism" (1935—written by Frank Owsley). But immediately they were forced to resort to exactly those "infringements" that Smith had indicated, and for which they had criticized "dictatorial" liberals like Barr as well as the planners and sociologists. The paramount necessity, Tate told W. T. Couch in 1934, was not only "getting tenants independent on the land" but also "keeping them independent there." The establishment of "peasant proprietorship" would require, literally, a "modified feudal tenure," Owsley wrote, under which land would be "non-mortgageable" and title would reside with the state. (It is noteworthy that the Agrarians associated themselves for a time with the monarchists and fascists of the British Distributist circle; and they as well as the various farm cooperatists like H. C. Nixon looked to France, Sweden, Norway, Denmark, Ireland, and other *European* countries for models of state-sponsored rural renaissance to, ironically, find the "way out" to a renewed American exceptionalism.) This land would be purchased from the landlords, loan companies, banks, and insurance firms that now owned it by federal authorities and state governments, although Owsley confessed privately to Couch that—having less confidence in "persuasion" than Mumford—"I am perfectly willing to see their lands confiscated . . . if they cannot be obtained in any other fashion." The new land system would necessitate protection from those same economic entities that had anchored tenancy and which were otherwise responsible for economic colonialism. For this purpose Owsley suggested "public ownership of railroads, power companies, gass companies steel corporations and public utilities" [sic], plus, most critically, "the creation of regional governments possessed of more autonomy than the states," essential not only because of "differences of economic interest" between the regions, "but because of differences of social and racial interests as well." These regional governments would have the power to nullify national legislation, levy their own tariffs, and constitute their own courts. "Once this foundation is securely built," Owsley wrote in the stirring and almost surreal conclusion of "Pillars" (surreal given the coercive and intrusive program he had just outlined), "the agrarian society will grow upon it spontaneously and with no further state intervention beyond that to which an agricultural population is accustomed. The old communities, the old churches, the old songs would arise from their moribund slumbers. . . . Leisure, good manners, and the good way of life might again be ours."[8]

The magnitude—and unlikelihood—of the "infringements" that would be necessary to restore this "good way of life" gave pause to a number of regionalists in the South and the West. Odum's ambivalence about the possibility of such a rural renaissance, voiced in the most basic and undeniable demographic terms, was repeated even more strongly in his colleague, Rupert Vance, and in others—Paul Taylor and Carey McWilliams especially—who began to face the "absolute facts" of global economic change, national urbanization, and farm mechanization, and to qualify and reduce their programmatic hopes accordingly. As has been noted, Vance supported "peasant proprietorship" in principle, but already in 1935 he was questioning the "feudal" measures that the Agrarians deemed necessary to "keeping" resettled farmers on their land. As he told Owsley, "I shrink from assigning these people a fixed status approaching serfdom in a world of mobility." He was all too aware of the "pressure toward migration" that had been building in the South for three decades or more and was increasing to catastrophic levels as a result of overpopulation, the dearth of regional capital, the collapse in world cotton markets and prices, the advent of government production quotas, and the spread of the tractor. Cumulatively, these enormous long- and short-term problems meant that the imperiled folk of the South could only be kept on the land at huge and unlikely cost, Vance believed. He estimated in a 1936 article that the rural rehabilitation measures proposed by the New Deal—much less thoroughgoing than what would be required for peasant proprietorship—even if capitalized at one billion dollars (a "generous" hypothetical figure), would be able to resettle only one and a quarter million farm family members in the South, leaving as many as seven million men, women, and children still poverty-stricken and landless. Given the lack of opportunities in the decrepit and devastated Southern economy, migration, Vance wrote, "remains the

area's sole immediate recourse"—"desirable, if not absolutely necessary."
Vance was in fact among the first to perceive the gathering of the next waves
of the historic Great Migration of millions of rural blacks and whites to the
North and the West, and he called for programs of training "to fit them for the
transition to urban and industrial environments . . . to which many of them, it
now seems, must go"—pushed by the "driving force" of simple demographics
and economics.[9]

Vance's figures appeared to undercut not only the possibilities for peasant
proprietorship but also for other projected configurations of the rural renaissance—as revealed in a further set of qualifications made most explicitly by
McWilliams and Taylor, writing from trend-setting California and a five-years
longer perspective. Surveying the "shock of change" erupting across the
southern United States, McWilliams concurred with Vance that "there is no
point whatever in attempting to reverse a clearly defined historical trend."
There was, he wrote, "nothing to be gained technically, nor, in the long run,
socially, by attempting to break up large holdings and to return to a concept of
farming that prevailed a century ago." The efficiencies demanded by modern
technology, the whole machine-centered "logic of our economic order"—all
argued against the old-fashioned political and cultural reasons for "relocating
displaced farm families on subsistence non-commercial farms." Sensing this
"fact," the Odum group, Nixon, and others had tended toward a cooperative
agriculture solution because it was conceived to be more appropriately and
viably modern, as well as more ethical and humane than unalloyed agribusiness. But from the viewpoint of the late 1930s and early 1940s—as the Great
Migration began to grow and swell—this method of keeping the dispossessed
on the land, indeed, the very idea of keeping people on the land, came to seem
increasingly obsolete. As Paul Taylor wrote, "The real opportunity for large-
scale absorption of the displaced must lie in the direction of industrial expansion, not in crowding them back onto the land where already they are surplus . . . produced but unneeded on the farms."[10]

Depopulation was thus an unavoidable "pattern" confronting rural America, in the short run likely only to worsen. The shortage of urban-industrial
jobs had acted to hold and to draw the impoverished to the countryside during
the "moment" of the depression, but with the coming of war in Europe,
McWilliams noted, "production of war materials has once again set the factories ablaze with light," which would only drain more and more people out of
rural areas. At the same time, Taylor predicted, "mechanization and industrialization on the land will spread," permanently dispossessing still more of
them. Yet Taylor "persisted" in projecting "new patterns" by which "to
preserve what we can of" a "very old American ideal"—"that our land shall
be farmed by working owners." Like many regionalists, including those who

had faced the "absolute facts" of the present, he had difficulty conceiving of an America without a substantial proportion of its population "living on the land." For McWilliams, however, facts were facts: 1942 was very late in the life of the American folk. "It is rather idle to speculate at the moment about ideal patterns of rural social relationships or idyllic rural utopias," he wrote at the end of *Ill Fares the Land,* adding presciently: "If such patterns were worked out and put into effect on an experimental basis"—as they had been at the Delta Cooperative Farm, at Norris, Tennessee, and at Radburn, New Jersey—"they would probably be destroyed, or perverted in their purpose" and "wither up and die." And so "there is, in fact, no 'solution' of this problem," McWilliams closed, no solution short of democratically overturning the "whole complex of our industrial order"—and concerning which he offered few suggestions.[11]

In his critique of the Agrarians, Henry Nash Smith, beginning a career-long examination of the functions and paradoxes of myth, had sought to define the "dilemma" of the "infringements" that they encountered when they attempted to "translate" their vision of a folk-regional society into the circumstances of the modern world, to discern why it was so "qualified." His analysis was applicable as well to the Mumford group, unable to confront the "plenitude of force" which would be necessary to realize their own "plans" for a noncoercive social order, and to the sociologists and Californians, watching the "driving force of history" stream away from the old yet new "patterns" into which they hoped to fashion it. In fact, with these words, Smith began to describe the dilemma facing the entire regionalist movement, and to write a eulogy for its abortive ideology. The Agrarians' myth, he declared,

> serves them well as a symbol through which to express their feeling that something is terribly wrong with the present industrial order, in this country as in the rest of the world, and we undoubtedly need every available expression of the vulgarity and cruelty which seem inseparable from the processes of industry. But the value of the myth disappears when one tries to use it as a blueprint for reform. For a myth is a work of art—a selection of human experiences. It is simplified by this selection. . . . The actual present is . . . too complex to be explained by myth. [A] program of reform is meaningless unless it is based on as complete a grasp as possible of the facts. Thus when the Agrarians are intent upon their myth, they can form no program; when they begin to consider practical measures, they have to turn their backs upon their myth. This is their dilemma.

What the Agrarians and other regionalist groups were attempting to do with their reforms was, in effect, to stop the "driving force of history," to redirect it, to gain control of the continental drift of cultural, political, and economic trends that the "absolute facts" of Odum showed to be leaving the older America behind. The drastic measures that would be required to bring about this change of inertia were a hallmark of just how far away the world of their "fathers and grandfathers" was, or, rather, how distant modern America was from the mythicized usable pasts that regionalists preserved from it—a telling distance, as Smith intimated: for them, those pasts, and their utopian projections into the future, supplied everything that was lacking in modernity; proselytized, they took on the aspect of a ghost dance. "It is aerophytic," Smith concluded of the Agrarian program, or any other: "it has its roots in wishes and dreams."[12]

If such an analogy is apt, regionalism was nevertheless a ghost dance which attracted few converts. The reasons for this failure should not, however, be entirely attributed to the "will to be naive" on the part of regionalists themselves, or to the consequent incoherences, tensions, and paradoxes of their doctrine. As unlikely as their utopias were in concrete economic or political terms, it is also true that every ideology encompasses mythic fictions, far-fetched metaphors, and unrealizable abstractions that, when legitimized, appear as universal truth and common sense. The mainstream liberal political culture of the 1930s, for example, was based in and proselytized such concepts as *progress*, *popular sovereignty*, the *social contract*, *individualism*, and *equality*, all of which were attenuated by the extensive "qualifications and reductions that ideals are subject to in the course of their translation" into reality. It was very much because of these attenuations, brought on by "internal erosion" as well as the corrosive and "perverting" context of capitalist urban-industrialism—the perceived "crisis" of liberalism—that the ideologization of regionalism was stimulated. *Why* regionalists with their utopian projections, their delegitimizing "hidden history" of national development, and their critique of genteel and mass culture were unable to convince Americans that these severe attenuations had taken place, that some of those ideals in themselves were in serious need of reformulation, is a question that, in short, cannot be completely answered by factors internal to their creed and movement, their "tenuousness" and fragility notwithstanding. Allen Tate's consolation from posterity was not misplaced: the efflorescing "glow" of the regionalist "ghost dance" left standing any number of artistic and intellectual monuments, works which gave expression to values and ideas and styles of lasting import. Among them were the histories of Webb and Mumford; the paintings of Benton and O'Keeffe; the poetry of Frost and Tate himself; the photography of Lange, Evans, and Bourke-White; the novels of Faulkner,

Steinbeck, Cather, and Wolfe; the folklore of Botkin and Rourke; the music of Copland and Guthrie; the sociology of Agee and Cash—even the Agrarians' own manifesto, the political movement it hoped to inspire all too evanescent, remained in print half a century after it was written. Granting all of the limitations of the political style of cultural radicalism and the regionalists' exorbitant expectations of a mass conversion, the questions remain: why did so few heed their often brilliant and devastating critique of modern America? Why did the grassroots upswell never materialize? Why did the legitimation of the would-be ideology of regionalism fail to take hold?

These were questions that regionalists, for all of their "persistence," asked themselves periodically throughout the 1930s. Despite the fact that the South, the national epitome of socioeconomic backwardness and cultural inertia, "had the best intellectual leadership it had ever possessed," wrote W. J. Cash in *The Mind of the South*, he was forced to conclude after a decade of observing their efforts that "intellectual leaderships are by themselves always helpless. Invariably they are quite incapable of taking their facts and ideas directly to the people, persuading them of their validity, and translating them into action." In this lack of "articulation between the new intellectual leaders and the body of the South," he believed, "the tragedy of the South as it stood in 1940 centrally resided." As early as 1935, when the last major national gathering of the movement convened in Baton Rouge (among those attending were Robert Penn Warren, Allen Tate, Frank Owsley, John Gould Fletcher, B. A. Botkin, W. T. Couch, Lambert Davis, editor of the *Virginia Quarterly Review*, Savoie Lottinville, Brandt's assistant at Oklahoma University Press, and John McGinnis, chief editor of the *Southwest Review*), Cash's tragedy, and its broader implications for the country as a whole, were already the top issue for discussion: "Is the problem of a lack of a proper public special to the South?" The present-day "dissociation of the artist from his public" (as Davis put it) was compared wistfully to the integrated "spiritual unity" that was presumed to exist between them in the seventeenth and eighteenth centuries. A "tone of bitterness" quickly entered the discussion as the participants began to consider the modern reasons for the "moribund humane tradition" and the "tremendous difficulty of establishing communication between the writer and the audience."[13]

On the eve of the conference, Fletcher had enumerated a number of their initial explanations in a letter to Van Wyck Brooks: "We are of course limited and hampered in every way," he wrote. "Not only are there few organs of public opinion down here, but the question of distributing the few there are, is very difficult. . . . Not many people read books, and bookstores are scarce and few." Fletcher here touched on two separate if closely related sets of problems, one institutional (and financial), the other cultural. The first received much comment at Baton Rouge and in correspondence among the various regional editors over the years: like any business, the "business of the regional renaissance" was not easy to pursue during the depression. The same crisis that provided the "moment" of opportunity to transform America's economy and society also hindered regionalists from getting the word out. At Baton Rouge, Couch reported simply that "books are not selling. The chief reason is lack of money." McGinnis's and Henry Nash Smith's *Southwest Review* had all of "four hundred paying subscribers—a good deal more of these in New York than in New Mexico, Louisiana, and Oklahoma," McGinnis corroborated rather sheepishly. John T. Frederick's *Midland* magazine promptly folded in 1931 when its subscriber base was unable to support a move from Iowa City to the higher rents of Chicago. With so few "patrons" among the general population, most regional magazines and presses had to rely on state support. But unfortunately, the depression was an era of fiscal retrenchment in the states; luxuries like universities and the arts were often among the first budget items to be cut. The conference host *Southern Review*'s generous endowment from the local dictator, Huey Long, was the exception proving the rule. Thus the common, commiserating refrain of the editors' letters: "The Governor ["Alfalfa Bill" Murray] is playing with the University," Botkin told H. G. Merriam in 1933. "You probably read of his order for the removal of education, engineering, and home economics. Who will be next?" Merriam replied of his own plight in Montana: "It looks as tho we *might* get thru with a 20% salary cut." In 1936 Couch's North Carolina Press was faced with "cutting off one-third of our staff, and cutting salaries and wages of the rest by about one-third" when it was rescued by a timely grant from the (ironically Northern-based and corporate-financed) Julius Rosenwald Fund—the dream of every editor: an independent "benefactor." But such windfalls were rare, and on the whole the hopes of regionalists to produce "a furious stream of publications" (as Ransom had foreseen for the Agrarians) remained thwarted.[14] In most cases, because these magazines and presses were "pioneering" institutions and therefore the sole media for serious publication in a given state or region, the promise and fulfillment of regional culture and consciousness rose and fell with them.

Yet this institutional weakness—the absence of bookstores and libraries, the paucity of subscribers, the underfunding, the tendency to treat such enterprises as luxury—was merely symptomatic of deeper, cultural obstacles to "spiritual unity," obstacles about which regionalists were quite cognizant. "The largest problem is the general lack of interest in books and the feeling that the intellectual life itself is of no importance," Couch grumbled at Baton Rouge. Much of this discussion echoed what Brooks and others had said a decade or more before in *Civilization in the United States*; little seemed to have changed, in spite of all the intervening efforts at cultural "reforestation."

In the South and Midwest particularly, culture remained "in the hands of the women's clubs and the men's dinner clubs," Botkin observed; it remained, in other words, marginal: "they still regard writers as freaks and curiosities instead of human beings with serious work to do." Howard Odum similarly had complained in his 1934 essay on planning: "The public pokes abundant fun at the experts and the specialists." And so regionalists were confronted by another "dilemma." To close the still-existing genteel, blindsided void between society and culture, they had chosen to use the "power of art" as their primary means, as their politics, to create simultaneously "a taste and a public." Yet they must "act" within a larger society in which those very means were regarded to be of secondary importance at best. The solution appeared obvious: to overcome marginality would require "great art," which one Baton Rouge participant defined as "a public and its artist having the same reactions."[15]

But it could not be so simple. Although regionalism certainly did include its share of "monuments," creating great art was easier said than done. The ever-persistent Botkin had admitted as early as 1932 that "a fundamental criticism of the whole regionalist movement [is] that, judged by purely literary standards, its productions often fail to measure up." At the same time, many of the monuments which were produced—*Absalom, Absalom!*, "Ode To the Confederate Dead," *The Culture of Cities*—might fail to constitute an aestheticized community for exactly the opposite reasons: they repelled the average reader not by inferior artistry (overwrought dialects, flowery scene setting, stock characterization), but because they were too complex and ambiguous, too "high-brow." Furthermore, good art or bad, regionalist productions had to compete for attention with the products of mass culture. A foreign observer, visiting the United States during the interwar years, would have had no trouble perceiving the true national "civic religion": the Great Depression notwithstanding, movie attendance reached record levels during the 1930s (65 percent of the total national population, once per week), radio came fully into its own (in 1929, 10 million in use; in 1939, 27.5 million, running four and one-half hours per day on average), and the last possession even the poorest of the poor would "leave behind" (the walls of their shacks papered with magazine ads and calenders) was their automobile. When they included all the modern conveniences in their "plans" for folk-regional reconstruction, regionalists were, in effect, striking an unavoidable bargain with the devil; if the poverty and misery of the depression (as well as a bow to political realism) had raised the issue of living standards in their awareness, "qualifying" their 1920s critique of mass culture, such a bargain could only serve to imperil further the culture that the folk made for themselves. As Fletcher reminded Botkin, "Modern inventions . . . do not exist separately from the metropolitan ideas

which they bring along with them"—"usually . . . highly abstract and utterly
unregional. . . . The moment a region swallows them, it becomes metropolitan
in its mind." And having swallowed them, a region became a more unlikely
candidate for "conversion" into a grassroots upswell, because in addition to
marginalizing artistic and intellectual production, mass cultural entertainment tended more and more to marginalize politics too, or at least the kind of
nineteenth-century–style participatory politics on which Mumford and others
staked their hopes ("Political life . . . must become as constant a process in
daily living as the housewife's visit to the grocer . . . and more frequent than
the man's visit to the barber").[16] Once the former entertainment value of that
participation was eclipsed, the possibility of reconstituting it even on theatrical, much less "rational" grounds, became more and more remote.

Were regionalists then (to paraphrase Allen Tate) merely creating pleasant
little laments for their own consumption? W. J. Cash had definite opinions
regarding their efficacy in the South: "If the people of the region were not
entirely unaffected by what the men who represented the new analytical and
inquiring spirit were doing, they were still affected by it only remotely and
sporadically."[17] Yet two developments of the 1930s seemed to signal the
contrary, although in the final analysis neither could have been of much
encouragement to aspirations of legitimating the regionalist ideology and
instilling a new "spiritual unity" in America. First, it should be noted that the
"bitterness" reigning at Baton Rouge was somewhat premature and misplaced: over the course of the decade several folk-regional works did, in fact,
find a public, a substantial public, achieving that rare formula of moral force,
artistry, timing, broad appeal, and critical acclaim by which "classics" sometimes become best-sellers. *The Good Earth*, *Tobacco Road*, and *The Grapes of
Wrath* each reached a mass audience (including play and moviegoers), and
each articulated the values of agrarian life, community, family, symbiosis,
cooperation, and others of which most regionalists would have approved and
of which, apparently, the public did as well. But none of the books had an
impact that could be described as substantively "political" or "programmatic"
(despite some clearly "propagandistic" overtones in both *Tobacco Road* and
The Grapes of Wrath). Instead, flying in the face of Odum's "absolute facts"
about the extent of urban industrialization, they tapped into some positive
mythic image of themselves that Americans very much wanted reinforced—
providing "temporary shelter" from the anomie of the depression, but falling
far short of announcing a "new stage in human culture." Each work was a
study more in survivalism than utopianism, the story of a personal faith
preserved in the midst of decay and catastrophe, yet hardly sweeping the
world before it: signature folk-regional narratives of stoicism and tragedy.

As a telling corollary to this palatable and diminished radicalism, regionalists were also confronted during the 1930s with an opposite barometer of how problematical their own practice of cultural radicalism could be: rather than winning converts (or striking a chord, at least), a number of their efforts evoked outright censorship attempts—the reaction of Americans when their positive mythic images were challenged. In 1927 W. T. Couch found himself apologizing to an author that higher-ups had ruled her work on a Darwinist "too dangerous for us to touch" and that consequently "publication would have to be stopped." In 1930 Henry Nash Smith was "submerged in a mess of Methodist politics" at Southern Methodist University when he was pressured to resign for writing the preface to an edition of Faulkner's "obscene and immoral" *Miss Zilphia Gant.* Botkin in 1932 was forced to cease publication of the *Folk-Say* series because the final volume (ordered withdrawn from sale) "got a 'little too wild for them,'" as he put it, including references to Marx, marijuana, and premarital sex. At the University of Montana, Merriam began a years-long feud with the State Board of Education over its 1935 resolution calling for the removal from the library of "certain objectionable or controversial books." Sandoz too got a taste of the "world-wide spread of intolerance and the will-to-persecute" in 1937, when the mayor of Omaha banned *Slogum House* from sale. Meanwhile, Angie Debo's *And Still the Waters Run* had to await publication for three years because it named the names of Oklahoma elites formerly involved in illegally expropriating Indian land ("There is a time when a book cannot be written," warned an Oklahoma University Press reader; "Our obligation to publish is moral," Joseph Brandt protested futilely). In light of these experiences, when J. Frank Dobie in 1945 recounted the events of the long-unfolding "Rainey controversy" at the University of Texas at Austin in terms of "high-handed Hitlerism" (a liberal president was fired by regents "for allowing an immoral book entitled U.S.A. by John Dos Passos to be taught in the University; also because cases of homosexuality had been found to exist" there), he merely underscored why perceptions of "these damned fascists at home" had become so palpable among regionalists by the early 1940s: "This is not a fight on a man named Rainey. It is a fight on freedom of mind and freedom of speech. It is a denial of the great truth chiseled in great letters across the Main Building of the University of Texas: YE SHALL KNOW THE TRUTH AND THE TRUTH SHALL MAKE YOU FREE."[18]

In the view of W. J. Cash, though, the "great truth" lay in the "denial"—in all of the "denials" that regionalists had encountered over the 1930s—rather than in this optimistic sentiment etched in stone. It was no accident that his low opinion of the efficacy of artists and intellectuals in the political arena appeared in a book chronicling the "sweep into the unreal" of *The Mind of the South.* And as Mari Sandoz might have told him (having made some of her own chilling discoveries in the Mind of the Midwest), his observations and conclusions need not have been limited to his home region. Cash's list of the defects of the Southern mentality, traced out of the antebellum period to the present, was 100 percent Americanism in a nutshell (with hints of the Nazism that preyed on his thoughts lurking often in the background). He characterized this mentality as the "patriotic will to hold rigidly to the ancient pattern":

> Violence, intolerance, aversion and suspicion toward new ideas, an incapacity for analysis, an inclination to act from feeling rather than from thought, an exaggerated individualism and a too narrow concept of social responsibility, attachment to fictions and false values, above all too great attachment to racial values and a tendency to justify cruelty and injustice in the name of those values, sentimentality and a lack of realism.

The "ancient pattern" that this mind-set would not turn loose was Cash's famous "savage ideal," the centerpiece of which was "exaggerated individualism" and "the great master faith of the nineteenth century," Progress. Despite the interwar crisis of culture, when "all the old ideas and faiths and systems were under attack, crumbling or even vanishing in places," Cash wrote, the response of the South had not been a willingness to seek out alternatives like the new Promised Land of the regional civilization, but instead "a passionate desire to keep on believing, willy nilly" in this ideal. This most recent reassertion was just the latest in the repeated "confirmation and revivification of the individualistic outlook" that had occurred throughout Southern history in the face of all manner of socioeconomic change. Confirming this, Robert and Helen Lynd, returning in 1937 to the "typical American" site of their original study to measure the extent of cultural change since the onset of the depression, discovered too that "Middletown is overwhelmingly living by the values by which it lived in 1925."[19]

Cash offered no complicated psychological explanations for this tendency toward denial, for the silence and censorship that greeted regionalist attempts at public education. "It was, after all, not surprising," he wrote, "that any body of people should prefer the comforts of complacency and illusion to facing highly unpleasant facts for which the remedy was far from being obvious." Yet the centrality of words like *illusion* and *fictions* and *false values* in Cash's analysis pointed to what was for him the "core of the tragedy" of Southern history, and that of "any body of people." The "hidden histories" and "unwritten stories" that regionalists had uncovered during the 1930s had shown what could be perpetrated on these blind sides, the disjunctions and paradoxes between ideal and reality that issued in misery and oppression. But for Cash, the most central, and frightening, revelation was the existence of the blind sides themselves. The South was a well-chosen locality to see this universal tendency in action; as Cash noted, Southerners were a people "long trained to believing what they liked to believe," a people who had, for example, clothed human slavery in aristocratic romance and paternalism.[20] Beyond recounting the long tradition of such "illusions" in the South, however, Cash's analysis did not seem able to penetrate—and perhaps, to his mind, could not penetrate, to find the "cause" of the blind sides, the "reason" for the irrational.

Seeking to convene utopia out in the provinces of America, to make Americans live up to their democratic ideals, regionalists had instead been stymied by this rather anti-utopian capacity of humans, the capacity—as they could see clearly in the unexceptional past and present of America, in the "upthrust into barbarism" taking place once again in Europe—to perpetrate any evil (Niebuhr's now-fashionable word) and still proclaim their innocence; or, in less lurid terms, to see in themselves the admirable qualities of a Ma Joad, a Jeeter Lester, or a Wang Lung, yet continue to participate in and uphold the values of a system that put such folk in peril. A few artists and intellectuals confronted this capacity head on—Sandoz, Faulkner, and Cash, for example—yet each was unable to sustain the gaze for very long. Sandoz, as noted, took refuge for a time with Crazy Horse, Faulkner (after *Absalom, Absalom!*) retreated back behind the blind sides ("Why do you hate the South?"—"I dont hate it. . . . I dont. I dont! I dont hate it! I dont hate it!"), and Cash, reportedly fearing that he was being pursued by Nazi agents, committed suicide in 1941. As the years passed, others too came to sense that the comforting disjunction between a people's "vision of themselves" and their actual social praxis (the resistances it offered to change, the crimes it could foster) had made problematic their pursuit of the new civic religion, of "rational politics," of cultural "reforestation." "I don't know how to get any real information into the heads of the dominant white leadership," W. T. Couch, one of the chief regional "educators," told Virginius Dabney, author of *Universal Education in the South*. He threw up his hands. "The only thing I know to do is to keep trying."[21]

Yet there was, in spite of all the feelings of frustration and impotence confronted by regionalists, a final and very good reason for this persistence. "Regionalism is certainly coming along very fast," John Gould Fletcher prefaced some remarks on the state of the movement to Donald Davidson in 1934, during an intermittent spell of optimism that struck any number of his counterparts especially in the early 1930s. He was writing of the New Deal, which seemed at that time to many to be, as Benton MacKaye wrote of the Tennessee Valley Authority (TVA), "a chance to make a start at least in surveying towards a new world." Odum too saw the TVA as "a great regional-national experiment," and Mumford pointed to the possibilities inherent in a number of other "new enterprises and new public agencies" established under the

auspices of the Roosevelt administration—such as the Public Works Administration and the U.S. Housing Authority—all aimed "experimentally" toward devising, he believed, "a more valuable pattern of social and economic
activities." Although one hesitates to conceive of this intersection of regionalism and the New Deal solely in terms of "influence" in one direction or
"appropriation" from the other, there is no doubt that a convergence of sorts
did occur. It was, after all, Franklin D. Roosevelt, tree farmer and governor of
New York, who gave the keynote speech in 1931 opening the University of
Virginia conference on regionalism, where (according to the hindsight of
several attendees) the idea of the TVA was born. With his neo-Jeffersonian
rhetoric and his advocacy of planning, one might almost be tempted to call
Roosevelt the "regionalist president." Standing for more than an hour before
the audience ("the longest time he had ever stood up with his braces," according to one onlooker), he set this perspective:

> It seems particularly appropriate that we at the University should be
> discussing plans, for the great planner of our nation, the first planner, was
> the father of the university; an architect of buildings, an architect of
> industry, and most of all an architect of government. And yet, after the
> age of Thomas Jefferson, it seems to me that our nation as a whole, and
> our several states forgot architecture in the sense in which it had been
> used and practiced by . . . Jefferson, and it is only in the last generation,
> our generation, that we have returned to thoughts of planning for the
> days to come.

Roosevelt told the delegates (gathered in one of the great halls designed by
Jefferson) that a primary concern of the nation must be the "problem of
maintaining a proper balance between city life and country life." Action must
be taken to establish "by cooperative effort some form of living which will
combine industry and agriculture." The ultimate end, he said, was to make
the citizenry of "our whole nation individual and independent."[22]

Few regionalists would have had qualms about such rhetoric; in fact, the
convergence of their movement and the New Deal may also be measured most
visibly by the number of regionalists who literally went to work for the New
Deal. Benton MacKaye worked for the TVA ("a golden & interesting opportunity," he told Fletcher); Rupert Vance consulted for the National Resources
Committee; Paul Taylor was employed by the Resettlement Administration
(RA); John Collier, of course, became head of the Bureau of Indian Affairs,
assisted by D'Arcy McNickle; B. A. Botkin was appointed national chief of the
folklore section of the Federal Writers' Project (FWP), while Couch was put in
charge of the entire FWP Southern contingent; and John Lomax evaluated
FWP-collected folk songs for placement in the Library of Congress archives.[23]

Several regional editors and writers became involved in the FWP at the state and regional level, editing and writing state guidebooks and other publications, including Angie Debo in Oklahoma, H. G. Merriam in Montana, and John T. Frederick in Illinois. Certainly too there were regionalist fellow travelers among the New Dealers—most prominent among them, Arthur E. Morgan, chairman of the TVA, student of Edward Bellamy, and author of *The Small Community: Foundation of Democratic Life* (1942). Regional planning, rural resettlement, the restoration of Indian tribal autonomy, and the cultivation and preservation of folk art and culture all found their place on the New Deal's unprecedented agenda, giving regionalism, in some form, an entry into the political arena, and regionalists some hope that the foundation for the "new stage in human culture" was being laid. In 1938, after previously being convened in various provincial cities, the National Folk Festival arrived in Washington, D.C., for an extended engagement.

A survey of the New Deal's rhetoric suggests its apparent commonality of interests with the regionalist movement, or at the very least a common, shared discourse. One major document, *The Future of the Great Plains* (1936), written by the Great Plains Committee, a group of officials from the Resettlement Administration and the U.S. Department of Agriculture, included a chapter on "Attitudes of Mind" among Plains dwellers that "must be subject to revision." For such attitudes, the report declared, "tend to crystallize, fail to take account of new conditions, cease to serve their original purposes, and frequently hinder necessary readjustments." They included the bankrupt notions

> That Man Conquers Nature. . . . That Natural Resources are Inexhaustible. . . . That Habitual Practices are Best. . . . That What is Good for the Individual is Good for Everybody. . . . That an Owner May Do with His Property as He Likes. . . . That Expanding Markets Will Continue Indefinitely. . . . That Values Will Increase Indefinitely. . . . That Tenancy is a Stepping Stone to Ownership. . . . That the Factory Farm is Generally Desirable.

Manifestly, most regionalists would find little to disagree with in these words, or with the report's conclusion that "in a democracy, education is more fundamental than legislation as a force directing rational progress." So too did other widely read New Deal writings, together with private utterances, seem to give voice to regionalist fears and articles of faith, such as TVA chairman David Lilienthal's *TVA: Democracy on the March* (1944) and the journals he wrote during his tenure (which show him reading Mumford and McWilliams, among others). In a 1940 entry he expressed worry over the efficacy of "tired liberals" trying to confront the "mass diseases of emotions" to which the public was prey and which were "beyond rational explanation at times." He later wondered to himself (after reading *Ill Fares the Land's* depiction of the independent family farm—the "basic unit" of the TVA—"fast passing away") in a style reminiscent of other would-be champions of the older America:

> What are we doing in TVA? Simply trying to fight a rear-guard action, a kind of retreat in which the outcome is foregone? Or are we simply sentimental and mushy about a beautiful past? Or do we think we can reverse the trend? Fighting hopeless battles sometimes is all there is left to do, and I would rather be in a hopeless fight if there were no alternative than to be on the winning side that seemed to me wrong.

Little of these doubts though found their way into the pages of *Democracy on the March*, an apology and manifesto in which Lilienthal lighted the "way out" to a *new* New World:

> A great Plan, a moral and indeed a religious purpose, deep and fundamental, is democracy's answer to home-grown would-be dictators and foreign anti-democracy alike. In the unified development of resources there is such a Great Plan: the Unity of Nature and Mankind. Under such a Plan in our valley we move forward. . . . If it is decentralized industry men want, "family farming," or pleasant cities not too large, an end to smoke and congestion and filth—there are modern tools which can be turned to just such ends . . . not only *for* the people but by the people. . . . Democracy can emerge revitalized.

Lilienthal had in past years stumped the country on behalf of this vision, seeking converts in a way that Mumford would have approved. In his journal, he recalled one speech given at Little Rock, Arkansas (October 22, 1941):

> . . . the men who were there, chiefly from Arkansas, Missouri, and Oklahoma, were definitely provincials in the same sense that I consider myself a provincial. Their reception . . . made it plain that I am making some headway in getting this decentralization idea over, and I am even getting something of the religious or emotional note which will be necessary before the issue is clearly understood and felt. Amusingly enough, at one stage in the address, when I was talking about the hazards of absentee government, I felt so much agreement coming up to me that I ad libbed a bit, and in the middle of this ad libbing some wind-blown Oklahoman intoned a great big "Amen."[24]

Yet to finish Fletcher's observation to Davidson on the prospects for their doctrine, "Regionalism is certainly coming along very fast, though it may not turn out to be the Bird you like"—in fact, few regionalists, in the end, were to like it.[25] Rather than the fulfillment of the "wishes and dreams" of the regionalist movement, the TVA and other New Deal programs proved to be, by and large, their denouement. All the apparent "agreement coming up to" Lilienthal notwithstanding, regionalists well knew that Americans were not "subjecting" their attitudes to "revision"—converting—in a manner that would allow the *new* New World to be realized, either in the Tennessee Valley or on the Plains. To some degree their support for the New Deal reflected their sense of frustration at the local-regional level, their expectation that with national backing and scope some political momentum toward the "new stage" might by built. As they had already discovered in their geography of power, the magnitude of the local vectors of power seemed to require some intervening force to redirect or overbalance them, bringing liberating change. The question remained as to how such intervention might occur without itself becoming onerous or, by turns, impotent. Regionalists maintained, and the New Deal incorporated (as Lilienthal shows), a professed faith in an activized grassroots upswell to find the elusive "equilibrium" between freedom and control.

At the 1931 Virginia conference, surely it had been a hopeful sign for regionalism and democracy generally—in the era of Hitler and Stalin—that the man who would soon be president had cast Jefferson ("that government is best which governs least") in the unlikely role of "first planner." (Standing before the First All-Union Conference of Managers of Socialist Industry four months earlier, Joseph Stalin had informed the assembled "shock brigade"— meeting during a temporary lull in the drive against "capitalist farming," a program which eventually left fourteen million peasants dead—that "it is time to adopt a new policy, a policy adapted to the present times—the policy of *interfering in everything*.") Yet in seeking to balance a utopian vision that demanded "interference" with a political philosophy that sought to limit it, and to operate within an economic and political power structure that legitimized the self-interest of innumerable large and petty fiefdoms in terms of that philosophy (fiefdoms which must fall if the utopian vision were to be enacted), the whole course of the New Deal was to demonstrate the programmatic fragility of "Jeffersonian planning," to show the concept to be something of an oxymoron. Theoretically, it occupied the same rarefied, metaphoric realm as the regionalist "symphonic nation" and "dynamic equilibrium," where rational control and social welfare could be reconciled with localism, independence, and individualism. In *practice*, however—or, as the New Dealers practiced it—the concept often worked against itself. Allegiance to Jeffersonian ideals inhibited planning, making it piecemeal (at most, reaching specific sectors of the economy such as agriculture) and subject to co-optation (under the rubric of noncoercive "cooperation") by the powerful national and local interests ("free individuals") which were presumably to be regulated. To the extent that planning was limited, corporate monopoly, concentration of wealth, and plutocratic control of the economy remained secure or increased, with a concomitant dwindling of Jeffersonian freedoms for the average citizen; regional plans also remained unfulfilled. Thus, while the constraining "least government" of "Jeffersonian planning" may have spared America the horrors of totalitarian repression, there was also such a thing as too *little* interference, especially in the eyes of those seeking basic social and economic reconstruction. Although the power that regionalists needed to change the inertia of history seemed at hand in the New Deal, much of the older America that they had hoped to preserve was, in the process—the *political* process—simply left behind. "Public works dictator" David Lilienthal, for one, was not going to be a martyr in its behalf. As he averred at the end of his reflections on the purpose of the TVA, showpiece of the New Deal, a thing of giant hydroelectric dams, fertilizer plants, and scientific farming: "There is a difference between bravely facing a losing fight and being a wooden-head about it."[26]

"In every move we make to bring about a change from waste to order we shall be treading on someone's toes, hurting someone who profits by it," Chairman Arthur E. Morgan (Lilienthal's predecessor and rival, and the real regionalist martyr at TVA) wrote somewhat truistically of the political realities confronting the "Great Plan" of the Valley Authority. The same might have been said of the other programs of regionalist reform that the New Deal attempted to implement.[27] Recognizing and seeking to accommodate these forces of potential resistance, the New Deal made or was forced to make compromises that could only tend to betray the interests of the peasants, migrants, Indians, tenants, and other remnants of the American folk. In the foreground of this denouement, any number of hard and immediate realities were relegating against the kind of interference that would be necessary in order for the New Deal (or any administration working within the strictures of the American political system) even to begin to implement the "utopias of reconstruction" advocated by regionalists. The nurturing of an elusive national "recovery," which preoccupied New Dealers, implied a certain allegiance to the basic structures of the contemporary economic order (for example, antitrust action taken against the more despised monopolies during the latter 1930s occurred often enough, but cut shallow). Any structural changes of the magnitude needed to institute a decentralized "symphonic nation" would have meant a great amount of social displacement and economic disruption. A dictator might ride out these pangs to long-term realization, but a president must in the short-term win elections and fight battles with Congress. Constitutional, federalist, and political (congressional) obstacles not unlike those that had thwarted the Southern cotton stabilization plan also hemmed in "radical" New Deal programs (such as public housing) at every turn. Roosevelt's rearguard attempts to move beyond the "Jeffersonian planning" approach by bolstering presidential authority through the use (ironically) of some of the "democratic instrumentalities" that regionalists hoped would transcend political infighting (the regional planning boards advocated by Louis Brownlow, for example) were turned aside with cries of fascism.

Given these resistances, and the vicissitudes of the economic cycle in the 1930s, the surprising fact is that the New Deal accomplished as much as it did: a regulatory apparatus for the worst corporate abuses, the first strands of the social safety net, federal fiscal management of basic economic parameters— these and other partial components of social democracy were grafted onto the preexistent industrial-capitalist structure. Among those components were various "projects" and "experiments" and "models" of the regional civilization, relatively small-scale (with the exception of the TVA), financially feasible, piecemeal programs that could with a minimum of disruption (though even these were opposed) provide better and more efficient "yardsticks" of economic development and social organization for public authorities and private industry. Thus were the agendas of the regionalist movement attenuated by the politics of the New Deal. ("I do not know what 'Regionalism' means," Roosevelt had admitted to the delegates at Virginia, who at the time probably took his words more as an expression of the candidate's infamous superficiality than as an omen.)[28]

If experiments and models existing "in the teeth" of the corporate-megalopolitan system hardly inaugurated the symphonic nation, it was in one sense an apt outcome. In the absence of a "broader cultural foundation," Mumford warned more truthfully than he knew in *The Culture of Cities*, "regional planning can have but a minor political significance," becoming a "barren externalism."[29] And in fact, as the regionalist utopia was "translated" into reality via mainstream politics-as-usual, a more ironic and sinister fate befell it than mere attenuation: many of the techniques and much of the language of the regional civilization came to be pressed into the service of Progress, of the local powers that be, of the regnant megalopolitan order, and of the national state, in ways that W. J. Cash would have appreciated.

The much-scrutinized TVA was a case in point. Ostensibly it was, as MacKaye and Mumford hoped, the first element of the "physical plan" of "water-control" that they and others had projected as the groundwork for the regional civilization; it was also to be an experiment in the political and economic "decentralization" (as Lilienthal's rhetoric indicated) that all regionalists envisioned as the essential transformative framework for the new order. But as sociologist Philip Selznick noted in his classic postwar critique of the Authority, *TVA and the Grass Roots* (1949), "In relation to the states, counties, and other local agencies, the TVA could not have operated successfully without framing its program within the existing pattern of government, including the powers and the traditional prerogatives of the local units"—prerogatives that in the South had upheld the tenant system and Jim Crow and the fiefdoms of local elites (the "preexisting pattern of leadership and control in the local area," as Selznick put it). In real-world terms, the "grass roots approach" constituted "a vital concession to the 'states rights' forces," Selznick argued, because any proposal for a planning authority to operate remotely from Washington ("absentee government") would have been defeated handily by the many "rugged individuals" in Congress who found the TVA—for all of Morgan's and Lilienthal's democratic rhetoric—already difficult enough to swallow. Although tantamount to a capitulation to the local powers that be, decentralization on these "qualified" terms—the terms of the courthouse circle, and of unregenerate, unconverted capitalist farmers, seeking not utopia but cheaper fertilizer and electricity, higher yields from their land—was the logical political eventuation of the noncoercive ethos of regionalism because, as Selznick (and most regionalists) well understood, "the alternative is force," applied to "tread on the toes" if not overthrow the local elites, and one therefore that no elected official could contemplate. Paradoxically, to a marveling Lilienthal, the local and national support which such a capitulation engendered meant that "politics" had been "kept out of TVA"; there would be no "taking care of the boys" by the Authority, he insisted, because "a river has no politics," only objective technical problems on which all could reach consensus.[30]

Yet Selznick argued quite the opposite (in a more controversial, but persuasive, interpretation): that the politics of "taking care of the boys" comprised the organizational core of the TVA. For proof, he observed the "close contact between leading agriculturists in the Authority and the national leadership of the American Farm Bureau Federation [AFBF]" (an organization devoted to protecting the interests of the more well-to-do farmer), contact which, in point of fact, was not limited to the higher levels but maintained throughout the organizational hierarchy of TVA, especially between government county agents and the AFBF-dominated state land grant agricultural extension services. To Selznick's mind, these special relationships represented a covert "cooptation" of the programs of the publicly financed TVA by a powerful private interest group—a common enough occurrence in American reform history, but one that the rhetoric of the TVA belied at every turn. "We appear to be uncovering and developing in this valley principles and practices for effecting a jointure of public interests with private, by methods that are voluntary and noncoercive," Lilienthal proclaimed. Thus, ironically, the grassroots concept so crucial to the regionalist utopia, the very key to the reintegration of culture and society, was itself made instead into what Selznick called a "protective ideology" (one of Cash's "fictions" or "illusions"), dedicated to ensuring the political survival of the TVA organization and upholding the interests of its powerful constituency, which were roles it performed "quite apart from the conscious sources of the official doctrine."[31]

It was and is difficult to doubt Lilienthal's sincerity, and Selznick suggests one reason for the (after all, merely ordinary) bifurcation of ideals and reality that found its inevitable way into the *new* New World of the Tennessee Valley. "'Results,' 'achievement,' and 'success' are heady words," he concluded. "They induce submission and consent . . . and they also enfeeble the intellect"—and, one might emphasize, self-criticality. There was no doubt of the success of the "physical plan" of the TVA, with its network of dams and power lines, its plants for processing nitrates and phosphates, yet it was a success bred of certain concessions of democracy. "At this moment the TVA's prestige and my own standing are at their highest point" since the inception of the program, Lilienthal noted with satisfaction in 1944, particularly pleased with a major newspaper's editorial calling for "more TVAs" and the continuing "stream of visitors from all over the world," from as far away as Egypt, who had come to see the exceptional experiment that America had wrought in the Tennessee Valley.[32] It remains unclear though what "principles and practices" they took away with them: surely the Egyptian officials were not planning to carry the gospel of grassroots democracy home to the *fellahin* peasantry, which had been oppressed and deprived for millennia; perhaps they were already contemplating the technologies required to build the Aswan High Dam, which would help to make Egypt a power in the emergent Middle East.

To be sure, the peasantry in America—the perennial victim of homegrown empire builders—was not faring too well itself under national government policies. In the Tennessee Valley (where tenant families, required to relocate from dam and lake sites, were often left to fend for themselves, the Great Plan notwithstanding) and elsewhere in the South and West, Vance, Raper, McWilliams, and other charters of the Great Migration were all too aware of the human consequences of the rural renaissance taking shape not on behalf of the migrants and tenants but for the larger owners and landlords. Yet while noting the paradoxical and sometimes damaging effects of many of its rural programs, it is nevertheless important not to cast the New Deal entirely in the role of villain. Government relief, migrant camps (such as the one offering refuge to the Joads), and other types of assistance—most of it "unprecedented"—helped millions to keep body and soul together during the depression. Some efforts were also made (through the Resettlement Administration and the Farm Security Administration [FSA]) to resettle families on their own homesteads and to provide loans to troubled small owners and "worthy" tenants to obtain land, though these efforts consistently met opposition and underfunding in Congress. On the other hand, it is also essential to see, as the observers of the embryonic Great Migration did, that such programs often treated the effects of other New Deal measures—AAA subsidies and NRA and other minimum-wage equalization legislation, for example—which tended to precipitate the "disintegrating feudalism" and dispossession that was the prelude to the "renaissance" of mechanization, price supports, fertilizers, crop quotas, long-term loans, soil conservation districts, and larger-scale parcels that would comprise the new pattern for American agriculture—in a depopulated, industrialized countryside. Despite the list of "attitudes" to be "revised" in *The Future of the Great Plains*, these new programs and techniques would necessitate relatively little "adaptation" on the part of Plains farmers, or farmers in other regions, already accustomed to the practice of capitalist agriculture and now armed with more intensive and efficient means.[33]

It was this perversion and warping of the "broader cultural foundation" of New Deal reform that disappointed many of its regionalist supporters, who, acknowledging the "driving force of history," began to see that it would offer no "way out" to the regional civilization. Already in 1936 Howard Odum was expressing the concern that the TVA might signify "the failure and futility of a possible abortive southern regionalism." Mumford too lamented (presciently enough) that the "the cultivation of the Tennessee Valley merely in terms of providing cheap electricity, or encouraging every family to have an electric refrigerator, is to reduce the whole enterprise to the scale of the nineteenth century civilization we are leaving behind us." And as the "utopian" Arthur Morgan (who envisioned small workshops and cooperative factories taking their place in the Valley) protested tellingly before he was forced out of the chairmanship, "It is planning for the total social results, and not for immediate personal advantage, that should characterize the New Deal." But at bottom, the New Deal's capitulation to "immediate personal advantage" and urban consumerism was immovably rooted in the very "allegiance" of New Dealers and Congress to the corporate-megalopolitan system, which was in turn just the political expression of the continuing, largely unshaken popular allegiance, as the Lynds reported from 1930s Middletown. "The New Deal is attempting to do nothing to *people*, and does not seek to alter their way of life, their wants and desires," FSA secretary Rexford Tugwell remarked—a good formula for political success, yet hardly the route to a "new world." Instead, it led to what was always the more likely of Odum's several projected American futures: not "general chaos" or "violent revolution" or "dictatorship," but "a new and increased dominance of corporate business and centralized power over society, making a new era of concentration, bigness, monopoly, commercialized agriculture and large scale industry."[34]

It is important nonetheless to note two admirable New Deal "projects" that emerged with at least limited success "in the teeth of" this gathering future, and that grew out of the New Deal's convergence with the regionalist movement. The first was the rudimentary folk "cultural foundation" laid down by the federal writers', arts, and theater projects of the Works Progress Administration (WPA). Surveying the work of the FWP in particular, a contemporary reviewer observed that "the Project would like to put the whole country in its books"—an aspiration that was both its strength and its weakness. Implicitly and explicitly, the State Guides and other publications issued by the FWP gave expression to a doctrine of national pluralism not unlike that animating the National Folk Festival. In his preface to *These Are Our Lives* (1939)—one of the FWP's more lasting contributions (published by the University of North Carolina Press)—W. T. Couch wrote in a typical Project vein that the compilation of transcribed interviews sought to convey the "rich variety of human experience": "The people, all the people, must be known, they must be heard. Somehow they must be given representation, somehow they must be given voice and allowed to speak, in their essential character."[35] The emphasis given by the FWP to oral history and recording also rendered important service to preserving the remnants of the older America, as was shown in B. A. Botkin's collection of ex-slave narratives, *Lay My Burden Down* (1943), which featured elderly and withered individuals speaking for the first time from beyond the blind side of the Old South myth.

Yet while such works as Couch's and Botkin's could and did provide a medium for the hidden histories of the recently and long-ago down-and-out, on the whole the FWP and the other federal artists programs were, not surprisingly, less than effective at or committed to the regionalists' projected delegitimation and "reorientation" of American values. This is not to say that works like the State Guides lacked critical commentary or a (often liberal or Marxist) politicized viewpoint. In fact, during the late 1930s, the FWP came under fire from the Dies Committee, a congressional subcommittee which had been created to spotlight "un-American activities" inside and outside of government ("I sincerely hope that the Federal Writers' Project will . . . not go to press with these guides until they are corrected so as to remove from them such propaganda and appeals to class hatred," said Chairman Dies in 1938). On balance, though, the documentarian virtues of the State Guides and other FWP works were also their ideological defect: usually written by multiple authors and edited with no clear agenda, encyclopedic and often antiquarian if not promotional in their attention to minute and quaint detail, their "massive" scope (a word frequently invoked by reviewers) tended to dilute any and all political content even as it gave expression to the vast diversity of America. As one reviewer wrote of the State Guides, capturing well their overall watered-down impact: "The books at their best avoid the overtones of both the social worker and the chamber of commerce. Their crowning virtue is in their wealth of story."[36] Conversely, when this "wealth of story" and other federally sponsored public art and architecture *were* pressed into the service of morale-boosting New Deal propaganda, they often attempted to communicate various positive, empowering themes to the citizenry—that Americans were a people of great endurance, for example, or that all-American hard work and know-how would solve all problems—and therefore they tended to encourage complacency and undercut the very public pressure for basic reform that New Dealers and regionalists alike desired.

But because the FWP faced much the same limitations in reaching an audience as did the more ambitious regionalist civic religion, it cannot be counted as an especially crucial influence toward foreclosing the "moment" of depression-era reform opportunity. More effective to the task of morale boosting were the Roosevelts' own direct mass media "fireside chats" and "My Day" columns, as were the relief measures that ameliorated the depression's worst symptoms. More crucial still to ending reform were the continuing lackluster performance of the economy, which seemed to indicate the "failure" of reforms already passed, and the not unrelated rise of a regrouped opposition in Congress, the so-called conservative coalition. The other laudable if less-than-successful regionalist "project" given a place on the New Deal's agenda, a project of outright social reform rather than mere cultural production, proved to be particularly susceptible to the increasing political inertia caused and heralded by these forces: John Collier's "Indian New Deal." Under the Indian Arts and Crafts Act of 1935 and other executive measures, Collier strove to "reverse" the historical trend toward complete assimilation by encouraging tribes to restore traditional religions, ceremonies, and craft making. The Indian Reorganization Act (IRA) of 1934 instituted the "decentralized" system of tribal council government, put an end to the atomizing and corrupt Dawes Act land allotment, and called upon tribes to reenter a communal tenure status. Many tribal groups, especially the more Americanized Five Civilized Tribes, were resistant particularly to the last provision, which became rather controversial and was heavily amended. A majority of tribes, however, did eventually adopt constitutions and charters of incorporation and otherwise sought to establish themselves on a more autonomous footing (the Navajo and the Five Civilized Tribes were very substantial holdouts).[37]

In contrast to the various schemes for the rural renaissance proposed to reverse the imperilment and uprooting of millions of poor people in the South and West, schemes that remained underfunded or unheeded, perhaps the reason for Collier's comparative success resided in the fact that bringing reform to his few hundred thousand Indians, many of them living in remote areas, simply "trod" on fewer "toes," upset fewer power structures, than the disruptions which would have been required to enact Morgan's cooperatives or Owsley's peasant proprietors. Yet what is indicative of the kinds of political obstacles confronting most New Deal policies—much less the more thoroughgoing measures that the more radical regionalists were hoping for—was shown in the continual pressures throughout the late 1930s and early 1940s to amend further, if not completely repeal, the Indian Reorganization Act: there was not, it seemed, even marginal room left in the United States for the older America. The ultra-conservative American Indian Federation called the IRA—in the typical conservative rhetoric of the day, directed against any policy that failed to uphold rugged individualism and free enterprise—an act which would inaugurate "Russian communistic life in the United States" or, variously, "Communism instead of Americanism."[38] Although Collier's opponents did not achieve outright repeal, they were able to keep the Indian Bureau's appropriations hobblingly low. Indeed, much the same tactics were used by the American Farm Bureau Federation to cripple the Resettlement Administration: not content with co-opting TVA programs, securing large government subsidies, and erecting large supportive bureaucracies in the name of "free enterprise," it must pursue and abort any alternative configuration to agribusiness-as-usual. Here, and in other instances of the latter 1930s conservative resurgence (the 1937 defeat of Roosevelt's proposals for seven "little TVAs," for example), can be seen most concretely the gradual dwindling of the "moment" for reform made possible by the crisis of the depression.

"Personally, I think the regionalism movement is almost played out," B. A. Botkin—one of the few members to keep track of the movement nationally—told Joseph Brandt in 1938, proposing to write its history. Certainly, Botkin's subsequent personal plight was another indicator of the increasingly chilly if not poisonous political atmosphere into which the "moment" was waning, announcing the looming approach of World War II. Botkin's job with the Federal Writers' Project had brought him to Washington, D.C., for a one-year stint as national folklore editor. He had for some time been associated with the League of American Writers and in Washington became prominent in the anti-isolationist American League for Peace and Democracy—two groups that, much to the chagrin of a number of liberal and regionalist members, later revealed themselves to be associated with the Communist Popular Front. Consequently, in the following year (1939), when Botkin was preparing to return to the University of Oklahoma to resume his teaching duties, he found that his "loyalty to our democratic institutions" was being called into question by the state board of regents. The sympathetic president of the university,

W. B. Bizzell, informed him that as early as the previous winter his name "was included in a list to me by the Governor of the State as being among those on the faculty . . . who are disloyal" (because of the paper he had given at the Second American Writers' Congress calling for the ideologization of regionalism). A renewal of his editorship allowed Botkin to remain in Washington, but in the fall of 1939 events took a turn for the worse. Simultaneously with a national press release (Bizzell later reported to him), an electric sign on the engineering building at the Norman campus "read as follows: 'Dr. B. A. Botkin, university English professor, listed by the Dies committee as a member of the communistic American League for Peace and Democracy." That alphabetical list, with his name at the top, cost Botkin his job (despite tenure) and severed all ties with the state he had adopted as his own nurturing regional landscape. The Thermidor represented by that list had also spawned Sandoz's nightmarish scenario from the heartland in *Capital City*, and the Roosevelt administration's 1938 proposal to circumvent local and congressional opponents via a direct (and ominous) projection of executive power through state-level regional planning boards. As the national mood became more and more shrill, it prompted Lewis Mumford, proselytizer of noncoercive "rational politics," to demand (in *Faith for Living*) the suppression of civil liberties and jail terms for all "Fascist agents" in the United States and a "forced conversion" of the fascist states abroad by the Western democracies before it was too late.[39]

Despite the last-ditch efforts of isolationists to preserve American exceptionalism by a literal separation from Europe, the United States was finally drawn into the war, and those "chaotic days" brought about a further waning of the regionalist impulse. Many of the reasons for this waning can only be described in terms of the vast forces and sea changes that are unleashed in a nation fighting the modern "total war." Whatever basis regionalist myths had in the objective reality, in the landscape, of interwar America, in the survivals of folk culture, in the sheer distances that still protected them, was largely wiped out by the *nationalizing* requirements of wartime. Whole populations were reshuffled out in the provinces, as war production drew millions to the cities of the North and military service took more millions to the bases and stations of the South and West, siphoning the growing flood of the Great Migration and pulling the very Indians off the reservations. The slow- or no-growth "mature economy," which was the keystone of many a regionalist economic analysis, was jump-started into a multiple increase of GNP. At the same time, corporate power—chastened and defensive during the depression years—underwent a great expansion and greater concentration, thanks to government cost-plus contracts and the efficiencies of scale needed for arms manufacture and war supplies. The national government itself, mobilized and enlarged beyond anything the conservative coalition had seen during the New Deal, reached down and touched the individual citizen as never before, emblematized by such mundane developments as ration coupons and recycling drives, and by more repressive signs of state power: even as the National Folk Festival was being staged for morale purposes in Washington, to "bind more closely . . . all the people who make up our country," to strengthen democracy with a "friendly mingling" in which "groups, regardless of race, creed, or nationality can come together" (as Sarah Gertrude Knott wrote), Japanese Americans were being taken to a rather different kind of gathering at internment camps spread across the Greater West.[40]

Perhaps because its waning came about not so much through an "internal erosion" of doctrine but because its proselytizers were bearing witness to this sudden remaking of the world, regionalism in fact enjoyed a brief afterglow of Indian summer during the war, as plans for postwar global reconstruction came to be generally discussed among American intellectuals. Regionalists were among those who shifted their concern from the inward regional-national focus of the 1920s and 1930s to the international context (where the rise of fascism had already turned it, and where soon, with the advent of the Cold War ethos, it was to remain for some time). Their recommendations for the coming postwar world centered on globalized versions of the regional civilization. Editorializing in a special Southwest issue of the *Saturday Review of Literature*, Henry Nash Smith wrote that "it is not absurd to think that internationalism and regionalism—resulting from a redistribution of the functions of the present national states—will prove to be necessary counterparts to one another." He foresaw a kind of patchwork quilt of regions, "economic and social units corresponding to diversities of physical environment . . . , some of them crossing international boundaries," encircling the globe. Meanwhile, D'Arcy McNickle, sitting in his office at the Department of the Interior, was sending utopian memoranda upstairs to his boss, John Collier:

This may be the time of crucial change. Not merely a time of building new structures (of world society, covenants, politico-economic undertakings) but of searching out new access channels to man's inner forces of courage, charity, forebearance, love. Both things must be done, the outward structure and the inward revisualization.

In answer to Collier's query, "What Indian [cultural] innovation has a chance on the world-winning side?," McNickle responded with undiminished faith:

Because he has never cleft the world in twain, distinguishing artificially (and falsely) between sacred and secular, between spiritual and physical, between "ideal" and "real," he has avoided the splitting of his own mind and soul. . . . If this wisdom can be adequately conceptualized, if it can be infused into the teaching of our day, if it can be put on the radio waves, written into the charters of institutions yet to be founded, then surely here is the answer, one answer at least to your question.[41]

Even as McNickle was writing these words, a terminus of sorts for the regionalist movement was taking shape out in that same sacred landscape around Santa Fe and Taos (nearer Los Alamos) where Collier had first discovered the aesthetic-symbiotic community, and the "power of art," back in 1919: the appearance, or perhaps, the *apparition*, of a new power in the world, an apparition in the presence of which the folk and the older America would have an ineradicable quaintness and obsolescence that no "will to be naive" could overcome; a power created by a large-scale organization, state-sponsored, kept secret from the grassroots, and given a fittingly alien and megalopolitan code name to jar against the beautiful and "unfenced" provincial setting into which the war state had penetrated: the Manhattan Project. The *new* New World molded and heralded by this power was to provide postwar Americans (still certain in their "illusions") with a rejuvenated sense of exceptionalism, despite its tenuous sources in standing armies, military-industrial complexes, Cold War nation-states, entangling alliances, the unimaginable force contained in the Bomb itself. From these rather unexceptional bearings, Americans were to define themselves as protector of the Free World pitted against the greater evil of the Soviet Union. To further inflate this hubris, the war-born prosperity and abundance of the United States, continuing into the unparalleled national spree of the postwar decades, would stand in stark contrast to the devastation of Europe and Japan. And so the "American individualism" which built the "American standard of living" that fostered the mass cultural "American way of life" was to become the utopian model which the nation offered the rest of the world. Thus reassured, a certain group of "reformers" would attempt in the 1950s to abolish John Collier's policies on behalf of preserving "world-winning" traditional Indian cultures and seek instead to assimilate Native Americans fully and finally into the modern world by a new policy known, appropriately, as "termination."

Epilogue

A Saving Remnant:
The Postwar Legacies of
the Regionalist Movement

And the woman which thou sawest is that great city,
which reigneth over the kings of the earth.
—Revelation 17:18

Scarcely more than twenty years separated B. A. Botkin's expression of admiration for a woodcut, sent to him
in 1930 by Percy MacKaye, that used "a female figure to
symbolize the folk spirit," and a theatrical masque conceived in 1951 by Walter Prescott Webb, based perhaps on
some disturbing boyhood memory out of Baptist West
Texas, which characterized "the Metropolis as a woman."
Along the axis of this drastic shift in conceit—from the
Earth Mother to the Whore of Babylon—one might trace
the "playing out" of the regionalist movement into the
postwar period, a dwindling that was also reflected by an
equally telling change in tone. In 1930, Botkin was afire
with the regionalist project of cultural reconstruction,
preparing to issue the second volume of *Folk-Say*, in
which he would feature the woodcut to illustrate the
organicist folk-say concept itself: "In this picture the
woman seems to be rising from the soil at the same time
that she seems crumbling into it," he wrote, "aptly suggestive of the intimate connection between lore and landscape, between the human being and his background, and
also of the continual rebirth of lore from the soil made
fertile by its own decay." In 1951, Webb was on the other
side of the World War II terminus of regionalism, the
efflorescing "moment" gone, and had just published his
last major work, *The Great Frontier*, after fourteen years
of effort. His recourse to apocalyptic imagery occurred in

the same letter in which he confessed, "I lean naturally to tragedy," and pictured as well the "Parabola of Individualism," according to the ineluctable curve of which Western man was now "disappearing in folds of modern corporate institutions."[1] Thus did the passing of the older America strike Webb, who was himself growing old. His continued "obsession" with the frontier, his tendency to let slip something like this dismal image from the Bible, or an anecdote of a nineteenth-century youth—these must have made him seem more and more old-fashioned to contemporaries, even as they continued to honor him for the contributions he had made during the years of the regional renaissance.

Many other regionalists, or former regionalists, were probably seen in the same light: distinguished now, the best work of their careers already behind them, back in those years of crisis that had evoked the renaissance. Yet most of them, like Webb, continued to think and write about much the same issues they always had, with perhaps a lesser art and passion and a trimming of expectations. Botkin in the postwar years, for example, compiled a number of folklore collections, focusing on each region of the country. Lewis Mumford, in 1945 still with thirty years of writing ahead of him, continued to find his themes in the City and, with a darker turn of vision, in the dehumanizing implications of modern technology. Mari Sandoz too retained as her setting and subject the trans-Missouri region of *Old Jules* and *Crazy Horse* but, again, never with quite the same fury she had once written of it.

But before marking the passage of these and other regionalists as a generation that had seen its day, it is important to emphasize how central the concept of the *region* had been to that generation's intellectual and political development, as an idea which crystallized and brought to a concrete focus their thought and art, and which then itself might fall away as its usefulness was spent or transcended. Sociologist Rupert Vance comes immediately to mind: Odum's regionalism provided him with a training ground in which to learn about the processes of demography, surveyed first in his early 1930s case studies of the operations of the South's cotton economy and then illuminated further by his observations of the Great Migration out of that region, social facts which gradually organized themselves for him around the more abstract yet universal "question of population redistribution," and which he could thereafter apply in any setting. (Regionalism as a sociological tool peaked in influence before the early 1950s, then was put aside.)[2]

Folklorist J. Frank Dobie received, by contrast, a more complicated, *political* education from the region. Along with Webb and Henry Nash Smith, he started the 1930s as for all intents and purposes a "good ol' boy"—albeit a highly educated good ol' boy—with a loyalty to the defunct Confederacy and the Code of the West and a conception of Texas as preeminently a white man's country, which showed in unfortunate undertones of "greasers" in his writings on the Hispanic influence in Southwestern lore and culture. He was as well in his own description "violently anti–New Deal." But by the mid-1930s the depression in general and Webb's *Divided We Stand* polemic in particular had politicized him, giving him a critical distance from his region; they had also instilled him with Webb's and Smith's hope of a decentralized, pluralist, and nonstatist "way out" of the crisis through a regional configuration of power. Seeing Texas with new and more critical eyes, he began to assume the "combative position" that would mark his final years at the University of Texas at Austin. From the perspective of "regional culture," he came to discover beyond his own former blind side the problems of racism in his home state (defeated in his attempt to have Spanish—crucial to understanding the Southwest—instituted as part of the university curriculum, he wrote, "What may you expect from the great majority of Texans who regard Latin America as Mexico and to whom all Mexicans are just 'greasers?' "). By the early 1940s Dobie the former good ol' boy was to be seen as one among several prominent "nigger lovers"—including Webb and Smith—fighting the local "fascists" (as one in the group described the pitch of the rhetoric) on behalf of such "universal" and "liberal" issues as minority enrollment at the state university.[3]

The career of Donald Davidson, however, showed that the intellectual and political "growth" fostered by the concept of the region did not have to take such liberal turns. Although the Agrarians appeared for a time to be willing to concede some kind of limited federal regulatory role to secure their system of peasant proprietorship, there was no mistaking the ultimate purpose of the "regional governments" that Davidson and Frank Owsley proposed in their mid-1930s manifestos. In those years the protection of "local autonomy . . . because of differences on social and racial interests" had been part of their much larger scheme of regional-sectional decentralization on behalf of a racially circumscribed national pluralism. But already by the late 1930s, as relatively race-blind New Deal policies continued to tread on the toes of white Southern conservatives, the regional-sectional configuration of Davidson's Agrarian vision shriveled down during the Thermidor to the single sectional issue of protecting racial segregation. In fact, by the middle of World War II, Davidson was proposing to reconstitute the disbanded Agrarians in the name of this one issue, calling for resistance to the "continuous and systematic war upon what you (and I, and others) stand for," as he was still railing in 1952 to Stark Young, "waged [by] the liberal-leftist-Communist-socialist crowd." By the mid- to late 1950s, in the course of the "new 'cold Civil War' " (what others liked to call the "Second Reconstruction") that had been launched against the South by federal power, Davidson made clear what it was he would "stand for," acting as state chairman of the prosegregationist Tennessee Federation for Constitutional Government "in these times that are, as you rightly say," he wrote Young of the persistent "subterranean life" of *I'll Take My Stand* in the postwar era, "much worse than when we unexpectedly burst forth."[4]

As Webb's own meditations and metaphors suggest, Davidson was not alone in his dark postregionalist perceptions of the postwar period (whatever their political content), and certainly other former members of the movement took note not only of the expended usefulness of the *region* but of a world that seemed to have moved on beyond it, heedlessly. For example, a poignant 1945 letter from H. G. Merriam to Joseph Brandt, who was working then as editor at Henry Holt in New York City (after heading the university presses at Oklahoma, Princeton, and Chicago—a rather ironic career track), seemed to indicate that some features of the nation's cultural map remained and were to remain largely unmodified despite the interwar regionalist revolt. In this letter, Merriam pitched a "crackbrained idea" for restarting his now-defunct *Frontier* magazine: "Why shouldn't a commercial publisher instead of running a commercial magazine, like *Harper's* . . . back five or six or seven regional magazines," he projected, "and publish itself a national magazine made up from the materials culled from the regional ones"—so went his proposal, a humble petition from the provinces addressed to the country's self-proclaimed cultural capital.[5]

Without doubt, from the perspective of some former regionalists, the megalopolitan regime seemed only to have extended and tightened its grip nationally and globally during the postwar era, perhaps most insidiously through the homogenizing mass cultural "world without a country" of television. In his last major postwar work, *The Pentagon of Power* (1970), Lewis Mumford—writing now not merely of the Machine but of the "megamachine," and quoting amply from fulfilled prophetic sections of *Technics and Civilization*—argued that instant "electronic communication has only hastened the speed . . . [of] total cultural dissolution." Rejecting much of Marshal McLuhan's media-made "global village" as "humbug," he warned that the mass media provided a dangerous "electronic illusion" of genuine communication, which was truly "possible only between people who share a common culture," those appropriating a culture's "complex inheritance" and participating in a "multi-dimensioned intercourse" that included writing, art, architecture, and technology. The electronic reduction of this genuine communication to an ephemeral audio-visual "controlled oral communication," which was no real dialogue but a "meticulously arranged monologue," could potentially put "every human soul on the planet" at the mercy of "the Dominant Minority," he believed; worse, it could cause humanity "to become increasingly illiterate and soon mutually unintelligible." Thus would humane culture dissolve—"*Is it not already dissolving?*—before our eyes," Mumford intoned, sounding more and more "old-fashioned" himself.

He concluded with words that Webb might have appreciated: "here in prospect is actually the electronic Tower of Babel."[6]

Ostensibly, Mumford's held-over postwar role as Cassandra seemed to signal some vitality or, at least, some stubborn faith in the essential insights that he and other regionalists had discovered within and lifted free of the region, universalizing and globalizing their implications. Yet other than in the variously regrettable and respectable postwar careers of former regionalists like Davidson, Dobie, or Mumford, did in fact the two-centuries-old regionalist tradition, or at a minimum its latest incarnation and apparent culmination in the interwar renaissance, still linger by even a "subterranean existence" into the thoroughly modern age following World War II? Was there (to borrow a phrase from Mumford, written during the more hopeful interwar years) a "saving remnant" of it left?

The question of legacies may be answered by references both direct and "subterranean." With regard to the regionalist cultural project, there was, first of all, the impressive and still significant corpus of literary and artistic "monuments" that it bequeathed to posterity, a number of them recognized as "masterpieces" (*Absalom, Absalom!*), others retaining a steady following (as Davidson noted, *I'll Take My Stand*), and still others undergoing unexpected revivals (John G. Neihardt's "psychedelic" *Black Elk Speaks*, during the 1960s). Second, not all regionalists did their most important work before World War II: Henry Nash Smith, for example, educated by regionalism in the problematics of myth, published *Virgin Land: The American West as Symbol and Myth* in 1950 and single-handedly helped to launch the still-infant inter-disciplinary field of American studies. In addition, such magazines as the *Southwest Review* and the *Southern Review*, as well as the university presses at North Carolina, Oklahoma, Nebraska, Louisiana State, and elsewhere, comprised an important institutional legacy that continued to enrich the cultural life of their respective regions and the nation for many years. And as late as the 1970s and 1980s, scholars were continuing to find at least some utility in the *region* as a concept, with sociologists like John Shelton Reed taking the measure of *The Enduring South* (1972, 1986) as a "subcultural persistence in mass society," with whole contingents of historians compiling a mammoth *Encyclopedia of Southern Culture* (1989), and with writers like *Washington Post* editor Joel Garreau proposing to redraw the national map more realistically as *The Nine Nations of North America* (1981).[7]

Regionalism as a politics, as an ideology or would-be ideology, also found expression in the postwar era, although in some cases, in rather typically ironic and paradoxical ways. The bifurcation of vision and technique that the regional planners had perceived in the Tennessee Valley Authority occurred during the postwar period to many of the conceptions that they themselves

had either championed or conceived. Intended to cultivate symbiosis and
"communal consciousness," these projections usually embodied more sophisticated and efficient methods of economic development than the "mine and
move" mentality could imagine. But those same superior plans thereby became prime candidates for appropriation by interests concerned *only* with
greater efficiency and increased development. The technology of waterpower,
for example, which in regionalist plans was meant to be the centerpiece of
the "unified development" of a whole "valley section"—with family farms,
planned communities, "smokeless factories," and "wilderness backbone" integrated together—came instead in the postwar years to represent the ultimate in congressional pork barrel, as project after project was constructed in
home districts often on flimsy budgetary and economic grounds but with
compelling political and bureaucratic rationales. The idea of "unified development" was perverted into a lobbying scheme for the rarely cost-effective sale
of hydroelectricity to nearby cities in order to bankroll the irrigation projects
of downstream agribusinesses—a sales pitch used more than once by the
Bureau of Reclamation or the Army Corps of Engineers to win initial (and
usually, irreversible) commitments to questionable projects.[8] Still more caricatured and bastardized than the "water-powered region" was the idea of the
"townless highway." The whole concept had been a tribute to the planners'
realist recognition of the centrality of the automobile in modern American
life—but perhaps they did not realize how central it was. As urban "free-
ways" and the components of the interstate highway system began to take
shape during the 1950s, certain key elements were added or subtracted from
their vision in the name of expanded capacity and profit. These proliferating
highways did not, of course, connect "highwayless towns" but rather created
new, long stretches of abutments for the construction of the "metropolitan
slum." If the main community-engendering and beautifying promise of the
planned town and freeway had been "inaccessibility," it was all too easily
short-circuited by the employment of the "access road."

Yet if in their "will to be naive" the planners, hoping to turn the automobile
to greater purposes, thus failed to recognize just how important were convenience, access, automobility, and other hallmarks of the consumer ethos, in
their more essential insight, articulated by Benton MacKaye, that humans
required and desired exposure to primeval-rural as well as urban environments, the regionalists seemed to have captured what would become an
increasingly important preoccupation of postwar Americans: "quality of life,"
the concern for personal health and well-being. As an issue, it was a "luxury"
that belonged more to an era of economic abundance than to the bread-and-
butter years of the Great Depression. But fundamentally, it also constituted a
critical component of the elusive "cultural foundation" which regionalists had

sought vainly to constitute for their own movement, and which would be the basis for the more successful efforts of their most direct postwar political heirs, the environmentalists. Ultimately, however, the failure of regionalists to acknowledge a cultural foundation built on consumerism was a hallmark of their refusal to grant too many concessions to modernity, to make those compromises with the "diabolical powers" of urban-industrialism that the more moderate adherents of mainstream postwar environmentalism were willing to make.

The larger dwindling away of regionalism into the postwar era may in fact be traced most clearly through its several ties to the environmental movement. One such link was the not inconsequential participation of Bernard DeVoto in the water and range fights of the West during the late 1940s and early 1950s. Possibly preoccupied and sated by his interminable literary feuds, DeVoto experienced something of a delayed politicization in the early 1940s, having held himself apart from much of the regionalist movement proper in previous years. A self-styled iconoclast and tough-minded realist ("a pluralist, a relativist, an empiricist"), he explained his apolitical stance of the interwar period with the excuse that "all my life I have quarreled with people who work with abstractions, generalizations, or systems"—and the 1930s were an era when political "systems" abounded. Given these sentiments, DeVoto remained skeptical of the efficacy of cultural radicalism. As he told his old rival Van Wyck Brooks (while refusing his invitation to a 1943 peace conference of writers), "Convocations of writers and intellectuals have always seemed to me ineffective, and not only ineffective but unrealistic, and not only unrealistic but irresponsibly frivolous." Nevertheless, DeVoto was at that moment (according to his longtime associate and biographer, Wallace Stegner) undergoing a thorough education in the modern Western landscape via personal tours and correspondence with National Park and National Forest Service officials, all of which would confront him with the prospect of an already-"plundered province" (as he had described it years earlier) being plundered again to a severity never known before, and which would compel him to become one of most vocal of the few outnumbered advocates for conservation in the boom days of the early postwar era.[9]

From his national podium at *Harper's Magazine* and in articles contributed to mass-circulation publications such as *Reader's Digest*, DeVoto carried out a campaign of column writing over the next several years, seeking to alert public opinion to the bold and subtle political ploys of the lumber companies, big cattlemen, mining concerns, farm bureaus, and power utilities that were laying waste to the West from its most picturesque parks and forests to its remotest scrublands. The central line of his analysis must have been all too familiar to fellow disenchanted Westerners like Sandoz or Webb (the latter was joining the fray of arid-region water politics by the 1950s), and relent-lessly his critique unrolled, year after year, as a tart commentary on the "self-deception that runs like a leitmotif through Western business." Taking advan-tage of yet bucking against the federal "paternalism" that had modernized the underdeveloped West during World War II, "and, being Western individualists and therefore gifted with illusion," DeVoto reported, big interests and small fry had joined together in the postwar years under a somewhat paradoxical federal platform: "get out and give us more money." He elaborated this doctrine as the "dream of economic liberation" through "continuous, con-tinually increasing federal subsidies [which] shall be made without safeguard or regulation." The political deals that were concocted out of these rarely so bluntly stated assumptions, as DeVoto depicted them, issued in irrigation projects, cheap range fees, mineral rights transfers, timber concessions, hy-droelectric dams, and other executively countenanced and congressionally approved inroads into "seventy years" of "wise use" conservation policies. For it was Pinchotesque conservationism that DeVoto was advocating and defending, invoking the old, eminently rational rhetoric of "sustained, perma-nent use," of an economy devoted to "steady, sustained, permanent yield." In the past, he argued, setting aside now-obsolete tirades against Eastern colo-nialism, "Federal intervention" on behalf of these conservation measures had "preserved . . . resources from locally owned liquidation by the West itself." But as "Western interests . . . hellbent on destroying the West" geared up in the late 1940s, the first of a series of postwar attempts to turn federal control of public lands wholesale over to more pliable Western state legislatures ("home rule"), DeVoto had only apprehension for his region, the future of which, he wrote, would depend on "whether it can defend itself against itself."[10]

It was this apprehension that had politicized DeVoto in the first place, and as he observed the course of conservation politics into the 1950s, he saw little to relieve it. One of the last polemical essays he wrote before his death was entitled "Conservation: Down and on the Way Out" (1954), a demoralizing chronicle of political "capture" and an analysis—not unlike Philip Selznick's on the TVA—of the "working principles" of Eisenhower administration con-servationism: " 'a friendly partnership' " with private businesses, " 'a greater measure of local participation and control,' " and, as DeVoto commented, in "an even more opaque phrase," increased efforts to " 'decentralize' " admin-istration to " 'operate at the grass roots.' " He interpreted the outcome of these principles in a manner that Selznick would have appreciated: "They would throw the gates wide open to the boys in the back room unless the Administration could get in first with programs of its own. It did not and the boys—the trade associations, the lobbies, the special interest groups—

rushed in with a loud whoop. . . . [A] considerable liquidation [of publicly owned resources] has been effected already and much more is in the works." As to the final disposition of Western resources, the aim of "the boys" became crystal clear to DeVoto: "the clock should be turned back somewhere beyond Theodore Roosevelt" to what DeVoto had once called the "economic cannibalism" of the Old West.[11]

And yet that same despairing analysis included an allusion to a long-running controversy still unresolved in DeVoto's lifetime, a controversy which he himself had helped instigate four years earlier, and which would be a galvanizing event for the not-yet embryonic postwar environmental movement: the battle over the proposed Echo Park dam on the upper Colorado River in Dinosaur National Monument. According to Wallace Stegner (himself a considerable presence in the Wilderness Society around that period), DeVoto had "started the uprising" with a widely read 1950 article that made "many million people" aware of "a threat to something most of them instinctively or out of personal experience valued highly." The Western landscape, harboring the last few wilderness bits and scraps of the frontier (with all of its popular mythic connotations still intact) had proven and would prove to be an especially potent rhetorical backdrop for turning such development battles into morality plays, as environmentalists were to discover. *Before* Dinosaur National Monument, what would become the environmental movement was described in these words by the man generally regarded as its "father," Aldo Leopold: "Despite nearly a century of propaganda, conservation still proceeds at a snail's pace; progress still consists largely of letterhead pieties and convention oratory"—exchanged among the small devoted membership of organizations like the Wilderness Society and the Sierra Club. *After* the successful fight to preserve Dinosaur, spearheaded by these groups and originally publicized by DeVoto, the modern environmental movement rolled forward as an undeniable political force, gathering momentum from controversy and catastrophe—atomic testing, *Silent Spring*, Santa Barbara oil spill, Mideast embargo, Alaska Lands Act, Three Mile Island—into the 1960s and 1970s. It would enjoy a popular base of support only dreamed of by the artists and intellectuals of the comparatively puny interwar regionalist "movement."[12]

But it was in the very success of battles like that over Dinosaur National Monument that the postwar dwindling away of the ideology of regionalism into the politics of environmentalism may be seen. The figure of Aldo Leopold provides both another link back to the earlier movement and, through his own career, an important commentary on the evolution and consequences of the postwar movement he "fathered." This place in history was secured for him by the publication of his work, *A Sand County Almanac* (1949, 1953), which became something of a Bible for nature lovers and which was to be grouped with the classic writings of Thoreau and Muir. Ironically, though, considering the success of the book as an environmentalist recruitment vehicle, the scattershot essays of *Sand County Almanac* cumulatively portray a man *retreating* from politics and policy-making—where Leopold had spent much of his professional life, as a forester—to seek the personal refuge of an authentic ethical life on a shaggy little Wisconsin farm, a place where even the weeds were spared destruction.

In the 1920s and 1930s, Leopold had been one of a number of foresters, including Benton MacKaye, who had started their careers in Gifford Pinchot's Forest Service and gradually grown disillusioned with it. Their ambivalence had been part of the ongoing fracturing of the concept and practice of multiple-use conservationism, a fracturing manifested most prominently by the famous lost battle over Hetch Hetchy Valley at Yosemite National Park in the 1910s, which revealed the readily "capturable" utilitarian and developmentalist core of the doctrine for all to see. Hetch Hetchy had also signaled the splitting off of a long-brewing and distinctive Muir-inspired *preservationism* for which there was a "highest use" of wilderness lands—*no* use, now or in the future, other than for recreation. To promote these more pure principles, Leopold, MacKaye, Robert Marshall, and others had joined together in 1935 to found the single-issue Wilderness Society. Thus had emerged the repentant Leopold of *Sand County Almanac* and the "land ethic," a man who in the course of his career had seen the destructiveness and ineffectuality of federal wildlife, range, and forest regulation, and who was himself guilty of eradicating a few populations of predators in his time. Leopold's formulation of the land ethic in *Sand County Almanac* was a kind of personal redemptive act, the painful acquisition of an "ecological conscience," and surely it is this theme that has given the book much of its power for modern audiences: a call for right living and "individual responsibility for the health of the land."[13]

Unfortunately—yet fittingly, given the importance of *A Sand County Almanac* to the modern environmental movement—Leopold's depiction of his own ecological redemption from past conservationist sins was intertwined with and in fact related to passages revealing his inability to translate his new "ethic" into effective policy or political action. On occasion in the book (which, compiled out of a lifetime of writings, was something of a cross-sectional history of his mind), Leopold's pronounced ambivalence regarding bureaucratic expertise and other keystones of Progressive and New Deal conservationism comes through: "At what point will governmental conservation, like the mastodon, become handicapped by its own dimensions. . . ? It tends to relegate to government many functions eventually too large, too complex, or too widely dispersed to be performed by government. . . . The answer, if there is any, seems to be in a land ethic, or some other force which assigns more obligation to the private landowner." Not surprisingly, for an American audience historically leery of regulation and bureaucracy, this subtheme of voluntarism was and always has been appealing. Yet the doubt expressed in that final sentence seems to have afflicted even Leopold's hopes for a "conversion" of the citizenry to his ethic. Despite a generation of education and exhortation, he wrote, the individual landowner "did not respond very well": "We have virtually no forestry, and mighty little range management, game management, wildflower management, pollution control, or erosion control being practiced voluntarily by private landowners."[14]

Thus, the famous land ethic—for all of the ideological and philosophical credit it later accrued from environmentalists—signified a last-ditch, not merely apolitical but desperately "*super*-political" attempt (as Davidson had dubbed a similar impulse in the interwar regional planners) to halt America's despoliation of nature, as Leopold admitted somewhat indirectly: "I had a bird dog named Gus. When Gus couldn't find pheasants he worked up an enthusiasm for . . . meadowlarks. This whipped-up zeal for unsatisfactory substitutes masked his failure to find the real thing. It assuaged his inner frustration. . . . We conservationists are like that." In the final analysis, Leopold's "inner frustration," which would be the frustration of the environmental movement, grew out of his recognition that he could not abandon politics and regulatory bureaucracies, as unsatisfactory as he had discovered them to be, compounded together with his realization that high-living capitalist Americans were less than likely to embrace the life-style demanded by the "ethic." In one of his final addresses before his death in 1947, delivered to the Conservation Committee of the Garden Club of America, Leopold sighed: "I have no illusions about the speed or accuracy with which an ecological conscience can become functional. It has required 19 centuries to define decent man-to-man conduct and the process is only half done; it may take as long to evolve a code of decency for man-to-land conduct."[15]

Again the dilemma, familiar to regionalists, was that of installing a proper "cultural foundation" in the public mind. Modern environmentalists found a solid bedrock for this foundation with the discovery of the personal *health* effects of disharmony with nature, insights that their regionalist precursors and Leopold had been largely oblivious to because the scientific data—and the scientific fields—did not yet exist in the interwar period. Alarming the postwar public with findings of pollution and contamination was to be by far the single most important means of recruiting a broad popular support base for environmental legislation. Yet as the environmental movement unfolded, it became more and more clear, to "crisis" proportions, that even the potent health issue was an insufficient cultural foundation for motivating basic change and solving persistent and worsening problems. One primary reason for this "snail's pace" of progress was the general failure of the widely fragmented American environmental movement to channel its groundswell of support behind a coherent ideology, or even the rudiments of one, which was in turn part and parcel of the environmentalists' reluctance to develop their love of nature and their yearning for quality of life into a full-fledged radical politics. Instead, the tendency of environmentalism was toward a piecemeal, single-issue approach—clean air, toxic waste, wilderness preservation—an approach that could lead to some measure of political success, to be sure, for that was what the modern political arena was designed for, that was the kind of politics which the enemy, the "special interests," twisted to advantage, forcing environmentalists to fight fire with fire. But such a single-issue strategy was also inherently reductive and, therefore, limited in its ability to deal with problems affecting whole ecological *systems*.

With their earlier attempts to construct regionalism as an ideology, MacKaye, Mumford, and other interwar planners had striven to bind up the unraveling of conservationism and preservationism, two doctrines that needed each other for political and ethical completeness: conservationism to be less compromisable, more righteous in its strictures on development; preservationism to be more realistic, less confined to pure-hearted rearguard actions against growth. To this revamped inheritance, regionalists had contributed their essential insight of the *city* as a component of the ecosystem, redirecting attention away from a previously exclusive focus on the hinterland as resource or refuge, and combining all within their systemic vision of traffic flows, backflows, iron glaciers, and backbones. It was this broadened vision that by the 1960s and 1970s seemed to have been lost to history with the regionalist movement, with the synthesizing, organicist concept of the *region* itself: that urban-industrial planning, resource conservation, and wilderness preservation must proceed together within a single, unified, uniquely and necessarily local *plan*.

One frequently remarked upon example of the paradoxical consequences of modern single-focus environmentalist politics, of its lack of such a comprehensive vision to reorient its half-finished cultural foundation, was what writer Edward Abbey called the phenomenon of "industrial tourism." Quite simply, if the successful advocacy of a Bernard DeVoto or the lobbying of Leopold and MacKaye's Wilderness Society might arouse public pressure to prevent the despoliation of a wilderness patch out in the hinterland (like Dinosaur National Monument), it little affected or referred to conditions, life-styles, and attitudes back in the urban cores. Because this setting (where most Americans lived fifty weeks of the year) was omitted, that wilderness patch remained vulnerable to all manner of urbanoid "glaciation," no matter how benevolently intended—it might begin with a mere few access roads to allow the public to see the sights the preservationists had promoted as worth saving. Thus the ill-prepared cultural foundation of environmentalism, based on quality of life, redounded against itself: on the one hand, postwar Americans desired health and well-being, and they "highly valued" pristine nature; conversely, they "highly valued" convenience, speed, and other benefits of the urban-consumerist culture of automobility. And so the swarms of cars arrived, filled with people escaping unlivable cities, to jam well-known picturesque parks like Yosemite, Yellowstone, or Smokie Mountains, as asphalt layers mean-while staked out more routes into less-famous places soon no longer to be off the beaten track.[16]

Certainly, preservationists over the years had proposed *restricted access* policies (the problem was becoming apparent as early as the 1920s and 1930s), yet again (as MacKaye might say) they were seeking only to "manage" the flow of traffic at its flooding mouth in the hinterland rather than control it at the source—in the cities and, at bottom, in the very mentality of automobility. Leopold himself commented famously on the problem in *Sand County Alma-nac* ("everywhere is the unspecialized motorist whose recreation is mileage, who has run the gamut of the National Parks in one summer"), but, ideologi-cally, he already had his hands full with some of the further ramifications of America's pursuit of quality of life, particularly the living standards required to support it, and what private landowners—farmers, ranchers, miners, lum-bermen—were willing to do to their property to supply its requisite unlimited growth.[17] Environmentalists could consequently look forward to an unending run of morality-play preservation battles, because (as DeVoto had begun warning in the earliest years of the postwar boom) after nothing was left to be extracted from those private lands, more could be found elsewhere, guaran-teeing that no parcel of postfrontier public land, no park, no free-flowing river, no obscure wetland, no patch of wilderness was ever entirely protected from the demand for quality of life, and that no political battle on their behalf was ever finally won.

It would not be accurate to imply that modern environmentalists were un-aware of the consequences of these blind sides and limitations to their move-ment's contradictory cultural foundation. The movement's very own "fa-ther," writing to fellow Wilderness Society member Benton MacKaye in 1946, pointed out the need for a more comprehensive agenda: "wilderness is merely one manifestation of a change of philosophy of land use . . . [and] the Wilder-ness Society, while focussing on wilderness as such, cannot ignore the other implications and should declare itself on them." MacKaye agreed: "Our ulti-mate job in the W.S. is the conservation of the earth as a fitting abode for humans." Later, especially in the years of the movement proper after 1960, others too came to recognize the necessity for a more profound reorientation of the movement both culturally and politically. One of the foremost political theorists of modern environmentalism, Murray Bookchin—in many ways, a utopianist heir and certainly a reader of Mumford—admitted forty-four years after the above Leopold-MacKaye exchange that "we desperately need coherence. . . . I mean a real *structure* of ideas that places philosophy, anthropology, history, ethics, a new rationality, and utopian visions in the service of freedom . . . for *natural* development as well as human." Bookchin and a few other theorists who got their start in the 1960s (such as Barry Commoner) looked to ecology for this ideological "synthesis of ideas," an ideology that would, they hoped (with their regionalist precursors), reveal and redefine power relations together with man-to-land conduct. So too had they believed, for a brief few years, that the 1960s counterculture would provide a truly alternative cultural foundation for their as yet vague political solutions to the concurrent "environmental crisis" (to use Commoner's phrase). As Bookchin noted admiringly of the counterculture in a 1965 essay, "Ecology and Revolutionary Thought":

> Their love of nature is a reaction against the highly synthetic qualities of our urban environment and its shabby products. Their informality of dress and manners is a reaction against the formalized, standardized nature of modern institutionalized living. Their predisposition to direct action is a reaction against the bureaucratization and centralization of society. Their tendency to drop out, to avoid toil and the rat race, reflects a growing anger towards the mindless industrial routine bred by modern mass manufacture in the factory, the office or the university. Their intense individualism is . . . a *de facto* decentralization of social life—a personal withdrawal from mass society.

Bookchin's own project, and that of other radical environmentalist theorists of those years, was clear, if somewhat problematic: through ecology, they must "convert this often nihilistic rejection of the status quo . . . into a reconstructive credo for a humanistic society."[18]

That the 1960s were another period in which many Americans had a longing to get "back-to-nature" (only to be outraged by the damage they found there) and that the decade also inaugurated a prolonged crisis of national exceptionalism (afflicting even the facile and incoherent Cold War variety) was no coincidence; it places this first broad awakening of environmentalism well within the regionalist tradition. Both tendencies—the return to nature and the antiexceptionalism—given their particular anarchic spin by the counterculture, can be seen in another spiritual heir to the regionalist sensibility,

Edward Abbey. In Abbey the regionalist mind took some familiar and some new and thoroughly modern turns—as any "tradition" must. Although many members of the counterculture did seek out nature as a nihilistic "personal withdrawal" to "tune-out" poverty, urban race riots, and the Vietnam War, the more "culturally radical" Abbey attempted in his novels and essays to advance Bookchin's project and portray the connections between them, the connections between rampant urban-industrialism, racism at home, imperialism abroad, and man-to-land misconduct.

Abbey's first widely read work, *Desert Solitaire* (1968), chronicled his own self-consciously "Thoreauvian" withdrawal to the remote canyon lands of DeVoto's home state, Utah. There, Arches National Monument remained, Abbey believed, one of the few wilderness places left beyond the highway system and the "howling streets of Megalomania, U.S.A.," in his words, "a desert place, clean, pure, totally useless, quite unprofitable"—what was left of Dobie's unfenced world. The "nature" that he encountered there during a summer's stay was at once the organically interconnected nature conceived by ecologists ("all living things on earth are kindred") and, turning his focus to the hard rock of the desert, a kind of existential anti-nature, "devoid of all humanly ascribed qualities . . . even the categories of scientific description," with "no heart," presenting a "riddle which has no answer," even the riddle "an illusion created by . . . the displaced human consciousness." For all of its impenetrability, however, the "anti-nature" of the desert had a sublimity that attracted Abbey, who dreamed of a "hard and brutal mysticism in which the naked self merges with a non-human world and yet somehow survives intact, individual, separate." The conceptual tension between this "non-human" anti-nature and the ecological nature in his accounts of desert wildlife suggests that the former was Abbey's own effort to mythicize a "saving remnant"—for in Abbey's 1960s America, nature had been drawn so far under human society's imperial dominion that it was ceasing to exist as a distinct entity. Thus he made nature *itself* a myth, a myth in which it was impermeable to human desires, utterly aloof from human activities. This saving remnant became Abbey's "bedrock and paradox" to stave off his despair at the fate of the other and imperiled nature of the "biotic community." As he wrote in the preface, "most of what I write about in this book is already gone or going under fast. This is not a travel guide but an elegy. A memorial. You're holding a tombstone in your hands."[19] One of his pastimes at Arches National Monument was to pull up the stakes laid out by road surveyors.

Such satisfying if futile acts of resistance formed the thematic core of Abbey's later and most famous work, the novel *The Monkey Wrench Gang* (1975), a political fantasy that was also a less-than-subtle commentary on the state of environmentalism in the 1970s. The 1960s moment of the countercul-

ture had passed away all too quickly, and Abbey, Bookchin, and others, hoping
to inspire a grassroots ecological politics, found their task complicated by the
Nixonian reaction, the Watergate scandal, and the contentious, highly complex, and often merely symbolic policy drafting of the Environmental Protection Agency. The post–Vietnam era left America's youth with less of an
appetite for participatory "direct action" (and all ages with a deepened disgust for politics), while previously daring countercultural tastes and mores
degenerated into the latest prepackaged stimuli for mass cultural consumption. Abbey's *Monkey Wrench Gang* was very much a book of this era, the
story of a small band of radical environmentalists engaged, pointedly, in what
were essentially (typically 1960s radical) anarchist politics, waging a struggle
only to break corrupted and corrupting power, not to own it. In the very
unexceptional America of the 1970s that Abbey depicted, anarchism seemed
the only effective way of doing battle with the corporate and imperial powers
that pervaded and controlled almost every corner of the landscape—by guer-
rilla action or, as it has come to be known, eco-terrorism or "ecotage."

Besides this grim and desperate response to unexceptionalism, what further strengthened Abbey's credentials as a spiritual heir of the regionalist
sensibility was his determination to cast his characters' radical leanings within
American political traditions. At the beginning of the novel, the carefully
named chief protagonist, George Washington Hayduke, "Vietnam, Special
Forces," returns home from the war to discover that "someone or something
was changing things":

> The city of Tucson from which he came, to which he returned, was ringed
> now with a circle of Titan ICBM bases. The open desert was being
> scraped bare of all vegetation, all life, by giant D-9 bulldozers reminding
> him of the Rome plows levelling Vietnam. These machine-made wastes
> grew up in tumbleweed and real-estate development. . . . Even the
> sky . . . was becoming a dump for the gaseous garbage of the copper
> smelters. . . . A smudge of poisoned air overhung his homeland.

Abbey described another of the novel's characters as "a true autochthonic pa-
triot" who "swears allegiance only to the land he knows," his loyalties not to
the United States but phasing out "toward the borders of the Colorado Plateau." Together he and Hayduke join a small loosely organized group dedicated to "creative destruction," sabotaging (without harming humans) construction equipment and effacing improvements from the desert landscape.
Abbey summed up their political philosophy, and his own, in these terms:

> One way or another they were going to slow if not halt the advance of
> Technology, the growth of Growth, the spread of the ideology of the

cancer cell. "I have sworn upon the altar of God," Hayduke bellows into the roaring wind . . . and he blinks, trying to remember Jefferson's words, "eternal hostility against *every fucking form of tyranny*"—getting it slightly wrong but absolutely right—"over the life of man."

But as the group's toll on private corporate property mounts, they are increasingly pursued across a landscape that only appears vast. The book ends in a characteristically regionalist way (an ending that Mari Sandoz or D'Arcy McNickle would have understood), with Hayduke surrounded by the same imperial forces that were abolishing nature itself and that America was projecting abroad to protect the "American way of life." As Hayduke reflects, just before he is killed by the fire of fifteen machine guns, "Oh it's 'Nam again all right all over again . . . with me as the last VC in the jungle." His body falls into a canyon and is never recovered.[20]

The Monkey Wrench Gang inspired and was inspired by the activities of actual radical and eco-terrorist organizations like Earth First!, groups which Abbey once described as "a motley crude Coxey's army of the malcontent, the discontent, the madly visionary," and which arose during the late 1960s and early 1970s out of frustration with the failure of the federal government to act forcefully and effectively to protect national forests from lumber interests and other areas of the public domain from similar private exploitation.[21] With the plot device of Hayduke's martyrdom on behalf of stopping the "growth of Growth," Abbey inadvertently argued that this style of individual direct action was no real solution against the enormous systemic forces of modern America, yet at the same time he and the Earth First!ers pointed to the *system* itself, the whole corporate-megalopolitan structure underlying the "American way of life," as the obstacle to an authentic, environmentally sound society. The regionalists of the 1920s and 1930s had mounted their own "Pickett's charge" against these "breastworks," realizing that the American way of life, already committed to living in megalopolitan concentrations, would have to change if it were to become truly "stable and settled and balanced and cultivated," as Mumford once had written. Yet the very existence of modern Cassandras like Abbey and the Earth First!ers showed that these larger questions were still not being asked, or answered, in the realm of mainstream environmental policy.

For if the consumer ethos of the "quality of life" had brought environmental issues fully into the national political discussion, it inherently limited that discussion to measures that would not jeopardize the "American standard of living" so necessary to the consumer's "well-being." This resulted in a reliance on the "technological fix"—for example, coal scrubbers or auto emission controls—which would in no way question the regnant urban-industrial order but merely treat the worst symptoms of the all-important but often antisymbiotic processes of economic growth and development. Much environmental protection policy was, moreover, necessarily conducted at the national level, because it involved highly technical issues, crossed state lines, implicated multinational corporations, and demanded expert bureaucratic monitoring and control. Yet up there, as DeVoto had warned, policy-making frequently became subject to co-optation by powerful lobbies that could delay regulations or write them in the regulatees' interest, well out of the sight and mind of the average citizen. Abbey and the Earth First!ers represented a vote of no confidence in the ability of politicians and bureaucrats to resist these forces. Similarly, the regionalists of the interwar years, for all of their old-fashioned republicanism and, in fact, because of it, did ask some basic questions about power. Regionalism, as an ideology, had been concerned with more than flood control or smokeless skies; it wanted to know, "Who Owns America?" And with their quaint ambivalence about consumerism and mass culture, which already in their own time was part of the immutable American way of life, regionalists had wanted to know as well, "In what way will we live in America?" Seeking to build a "quality civilization in a quantity world," to paraphrase Howard Odum, regionalists thought (naively) that the answers were best turned over to the people themselves.[22]

This is not to imply that some progress has not been made by their less-than-utopian mainstream environmentalist heirs, that corporate (even personal) behavior has not been altered, or that the environment has not improved a respectable amount since the inauguration of the movement—a movement which was by the 1990s still unfolding. Some might argue that a "less-than-utopian" strategy of accommodation with interest group politics and urban consumerism was a sign of realist political sophistication rather than ideological timidity. Furthermore, to a growing extent in the 1970s and 1980s, environmental organizations did find themselves broadening out their agendas, directing lobbyists and legal staffs to deal with the array of interconnected problems that were ramifying throughout national and *global* ecosystems (postwar space science having revealed not merely regional- or continental-but *planetary*-scaled ecologies). Although American environmentalists remained reluctant to make the foray into electoral politics and establish a full-fledged "green" political movement, they were by the 1980s resorting increasingly to national coalitions that proved to be formidable in shaping policy (as in the Alaska lands battle) and resisting the malign federal neglect of the Reagan-Bush years.[23]

Meanwhile, Bookchin's incisive "social ecology," Commoner's vision of a reformed "technosphere," Wendell Berry's celebration of the "small farm," and Daniel Botkin's humblingly complex "stochastic" ecosystems all suggested that a healthy ferment of ideas within environmental science, philosophy, and ideology was continuing. And by the late 1970s and on into the 1980s, as a 1989 article appearing in the *New Yorker* magazine reported, a small and "informal coalition of local government leaders, college researchers, environmentalists, and volunteers," as well as landscape architects and urban planners, who called themselves "regionalists," was also slowly emerging in America, seeking to find some middle way between the extreme but futile tactics and life-styles of the radicals, the inertia and complacency of most of the rest of the public-at-large, and the remote and unaccountable policies of distant regulators and powerful developers. These new regionalists disputed the notion that "progress demands degraded surroundings," which must be escaped from either periodically or permanently. Instead, they strove to find environmentally viable solutions to the damage and displacement of economic development, yet without halting that development—"both/and" solutions rather than "either/or." The key, they believed, lay in instilling the public, a local public, with a sense of "connectedness"—aesthetic, historical, and personal—to the place where they lived. This was "basically a democratic procedure rather than something outsiders can control or impose," the new regionalists assumed, because it was already latent in the concrete way the local people lived their lives. In reality, the regionalist's chief task "involved reconnecting people with their own sense of connectedness" and overcoming the "full force of discouragement built into people after two hundred years of development decisions that ignored connectedness."[24]

These new regionalists realized that they had not been the first to arrive at such conclusions, that they were "descendants" of sorts. According to Tony Hiss, author of the *New Yorker* article, a "recently rediscovered and now much pored-over book" called *The New Exploration* had shown them that the new regionalists were "not doing anything innovative, after all; they're only resuming work . . . fully spelled out in MacKaye's work." One of the new regionalists, planner Robert Yaro, recounted an experience that would have been all too familiar to any regionalist of the interwar years—a story involving his grandparents' Connecticut farm, the older America, and the megalopolitan "world without a country":

When I was growing up, in the nineteen fifties, my grandparents had a farm outside Hartford, in a place called Andrews Corners, where their farm was actually one of the four corners of a crossroads. The farm was surrounded by orchards, and there was a skating pond for the winter, and blueberry bushes for July and August picking. By the time I was a teen-

ager, the three other corners were being filled in, and there were super-
markets and gas stations standing on old farmland. By the time I got out
of college, my grandparents' farm had become a regional shopping mall.

He added, "Almost all the regionalists I know have had this kind of experience
growing up—it's what gets them started." Indeed, Edward Abbey articulated much the same experience of "cultural dispersion," of "connectedness"
violated, through Hayduke, returning to a monstrously transformed post-
Vietnam Tucson, a place to inspire masques like Walter Prescott Webb's.
Instead, however, the shock had launched Hayduke on his crusade of "creative
destruction," which in turn apparently struck a chord with a number of "local
people" in the West. In the years following the publication of *The Monkey
Wrench Gang*, a bumper sticker began appearing on automobiles in that
region, expressing a defiance that Abbey was finally obliged to acknowledge
with a sequel, entitled with the bumper sticker's same two words, and published in the year after Abbey's death: *Hayduke Lives!* (1990).[25]

Notes

Abbreviations

BLYU	Beinecke Library, Yale University, New Haven
BTHC	Eugene C. Barker Texas History Center, Austin
HHU	Houghton Library, Harvard University, Cambridge
HL	Huntington Library, San Marino
HRCTA	Harry Ransom Humanities Research Center, Texas-Austin
MNML	Museum of New Mexico Library, Santa Fe
MS	Unpublished manuscript
NSHS	Nebraska State Historical Society, Lincoln
OSUSC	Oklahoma State University Special Collections, Stillwater
OUL	University of Oklahoma Libraries, Norman
SHCCH	Southern Historical Collection, Chapel Hill
SMUDL	Southern Methodist University DeGolyer Library, Dallas
SMUFL	Southern Methodist University Fondren Library, Dallas
TSA	Texas State Archives, Austin
UASCF	University of Arkansas Special Collections, Fayetteville
UMA	University of Montana Archives, Missoula
UMWHC	University of Missouri Western Historical Collection, Columbia
UNAL	University of Nebraska Archives, Lincoln
UNCL	University of North Carolina Library, Chapel Hill
UNMSC	University of New Mexico Special Collections, Albuquerque
UVSC	University of Virginia Special Collections, Charlottesville
VSC	Vanderbilt Special Collections, Nashville
WHCO	Western History Collection, University of Oklahoma, Norman
YUL	Yale University Library, New Haven

Introduction

1. Crèvecoeur, *Letters*, pp. 63, 77, 67; Mumford, *Golden Day*, pp. 43, 31, 275. For biographical information, see Asselineau and Wilson, *St. John de Crèvecoeur*, especially pp. 34–35, and Mumford, *Sketches*, pp. 410–11. On Mumford in general, see also Miller, *Mumford: A Life*. On a regionally differentiated colonial America, see David Hackett Fischer's mammoth *Albion's Seed: Four British Folkways in America* (New York, 1989).

2. Crèvecoeur, *Letters*, pp. 36, 62, 74–75, 63–64.

3. Ibid., pp. 64–66, 96. On Rousseau, see Shklar, *Men and Citizens*.

4. Crèvecoeur, *Letters*, p. 63. On republicanism, see Bernard Bailyn, *The Ideological Origins of the American Revolution* (Cambridge, Mass., 1982), and Gordon S. Wood, *The Creation of the American Republic* (New York, 1972). Regarding the colonies as an

expanding periphery of the British Empire, see Bailyn, *The Peopling of British North America* (New York, 1987).

5. Crèvecoeur, *Letters*, pp. 420, 424–25, 198, 208, 221–22.

6. Mumford, *Golden Day*, pp. 119–20, 79. For analysis of the influence of James Harrington, see J. G. A. Pocock, *The Machiavellian Moment* (Princeton, 1975), and Noble, *End of American History*.

7. Mumford, *Sketches*, p. 410, and *Golden Day*, pp. 275, 281, 25, 80–81, 12, 275. On "catastrophist" history, see Thomas, "The Uses of Catastrophism."

8. Mumford, *Golden Day*, pp. 80, 119, 281–82, 274, 87, 158, 278.

9. Ibid., pp. 281, 93, 90, 86, 93, 74, 279, 92, 158.

10. Ibid., p. 91; Crèvecoeur, *Letters*, p. 67; Mumford, *Golden Day*, pp. 158–60, *Sketches*, pp. 410–11, and *Golden Day*, pp. 277, 273–74, 283.

11. Hawthorne quoted in Jensen, *Regionalism*, p. 220.

12. Botkin, *Folk-Say*, p. 12n (Dobie quotation); Mumford, *Golden Day*, p. 38; Odum and Jocher, *Regional Balance*, p. 15.

13. Mumford, *Golden Day*, pp. 43, 58, 38.

14. Emerson, *Essays and Lectures*, p. 69; Dobie to Walter Prescott Webb, October 30, 1923, W. P. Webb Collection, BTHC. For definitions of "conservatism" and "styles of thought," see Karl Mannheim, "Conservative Thought," in Paul Kecskemeti, ed., *Essays on Sociology and Social Psychology* (London, n.d.), pp. 74–164.

15. Tate to John Gould Fletcher, August 27, 1927, Fletcher Collection, UASCF; Jensen, *Regionalism*, p. 230 (Howells quotation); Parrington, *Currents*; Frederick, "Ruth Suckow and the Middle Western Literary Movement," pp. 2–3; Davidson, *Leviathan*, p. 235.

16. Davidson, *Leviathan*, pp. 17, 21–22, 232.

17. Brooks, *The Flowering of New England* (New York, 1936); Mathiessen, *American Renaissance* (New York, 1941); Davidson, *Leviathan*, pp. 234–35, 238; Tate, *Essays*, p. 533; Cather, *My Ántonia*, p. 169; Botkin, *Folk-Say*, p. 11; Smith to Padraic Colum, April 30, 1931, Southern Methodist University Press Collection, SMUDL; Davidson, *Leviathan*, p. 15 (Turner quotation). For an important discussion of the influence of the ideas of Herder on Southern regionalism, see Michael O'Brien, *Idea of the American South.*

18. Jensen, *Regionalism* (Simms quotation), p. 225; Garland, *Idols*, p. 118; Spencer, *Nationality* (Linn, Webster, and Masters quotations), pp. 29, 27–28, 102, 249. See Spencer for a good general discussion of literary nationalism in the eighteenth and nineteenth centuries.

19. Emerson, *Essays*, pp. 68, 53.

20. Davidson, *Leviathan*, pp. 237, 12.

21. Jensen, *Regionalism*, pp. 226 (Coggeshall quotation), 227.

22. Davidson, *Leviathan*, 18–19; Mumford, *Golden Day*, 158–59; Spengler, *Decline of the West*, 1:32–33. For a global "core versus periphery" analysis, see Daniel Chirot, *Social Change in the Twentieth Century* (New York, 1977).

23. Davidson, *Leviathan*, p. 15; Garland, *Idols*, pp. 119, 131, 128, 122, 120, 134.

24. Turner quoted in Davidson, *Leviathan*, pp. 13–14, 28.

25. Davidson, *Leviathan*, p. 13 (Turner quotation); Anderson, *Winesburg, Ohio*, p. 71; Lewis, *Zenith*, p. 523; Lewis to Mary Austin, December 15, 1920, BLYU.

26. Douglas L. Wilson, *Essays by George Santayana*, pp. 52, 39–40, 43–44; Brooks,

Coming-of-Age, pp. 7, 164. On the prewar revolt, see May, *End of American Inno-cence*; Abrahams, *Lyrical Left*; Blake, *Beloved Community*.

27. Stearns, *Civilization*, pp. vii, 140; Brooks, *Coming-of-Age*, p. 163.

28. Brooks in Stearns, *Civilization*, pp. 219, 182–96.

29. Douglas L. Wilson, *Essays by George Santayana*, p. 63; Locke, *New Negro*, pp. 199, 242, xvi. Two works provide a comprehensive view of the New York intellectual scene during the interwar years: Communists and leftists generally are examined in Wald, *New York Intellectuals*, and "cosmopolitans" are given sophisticated treatment in Cooney, *Rise of the New York Intellectuals*. On the relationship of some of the Agrarians to the cosmopolitans, see particularly Cooney, *Rise*, pp. 208–9. For a defini-tion and discussion of cultural radicalism, see Abrahams, *Lyrical Left*. On the Harlem Renaissance, see Jervis Anderson, *This Was Harlem*. For a general overview of intellectual life during the interwar years, see Pells, *Radical Visions*; Susman, *Culture as History*; Perry, *Intellectual Life*.

30. Cooney, *Rise of the New York Intellectuals*, pp. 58–60; Locke, *New Negro*, p. 285; Mumford quoted in "The Regional Community," *Survey Graphic* 7 (May 1925): 129.

31. Cooney, *Rise of the New York Intellectuals*, pp. 58–60, 208.

32. Lippmann, *A Preface to Morals*, pp. 19–20.

33. On the Arts and Crafts movement, see Orvell, *The Real Thing*; on the influence of Ebenezer Howard and the garden city concept, see Buder, *Visionaries and Planners*. For preregionalist movement cultural currents toward "simplicity," see Shi, *Simple Life*. For pre–World War I intellectual and artistic confrontations with the folk in one region, see Shapiro, *Appalachia on Our Mind*.

34. Mumford, *Technics*, p. 430, "Toward a New Regionalism," pp. 156–57, and *Golden Day*, p. 279.

Chapter 1

1. Woodress, *Willa Cather* (quoted biographical information), pp. 25, 35–38; Cather, *Lark*, p. 362. The Woodress biography provides a thorough and balanced treatment of Cather's life. See also Brown, *Willa Cather*, and Sharon O'Brien, *Willa Cather*.

2. Cather, *Lark*, pp. 374–83.

3. Cather, *Lark*, p. 374, *O Pioneers!*, pp. 3, 71, and *My Ántonia*, pp. 169–70, 197, 226.

4. Cather, *My Ántonia*, pp. 155–56, 238, 197, 205; Cather, *Later Novels*, p. 95; quoted in Woodress, *Willa Cather*, p. 335; Cather, *Later Novels*, p. 261.

5. Cather, *Later Novels*, p. 263; Cather to E. K. Brown, October 7, 1946, E. K. Brown Papers, YUL (paraphrased); Cather, *Archbishop*, pp. 232–33, 98, 294–97.

6. Cather, *Later Novels*, p. 138; quoted in Woodress, *Willa Cather*, p. 343; Cather, *Archbishop*, pp. 275–76.

7. Lomax, *Ballad Hunter*, p. 1; Robert Frost, "The Road Not Taken," in *The Poetry of Robert Frost* (New York, 1979), p. 105.

8. Faulkner quoted in Watkins, "What Stand Did Faulkner Take?," p. 49. Watkins provides a useful discussion of Faulkner's relationship to regionalism.

9. Mary Austin to Alice Corbin Henderson, February 19, 1919, Henderson Papers, HRCTA; Austin to Carey McWilliams, January 13, 1931, Austin Collection, UNMSC. For a good biographical portrait of Austin, see Gibson, *Colonies*.

10. Austin, *Horizon*, pp. 136, 349.

11. Ibid., pp. 336, 349, 68, 76, 82–83, 124, 176, 181.

12. Ibid., pp. 187–89, 197–98.

13. Ibid., pp. 197–98, 289, 33.

14. Quoted in Gibson, *Colonies*, p. 200. For more elaborate examinations of the personal lives of Sandoz and Rourke, see Stauffer, *Mari Sandoz*, and Joan S. Rubin, *Constance Rourke*.

15. Austin, *Horizon*, pp. 330, 349, 234, quoted in Gibson, *Colonies*, pp. 204–5.

16. McGinnis to J. Frank Dobie, May 11, 1945, Dobie Collection, HRCTA.

17. McWilliams, *Education*, pp. 27, 33, 42, 54, 66, and "Young Man, Stay West," p. 301.

18. Henry Smith to W. S. Campbell, June 16, 1938, Campbell Collection, WHCO; Smith, "McGinnis and the Southwest Review," p. 302; Smith to Mary Austin, August 7, 1930, copy from Huntington Library in Pearce Papers, UNMSC; Smith, "Living in America," pp. 25–31. Smith apparently did not begin consistently using his middle name—Nash—until after 1940. For a biographical portrait of Henry Nash Smith, see Bridgman, "American Studies."

19. Smith, "Living in America," pp. 24–30.

20. Ibid., p. 28; Merriam to Lew Sarett, September 30, 1927, Merriam Papers, UMA; Merriam, "The Origin of The Frontier" and "Why the Frontier Adventure?," MSS (1958?); Merriam to Ezra Pound, March 26, 1931, Merriam Papers, UMA.

21. Botkin to Henry Smith, July 3, 1929, Southern Methodist University Archives, SMUFL; Botkin to Alexander Krappe, July 17, 1921, Botkin Collection, UNAL. For an excellent discussion of Botkin's folklore interests and possible Jewish cultural influences on it, see Hirsch, "Folkore in the Making."

22. Botkin to Thor Hultgen (December 30, 1921), Botkin to Alexander Krappe (October 28, 1921), and Botkin to "Miss Whitehead" (February 18, 1922), Botkin Collection, UNAL.

23. Botkin to Smith, July 2, 1929, Southern Methodist University Archives, SMUFL; Botkin to Austin, March 1, 1932, Botkin Collection, UNAL.

24. Davidson to Fletcher, June 13, 1927, Fletcher Collection, UASCF.

25. Writing on cultural critics in late nineteenth-century Germany, Fritz Stern called this phenomenon "cultural despair" in his classic work, *The Politics of Cultural Despair*, which provides analysis of the reception of modernization in a European cultural context.

26. Tate, *The Fathers*, pp. 266, 183, 135; Tate to Donald Davidson, May 14, 1926, in Fain and Young, *Literary Correspondence*, p. 166; Davidson to Tate, February 15, 1927, in Fain and Young, *Literary Correspondence*, pp. 186–87. The Agrarians have been written about extensively, but for two works that are particularly insightful in their integration of biographical portraits of selected Agrarians and the themes of modernism and regionalism, see Singal, *War Within*, and Michael O'Brien, *Idea of the American South*. Other very helpful background information and analysis may be found in Louis D. Rubin, Jr., *Wary Fugitives*; Conkin, *Southern Agrarians*; Young, *Gentleman in a Dustcoat*, on Ransom; and Young and Inge, *Donald Davidson*. See King, *A Southern Renaissance*, for the interwar years placed in a more literary thematic context. On Tate, see especially Singal, *War Within*, pp. 232–60.

27. Ransom to Allen Tate, February 20, 1927, copy from Princeton University in T. D. Young Collection, VSC; Singal, *War Within*, 203 (Ransom quotation); Ransom to Tate, February 20, 1927, July 4, 1929, copies from Princeton University in T. D. Young

Collection, VSC; Fletcher to Brooks (March 21, 1924) and Davidson to Fletcher (June 13, 1927), Fletcher Collection, UASCF; Ransom to James Southal Wilson, November 3, 1926, *Virginia Quarterly Review* Papers, UVSC. See Young, *Gentlemen in a Dustcoat*, for a complete treatment of Ransom. See also Singal, *War Within*, pp. 203–19. For biographical background of Fletcher, see Carpenter and Rudolph, introduction to *Selected Poems of . . . Fletcher*.

28. Davidson to Fletcher, March 21, 1926, Davidson Papers, VSC; Davidson to Tate, February 23, 1920, in Fain and Young, *Literary Correspondence*, pp. 324–24; Davidson to Margery Swett, June 28, 1923, Davidson Papers, VSC; Davidson to Tate, March 4, 1927, in Fain and Young, *Correspondence*, p. 193; Davidson to R. N. Linscott, April 9, 1927, Davidson Papers, VSC. For a fuller portrait of Davidson and his thought, see Michael O'Brien, *Idea of the America South*, and Young and Inge, *Donald Davidson*.

29. Singal, *War Within*, p. 249 (Tate quotation); Botkin, "The Folk in Literature," p. 9; Singal, *War Within*, pp. 133–34 (Odum quotation); Mumford, "Regions—To Live In," p. 152.

30. Howard Odum to Gerald W. Johnson, January 4, 1928, Odum Papers, SHCCH. See Singal, *War Within*, for a ground-breaking biographical discussion of Odum and other members of his circle, including Rupert Vance. See also Michael O'Brien, *Idea of the American South*, for his analysis of Southern sociology.

31. Odum and Jocher, *Regional Balance*, p. 15; Odum and Moore, *American Regionalism*, pp. 3–31; Singal, *War Within*, p. 124 (Odum quotation).

32. Mumford, *Sketches*, pp. 3, 35, 86, 4–5, 129–30. See Miller, *Mumford: A Life*, for an excellent treatment of Mumford's life and works.

33. "The Regional Community," p. 129 (first Mumford quotations); Mumford, "Regions—To Live In," pp. 151–52.

34. Mumford, *Sketches*, pp. 282–83.

Chapter 2

1. Bynner, *Selected Poems*, p. 130 (opening quotation); Alexander and Whitaker, *Sculpture*, p. 3; Whitaker, *Goodhue—Architect*, p. 40; Alexander and Whitaker, *Sculpture*, p. 2; Nelson, *Memorial*, pp. 11, 14. For a general history of the building, see Luebke et al., *Harmony of the Arts*.

2. Alexander and Whitaker, *Sculpture*, pp. 3–4; Nelson, *Memorial*, pp. 25–30.

3. Alexander and Whitaker, *Sculpture*, p. 5; Cunningham, *Capitol*, pp. 13–14; Nelson, *Memorial*, pp. 105–11; Alexander and Whitaker, *Sculpture*, pp. 5–6, 8.

4. Oliver, *Goodhue*, p. 232 (Mumford quotation); Whitaker, *Goodhue—Architect*, pp. 45, 40; Oliver, *Goodhue*, p. 187; Cunningham, *Capitol*, pp. 4–6.

5. Neihardt, *Poetic Values*, pp. 143, 120–21.

6. Neihardt to George Steele Seymour, April 19, 1921, copy from Knox College, Neihardt Papers, UMWHC; John Collier, "Does the Government Welcome the Indian Artist?," May 14, 1934, MS, Collier Papers, YUL; Neihardt, *Black Elk*, p. 1.

7. E. P. Dutton & Co. to Edgar Hewett, September 14, 1925, Hewett Collection, MNML (Alexander quotation); Luhan to Austin, December 1922 or 1923, Pearce Collection, UNMSC.

8. Alexander to Hewett (June 2, 1923) and Austin to Hewett (December 12, 1920), Hewett Collection, MNML.

9. Wissler, *American Indian*, p. xix; Hewett, *Ancient Life*, pp. 374, 94, 53. On Hewett's life, see Chauvenet, *Hewett and Friends*.

10. Hewett, *Ancient Life*, pp. 52, 27, 23–24; Austin, *American Rhythm*, p. 54; Hewett, *Ancient Life*, p. 24.

11. Hewett, *Ancient Life*, pp. 31, 23, 42–43, 51.

12. Ibid., *Ancient Life*, pp. 61, 44; Austin, *American Rhythm*, p. 36.

13. Worster, *Nature's Economy*, 204. See Worster for a very helpful overview of changing conceptions of nature and the historical emergence of ecological thinking.

14. Alexander and Whitaker, *Sculpture*, p. 3.

15. John Collier, "Man Can Half Control His Doom" (May 21, 1942) and "Does the Government Welcome the Indian Artist?" (May 14, 1934), MSS, Collier Papers, YUL; Austin, *American Rhythm*, p. 54; Hewett, *Ancient Life*, pp. 27, 47.

16. Sandoz to H. L. Mencken, February 13, 1933, Sandoz Collection, UNAL. See Stauffer, *Mari Sandoz*, for her background and analysis of Sandoz's efforts.

17. Sandoz to Mencken, February 13, 1933, Sandoz Collection, UNAL; Brandt to William Bennett Bizzell (September 7, 1929), Brandt to Bizzell (November 13, 1928), and Brandt to Grant Foreman (February 16, 1934), University of Oklahoma Press Collection, OUL.

18. Sarett to Merriam, September 24, 1928, Merriam Papers, UMA. On Weber's concept of disenchantment and "rationalization," based on an idea borrowed from Friedrich Schiller, see the introduction to Gerth and Mills, *From Max Weber*, p. 51.

19. Terry P. Wilson, "Osage Oxonian," p. 272 (Mathews quotation); Mathews to W. S. Campbell, December 3, 1930, Campbell Collection, WHCO. Wilson's essay provides a first-rate portrait of Mathews.

20. La Farge, *Laughing Boy* (1957), pp. 109, 268, 222, 200, 164, 199; and (1971), pp. 85, 109.

21. Austin to Robinson Jeffers, June 23, 1930, copy of Huntington Library material, Pearce Collection, UNMSC; Sandoz to *Saturday Evening Post*, July 1928, 1930, Sandoz Collection, UNAL; Neihardt to Julius T. House, June 1931, Neihardt Papers, UMWHC.

22. Neihardt to Nick Black Elk (November 6, 1930) and Neihardt to House (June 1931), Neihardt Papers, UMWHC.

23. Sandoz to Mencken, February 13, 1933, Sandoz Collection, UNAL; Mathews, *Wah'Kon-Tah*, pp. 300–301.

24. Brandt, "Pioneering Regional Press," p. 206.

25. On modernism, see Schwartz, *Matrix of Modernism*; Orvell, *The Real Thing*; and Singal, "American Modernism," pp. 7–26.

26. Connor, *Postmodernist Culture*, p. 68 (Gropius quotation); Huxley, *Brave New World*, pp. 81–82, vii. Suggestive on the concept of the civic (or "civil") religion is Charles Reagan Wilson, "The Religion of the Lost Cause." On the political function of aesthetic experience, see Chytry, *Aesthetic State*, as well as Friedrich Schiller, *On the Aesthetic Education of Man* (New York, 1983).

27. Austin, *Horizon*, p. 336; Lawrence, *Plumed Serpent*, pp. 373, 8, 461, 68, 457–58, 78, 153.

28. Lawrence, *Plumed Serpent*, pp. 113, 455, 457.

29. Ibid., p. 461; La Farge to Collier, November 26, 1934, Collier Papers, YUL; Wissler, *Indians of the United States*, p. 274.

30. Neihardt to George Sterling, October 21, 1920, Neihardt Papers, UMWHC; Pearce, "Folklore and Fascism," pp. 85, 88.

31. Pearce, "Folklore and Fascism," 84; Mathews, *Wah'Kon-Tah*, p. 303.

32. Brandt to N. G. Henthorne (February 4, 1935) and Brandt to W. B. Bizzell (August 22, 1934), University of Oklahoma Press Collection, OUL. On Ezra Pound's prince as artist, see Schwartz, *Matrix of Modernism*, pp. 126–28. On "aesthetic education," see Schiller, *Aesthetic Education*.

33. Hewett, *Ancient Life*, pp. 27, 47; Alexander and Whitaker, *Sculpture*, p. 3.

Chapter 3

1. Ransom, "Aesthetic," pp. 290–93.

2. Ibid., pp. 307, 293. On the New Mexico conference, see B. A. Botkin, "The New Mexico Round Table," pp. 152–59.

3. Botkin, *Folk-Say* (1930), p. 15; Botkin to Walter Evans Kidd, November 22, 1929, Botkin Collection, UNAL.

4. Woodress, *Willa Cather*, p. 335 (Cather quotation); Alexander and Whitaker, *Sculpture*, pp. 2–3.

5. Frank, *Re-Discovery*, pp. 57, 64–65. For a useful discussion of the larger interwar critique of the frontier myth and Turner's thesis, see Susman, *Culture as History*, pp. 27–38. For a general and penetrating analysis of the frontier myth, see Slotkin, *Fatal Environment*.

6. Stearns, *Civilization*, p. 140; Brooks, *Mark Twain*, pp. 211, 59–60; Stearns, *Civilization*, p. 185 (Brooks quotation); MacKaye, *New Exploration*, p. iv.

7. Mumford, *Sketches*, p. 381; DeVoto, *Twain's America*, pp. 42, 91, 241, 32. The term *usable past* was coined by Van Wyck Brooks in his essay "On Creating a Usable Past," *Dial* 64 (April 11, 1918): 337–41.

8. Vance, *Geography*, p. 69; Parrington, *Currents*, 3:8; Sandoz, *Old Jules*, p. 19; Braunlich, *Lynn Riggs*, p. 77.

9. Parrington, *Currents*, 3:102–3, 368.

10. Ibid., 2:474, 3:3–4, 1:131; quoted in Hofstadter, *The Progressive Historians*, pp. 368; Parrington, *Currents*, 3:368, 26, 413. See Hofstadter for a good biographical portrait of Parrington.

11. Parrington, *Currents*, 3:403, 364; Rölvaag, *Giants*, pp. 279, 200, 250.

12. DeVoto, *Twain's America*, p. 172; Rourke, *American Humor*, pp. 227, 231, 297, 108, 232–33, 220, 282; Rourke to Merriam, July 5, 1933, Merriam Papers, UMA; DeVoto, *Twain's America*, pp. 92–93. For an excellent portrait and analysis of Rourke's life and works, see Joan S. Rubin, *Constance Rourke*.

13. Rourke to Merriam, July 5, 1933, Merriam Papers, UMA; DeVoto, *Twain's America*, pp. 240–41; Rourke, *American Humor*, pp. 201, 205, 282, 288.

14. Alexander Haggerty Krappe, "'American' Folklore," in Botkin, *Folk-Say* (1930), p. 291; Botkin, *Folk-Say* (1930), p. 16.

15. Webb, *Great Plains*, pp. iv, 508.

16. Webb to E. E. Dale, March 16, 1924. On Sandoz's blindness and hard frontier life, see Stauffer, *Mari Sandoz*, especially p. 33.

17. Oliver, *Goodhue*, p. 232 (Mumford quotation); Donald Davidson to John Gould Fletcher, June 13, 1927, Fletcher Collection, UASCF. On the Indian war and Gilded Age cultural consensus, and for an extremely helpful general discussion of the theories of myth, see Slotkin, *Fatal Environment*, particularly pp. 18–32.

18. Botkin to Henry Nash Smith, January 11, 1931, Southern Methodist University Archives, SMUFL; Botkin, *Folk-Say* (1930) advertisement flyer.

19. Vance, *Geography*, p. 62; Turner, *Frontier and Section*, p. 116; Vance, *Geography*, pp. 75–76, 69; Cather, *O Pioneers!*, pp. 75, 211.

20. Lomax, *Ballad Hunter*, pp. 40–41, 112–13; Randolph, *Ozarks*, pp. 22, 309. On Odum and Left-Wing Gordon, see Singal, *War Within*, especially pp. 143–46.

21. Ransom, "Aesthetic," pp. 296–97, 307, and "South Defends Its Heritage," pp. 110, 109, 115.

22. Braunlich, *Lynn Riggs*, pp. 102–3; Odum, *Songs*, p. 38; Lytle, "The Hind-Tit," in Twelve Southerners, *I'll Take My Stand*, pp. 224, 231; Odum, *Songs*, pp. 158–59, *Cold Blue Moon*, p. 18, and *Songs*, pp. 247, 263.

23. Randolph, *Ozarks*, p. 308; Young, *So Red the Rose*, p. 18; Rölvaag, *Giants*, pp. 43, 275; Dobie, *Vaquero*, p. 297; Faulkner, *Absalom, Absalom!*, p. 221.

24. Randolph, *Ozarks*, pp. 299, 309.

25. Parrington, *Currents*, 3:xxiv.

26. Stegner, *Uneasy Chair*, p. 72 (first DeVoto quotation); DeVoto, *The Year of Decision: 1846*, p. 4; Botkin, "The Folk and the Individual," p. 132; MacKaye, *Exploration*, p. 16; Randolph, *Ozarks*, pp. 299, 309. For one of the best discussions of the function of "felt" history, see Joan S. Rubin, *Constance Rourke*, especially the chapter entitled "Style."

27. Parrington, *Currents*, 3:369; Dos Passos, *The Big Money*, p. 469; Parrington, *Currents*, 3:7; Lytle, "The Hind-Tit," pp. 244–45.

28. Frank, *Re-Discovery*, pp. 128–29, 201, 153, 215, 154. On Frank, see Blake, *Beloved Community*, and Frank, *Memoirs*.

29. Frank, *Re-Discovery*, pp. 222, 127, 213, 223, 310, 205, 208.

Chapter 4

1. Ransom to Tate, February 20, 1927, Ransom Papers, copy from Princeton University in T. D. Young Collection, VSC; Buck, *Good Earth*, p. 80; Summerfield, *AE*, pp. 254–58; *Lincoln Star and Journal*, October 21, 1930; Gibson, *AE*, p. 359.

2. Gibson, *AE*, p. 358; Buck, *Good Earth*, p. 260; Gibson, *AE*, pp. 359–62; Buck, *Good Earth*, p. 152.

3. Sandoz to Philip S. Rose, August 23, 1932, Sandoz Collection, UNAL.

4. Lynd and Lynd, *Middletown*, p. 498.

5. Odum, *Wings on My Feet*, p. 57; Dorman, "Agrarianism," pp. 255, 258 (Murray quotations).

6. Dorman, "Agrarianism," p. 253 (Murray quotation); Lewis, *Zenith*, p. 520.

7. Botkin, *Folk-Say* (1929), pp. 17, 14, "Folk-Say and Space," p. 322, and "Serenity and Light," p. 493; Smith, "Living in America," p. 27.

8. Davidson to Tate, February 5, 1929, in Fain and Young, *Literary Correspondence*, p. 221. On civic religion of the Confederacy, see Charles Reagan Wilson, "The Religion of the Lost Cause."

9. Fletcher to Tate, August 30, 1927, Fletcher Collection, UASCF; Ransom to Tate, July 4, 1929, copy from Princeton University in T. D. Young Collection, VSC; Davidson to R. N. Linscott, April 9, 1927, Davidson Papers, VSC; Davidson to Tate, February 5, 1929, in Fain and Young, *Literary Correspondence*, p. 221; Davidson to Fletcher (March 23, 1931) and Davidson to Ransom (July 5, 1929), Davidson Papers, VSC;

Ransom, "South Defends Its Heritage," pp. 117–18, 115; "Articles of an Agrarian Restoration," MS (1929), Davidson Papers, VSC.

10. Smith, "Note on the Southwest," p. 275.

11. Williams, *American Grain*, pp. 214, 212–13.

12. Frederick, *Green Bush*, pp. 73–74, 96–97.

13. Ibid., pp. 210–11, 231, 236–37, 277, 286–87, 303, 82.

14. Merriam, "Covered Wagon," p. 1; Williams, *American Grain*, p. v.

15. Sarett to Merriam, September 17, 1927, Merriam Papers, UMA.

16. Merriam, "Covered Wagon," p. 1; Merriam to H. L. Davis, November 17, 1927, Merriam Papers, UMA; Merriam, "Covered Wagon," p. 1; Merriam to Norman Mac-Leod (May 5, 1929), Merriam to H. L. Davis (June 11, 1930), Merriam to Carey McWilliams (September 28, 1930), Merriam to James Rorty (April 29, 1929), and Merriam, article for *The New Student* (MS, January 23, 1928), Merriam Papers, UMA; Merriam, "Covered Wagon," p. 1.

17. Hartley Alexander to Neihardt (October 31, 1927), Carl Sandburg to Neihardt (October 10, 1927), and Neihardt to Austin (October 24, 1927), Neihardt Papers, UMWHC; H. G. Merriam, "Writers Conference," MS, 1931, Merriam Papers, UMA.

18. Buck, "Valley History," p. 240; Sarett to Merriam, December 11, 1927, Merriam Papers, UMA; McWilliams, "Young Man, Stay West," pp. 307–8; Benton, *An American in Art*, pp. 191, 151; DeVoto to Jarvis Thurston, May 24, 1943, in Stegner, *Letters of Bernard DeVoto*, p. 25.

19. Benton, *American in Art*, pp. 191, 151. On cosmopolitans, see Cooney, *Rise of the New York Intellectuals*, pp. 58–60.

20. Botkin, "The Folk and the Individual," pp. 132–33; McWilliams, *New Regionalism*, p. 21.

21. Botkin, *Folk-Say* (1930), p. 17, and *Folk-Say* (1929), pp. 9–10; Lomax and Lomax, *Singing Country*, p. xxi.

22. Botkin, *Folk-Say* (1929), pp. 9–10.

23. Dobie to Walter Prescott Webb, October 30, 1923, Dobie Collection, HRCTA; Dobie, *Coronado's Children*, p. xvii; Dobie, ed., *Man, Bird, and Beast* (Austin, 1930), p. 6; Dobie, "To justify interest in legends," MS, 1924, Dobie Collection, HRCTA; Dobie, *Coronado's Children*, p. xvii; Rourke, *American Humor*, p. 201; Dobie to John Young (May 7, 1926) and Dobie, "Legends of the Southwest" (MS, June 18, 1925), Dobie Collection, HRCTA.

24. Rourke, *Roots*, p. 250. See Joan S. Rubin, *Constance Rourke*, for a discussion of Rourke's critical theory as subversive of genteel hierarchy.

25. Benton, *An American in Art*, pp. 156, 187, 189, 155; Buck, "Valley History," pp. 232, 228, 237–39; McWilliams, "Young Man, Stay West," p. 309.

26. Lewis, *Zenith*, pp. 527–28; Percy MacKaye to Botkin, February 14, 1930, Botkin Collection, UNAL.

27. Lynd and Lynd, *Middletown*, pp. 5, 17, 41, 6, 493, 491.

28. MacKaye, *New Exploration*, pp. 225, 73.

29. Ibid., p. 71; Summerfield, *AE*, p. 256; Leavis, *Mass Civilization*, p. 7; Joad, *Horrors*, pp. 27, 15–16, 43–44. See Brantlinger, *Bread and Circuses*, for a discussion of intellectual critiques of mass culture.

30. Botkin, "We Talk About Regionalism," p. 288 (Tate quotation); Summerfield, *AE*, p. 255; Frank, *Re-Discovery*, p. 72; Neihardt to George Sterling, August 30, 1921, Neihardt Papers, UMWHC.

31. Bernard Bailyn et al., *The Great Republic* (New York, 1985), pp. 710, 713 (statistics cited); Mumford, "New Regionalism," p. 158; Frank, *Re-Discovery*, p. 73.

32. MacKaye, *New Exploration*, pp. 72–73, 151; Willa Cather, *Destinies*, p. 31; MacKaye, *New Exploration*, p. 15; "Articles" (1929), MS, Davidson Papers, VSC; Lytle, "The Hind-Tit," in Twelve Southerners, *I'll Take My Stand*, p. 237. For Hewett, Ransom, and Austin, see chapters 2 and 3.

33. Lynd and Lynd, *Middletown*, p. 88; Cather, *Destinies*, p. 40.

34. Lynd and Lynd, *Middletown*, p. 478; Lewis, *Zenith*, p. 340; Lynd and Lynd, *Middletown*, p. 272; Parrington, *Currents*, 3:368; Lynd and Lynd, *Middletown*, p. 274.

35. Parrington, *Currents*, 3:189, 392; MacKaye, *New Exploration*, p. 14; Parrington, *Currents*, 2:474, 1:350; Dobie, *Publications of the Texas Folklore Society* (May 1925), pp. 7–8.

36. Spengler, *Decline of the West*, 1:32–33; 2:99, 464, 506.

37. MacKaye, *New Exploration*, pp. 72–73.

38. Turner, *Frontier and Section*, pp. 131, 126–27, 134–35.

39. Ibid., pp. 152, 135, 153.

40. Ibid., p. 153; Fletcher to Van Wyck Brooks, March 21, 1924, Fletcher Collection, UASCF. On Turner and exceptionalism, see Noble, *End of American History*, pp. 16–40. See also Pickens, "Westward Expansion," pp. 409–18.

41. Lytle, "The Hind-Tit," p. 244; Alexander and Whitaker, *Sculpture*, p. 3; Ransom, "South Defends Its Heritage," p. 115.

42. MacKaye, *New Exploration*, pp. 144, 119, 224–25, 75, 147, 224.

43. Vance, *Geography*, p. 483; Fred A. Shannon, *Appraisal*, p. 113 (Webb quotation); Vance, *Geography*, pp. 6–7, 482. For biographical background of MacKaye, see Thomas, "Lewis Mumford, Benton MacKaye, and the Regional Vision."

44. Vance, *Geography*, pp. 11, ix.

45. Ibid., p. 60; Odum, *Epoch*, pp. 313, 329–30, 65, 314. On Odum and regional portraiture, see Singal, *War Within*, pp. 129–35; and Michael O'Brien, *Idea of the American South*, pp. 60–69.

46. Mumford, *Sketches*, pp. 341–42, and "Fourth Migration," p. 130; MacKaye, *New Exploration*, pp. 59–60, 47, 133.

47. MacKaye, *New Exploration*, pp. 70–71, 33–35, 59, 225, 71.

48. Vance, *Geography*, p. 511; Odum, *Epoch*, p. 335; Vance, *Geography*, pp. 495–96, 286–87; Odum, *Epoch*, p. 128; Vance, *Geography*, pp. 491, 508–10, 507.

49. Mumford, "Fourth Migration," p. 131–32, "Regions—To Live In," pp. 151–52, and *Technics*, pp. 359, 414–15, 410–11.

50. MacKaye, *New Exploration*, p. 208; Vance, *Geography*, p. 495.

51. Vance, *Geography*, pp. 490, 483; MacKaye, *New Exploration*, p. 225. Max Weber is credited with the concept of modern "disenchantment of the world"; see his famous essay, "Science as a Vocation," for his own pessimistic evaluation of the prospects of "re-enchantment" through monumentalist art in Gerth and Mills, *From Max Weber*.

Chapter 5

1. Klein, *Woody Guthrie* (New York, 1990), p. 174 (opening quotation); Sandoz, "Mist," pp. 41, 42, 44, and *Old Jules*, p. 325.

2. Sandoz, "Mist," pp. 47, 45.

3. Ibid., pp. 42–43, 47.

4. Ibid., pp. 48–50.

5. Odum, "Regional-National Social Planning," pp. 7–8.

6. Hitler quoted in Jonge, *Weimar Chronicle*, pp. 195, 217, Kershaw, *Hitler Myth*, p. 41, and Pearce, "Folklore and Fascism," p. 84; Communist quoted in Conquest, *Harvest of Sorrow*, pp. 147–48; Odum, "Regional-National Social Planning," p. 9.

7. B. A. Botkin, "Next Step," p. 86.

8. Ibid., pp. 86–87; Botkin, "Regionalism and Culture," pp. 143, 156.

9. Botkin, "Next Step," p. 86, and "Regionalism and Culture," pp. 157, 156. Rosenblum, *Another Liberalism*, is very suggestive about the lack of a communitarian ethos in modern liberalism.

10. Botkin, "Next Step," pp. 86–87. For some suggestive essays on the nature and function of ideology, see Bercovitch and Jehlen, *Classic American Literature*; see also Mannheim, *Ideology and Utopia*.

11. Botkin, "Next Step," p. 86, and "Regionalism and Culture," pp. 157, 156. Dobie to Tom Lea (April 4, 1943) and Dobie to Webb (October 28, 1937), Dobie Collection, HRCTA.

12. Wolfe quoted in Donald, *Look Homeward*, p. 438.

13. Webb, *Divided We Stand*, p. 158.

14. Webb quoted in Kingston, *Webb in Stephens County*, pp. 56, 4, 3, 44. Kingston provides a very useful biographical treatment of the young Webb. See also William A. Owens, *Three Friends: Bedichek, Dobie, Webb* (Garden City, N.Y., 1969), and Necah Stewart Furman, *Walter Prescott Webb: His Life and Impact* (Albuquerque, 1967).

15. Webb to Roy Bedichek, April 23, 1945, quoted in Owens, *Three Friends*, pp. 97–98; Webb, *Great Plains*, p. 227; Kingston, *Webb in Stephens County*, p. 45; Webb, *Divided We Stand*, pp. 167, 161.

16. Andy Adams to Webb, March 2, 1924, Webb Collection, BTHC; Webb, *Great Plains*, pp. 507, 8, vi, 141, 226, 206, 497, 227. For analysis of *The Great Plains*, see Tobin, *Making of a History*, and Wolfskill, "Webb and *The Great Plains*."

17. Webb, *Divided We Stand*, pp. 167, 157.

18. Ibid., pp. 168–69.

19. Ibid., pp. 3, 12–13, 87.

20. Ibid., pp. 110–11, 39–40.

21. Ibid., pp. 94, 25, 131.

22. Davidson, *Leviathan*, p. 42; Couch to Frank W. Prescott, November 10, 1937, Couch Papers, SHCCH.

23. Davidson to Webb, October 25, 1938, Webb Collection, BTHC; Davidson, *Leviathan*, pp. 176, 174.

24. Davidson, *Leviathan*, pp. 333, 331, 330, 113, 328.

25. Davidson, *Leviathan*, pp. 134, 338, 327.

26. Davidson, *Leviathan*, p. 134; McWilliams, *Factories*, p. 4; Odum, *Southern Regions*, p. 2; Lange and Taylor, *American Exodus*, p. 15 (unless otherwise noted, all page citations are to 1969 revised edition); Odum, *Southern Regions*, p. 255.

27. Webb, *Great Plains*, pp. 141, 48, 478, 58.

28. Correspondent quoted in Rydell, *World's a Fair*, pp. 63–64; Meriam Report quoted in Prucha, *Great Father*, p. 287. For biographical background of Dale, see Dale, *West Wind Blows*.

29. Debo, "Edward Everett Dale, Historian of Progress," 1930–31, MS, Debo Papers, OSUSC; Dale, "Spirit of Soonerland," pp. 170–71.

30. Debo to Dale, December 6, 1932, Dale Collection, WHCO; Debo, *Waters*, pp. 92–93, xi.

31. Debo, *Waters*, pp. 7, 9, 14, 21, x.

32. Mathews, *Sundown*, p. 274.

33. Ibid., pp. 1, 65, 67.

34. Ibid., pp. 90, 117, 245.

35. Ibid., pp. 274, 296–97, 42.

36. McNickle, *The Surrounded*, pp. 216–17.

37. Ibid., pp. 124–28, 117.

38. Ibid., p. 173.

39. Ibid., pp. 111, 189, 138–39.

40. Ibid., pp. 175–76, 208–9, 218, 236, 259, 275, 287–97.

41. Odum, *Southern Regions*, p. 173.

42. Ibid., pp. 213, 2, 135.

43. Ibid., p. 16; Kirby, *Rural Worlds Lost*, p. 137 (Percy quotation); Odum, *Southern Regions*, pp. 23, 55.

44. Vance, "Is Agrarianism for Farmers?," in Reed and Singal, *Papers of Rupert Vance*, p. 70; Raper and Reid, *Sharecroppers All*, pp. 16, 20; Vance, "Agrarianism," p. 70.

45. Vance, "Agrarianism," pp. 70–71, 65; Raper, *Peasantry*, p. 4; Faulkner, *Absalom, Absalom!*, p. 72; Cash, *Mind of the South*, p. 14. On the Odum circle's and the general interwar critique of the Old South, see Singal, *War Within*; O'Brien, *Idea of the American South*; and King, *A Southern Renaissance*.

46. Odum, *Southern Regions*, p. 227; Raper and Reid, *Sharecroppers All*, pp. 79, 247.

47. Raper and Reid, *Sharecroppers All*, p. 79; Odum, *Southern Regions*, pp. 487 (Johnson quotation), 483, 481. On Odum's cautious and diplomatic approach on racial and other sensitive regional issues, and the context of institutional constraints he operated under, see Singal, *War Within*, pp. 126–28, and O'Brien, *Idea of the American South*, pp. 70–79. On Johnson's moderate racial positions, see Singal, *War Within*, pp. 323–27.

48. Raper and Reid, *Sharecroppers All*, pp. 247, 81, 246.

49. Ibid., p. 140; Vance, "Agrarianism," pp. 73, 71.

50. Raper and Reid, *Sharecroppers All*, pp. 212, 221; Vance, "Agrarianism," p. 68; Raper, *Peasantry*, p. 170.

51. Vance, "Agrarianism," p. 69; Kingston, *Webb in Stephens County*, p. 44; Caldwell, *Tobacco Road*, p. 163.

52. Raper, *Peasantry*, pp. 171, 34; Raper and Reid, *Sharecroppers All*, p. 37.

53. Raper and Reid, *Sharecroppers All*, p. 25; Raper, *Peasantry*, p. 122; Lange and Taylor, *American Exodus*, p. 24.

54. Vance, "The Old Cotton Belt," in Reed and Singal, *Papers of Rupert Vance*, p. 86; Raper, *Peasantry*, pp. 34, 252.

55. Raper, *Peasantry*, pp. 252–53; Odum, *Southern Regions*, p. 63; Lange and Taylor, *American Exodus*, pp. 35, 37.

56. Raper, *Peasantry*, pp. 171, 252–53; Raper and Reid, *Sharecroppers All*, p. 46. Two excellent analyses of the sharecropper and tenant system in this period are found in Kirby, *Rural Worlds Lost*, and Wright, *Old South, New South*.

57. Bulletin quoted in Lange and Taylor, *American Exodus*, p. 32 (1939 edition); Raper and Reid, *Sharecroppers All*, p. 217.

58. Lange and Taylor, *American Exodus*, pp. 103, 20, 33, 110, 18, 113.

59. Odum, *Southern Regions*, p. 61; Raper and Reid, *Sharecroppers All*, pp. 220–21.

60. Sears, *Deserts*, pp. 230, 168, 1, 194, 92; Rogers, "Good Gulf Show," in Gragert, *Radio Broadcasts*, pp. 120–22. For a superb analysis of the ecological origins of the Dust Bowl disaster and intellectual responses to it, see Worster, *Dust Bowl*.

61. Lange and Taylor, *American Exodus*, p. 113.

62. Ibid., pp. 70–72; p. 91 (1939 edition).

63. Steinbeck, *Grapes of Wrath*, pp. 166, 34–35, 40, 36–37.

64. Ibid., p. 166; Lange and Taylor, *American Exodus*, p. 113; McWilliams, *Factories*, pp. 48, 3–4.

65. McWilliams, *Factories*, pp. 11–13, 5.

66. Ibid., pp. 5, 25, 90, 48.

67. Lange and Taylor, *American Exodus*, p. 141 (1939 edition); McWilliams, *Factories*, p. 306; Lange and Taylor, *American Exodus*, p. 155 (1939 edition).

68. Raper and Reid, *Sharecroppers All*, pp. 46–47; McWilliams, *Ill Fares the Land*, p. 199.

69. Caldwell, *Tobacco Road*, p. 62.

70. Odum, *Southern Regions*, p. 475; Steinbeck, *Grapes of Wrath*, p. 96.

Chapter 6

1. Steinbeck, *Grapes of Wrath*, pp. 96, 165.

2. Webb to Abe Melton, October 8, 1943, Webb Collection, BTHC.

3. Webb, "Application for Guggenheim Fellowship" (1937), Webb Collection, BTHC.

4. Webb to E. E. Dale, February 15, 1939, Dale Collection, WHCO; Webb, *Divided We Stand*, pp. 217–18.

5. Webb, *Divided We Stand*, pp. 168, 161.

6. Ibid., pp. 163–64; Webb to Dale, February 15, 1939, Dale Collection, WHCO; Webb, *Divided We Stand*, pp. 239, 236, 163.

7. Webb to Melton, October 8, 1943, Webb Collection, BTHC; Webb, *Divided We Stand*, p. 164; Webb to Dale, February 15, 1939, Dale Collection, WHCO.

8. Webb, *Divided We Stand*, pp. 238–39.

9. Ibid.; Webb to Ralph Tester, February 25, 1951, Webb Collection, BTHC; Webb, "Application for Guggenheim Fellowship."

10. Mumford, *Cities*, p. 9; *Technics*, pp. 109, 211, 154, 210, 213, 215, 241, 211.

11. Mumford, *Cities*, pp. 5, 233, 289, 292, 283, 279, 290, 255, 273–75, 277. On the jeremiad as a commonly used narrative device among American historians and intellectuals, see the classic by Bercovitch, *American Jeremiad*. See also Noble, *End of American History*. For an analysis of *The Culture of Cities*, see Miller, *Mumford: A Life*, pp. 354–73.

12. Mumford, *Cities*, pp. 292, 295, 299.

13. Ibid., pp. 298, 11, 293.

14. McWilliams, *Factories*, p. 306; Raper and Reid, *Sharecroppers All*, p. 248.

15. Raper and Reid, *Sharecroppers All*, p. 248; Debo, *Waters*, p. 395; McWilliams, *Factories*, pp. 306, 325; Lange and Taylor, *American Exodus*, p. 136 (1939 edition).

16. Mumford, *Cities*, pp. 382–87, 348.

17. Gerth and Mills, *From Max Weber*, p. 123 (first quotation); Fletcher to Tate, December 19, 1930, Fletcher Collection, UASCF.

18. Mari Sandoz to Mrs. Eugene Thorp, April 5, 1940, Sandoz Collection, UNAL.

19. Kingston, *Webb in Stephens County*, p. 4; Webb, *Great Plains*, p. 509; Sandoz, *Old Jules*, p. 215; Sandoz to Verona Kirkpatrick, March 4, 1936, Sandoz Collection, UNAL; Sandoz, *Old Jules*, pp. 406, 325.

20. Sandoz, *Old Jules*, pp. 325, 74, 76, 53, 236.

21. Sandoz to Harper's Monthly Magazine, October 19, 1932; Sandoz to J. R. de la Torre Bueno, Jr., July 21, 1942; Sandoz, *Slogum*, pp. 281–83; Sandoz to Martin Nelson, March 9, 1938. All letters from Sandoz Collection, UNAL.

22. Sandoz, *Slogum House*, pp. 209, 298, 239.

23. Ibid., pp. 298, 327–28, 331, 336.

24. Sandoz to the Daughter of James Manahan, October 24, 1936; Hicks, *Populist Revolt*, p. 422; Sandoz to Eva Mahoney, November 16, 1939; Sandoz to Helen Mary Hayes, August 28, 1940; Sandoz, *Capital City*, pp. 278, 48. All letters from Sandoz Collection, UNAL.

25. Sandoz, *Capital City*, p. 48; McWilliams, *Factories*, p. 325; Mumford, *Cities*, p. 328.

26. Sandoz to Mrs. Eugene Thorp, April 5, 1940, Sandoz Collection, UNAL.

27. Sandoz, *Capital City*, p. 270; Mumford, *Cities*, p. 329.

28. Sandoz, *Old Jules*, p. 46; Sandoz to Mrs. O. W. Adams, December 30, 1935; Sandoz, "Nebraska's Place in the New Literature," speech quoted in *Lincoln Star and Journal*, May 23, 1937; Sandoz to Verona Kirkpatrick, March 4, 1936; Freud, *Civilization*, p. 36; Sandoz, *Old Jules*, p. 216. All letters from Sandoz Collection, UNAL.

29. Sandoz to Vida Belk, January 20, 1941, Sandoz Collection, UNAL; Sandoz, *Capital City*, pp. 48, 322

30. Sandoz, *Capital City*, p. 334.

31. Ibid., pp. 234, 316, 324, 342–43.

32. Sandoz to Fred Ballard (December 27, 1941), Sandoz to Botkin (May 19, 1936), Sandoz to Charlie Morton (July 7, 1941), and Sandoz to Paul Hoffman (January 17, 1942), Sandoz Collection, UNAL. For biographical details of Sandoz during the late 1930s and early 1940s and analysis of various works, see Stauffer, *Mari Sandoz*, pp. 111–62.

33. Clark, *Ox-Bow Incident*, pp. 219, 224.

Chapter 7

1. Kesten and Winston, *Thomas Mann Diaries*, p. 284; Mann, *Democracy*, pp. 66, 7, and *Freedom*, p. 11.

2. Mann, *Magic Mountain*, p. 719, *Democracy*, pp. 8–9, 57–58, 63–64, and *Freedom*, pp. 10, 5.

3. Knott to Green, July 1933, Green Papers, SHCCH; Knott to Botkin, June 13, 1933, Botkin Collection, UNAL; Knott to Green (June 25, 1933, and September 1933), Green to Knott (September 15, 1933), and Knott to Green (1933), Green Papers, SHCCH. On Botkin's pluralism, see Hirsch, "Folklore in the Making."

4. *Washington Post*, May 6, 1938, April 25, 1940.

5. Mumford, *Cities*, pp. 377–78.

6. Collier, "Man Can Half Control His Doom," MS, May 21, 1942, Debo Papers, OSUSC; Mumford, *Technics*, p. 430; McWilliams, *Factories*, p. 306; Mann, *Freedom*, p. 10.

7. Neihardt to H. S. Latham, May 1935, Neihardt Papers, UMWHC; Odum, *Southern Regions*, p. 235; Agar and Tate, *Who Owns America?*, p. 108; Mumford, "Social Purposes," p. 119.

8. Brooks to Mumford, March 30, 1938, in Spiller, *Brooks-Mumford Letters*, p. 151; Mumford, *Cities*, p. 387.

9. Davidson to Mr. Finney, November 6, 1930, Davidson Papers, VSC; Ransom to Tate, January 5, 1929, Ransom Papers, copy from Princeton University in T. D. Young Collection, VSC. For one of the most thorough and insightful accounts of the Agrarian "Cause," see Louis Rubin, *Wary Fugitives*. Also very useful is Conkin, *Southern Agrarians*, especially pp. 89–143.

10. Davidson to Tate, October 29, 1932, in Fain and Young, *Literary Correspondence*, p. 276; Fletcher to Owsley (December 1, 1933) and Ransom to Fletcher (March 7, 1934), Fletcher Collection, UASCF.

11. Tate to Davidson, September 28, 1935, Davidson Papers, VSC; Davidson to Tate (January 2, 1943) and Tate to Davidson (December 4, 1942), in Fain and Young, *Literary Correspondence*, pp. 328–30.

12. Tate to Davidson, September 28, 1935, Davidson Papers, VSC.

13. Ransom to Fletcher, October 25, 1933, Fletcher Collection, UASCF.

14. Odum to President Chase, February 1926, Odum Papers, SHCCH; Fletcher to Mumford, February 16, 1931, Fletcher Collection, UASCF.

15. Huxley, *Brave New World*, p. vii.

16. Mumford, *Cities*, pp. 386–87; Agar and Tate, *Who Owns America?*, pp. 107–8; Odum, *Southern Regions*, pp. 579–80, 534.

17. MacKaye, "Tennessee," pp. 252–94.

18. Nixon, *Forty Acres*, p. 78; Owsley, "The Pillars of Agrarianism," in Harriet Chappell Owsley, *Essays of Frank Lawrence Owsley*, p. 183; Vance, "Is Agrarianism for Farmers?," in Reed and Singal, *Papers of Rupert Vance*, p. 72; Ransom, "Regionalism in the South," p. 112; Davidson to Mr. Finney, November 6, 1930, Davidson Papers, VSC; Odum, "Planning," pp. 20–21; Agar and Tate, *Who Owns America?*, p. 181. On the Agrarians and the "proprietary" ideal, see Conkin, *Southern Agrarians*.

19. Raper and Reid, *Sharecroppers All*, p. 249; Nixon, *Forty Acres*, pp. 8, 67, 76, 78; Lange and Taylor, *American Exodus*, pp. 153–55 (1939 edition); McWilliams, *Factories*, p. 325. For background on Nixon, see Sarah Newman Shouse, *Hillbilly Realist: Herman Clarence Nixon* (University, Ala., 1986).

20. La Farge to *Boston Evening Transcript*, October 28, 1936; La Farge to Collier, November 26, 1934; Collier, "Decentralization," MS, July 1936; La Farge to Collier, February 28, 1935; and La Farge to Charlotte Westwood, June 3, 1936—all in Collier Papers, YUL. On Collier's policy, see Kelly, *Assault on Assimilation*; Philp, *John Collier's Crusade*; and Prucha, *Great Father*, pp. 311–39.

21. Odum, *Southern Regions*, p. 259.

22. Smith to Austin, September 28, 1933, copies from Huntington Library in Pearce Collection, UNMSC; Smith, "The Southwest," p. 6.

23. Mumford, *Cities*, p. 312.

24. Ibid., pp. 390, 380; Couch to Donald Davidson, January 13, 1934, Couch Papers, SHCCH; Mumford, *Cities*, pp. 330, 328, 377, 380.

25. Weber, "Politics as a Vocation," in Gerth and Mills, *From Max Weber*, p. 128; Vance, *Geography*, p. 490; quoted in Wright, *Old South, New South*, p. 227.

26. Fletcher to Tate (August 10, 1927), Fletcher to Owsley (December 12, 1933), Fletcher to Donald Davidson (December 17, 1937), Fletcher to Mumford (January 11, 1933), and Fletcher to Tate (July 11, 1931), Fletcher Collection, UASCF. For biographical information, see introduction to Carpenter and Rudolph, *Selected Poems*.

Chapter 8

1. Fletcher Collection, UASCF (opening quotation); Mumford, "Regional Planning," MS, July 8, 1931, University of Virginia Institute of Public Affairs Papers, UVSC; Botkin to Mumford, May 9, 1931, Botkin Collection, UNAL.

2. Fletcher to Tate (August 10, 1927), Fletcher to Owsley (December 12, 1933), Fletcher to Mumford (February 26, 1930, and May 9, 1934), Fletcher to Brooks (April 24, 1935), Fletcher to Botkin (April 2, 1933), Fletcher to Mumford (July 5, 1933), and Fletcher to Tate (March 13, 1935), Fletcher Collection, UASCF; Davidson to Owsley, August 3, 1936, Davidson Papers, VSC; Warren, "Literature as a Symptom," in Agar and Tate, *Who Owns America?*, p. 275.

3. Davidson to Tate, October 29, 1932, in Fain and Young, *Literary Correspondence*, p. 276; Mumford, *Cities*, p. 380; Henry Nash Smith to Mary Austin, September 28, 1933, copies from Huntington Library in Pearce Collection, UNMSC.

4. Davidson, *Leviathan*, pp. 306–7; Mumford, *Cities*, pp. 485–86. On Davidson's critique of the "super-political" nature of planning, see Singal, *War Within*, pp. 149–50.

5. Mumford, *Cities*, p. 485; Davidson to Couch, May 7, 1939, University of North Carolina Press Papers, UNCL; Conquest, *Harvest of Sorrow*, p. 347 (Burke quotation); Fletcher to Mumford, July 5, 1933, Fletcher Collection, UASCF; Mumford, *Cities*, p. 380.

6. Barr's contribution to *I'll Take My Stand* was entitled "Shall Slavery Come South?"; see Barr to Michael Plunkett, March 10, 1975, Barr Collection, UVSC. On the debate, see *Chattanooga News*, November 22, 1930, clippings in Davidson Papers, VSC; and Barr to Davidson (March 11, 1930) and Barr to Davidson, Ransom, and Tate (September 25, 1930), Davidson Papers, VSC.

7. Odum, *Southern Regions*, pp. 227, 425–26; Smith, "Dilemma of Agrarianism," p. 228.

8. Tate to Davidson, February 23, 1936, in Fain and Young, *Literary Correspondence*, p. 296; Tate to Couch, June 17, 1934, Couch Papers, SHCCH; Owsley, "The Pillars of Agrarianism," in Harriet Chappell Owsley, *Essays of Frank Lawrence Owsley*, p. 188; Owsley to Couch, March 11, 1935, Couch Papers, SHCCH. On Owsley, see chapter in Michael O'Brien, *Idea of the American South*. On the influence of Distributist ideas, see especially Conkin, *Southern Agrarians*.

9. Vance to Owsley, March 29, 1935, Owsley Papers, VSC; Vance, "The Old Cotton Belt," in Reed and Singal, *Papers of Rupert Vance*, pp. 87, 123–24.

10. McWilliams, *Ill Fares the Land*, pp. 387–88; Lange and Taylor, *American Exodus*, pp. 156, 154 (1939 edition).

11. McWilliams, *Ill Fares the Land*, pp. 386–88; Lange and Taylor, *American Exodus*, p. 155 (1939 edition).

12. Smith, "Dilemma of Agrarianism," pp. 231–32.

13. Cash, *Mind of the South*, p. 432; Robert Penn Warren to Botkin, April 4, 1935, Botkin Collection, UNAL; Simpson, Olney, and Gulledge, *Southern Review*, pp. 53, 52, 63, 71.

14. Fletcher to Brooks, March 22, 1935, Fletcher Collection, UASCF; Simpson, Olney, and Gulledge, *Southern Review*, pp. 47, 55; Botkin to Merriam, March 18, 1933, Botkin Collection, UNAL; Couch to Edwin R. Embree, January 29, 1936, Nixon Papers, VSC; Ransom to Tate, January 5, 1930, Ransom Papers, copies from Princeton University in T. D. Young Collection, VSC.

15. Simpson, Olney, and Gulledge, *Southern Review*, pp. 68, 60–61, 41; Odum, "Regional-National Social Planning," p. 8.

16. Botkin to Paul Horgan, December 16, 1932, Botkin Collection, UNAL; James T. Patterson, *America in the Twentieth Century* (New York, 1983), p. 190 (statistics); Fletcher to Botkin, July 12, 1933, Botkin Collection, UNAL; Mumford, *Cities*, p. 382.

17. Cash, *Mind of the South*, p. 429.

18. Couch to Nell Battle Lewis, January 16, 1927, Couch Papers, SHCCH; Smith to Mary Austin, October 2, 1930, copies from Huntington Library in Pearce Collection, UNMSC; Botkin to H. H. Lewis (November 17, 1932) and Botkin to Haniel Long (November 17, 1932), Botkin Collection, UNAL; George Finlay Simmons to Merriam, April 16, 1936, Merriam Papers, UMA; Sandoz to Rabbi David A. Goldstein, 1937, Sandoz Collection, UNAL; Morris L. Wardell, reader's report (MS, 1937), and Brandt to W. B. Bizzell (July 20, 1937), University of Oklahoma Press Collection, OUL; Dobie, "Regents vs. University" (MS, January 15, 1945), and Dobie to Tom Lea (January 10, 1943), Dobie Collection, HRCTA.

19. Cash, *Mind of the South*, pp. 65, 327, 439–40, 301, 22; Leuchtenberg, *Roosevelt and the New Deal*, p. 273 (Lynds' quotation).

20. Cash, *Mind of the South*, pp. 431–32.

21. Faulkner, *Absalom, Absalom!*, p. 311; Couch to Dabney, March 13, 1935, University of North Carolina Press Papers, UNCL. On Cash, see Michael O'Brien, "A Private Passion: W. J. Cash," in *Rethinking the South*; see also the chapter in King, *A Southern Renaissance*, and, for the most complete treatment, Clayton, *Cash: A Life*.

22. Fletcher to Davidson, December 5, 1934, Fletcher Collection, UASCF; Odum, *Southern Regions*, p. 165; Mumford, "Social Purposes," pp. 119, 128; Brownlow, *Passion for Anonymity*, p. 270; Roosevelt, "State Planning," MS, July 6, 1931, University of Virginia Institute of Public Affairs Papers, UVSC.

23. MacKaye to Fletcher, July 20, 1934, Fletcher Collection, UASCF.

24. Great Plains Committee, *Future of the Great Plains*, pp. 63–67, 127; Lilienthal, *Journals*, pp. 173, 469, 389, and *TVA*, pp. 197, 224–25.

25. Fletcher to Davidson, December 5, 1934, Fletcher Collection, UASCF.

26. Daniels, *Documentary History of Communism*, p. 231 (Stalin quotation); Lilienthal, *Journals*, p. 469.

27. Morgan, "Benchmarks . . . : The Strength of the Hills," p. 46.

28. Roosevelt, "State Planning."

29. Mumford, *Cities*, p. 386.

30. Selznick, *Grassroots*, pp. 55, 119, 61; Lilienthal, *TVA*, p. 179.

31. Lilienthal, *TVA*, p. 106; Selznick, *Grassroots*, pp. 61, 262.

344   Notes to Pages 298–310

32. Selznick, *Grassroots*, p. 7; Lilienthal, *Journals*, pp. 640–41.

33. On the fate of tenant farmers in the Tennessee Valley, see McDonald and Muldowny, *TVA and the Dispossessed*.

34. Odum, *Southern Regions*, p. 165; Mumford, "Social Purposes," p. 129; Morgan, "Benchmarks . . . : Roads to Prosperity in the TVA," p. 576; Leuchtenberg, *Roosevelt and the New Deal*, p. 339 (Tugwell quotation); Odum, "Regional-National Social Planning," p. 8. For what remains one of the best balanced interpretations of the New Deal, see Leuchtenberg, *Roosevelt and the New Deal*.

35. Bolles, "Federal Writers' Project," p. 19; Couch, *These Are Our Lives*, pp. xiii–xiv. On the "documentary" impulse of the 1930s, see the classic by William Stott, *Documentary Expression and Thirties America* (New York, 1973). On folklore and the FWP, see Hirsch, "Cultural Pluralism."

36. Umland, "Editing WPA Guide Books," p. 168 (Dies quoted); Bolles, "Federal Writers' Project," p. 18.

37. On the Indian New Deal, see Prucha, *Great Father*; Philp, *John Collier's Crusade*; and Kelly, *Assault on Assimilation*.

38. Philp, *John Collier's Crusade*, p. 172 (quotations). See Grant McConnell, *The Decline of Agrarian Democracy* (Berkeley, Calif., 1953), for a critical study of the influence of the American Farm Bureau Federation.

39. Botkin to Brandt, March 1, 1938, University of Oklahoma Press Collection, OUL; Bizzell to Botkin (July 1, 1939) and Bizzell to Botkin (October 28, 1939), Botkin Collection, UNAL; Miller, *Mumford: A Life*, p. 397 (Mumford quotation). On the late 1930s as Thermidor, see Karl, *The Uneasy State*. See also Karl, *Executive Reorganization and Reform in the New Deal* (Chicago, 1966), on the Brownlow proposal for executive reform through regional planning boards.

40. Knott, "National Folk Festival Association Can Aid in Emergency," MS, 1942, Green Papers, SHCCH.

41. Smith, "The Southwest," p. 6; McNickle to Collier, September 27, 1943, Collier Papers, YUL.

Epilogue

1. Botkin to Percy MacKaye, March 15, 1930, Botkin Collection, UNAL; Webb to Ralph Tester, February 25, 1951, Webb Collection, BTHC.

2. Vance, "The Old Cotton Belt," in Reed and Singal, *Papers of Rupert Vance*, p. 86. On Vance's postregionalist work, see Singal, *War Within*, pp. 314–15.

3. Dobie to Webb, October 28, 1937, Webb Collection, BTHC; Roy Bedichek to William Owens, June 12, 1945, in Owens and Grant, *Letters of Roy Bedichek*, p. 266. On Dobie's maturation, see Winston Bode, *J. Frank Dobie: A Portrait of Pancho* (Austin, 1968); Ronnie Dugger, ed., *Three Men in Texas: Bedichek, Webb, and Dobie* (Austin, 1967); and William A. Owens, *Three Friends: Bedichek, Dobie, Webb* (Garden City, N.Y., 1969). See also Dobie, *A Texan in England* (Boston, 1944).

4. Owsley, "Pillars of Agrarianism," in Harriet Chappell Owsley, *Essays of Frank Lawrence Owsley*, p. 188; Davidson to Stark Young (September 29, 1952) and Davidson to Stark Young (September 29, 1957), Young Collection, HRCTA. On Davidson's post-Agrarian career as a segregationist, see Young and Inge, *Donald Davidson*. See also

Conkin, *Southern Agrarians*, pp. 148–57; and Michael O'Brien, *Idea of the American South*, pp. 208–9.

5. Merriam to Brandt, September 23, 1945, Merriam Papers, UMA.

6. Mumford, *Pentagon of Power*, pp. 293–99.

7. See Henry Nash Smith, *Virgin Land: The American West as Symbol and Myth* (Cambridge, Mass., 1982), and on Smith's impact, see Bridgman, "American Studies"; Charles Reagan Wilson and William Ferris, eds., *Encyclopedia of Southern Culture* (Chapel Hill, 1989); and Joel Garreau, *The Nine Nations of North America* (New York, 1981).

8. For an excellent analysis of Western reclamation politics in the postwar period, see Reisner, *Cadillac Desert*.

9. DeVoto to a Miss Burke (March 27, 1944) and DeVoto to Brooks (August 2, 1943), in Stegner, *Letters of Bernard DeVoto*, pp. 29, 123. See Stegner, *Uneasy Chair*, pp. 287–322, for background on DeVoto's conservationist efforts.

10. DeVoto, "West," in *Easy Chair*, pp. 234–35, 244–45, 254–55.

11. DeVoto, "Conservation," in *Easy Chair*, pp. 329–30; DeVoto, "West," in *Easy Chair*, p. 245.

12. Stegner, *Uneasy Chair*, pp. 321, 314; Leopold, *Almanac*, p. 243. On postwar environmentalism, see the indispensable work by Hays, *Beauty, Health and Permanence*, especially pp. 13–39.

13. Leopold, *Almanac*, pp. 243, 258; for biographical treatment of Leopold, see Meine, *Aldo Leopold*. On the famous Progressive Era "schism" between conservationism and wilderness preservation, see Nash, *Wilderness and the American Mind*, particularly pp. 161–81. Nash has recently backed away from too strict a distinction between the two movements—with some justification—but the fact that there has been a perceived need to launch single-issue wilderness organizations, and the basic disagreement over proper human use—economic development and raw materials versus recreation and scenery—would seem to indicate that the distinction is still interpretively useful. See Roderick Nash, *American Environmentalism* (New York, 1990), pp. 6–7.

14. Leopold, *Almanac*, pp. 250, 200.

15. Ibid., p. 200; Leopold, "The Ecological Conscience," in Flader and Callicott, *River of the Mother of God*, p. 345.

16. Abbey, *Desert Solitaire*, pp. 45–67.

17. Leopold, *Almanac*, p. 282.

18. Meine, *Leopold*, p. 480 (Leopold and MacKaye quotations); Bookchin, *Remaking Society*, p. 18; Commoner, *Closing Circle*, p. 178; Bookchin, *Post-Scarcity Anarchism*, p. 92.

19. Abbey, *Desert Solitaire*, pp. 298, 33, 24, 272–73, 6, xii. Suggestive on the theme of an "abolished" nature is McKibben, *The End of Nature*.

20. Abbey, *Monkey Wrench Gang*, pp. 15, 358, 207, 368.

21. Abbey, *Hayduke Lives!*, p. 186. On radical environmentalism, see Christopher Manes, *Green Rage: Radical Environmentalism and the Unmaking of Civilization* (Boston, 1990).

22. Odum, *Southern Regions*, p. 27.

23. For a level-headed evaluation of the successes and limits of environmentalist politics, and for an overview of the attempted "Reagan antienvironmental revolution," see Hays, *Beauty, Health, and Permanence*, especially pp. 427–543.

24. Hiss, "Countryside," pp. 37, 57. See also Hiss, *Experience of Place*; Bookchin, *Remaking Society*; Commoner, *Making Peace with the Planet*; Berry, *The Gift of Good Land*; and Daniel B. Botkin, *Discordant Harmonies*. (Daniel Botkin, incidentally, is the son of B. A. Botkin.)

25. Hiss, "Countryside," pp. 44, 57. For Abbey's own allusions to the Hayduke "cult," see *Hayduke Lives!*, pp. 29, 189, 200.

Bibliography

This bibliography is organized as follows:
Manuscript Collections
Primary Sources
Selected Secondary Sources

Manuscript Collections

Albuquerque, New Mexico
  University of New Mexico Special Collections
    Mary Austin Collection
    T. M. Pearce Collection
Austin, Texas
  Eugene C. Barker Texas History Center, University of Texas at Austin
    Walter Prescott Webb Collection
  Harry Ransom Humanities Research Center, University of Texas at Austin
    Contempo Collection
    Rupert Croft-Cooke Papers
    J. Frank Dobie Collection
    Alice Corbin Henderson Papers
    Robinson Jeffers Papers
    Oliver La Farge Papers
    E. Nehls Papers
    Leonidas Warren Payne Papers
    Stark Young Papers
  Texas State Archives
    Walter Prescott Webb Papers
Cambridge, Massachusetts
  Houghton Library, Harvard University
    Witter Bynner Papers
Chapel Hill, North Carolina
  Southern Historical Collection, University of North Carolina at Chapel Hill
    W. T. Couch Papers
    Paul Green Papers
    Howard Odum Papers
  University of North Carolina at Chapel Hill Library
    University of North Carolina Press Papers
Charlottesville, Virginia
  University of Virginia Special Collections
    F. Stringfellow Barr Collection
    Southern Writers' Convention Papers

University of Virginia Institute of Public Affairs Papers
Virginia Quarterly Review Papers
James Southal Wilson Papers
Columbia, Missouri
  University of Missouri Western Historical Collection
    John G. Neihardt Papers
Dallas, Texas
  Fikes Hall of Special Collections, DeGolyer Library, Southern Methodist University
    Southern Methodist University Press Records
  Fondren Library, Southern Methodist University
    Southern Methodist University Archives
Fayetteville, Arkansas
  University of Arkansas Special Collections Department, University of Arkansas–Fayetteville
    John Gould Fletcher Collection
Lincoln, Nebraska
  Nebraska State Historical Society
    Mamie Jane Meredith Papers
    Louise Pound Papers
  University of Nebraska Archives, University of Nebraska at Lincoln
    B. A. Botkin Collection
    Willa Cather Collection, B. Slote Papers
    Mari Sandoz Collection
Missoula, Montana
  University of Montana Archives, Mansfield Library
    H. G. Merriam Papers
Nashville, Tennessee
  Vanderbilt Special Collections, Vanderbilt University
    Donald Davidson Papers
    Herman Clarence Nixon Papers
    Frank Owsley Papers
    John Crowe Ransom Papers (copies), T. D. Young Collection
New Haven, Connecticut
  Beinecke Library, Yale University
    E. K. Brown Papers
    Barrett H. Clark Papers
    Arthur D. Ficke Papers
    Sinclair Lewis Papers
  Yale University Library
    John Collier Papers
Norman, Oklahoma
  University of Oklahoma Libraries
    University of Oklahoma Press Collection
  Western History Collection, University of Oklahoma
    W. S. Campbell Collection
    E. E. Dale Collection

San Marino, California
  Huntington Library
    Mary Austin Collection
Santa Fe, New Mexico
  Museum of New Mexico Library
    Edgar L. Hewett Collection
Stillwater, Oklahoma
  Oklahoma State University Special Collections
    Angie Debo Papers

Primary Sources

Abbey, Edward. *Desert Solitaire*. 1968. Reprint. New York, 1985.

———. *Hayduke Lives!* Boston, 1990.

———. *The Monkey Wrench Gang*. 1975. Reprint. New York, 1976.

Agar, Herbert, and Allen Tate, eds. *Who Owns America? A New Declaration of Independence*. Boston, 1936.

Agee, James, and Walker Evans. *Let Us Now Praise Famous Men*. 1941. Reprint. Boston, 1980.

Alexander, Hartley Burr, and Charles Whitaker. *The Architectural Sculpture of the State Capitol at Lincoln, Nebraska*. New York, 1926.

Anderson, Sherwood. *Winesburg, Ohio*. 1919. Reprint. New York, 1984.

Austin, Mary. *The American Rhythm*. New York, 1930.

———. *Earth Horizon*. New York, 1932.

Barr, Stringfellow. "Shall Slavery Come South?" *Virginia Quarterly Review* 6 (October 1930): 481–94.

———. "The Uncultured South." *Virginia Quarterly Review* 5 (April 1929): 192–200.

Benton, Thomas Hart. *An American in Art*. Kansas City, 1969.

Berry, Wendell. *The Gift of Good Land*. San Francisco, 1981.

Bolles, Blair. "The Federal Writers' Project." *Saturday Review of Literature* 18 (July 9, 1938): 3–4, 18–19.

Bookchin, Murray. *Post-Scarcity Anarchism*. Montreal, 1990.

———. *Remaking Society: Pathways to a Green Future*. Boston, 1990.

Botkin, B. A. "The Folk and the Individual: Their Creative Reciprocity." *English Journal* 27 (February 1938): 121–35.

———. "The Folk in Literature: An Introduction to the New Regionalism." In *Folk-Say: A Regional Miscellany*, edited by B. A. Botkin, pp. 9–20. Norman, Okla., 1929.

———. "The Folkness of the Folk." *English Journal* 26 (June 1937): 461–69.

———. "Folk-Say and Space: Their Genesis and Exodus." *Southwest Review* 20 (July 1935): 321–35.

———. "The New Mexico Round Table on Regionalism." *New Mexico Quarterly* 3 (August 1933): 152–59.

———. "Regionalism: Cult or Culture?" *English Journal* 25 (March 1936): 181–85.

———. "Regionalism and Culture." In *The Writer in a Changing World*, edited by Henry Hart, pp. 140–57. New York, 1946.

————. "Regionalism: The Next Step." *Space* 1 (December 1934): 86–88.

————. "Serenity and Light." *Southwest Review* 14 (Summer 1929): 492–93.

————. "We Talk about Regionalism—North, East, South, and West." *Frontier* 13 (May 1933): 286–96.

————, ed. *Folk-Say: A Regional Miscellany*. Norman, Okla., 1929.

————, ed. *Folk-Say: A Regional Miscellany, 1930*. Norman, Okla., 1930.

Botkin, Daniel B. *Discordant Harmonies*. New York, 1990.

Brandt, Joseph. "A Pioneering Regional Press." *Southwest Review* (Autumn 1940): 26–36.

Braunlich, Phyllis Cole. *The Life and Letters of Lynn Riggs*. Norman, Okla., 1988.

Brooks, Van Wyck. *America's Coming-of-Age*. 1915. Reprint. New York, 1930.

————. *The Ordeal of Mark Twain*. New York, 1920.

Brownlow, Louis. *A Passion for Anonymity: The Autobiography of Louis Brownlow, Second Half*. Chicago, 1962.

Buck, Pearl S. *The Good Earth*. 1931. Reprint. New York, 1973.

Buck, Solon J. "Progress and Possibilities of Mississippi Valley History." *Chronicles of Oklahoma* 1 (June 1923): 227–42.

Bynner, Witter. *Selected Poems*. Edited by Robert Hunt. New York, 1936.

Caldwell, Erskine. *Tobacco Road*. 1932. Reprint. New York, 1959.

Caldwell, Erskine, and Margaret Bourke-White. *You Have Seen Their Faces*. New York, 1937.

Cash, W. J. *The Mind of the South*. 1940. Reprint. New York, 1969.

Cather, Willa. *Death Comes for the Archbishop*. 1927. Reprint. New York, 1971.

————. *Early Novels*. New York, 1987.

————. *Later Novels*. New York, 1990.

————. *My Ántonia*. 1918. Reprint. Boston, 1988.

————. *Obscure Destinies*. New York, 1974.

————. *O Pioneers!* 1913. Reprint. Boston, 1976.

————. *The Song of the Lark*. 1915. Reprint. Boston, 1983.

Clark, Walter Van Tilburg. *The Ox-Bow Incident*. 1940. Reprint. New York, 1960.

Collier, John. "The American Congo." *Survey Graphic* 3 (August 1923): 467–76.

————. "The Red Atlantis." *Survey Graphic* 2 (October 1922): 15–66.

Commoner, Barry. *The Closing Circle: Nature, Man, and Technology*. New York, 1971.

————. *Making Peace with the Planet*. New York, 1975.

Couch, W. T., ed. *Culture in the South*. Chapel Hill, 1934.

————. *These Are Our Lives*. Chapel Hill, 1939.

Covert, Alice Lent. *Return to Dust*. New York, 1939.

Crèvecoeur, J. Hector St. John. *Letters from an American Farmer and Sketches of Eighteenth-Century America*. 1782. Reprint. New York, 1963.

Cunningham, Harry F. *The Capitol*. Lincoln, Nebr., 1931.

Dabney, Virginius. *Liberalism in the South*. Chapel Hill, 1932.

Dale, E. E. "The Spirit of Soonerland." *Chronicles of Oklahoma* 1 (June 1923): 167–78.

————. *The West Wind Blows: The Autobiography of E. E. Dale*. Oklahoma City, 1984.

Daniels, Robert V., ed. *A Documentary History of Communism*. Hanover, N.H., 1984.

Davidson, Donald. *The Attack on Leviathan*. Chapel Hill, 1938.

———. *The Tall Men*. Boston, 1927.

Debo, Angie. *And Still the Waters Run: The Betrayal of the Five Civilized Tribes*. 1940. Reprint. Norman, Okla., 1984.

DeVoto, Bernard. *The Easy Chair*. Boston, 1955.

———. *Mark Twain's America*. Boston, 1932.

———. *The Year of Decision: 1846*. New York, 1943.

Dobie, J. Frank. *Coronado's Children*. 1930. Reprint. Austin, Tex., 1978.

———. *A Vaquero of the Brush Country*. 1929. Reprint. Austin, Tex., 1981.

Dos Passos, John. *The Big Money*. 1936. Reprint. New York, 1979.

Emerson, Ralph Waldo. *Essays and Lectures*. New York, 1983.

Fain, John Tyree, and Thomas Daniel Young, eds. *The Literary Correspondence of Donald Davidson and Allen Tate*. Athens, Ga., 1974.

Faulkner, William. *Absalom, Absalom!* 1936. Reprint. New York, 1972.

Flader, Susan L., and J. Baird Callicott, eds. *The River of the Mother of God and Other Essays by Aldo Leopold*. Madison, Wis., 1991.

Fletcher, John Gould. *Europe's Two Frontiers*. London, 1930.

Frank, Waldo. *Memoirs of Waldo Frank*. Edited by Alan Trachtenberg. Amherst, Mass., 1973.

———. *The Re-Discovery of America*. New York, 1929.

Frederick, John T. *Green Bush*. New York, 1925.

———. "Ruth Suckow and the Middle Western Literary Movement." *English Journal* 20 (January 1931): 1–8.

Freud, Sigmund. *Civilization and Its Discontents*. 1930. Reprint. London, 1951.

Garland, Hamlin. *Crumbling Idols*. 1894. Reprint. Cambridge, Mass., 1960.

Gerth, H. H., and C. Wright Mills, eds. and trans. *From Max Weber*. New York, 1946.

Gibson, Mark, ed. *The Living Torch: A.E.* New York, 1938.

Gragert, Steven K., ed. *Radio Broadcasts of Will Rogers*. Stillwater, Okla., 1983.

Great Plains Committee. *The Future of the Great Plains*. Washington, D.C., 1936.

Hart, Henry, ed. *The Writer in a Changing World*. New York, 1937.

Hewett, Edgar L. *Ancient Life in the American Southwest*. Indianapolis, 1930.

Hicks, John. *The Populist Revolt*. Minneapolis, 1931.

Hiss, Tony. "Encountering the Countryside, II." *New Yorker* 65 (August 28, 1989): 37–63.

———. *The Experience of Place*. New York, 1990.

Huxley, Aldous. *Brave New World*. 1932. Reprint. New York, 1969.

Joad, C. E. M. *The Horrors of the Countryside*. London, 1931.

Kesten, Hermann, ed., and Richard Winston and Clara Winston, trans. *Thomas Mann Diaries, 1918–1939*. New York, 1982.

Krappe, Alexander Haggerty. "'American' Folklore." In *Folk-Say: A Regional Miscellany*, edited by B. A. Botkin, pp. 291–97. Norman, Okla., 1930.

La Farge, Oliver. *Laughing Boy*. 1929. Reprint. New York, 1957, 1971.

Lange, Dorothea, and Paul Schuster Taylor. *An American Exodus: A Record of Human Erosion*. New York, 1939.

———. *An American Exodus: A Record of Human Erosion*. Rev. ed. New Haven. 1969.

Lawrence, D. H. *The Plumed Serpent*. 1926. Reprint. New York, 1959.

Leavis, F. R. *Mass Civilization and Minority Culture*. Cambridge, 1930.

Leopold, Aldo. *A Sand County Almanac*. 1949, 1953. Reprint. New York, 1984.

Lewis, Sinclair. *It Can't Happen Here*. 1935. Reprint. New York, 1970.

————. *Lewis At Zenith*. New York, 1961.

Lilienthal, David E. *The Journals of David E. Lilienthal: The TVA Years, 1939–1945*. New York, 1964.

————. *TVA: Democracy on the March*. New York, 1944.

Lippmann, Walter. *A Preface To Morals*. New York, 1929.

Locke, Alain, ed. *The New Negro*. 1925. Reprint. New York, 1983.

Lomax, John. *Adventures of a Ballad Hunter*. New York, 1947.

Lomax, John A., and Alan Lomax. *Our Singing Country*. New York, 1941.

Lynd, Robert S., and Helen Merrell Lynd. *Middletown*. 1929. Reprint. New York, 1982.

MacKaye, Benton. "End or Peak of Civilization?" *Survey Graphic* 21 (October 1932): 441–44.

————. *The New Exploration*. 1928. Reprint. Urbana, Ill., 1962.

————. "Region Building in River Valleys." *Survey Graphic* 29 (February 1940): 107–8.

————. "Tennessee—Seed of a National Plan." *Survey Graphic* 22 (May 1933): 251–94.

McNickle, D'Arcy. *The Surrounded*. 1936. Reprint. Albuquerque, 1978.

McWilliams, Carey. *The Education of Carey McWilliams*. New York, 1978.

————. *Factories in the Field*. Boston, 1939.

————. *Ill Fares the Land*. Boston, 1942.

————. *The New Regionalism in American Literature*. Seattle, 1931.

————. "Provincialism: New Style." *Frontier and Midland* 14 (November 1933): 17–22.

————. "Young Man, Stay West." *Southwest Review* 15 (Spring 1930): 301–9.

Mann, Thomas. *The Coming Victory of Democracy*. New York, 1938.

————. *The Magic Mountain*. 1924. Reprint. New York, 1969.

————. *The Problem of Freedom*. Geneva, N.Y., 1939.

Mathews, John Joseph. *Sundown*. 1934. Reprint. Norman, Okla., 1988.

————. *Wah'Kon-Tah: The Osage and the White Man's Road*. Norman, Okla., 1932.

Merriam, H. G. "Endlessly the Covered Wagon." *Frontier* (November 1927): 1.

————, ed. *Northwest Verse*. Caldwell, Idaho, 1942.

Morgan, Arthur E. "The American Bent for Planning." *Survey Graphic* 25 (April 1936): 236–88.

————. "Benchmarks in the Tennessee Valley: Roads To Prosperity in the TVA." *Survey Graphic* 23 (November 1934): 548–76.

————. "Benchmarks in the Tennessee Valley: The Strength of the Hills." *Survey Graphic* 23 (January 1934): 5–46.

————. *The Making of the TVA*. Buffalo, N.Y., 1974.

————. *The Small Community: Foundation of Democratic Life*. New York, 1942.

Mumford, Lewis. *The Culture of Cities*. New York, 1938.

————. "The Fourth Migration." *Survey Graphic* 7 (May 1925): 130–33.

————. *The Golden Day*. New York, 1926.

————. *The Pentagon of Power*. New York, 1970.

————. "Regions—To Live In." *Survey Graphic* 7 (May 1925): 151–52.

———. *Sketches from Life*. New York, 1982.

———. "Social Purposes and New Plans." *Survey Graphic* 29 (February 1940): 119–30.

———. *The Story of Utopias*. New York, 1922.

———. *Technics and Civilization*. New York, 1934.

———. "Toward a New Regionalism." *New Republic* (March 25, 1931): 156–57.

Neihardt, John G. *Black Elk Speaks*. 1932. Reprint. New York, 1972.

———. *The Mountain Men*. 1925, 1941. Reprint. Lincoln, Nebr., 1971.

———. *Poetic Values*. New York, 1925.

———. *The Twilight of the Sioux*. 1935. Reprint. Lincoln, Nebr., 1971.

Nelson, Leonard R. *Nebraska's Memorial Capitol*. Lincoln, 1931.

Nixon, Herman Clarence. *Forty Acres and Steel Mules*. Chapel Hill, 1938.

———. *Possum Trot: Rural Community, South*. Norman, Okla., 1941.

Odum, Howard. *An American Epoch*. New York, 1930.

———. "The Case For Regional-National Social Planning." *Social Forces* 13 (October 1934): 6–23.

———. *Cold Blue Moon*. Indianapolis, 1931.

———. *The Negro and His Songs*. Chapel Hill, 1925.

———. "Regionalism vs. Sectionalism in the South's Place in the National Economy." *Social Forces* 12 (March 1933): 338–54.

———. *Southern Regions of the United States*. Chapel Hill, 1936.

———. *Wings On My Feet*. Indianapolis, 1929.

Odum, Howard, and Katherine Jocher, eds. *Regional Balance in America*. Chapel Hill, 1945.

Odum, Howard, and Harry Estill Moore. *American Regionalism*. New York, 1938.

Owens, William A., and Lyman Grant, eds. *Letters of Roy Bedichek*. Austin, Tex., 1985.

Owsley, Harriet Chappell, ed.. *The South: Old and New Frontiers: Selected Essays of Frank Lawrence Owsley*. Athens, Ga., 1969.

Parrington, Vernon L. *Main Currents in American Thought*. 3 vols. 1927, 1930. Reprint. Norman, Okla., 1987.

Pearce, T. M. "Folklore and Fascism." *New Mexico Quarterly* 8 (May 1938): 82–88.

———. "Southwestern Culture: An Artificial or Natural Growth?" *New Mexico Quarterly* 1 (August 1931): 195–209.

Randolph, Vance. *The Ozarks: An American Survival of Primitive Society*. New York, 1931.

Ransom, John Crowe. "The Aesthetic of Regionalism." *American Review* 2 (January 1934): 290–310.

———. "Regionalism in the South." *New Mexico Quarterly* 4 (May 1934): 108–13.

———. "The South Defends Its Heritage." *Harper's Magazine* 159 (June 1929): 108–18.

Raper, Arthur F. *Preface to Peasantry*. Chapel Hill, 1936.

Raper, Arthur F., and Ira De A. Reid. *Sharecroppers All*. Chapel Hill, 1941.

Reed, John Shelton, and Daniel Joseph Singal, eds. *Regionalism and the South: Selected Papers of Rupert Vance*. Chapel Hill, 1982.

Rölvaag, O. E. *Giants in the Earth*. 1927. Reprint. New York, 1955.

Rourke, Constance. *American Humor*. New York, 1931.

———. *The Roots of American Culture and Other Essays*. New York, 1942.

———. "The Significance of Sections." *New Republic* (September 20, 1933): 148–51.
Sandoz, Mari. *Capital City.* 1939. Reprint. Lincoln, Nebr., 1982.
———. *Crazy Horse: Strange Man of the Oglalas.* 1942. Reprint. Lincoln, Nebr., 1961.
———. "Mist and the Tall White Tower." *Story* 9 (September 1936): 41–50.
———. *Old Jules.* 1935. Reprint. Lincoln, Nebr., 1985.
———. *Slogum House.* 1937. Reprint. Lincoln, Nebr., 1981.
Sears, Paul. *Deserts on the March.* Norman, Okla., 1935.
Selznick, Philip. *TVA and the Grassroots.* Berkeley, Calif., 1949.
Shannon, Fred A. *An Appraisal of Walter Prescott Webb's The Great Plains.* New York, 1940.
Simpson, Lewis P., James Olney, and Jo Gulledge, eds. *The Southern Review and Modern Literature, 1935–1985.* Baton Rouge, 1988.
Smith, Henry Nash. "The Dilemma of Agrarianism." *Southwest Review* 19 (April 1934): 215–32.
———. "McGinnis and the Southwest Review: A Reminiscence." *Southwest Review* 40 (Autumn 1955): 299–310.
———. "A Note on the Southwest." *Southwest Review* 14 (Spring 1929): 267–78.
———. "On Living in America." *Southwest Review* 16 (October 1930): 22–31.
———. "The Southwest: An Introduction." *Saturday Review of Literature* 25 (May 16, 1942): 5–6.
Spengler, Oswald. *The Decline of the West.* 2 vols. 1926. Reprint. New York, 1973.
Spiller, Robert E., ed. *The Van Wyck Brooks–Lewis Mumford Letters.* New York, 1970.
Stearns, Harold E., ed. *Civilization in the United States.* New York, 1922.
Stegner, Wallace, ed. *The Letters of Bernard DeVoto.* Garden City, N.Y., 1975.
Steinbeck, John. *The Grapes of Wrath.* 1939. Reprint. New York, 1977.
Tate, Allen. *Essays of Four Decades.* New York, 1968.
———. *The Fathers.* 1938. Reprint. Baton Rouge, 1982.
———. "Regionalism and Sectionalism." *New Republic* 69 (December 23, 1931): 158–61.
Turner, Frederick Jackson. *Frontier and Section.* Edited by Ray Allen Billington. Englewood Cliffs, N.J., 1961.
Twelve Southerners. *I'll Take My Stand.* 1930. Reprint. Baton Rouge, 1983.
Umland, Rudolph. "On Editing WPA Guide Books." *Prairie Schooner* 13 (Fall 1939): 160–69.
Vance, Rupert. *Human Geography of the South.* Chapel Hill, 1932, 1935.
———. "Human Resources and Public Policy: An Essay toward Regional-National Planning." *Social Forces* 22 (October 1943): 20–25.
———. "Planning the Southern Economy." *Southwest Review* 20 (January 1935): 111–23.
Virgil. *The Georgics.* New York, 1982.
Webb, Walter Prescott. *Divided We Stand: The Crisis of a Frontierless Democracy.* New York, 1937.
———. *The Great Frontier.* 1951. Reprint. Austin, Tex., 1979.
———. *The Great Plains.* 1931. Reprint. Lincoln, Nebr., 1981.
Whitaker, Charles Harris, ed. *Bertram Grosvenor Goodhue—Architect and Master of Many Arts.* New York, 1925.

Williams, William Carlos. *In the American Grain*. 1925. Reprint. New York, 1956.
Wilson, Douglas L., ed. *The Genteel Tradition: Nine Essays by George Santayana*. Cambridge, Mass., 1967.
Wissler, Clark. *The American Indian*. Oxford, 1922.
———. *Indians of the United States*. New York, 1940.
Young, Stark. *So Red the Rose*. New York, 1934.
Young, Thomas Daniel, and Elizabeth Sarcone, eds. *The Lytle-Tate Letters*. Jackson, Miss., 1987.

Selected Secondary Sources

Abrahams, Edward. *The Lyrical Left: Randolph Bourne, Alfred Stieglitz, and the Origins of Cultural Radicalism in America*. Charlottesville, 1988.
Anderson, Jervis. *This Was Harlem: A Cultural Portrait, 1900–1950*. New York, 1983.
Asselineau, Roger, and Gay Allen Wilson. *St. John de Crèvecoeur*. New York, 1987.
Bensel, Richard Franklin. *Sectionalism and American Political Development, 1880–1980*. Madison, Wis., 1984.
Bercovitch, Sacvan. *The American Jeremiad*. Madison, Wis., 1980.
Bercovitch, Sacvan, and Myra Jehlen, eds. *Ideology and Classic American Literature*. Cambridge, 1989.
Blake, Casey Nelson. *Beloved Community: The Cultural Criticism of Randolph Bourne, Van Wyck Brooks, Waldo Frank, and Lewis Mumford*. Chapel Hill, 1990.
Brantlinger, Patrick. *Bread and Circuses: Theories of Mass Culture as Social Decay*. Ithaca, N.Y., 1983.
Bridgman, Richard. "The American Studies of Henry Nash Smith." *American Scholar* 56 (Spring 1987): 259–68.
Brown, E. K. *Willa Cather: A Critical Biography*. Lincoln, Nebr., 1987.
Buder, Stanley. *Visionaries and Planners: The Garden City Movement and the Modern Community*. New York, 1990.
Carpenter, Lucas, and Leighton Rudolph, eds. *Selected Poems of John Gould Fletcher*. Fayetteville, Ark., 1988.
Chauvenet, Beatrice. *Hewett and Friends*. Santa Fe, N.Mex., 1983.
Chytry, Josef. *The Aesthetic State*. Berkeley, Calif., 1989.
Clayton, Bruce. *W. J. Cash: A Life*. Baton Rouge, 1991.
Conkin, Paul K. *The Southern Agrarians*. Knoxville, Tenn., 1988.
Connor, Steven. *Postmodernist Culture: An Introduction to Theories of the Contemporary*. Oxford, 1990.
Conquest, Robert. *The Harvest of Sorrow: Soviet Collectivization and the Terror-Famine*. New York, 1986.
Cooney, Terry A. *The Rise of the New York Intellectuals: Partisan Review and Its Circle*. Madison, Wis., 1986.
Corrin, Jay P. *G. K. Chesterton and Hillaire Belloc: The Battle Against Modernity*. Athens, Ohio, 1981.
Donald, David Herbert. *Look Homeward: A Life of Thomas Wolfe*. New York, 1987.
Dorman, Robert L. "The Tragical Agrarianism of Alfalfa Bill Murray, the Sage of Tishomingo." *Chronicles of Oklahoma* 66 (Fall 1988): 240–67.

Gibson, Arrell Morgan. *The Santa Fe and Taos Colonies: Age of the Muses, 1900–1942*. Norman, Okla., 1988.

Hamilton, Nigel. *The Brothers Mann*. New Haven, 1979.

Hays, Samuel P. *Beauty, Health, and Permanence: Environmental Politics in the United States, 1955–1985*. Cambridge, 1987.

Hirsch, Jerrold. "Cultural Pluralism and Applied Folklore." In *The Conservation of Culture*, edited by Burt Feintuch, pp. 46–67. Lexington, 1988.

———. "Folklore in the Making: B. A. Botkin." *Journal of American Folklore* 100 (January–March 1987): 3–38.

Hoffman, Frederick J., Charles Allen, and Carolyn F. Ulrich, eds. *The Little Magazine: A History and Bibliography*. Princeton, N.J., 1947.

Hofstadter, Richard. *The Progressive Historians: Turner, Beard, Parrington*. Chicago, 1968.

Jensen, Merrill, ed. *Regionalism in America*. Madison, Wis., 1951.

Jonge, Alex de. *The Weimar Chronicle*. New York, 1978.

Karl, Barry. *The Uneasy State*. Chicago, 1985.

Kelly, Lawrence C. *The Assault on Assimilation*. Albuquerque, 1983.

Kelley, Robin D. G. *Hammer and Hoe: Alabama Communists during the Great Depression*. Chapel Hill, 1990.

Kershaw, Ian. *The Hitler Myth*. New York, 1989.

King, Richard H. *A Southern Renaissance: The Cultural Awakening of the American South, 1930–1955*. New York, 1982.

Kingston, Mike. *Walter Prescott Webb in Stephens County*. Austin, Tex., 1985.

Kirby, Jack Temple. *Rural Worlds Lost: The American South, 1920–1960*. Baton Rouge, 1987.

Klein, Joe. *Woody Guthrie: A Life*. New York, 1980.

Leuchtenburg, William E. *Franklin D. Roosevelt and the New Deal, 1932–1940*. New York, 1963.

Lowitt, Richard. *The New Deal and the West*. Bloomington, Ind., 1984.

Luebke, Frederick C., ed. *A Harmony of the Arts: The Nebraska State Capitol*. Lincoln, 1990.

McCraw, Thomas K. *Morgan vs. Lilienthal: The Feud within the TVA*. Chicago, 1970.

McDonald, Michael J., and John Muldowney. *TVA and the Dispossessed*. Knoxville, Tenn., 1982.

McKibben, Bill. *The End of Nature*. New York, 1989.

Mannheim, Karl. *Ideology and Utopia*. New York, 1936.

May, Henry F. *The End of American Innocence*. Chicago, 1964.

Meine, Curt. *Aldo Leopold: His Life and Work*. Madison, Wis., 1988.

Miller, Donald L. *Lewis Mumford: A Life*. New York, 1989.

Nash, Roderick. *Wilderness and the American Mind*. New Haven, 1982.

Noble, David W. *The End of American History*. Minneapolis, 1985.

O'Brien, Michael. *The Idea of the American South, 1920–1941*. Baltimore, 1979.

———. *Rethinking the South: Essays in Intellectual History*. Baltimore, 1988.

O'Brien, Sharon. *Willa Cather: The Emerging Voice*. New York, 1987.

Oliver, Richard. *Bertram Grosvenor Goodhue*. Cambridge, Mass., 1983.

Orvell, Miles. *The Real Thing: Imitation and Authenticity in American Culture, 1880–1940*. Chapel Hill, 1989.

Pells, Richard. *Radical Visions and American Dreams*. New York, 1973.

Perry, Lewis. *Intellectual Life in America: A History*. Chicago, 1989.

Philp, Kenneth R. *John Collier's Crusade for Indian Reform, 1920–1954*. Tucson, 1977.

Pickens, Donald K. "Westward Expansion and the End of American Exceptionalism: Sumner, Turner, Webb." *Western Historical Quarterly* 12 (October 1981): 409–18.

Prucha, Francis Paul. *The Great Father: The United States Government and the American Indians*. Lincoln, Nebr., 1986.

Reed, John Shelton. *The Enduring South: Subcultural Persistence in Mass Society*. Chapel Hill, 1986.

Reisner, Marc. *Cadillac Desert: The American West and Its Disappearing Water*. New York, 1986.

Rosemblum, Nancy L. *Another Liberalism: Romanticism and the Reconstruction of Liberal Thought*. Cambridge, Mass., 1987.

Rubin, Joan S. *Constance Rourke and American Culture*. Chapel Hill, 1980.

Rubin, Louis D., Jr. *The Wary Fugitives: Four Poets and the South*. Baton Rouge, 1978.

Rydell, Robert W. *All the World's a Fair: Visions of Empire at American International Expositions, 1876–1916*. Chicago, 1984.

Schwartz, Sanford. *The Matrix of Modernism: Pound, Eliot, and Early Twentieth-century Thought*. Princeton, N.J., 1985.

Shapiro, Henry D. *Appalachia on Our Mind: The Southern Mountains and Mountaineers in the American Consciousness, 1870–1920*. Chapel Hill, 1986.

Shi, David. *The Simple Life: Plain Living and High Thinking in American Culture*. Oxford, 1985.

Shklar, Judith. *Men and Citizens*. London, 1969.

Singal, Daniel Joseph. "Towards a Definition of American Modernism." *American Quarterly* 39 (1987): 7–26.

———. *The War Within: From Victorian to Modernist Thought in the South, 1919–1945*. Chapel Hill, 1982.

Slotkin, Richard. *The Fatal Environment: The Myth of the Frontier in the Age of Industrialization, 1800–1890*. Middletown, Conn., 1986.

Spencer, Benjamin T. *The Quest for Nationality*. Syracuse, N.Y., 1957.

Stauffer, Helen Winter. *Mari Sandoz: Story Catcher of the Plains*. Lincoln, Nebr., 1982.

Stegner, Wallace. *The Uneasy Chair*. Garden City, N.Y., 1974.

Stern, Fritz. *The Politics of Cultural Despair*. Berkeley, Calif., 1974.

Stott, William. *Documentary Expression and Thirties America*. New York, 1986.

Summerfield, Henry. *That Myriad-Minded Man: A.E.* London, 1975.

Susman, Warren. *Culture as History: The Transformation of American Society in the Twentieth Century*. New York, 1984.

Thomas, John L. "Lewis Mumford, Benton MacKaye, and the Regional Vision." In *Lewis Mumford: Public Intellectual*, edited by Thomas P. Hughes and Agatha C. Hughes, pp. 66–99. New York, 1990.

———. "Lewis Mumford: Regionalist Historian." *Reviews in American History* 16 (March 1988): 158–72.

———. "The Uses of Catastrophism: Lewis Mumford, Vernon L. Parrington, Van Wyck Brooks, and the End of American Regionalism." *American Quarterly* (June 1990): 223–51.

Tobin, Gregory M. *The Making of a History.* Austin, Tex., 1976.

Wald, Alan M. *The New York Intellectuals: The Rise and Decline of the Anti-Stalinist Left from the 1930s to the 1980s.* Chapel Hill, 1987.

Watkins, Floyd C. "What Stand Did Faulkner Take?" In *Faulkner and the Southern Renaissance,* edited by Doreen Fowler and Ann J. Abadie, eds., pp. 40–62. Jackson, Miss., 1982.

Wellek, René. *A History of Modern Criticism.* Vol. 6, *American Criticism, 1900–1950.* New Haven, 1986.

Wilson, Charles Reagan. "The Religion of the Lost Cause." In *Myth and Southern History,* edited by Patrick Gerster and Nicholas Cords. Urbana, Ill., 1989.

Wilson, Terry P. "Osage Oxonian: The Heritage of John Joseph Mathews." *Chronicles of Oklahoma* 59 (Fall 1981): 264–93.

Wolfskill, George. "Walter Prescott Webb and *The Great Plains*: Then and Now." *Reviews in American History* 12 (June 1984): 296–307.

Woodress, James. *Willa Cather: A Literary Life.* Lincoln, Nebr., 1987.

Worster, Donald. *Dust Bowl: The Southern Plains in the 1930s.* New York, 1982.

———. *Nature's Economy: A History of Ecological Ideas.* Cambridge, 1977.

Wright, Gavin. *Old South, New South: Revolutions in the Southern Economy Since the Civil War.* New York, 1986.

Young, Thomas Daniel. *Gentleman in a Dustcoat: A Biography of John Crowe Ransom.* Baton Rouge, 1976.

Young, Thomas Daniel, and M. Thomas Inge. *Donald Davidson.* New York, 1971.

Index

338 (n. 46); on cooperative rural renaissance, 266–67, 281–82; hopes to avoid governmental coercion, 269–70; on TVA, 291, 300

O'Keeffe, Georgia, xiii, 35, 74, 284

Owsley, Frank, 260, 285; on rural renaissance, 266–67, 272, 341 (n. 18); "Pillars of Agrarianism," 280–81, 309

Parrington, Vernon L.: *Main Currents in American Thought*, 11–12, 87–89, 99, 100, 102, 128; as regionalist fellow traveler, 35; catastrophic view of history, 84; exceptionalist myths, 94; as Progressive historian, 170; and Turner thesis, 172

Pearce, T. M. (*New Mexico Quarterly*), 45; on Native American folk culture and social democracy, 78

Percy, Alexander, 183, 187

Pound, Ezra, 43, 79

Preservationism, xiii, 138; of John Muir, 24, 134, 316, 345 (n. 13)

Randolph, Vance: *The Ozarks*, 97–98, 100

Ransom, John Crowe: and Agrarian experience of cultural dispersion, 47; biography of, 48, 212; on Southern resistance to progress, 49, 111–12; "Aesthetic of Regionalism," 81–82, 96, 98, 268; "The South Defends Its Heritage," 98, 126; on poets and cultural leadership, 105; as member of Southern Agrarian circle, 259–60, 276, 286; projection of rural renaissance, 266–67; debate with Stringfellow Barr (1930), 278–79

Raper, Arthur F., 51, 183, 208, 239; as critic of frontier myth, 184, 188, 196, 221; on Old South myth, 184–85; on Southern racism, 185, 187; *Sharecroppers All*, 187, 267; *Preface to Peasantry*, 189; analysis of farm tenancy system, 189–94, 338 (n. 55); on American peasantry, 203; on grassroots cooperation, 230; as political realist, 232; position on rural renaissance, 267; perceives Great Migration, 299

Region: definitions of, xii, 5, 34, 84–85, 134–35, 318. *See also* Folk; Regionalism

Regionalism: as ideology, xii-xiii, 25, 74, 149, 150–54, 228, 251–58, 318, 324, 337 (n. 10); definitions of, 2, 7–11, 12–13, 25, 50, 133–41, 283–84; as movement, 34, 116–17, 275–77

Regional planning: defined, 133–34, 138–39, 270–71, 318

Regional Planning Association of America (RPAA), 8, 23, 46, 53, 137–38

Riggs, Lynn, 87, 94, 98–99; *Green Grow the Lilacs*, 98, 105

Rogers, Will, 196–97

Rölvaag, O. E.: *Giants in the Earth*, 90, 100, 159; and folk resistance to acculturation, 92, 96

Roosevelt, Franklin Delano, 162, 253; on regional planning, 292, 297

Rourke, Constance: biography of, 38, 51, 209; *American Humor*, 90–92; on folk cultural persistence, 91, 96; myth in interpretations, 94; on folklore as art, 119–21; and National Folk Festival, 252

Russell, George William. *See* AE

Sandburg, Carl, 12, 35, 67

Sandoz, Mari: biography of, 38, 40, 68, 212, 233; as part of Midwestern wing, 45; as field collector, 72, 97; *Crazy Horse*, 73, 94, 244, 291, 308; *Old Jules*, 87, 146, 233–34, 241–42, 308; on 1920s, 107, 158; and "felt" history, 136, 244; "Mist and the Tall White Tower," 145–48, 232, 243; Nebraska capitol as symbol for, 145–48, 236–39, 242–44; *Capital City*, 146, 234, 238–44, 250; *Slogum House*, 146, 234–37; as regionalist Cassandra, 232; concern over fascism, 234–35, 241–44; on frontier myth, 235–36; Midwestern liberal tradition, 236, 238, 240; regional civilization, 240, 257; philosophical pessimism of, 255, 263; banning of *Slogum House*, 289; late 1930s as Thermidor, 304; postwar career, 308, 313

(n. 17), 336 (n. 51); "Politics as a Voca-
tion," 271–72, 313
Whitman, Walt, 8, 81, 86, 102, 104, 106,
113
Wilderness Society, 315–16, 318
Williams, William Carlos: *In the Ameri-
can Grain*, 113, 115, 118, 121
Wilson, James Southal (*Virginia Quar-
terly Review*), 111
Wissler, Clark, 63, 78

Wolfe, Thomas, xiii, 34, 154, 285
Wood, Grant, 45, 118
World War II: effects on regionalist
movement, 304–6

Yaro, Robert: as postwar new regionalist, 325–26
Young, Stark: *So Red the Rose*, 100; in
postwar period, 309–10